Drive Around
California

YOU R GUIDE TO GREAT DRIVES

Titles in this series include:

For further information about these and other Thomas Cook publications, write to Thomas Cook Publishing, PO Box 227, The Thomas Cook Business Park, 9 Coningsby Road, Peterborough PE3 8SB, United Kingdom.

Drive Around
California

The best of California,
including Los Angeles and
San Francisco, Palm Springs
and Hollywood, Disneyland
and Universal Studios, the
Grand Canyon, Death Valley
and the Napa Valley

Maxine Cass and Fred Gebhart

Thomas Cook
Publishing
www.thomascookpublishing.com

Written, researched and updated by Maxine Cass and Fred Gebhart

Published by Thomas Cook Publishing
A division of Thomas Cook Tour Operations Limited.
Company registration no. 1450464 England
The Thomas Cook Business Park, Unit 9, Coningsby Road,
Peterborough PE3 8SB, United Kingdom
E-mail: books@thomascook.com, Tel: + 44 (0) 1733 416477
www.thomascookpublishing.com

Produced by Cambridge Publishing Management Limited
Burr Elm Court, Main Street, Caldecote CB23 7NU

ISBN: 978-1-84848-063-6

© 2005, 2007 Thomas Cook P
This third edition © 2009
Text © Thomas Cook Publishi
Road maps supplied by Lovell
Map data © MapQuest.com.Ir
City maps © Thomas Cook Pu

Series Editor: Adam Royal
Production/DTP: Steven Colli

Printed and bound in India b

Cover photography: Front: © Getty Images/Ron and Patty Thomas; Back: © Thomas Cook

Although every care has been taken in compiling this publication, and the contents are believed to be correct at the time of printing, Thomas Cook Tour Operations Limited cannot accept any responsibility for errors or omissions, however caused, or for changes in details given in the guidebook, or for the consequences of any reliance on the information provided. Descriptions and assessments are based on the authors' views and experiences when writing and do not necessarily represent those of Thomas Cook Tour Operations Limited.

About the authors

Maxine Cass is a rare specimen, a California native. Since she was born on the Stanford University campus in Palo Alto, Maxine has studied Medieval European History at the University of California, Santa Barbara, lived in Greece and Senegal, and become a widely published photojournalist and author. Maxine is the author of the *AAA Photo Journey to San Francisco, Time for Food: San Francisco*, and other guidebooks to Florida, Western Canada, the Pacific Northwest and Mexico. She contributes to various travel and business publications in Europe, the US, Canada and Asia. Between research trips around the world, Maxine gardens at the home in San Francisco she shares with her husband and series co-author, Fred Gebhart.

Fred Gebhart has lived in California for more than 40 years, interrupted by extended sojourns in Europe and West Africa that have eventually sent him back to his adopted state. He has logged thousands of miles in California, as a child as well as an adult, travelling by foot, horseback, balloon, bicycle, sailboat, RV and car. A freelance photojournalist for more than 25 years, Fred covers California and the Western United States for publications in Asia and Europe while focusing on Australasia for US readers. With his wife, Maxine Cass, Fred has written a number of Thomas Cook titles, including *On the Road around California, Must See Florida,* and *Drive Around Guides Vancouver* and *British Columbia.*

Acknowledgements

The authors and publishers would like to thank the following people and organisations for their assistance:
Laurie Armstrong, San Francisco CVB; Molly Blaisdell; Kate Buska & Joe Timko, San Diego CVB; Calaveras Visitors Bureau; Kelly Chamberlain; Lara Chanley, Santa Monica CVB; Chris Chrystal, Nevada Commission on Tourism; Ellen Clark & Geoffrey Williams; Delaware North Companies; Robert Deuel, the Disneyland Resort; Bob Fish, USS *Hornet*; Kris Fister, Sequoia & Kings Canyon National Parks; Lee Foster; Lou Gebhart; Mark Graves, Palm Springs Desert Resort Communities CVA; Elizabeth Harryman & Paul Lasley; Kenny Karst, DNC Parks & Resorts at Yosemite; Brian M Logan, BLM Arcata; Carol Martinez, LA, Inc.; Paul & Virginia McCarthy; Mendo & Panther; Monterey Bay Aquarium; John Poimiroo; Mary Ellen Quesada; Sharon Rooney; Sue Russell, El Dorado County Chamber of Commerce; San Diego Zoo's Wild Animal Park; San Diego Zoological Society; Fred Sater; Stanford Inn by the Sea; Lucy Steffens, Sacramento CVB; Richard Stenger, Humboldt County CVB; Town & Country Hotel; Marilyn Wagner; Keith Walklet; Welk Resort Center; Whale Watch Inn.

Contents

Above
The stark beauty of the desert

About Drive Around Guides

Thomas Cook's Drive Around Guides are designed to provide you with a comprehensive but flexible reference source to guide you as you tour a country or region by car. This guide divides California into touring areas – one per chapter. Major cultural centres or cities form chapters in their own right. Each chapter contains enough attractions to provide at least a day's worth of activities – often more.

Symbol key

 ℹ Tourist Information Centre

 Ⓦ Website

 ✉ Advice on arriving or departing

 Ⓟ Parking locations

 Ⓠ Advice on getting around

 ⤷ Directions

 ⓣ Sights and attractions

 ◖ Accommodation

 Ⓜ Eating

 ◯ Shopping

 Ⓢ Sport

 ◬ Entertainment

Ratings

To make it easier for you to plan your time and decide what to see, every area is rated according to its attractions in categories such as Architecture, Entertainment and Children.

Chapter contents

Every chapter has an introduction summing up the main attractions of the area, and a ratings box, which will highlight the area's strengths and weaknesses – some areas may be more attractive to families travelling with children, others to wine-lovers visiting vineyards, and others to people interested in finding castles, churches, nature reserves or good beaches.

Each chapter is then divided into an alphabetical gazetteer, and most chapters feature a suggested tour. You can select whether you just want to visit a particular sight or attraction, choosing from those described in the gazetteer, or whether you want to tour the area comprehensively. If the latter, you can construct your own itinerary, or follow the author's suggested tour, which comes at the end of most area chapters.

Practical information

The practical information in the page margins, or sidebars, will help you locate the services you need as an independent traveller – including the tourist information centre, car parks and public transport facilities. You will also find the opening times of sights, museums, churches and other attractions, as well as useful tips on shopping, market days, cultural events, entertainment, festivals and sports facilities.

The gazetteer

The gazetteer section describes all the major attractions in the area – the villages, towns, historic sites, nature reserves, parks or museums that you are most likely to want to see. Maps of the area highlight all the places mentioned in the text. Using this comprehensive overview of the area, you may choose just to visit one or two sights.

One way to use the guide is simply to find individual sights that interest you, using the index or overview map, and read what our authors have to say about them. This will help you decide whether to visit the sight. If you do, you will find plenty of practical information, such as the street address, the telephone number for enquiries and opening times.

Alternatively, you can choose a hotel, perhaps with the help of the accommodation recommendations contained in this guide. You can then turn to the overall map on pages 10–11 to help you work out which chapters in the book describe those cities and regions that lie closest to your chosen touring base.

Driving tours

The suggested tour is just that – a suggestion. The routes are designed to link the attractions described in the gazetteer section, and to cover outstandingly scenic coastal, mountain and rural landscapes. The total distance is given for each tour, as is the time it will take you to drive the complete route, but bear in mind that this indication is just for the driving time: you will need to add on extra time for visiting attractions along the way.

Many of the routes are circular, so that you can join them at any point. Where the nature of the terrain dictates that the route has to be linear, the route can either be followed out and back, or you can use it as a link route, to get from one area in the book to another.

Accommodation and food

In every chapter you will find lodging and eating recommendations for individual towns, or for the area as a whole. These are designed to cover a range of price brackets and concentrate on more characterful small or individualistic hotels and restaurants. In addition, you will find information in the *Travel facts* chapter on chain hotels, with an address to which you can write for a guide, map or directory. The price indications used in the guide have the following meanings:

$ budget level
$$ typical/average prices
$$$ de luxe.

Introduction

Above
Mission Carmel: San Carlos
Borromeo Mission

California is an asylum where the inmates have permanent control and the rest of the world is clamouring to get in. It's a hypermarket of people, places and experiences, from the vast horizons of the northeast to the teeming streets of Los Angeles and San Diego, from manicured vineyard rows to trackless forests that have never been properly mapped.

It's a land rife with myths, half-truths and outright lies stirred together to create a morality tale that is part admonition and part salacious entertainment. Even the handful of Californians who were born here can't always discern one tale from another. Most don't care. When Californians heard that 'perception is reality', they took it to heart as their own reality. California is a land of change, always moving toward an ever-better future. From that shared belief has sprung the California Dream, an ever-evolving mix of fact, fantasy and hope that suffuses the Golden State in a golden glow of arrested adolescence.

Named after a mythical land and nourished by generations of dreamers and schemers, California has come to epitomise a place where anything can happen – and usually does. Fortunes have been won, lost and won again by every means imaginable. More than a few sprang full-grown from the minds of men whose ambition overreached their good sense. Avarice, lust and fraud are as much part of the California Dream as peace, love and happiness. What all six share is an unshakeable faith in the positive power of change, a maniacal belief that tomorrow *will* be a better day.

Until the arrival of steamships and transcontinental railways, simply travelling to California required an unhealthy dose of optimism. The journey from the Atlantic coast of North America offered the prospect of gruelling physical hardship by land or gnawing boredom by sea, both leavened by the very real prospects of death by disaster, disease or foul play along the way. Once arrived, rugged terrain and treacherous coastal shoals made travel up and down the state equally problematic. Despite the obvious difficulties, California has been portrayed as the Golden State – a paradise on earth – since it was first viewed by Europeans more than four centuries ago. It didn't seem to matter that just getting to California required either an extraordinary leap of faith or an equally extraordinary act of desperation. Once arrived, fame and fortune somehow seemed assured.

Generations of stubborn determination have turned that impenetrable faith in the future into a self-fulfilling prophecy that feeds upon itself and infects legions of newcomers from around the globe. The soaring spires of the Yosemite Valley and the cathedral silence of a grove of redwood trees wreathed in mist and spotlit by beams of sunlight are as much a part of modern California as the imagination, engineering and sheer sweat that created Disneyland, Industrial Light & Magic and generations of silicon chips.

California is a study in contradictions. It's the most populous state in America, yet has vast tracts of untouched wilderness. It produced the cult of youth, beauty and health that is sweeping the globe, yet has one of America's fastest-growing populations of retired persons. It's a land built by immigrants whose political leaders fan the flames of anti-immigrant sentiment at election time. It's among the richest economies on earth, yet it refuses to feed, house and educate a growing minority of its population.

None of this is news to Californians. They revel in quirks and contradictions. Most of them are here by choice, not by birth. That they remain only reinforces the optimism that drew them, or their parents, here in the first place. One of the seldom-acknowledged joys of California is that everything that is said about the place is both true and untrue at the same time.

Below
Golden Gate Bridge,
San Francisco

Travel facts

Accommodation

Thousands of chain hotels and motels provide the most reliable accommodation. Expect to pay $100–$250 per night in major cities, $70–$150 in smaller towns, single or double occupancy.

Camping pitches and RV sites must be booked in advance for popular national, state and local parks. RV parks are common in rural areas but rare in cities (*see Recreational vehicles, page 21*). Bed and breakfast is often among the most expensive options; several hundred are listed on the California Association of Bed and Breakfast Inns, *www.cabbi.com*. Fax or use the toll-free telephone numbers for booking; you can also book via e-mail or a website. Local tourist offices usually have lists of area accommodation and some make bookings.

Airports

Heightened airport security in the US may mean delays and unpredictable waits. Plan plenty of time to make connections, and be prepared to remove footwear and laptop computers at security checkpoints, where cabin baggage may also be hand-searched. Before departure for the United States, check at *www.tsa.gov* for current restrictions on liquids, food, beverages and medication that may be hand-carried onto an aircraft. Most international visitors fly into Los Angeles International Airport (LAX) or San Francisco International Airport (SFO). Luggage trolleys are free for international arrivals; expect to pay $3 at domestic terminals. For flight information and bookings, contact individual airlines. Major airports have foreign exchange, banking services and cash machines (ATMs) as well as car-hire facilities. Secondary airports may be less congested.

Children

Most attractions offer children's rates. Many hotels and motels can arrange for babysitters, a pricey service. Children up to 18 stay free in their parents' room with many motel chains.

Picnics offer mealtime flexibility. So does a small cooler filled with cold drinks and snacks. Most towns have roadside restaurants with long hours, cheap children's menus and familiar names.

Currency

US dollars, all the same size, come in denominations of $1, $2 (rare), $5, $10, $20, $50 and $100. Older versions of $50 and $20 and the other denominations are all the same colour, green and white. Updated bills have added colours to designs. All bills have a different US president on the front and design on the back. There are 100 cents to the dollar. Coins are: 1 cent (penny), 5 cents (nickel), 10 cents (dime), 25 cents (quarter), 50 cents (half-dollar – rare), and a rare quarter-sized Susan B. Anthony dollar. Oversized silver dollar coins are common in Nevada.

The safest forms of money are traveller's cheques and credit or debit cards. Carry at least one, preferably two, major credit cards such as **Access (MasterCard)**, **American Express** or **Visa**. Car-hire companies, hotels and motels require a credit card or a substantial cash deposit, even if the bill has been prepaid or will be settled in cash.

Banks can exchange foreign currency or traveller's cheques, but expect delays at small town branches. US dollar traveller's cheques from well-known issuers such as Thomas Cook are acceptable everywhere.

Customs allowances

Allowances can change. Before travelling, check with the US Department of Homeland Security, Customs and Border Protection, *tel: (202) 354-1000; www.cbp.gov/xp/cgov/travel*. Non-resident visitors to the US may bring 1 litre of spirits, beer or wine, 200 cigarettes and 100 non-Cuban cigars and up to $100 worth of gifts duty-free. The age limit for alcohol is 21 and 18 for tobacco. Be aware that the state of California enforces a strict smoking ban in all public places, including outdoor restaurants.

Check with customs officials at home for returning duty-free allowances. Alcohol, tobacco, perfume, electronics and similar items are cheaper at supermarkets and department stores than at airport and downtown duty-free shops.

Disabled travellers

Federal and state laws require that public businesses and services be readily accessible by persons with disabilities. Hotels, restaurants, offices, shops, cinemas, museums, post offices and other buildings must have access ramps and toilets designed for wheelchairs. Most cities also have kerb ramps at street corners. Major parks have at least a few sealed pathways for disabled visitors. For specific information, contact **SATH** (Society for Accessible Travel & Hospitality), *347 5th Ave, Suite 605, New York NY 10016; tel: (212) 447-7284; www.sath.org* or **RADAR**, *12 City Forum, 250 City Rd, London EC1V 8AF; tel: (020) 7250-3222; www.radar.org.uk*. California State Parks strive to be access friendly; *tel: (916) 445-8949; access@parks.ca.gov; access.parks.ca.gov*

Above
Lunching alfresco in
North Beach

Left
Native American-style
art in Grand Canyon
National Park

Electricity

America uses 110 volt 60
hertz current with two- or
three-prong plugs. Power
and plug converters are
seldom available.

Beware of buying electrical
equipment – it probably
won't operate on your
voltage at home. Exceptions
are battery-operated items
such as radios, cameras and
portable computers.

Be equally wary of DVDs.
DVD players are designated
by region. The US is in
region D1, the UK and
Western Europe are region
D2. Look for a 'region-free'
DVD, otherwise it's unlikely
the DVD will play on your
DVD player. America uses
the NTSC format, most
other countries use PAL or
SECAM. Make sure you
check your home country
High Definition (HD)
equipment standard for
compatibility if you plan to
shop in the United States.

Drinking laws

The drinking age is 21 and it is strictly enforced. Beer, wine and spirits
can be purchased in food, drug and convenience stores as well as in
liquor stores. Licensed establishments, bars, lounges, saloons and pubs
may open between 0600 and 0200 in California and any hours in
Nevada. Laws against drinking and driving are severe and are also
strictly enforced (*see Drinking and driving, page 25*).

Earthquakes

Most of the 5000-plus earthquakes that shake California yearly are too
small to be noticed. If the tremors are mild, i.e. dishes aren't rattling,
treat it like an amusement park ride and thrill friends at home with
tales of terror.

If it becomes difficult to stand or items fall from shelves, take cover
beneath the nearest solid table. If there's no table, brace yourself in an
interior doorway. Stay away from windows, bookcases or anything else
that could collapse. *Don't* run outside, where glass, masonry and
power lines could be falling.

If driving, pull off the road and stop on solid ground – you can't
drive safely when the road is moving. If you are about to cross a bridge
or flyover, stop, or get to the other side as quickly as possible. Then
get ready for the next shake. There are always aftershocks, sometimes
as strong as the mother quake.

Eating out

Expect to eat too much. The US periodically indulges in fad diets,
touting fad-related dishes on menus. Otherwise, an 'American
breakfast' combines bacon, sausages or ham, hash browns, eggs,
pancakes or French toast and toast. English muffins (crumpets),
waffles, bagels, fresh fruit, yoghurt, porridge and cereal are other
possibilities. A 'Continental breakfast' is juice, coffee or tea and bread
or a pastry.

Lunch and dinner menus feature appetisers, salads, soups, pastas,
entrées and desserts. Salads come at the beginning of the meal.
Sunday brunch, self-service buffets piled high with hot and cold
dishes, can be good value for hearty eaters (usually served 1100–1400).

Many fast-food outlets have drive-up windows. Look for A&W,
Arby's Roast Beef, Burger King, Carl's Jr, In-N-Out Burger, Jack-in-the-
Box, KFC (Kentucky Fried Chicken), McDonald's, Pizza Hut, Quiznos
Sub, Subway and Taco Bell.

Chain restaurants, ubiquitous along freeways, include Chevy's
(Mexican), Applebee's, Denny's (both American), Fresh Choice (salads,
soups and pastas), Olive Garden (Italian), Red Lobster (seafood) and
Sizzler (American).

Above
Rock climbing in Joshua Tree National Park

Museums

Most museums are closed one day per week, usually Mon or Tue. Rural museums may open only on weekends or during the busy summer season. Most charge an entry fee.

Entry formalities

Non-US citizens generally need a passport, visa and proof of return travel to enter the country. Check details with the US Customs and Border Protection (*www.cbp.gov/xp/cgov/travel*) and your nearest US consulate or embassy at least three months before departure, as regulations change frequently. Weapons, narcotics, many foodstuffs, and certain pharmaceutical products may not be imported. Carry documentation such as a doctor's prescription to prove that medications are legitimate.

Health

In the event of a life-threatening emergency, telephone 911 for an ambulance. If a life is at stake, treatment will be swift and professional, with payment problems left for later. For more mundane problems, urban areas and most rural communities have 24-hour walk-in clinics.

Because US medical providers do not accept non-US health plan coverage, health insurance is mandatory to ensure provision of non-emergency health services. Most travel agents who sell international travel offer travel insurance policies covering US medical costs.

Bring prescription medication for the entire trip, plus a few extra days and a copy of the prescription for emergencies. As names of drugs vary from country to country, the prescription should show the generic (chemical) name and formulation, not just a brand name.

California is basically a healthy place. No inoculations are required and common sense is enough to avoid most health problems. Eat normally and don't drink water that hasn't come from the tap or a bottle. Most groundwater is contaminated with *giardia* and other intestinal parasites. Check the US Centers for Disease Control website (*www.cdc.gov*) for recommended repellents and precautions against Lyme Disease (deer tick-borne) and West Nile virus (mosquito-borne).

Sunglasses, broadbrimmed hats and sunscreen help prevent sunburn, sunstroke and heat prostration. Be sure to drink plenty of non-alcoholic liquids, especially in hot weather.

Information

California Travel & Tourism Commission, *980 9th St, Ste 480, Sacramento CA 95814; tel: (916) 444-4429;* **California Tourism,** *PO Box 1499, Sacramento CA 95812-1499; tel: (800) 862-2543; www.visitcalifornia.com.* California has 13 **California Welcome Centers**, listed with links to each location and its region, at *www.visitcwc.com.* **Nevada Commission on Tourism,** *401 N. Carson St, Carson City NV 89701; tel: (775) 687-4322* or *(800) 638-2328; www.travelnevada.com.* Annual California and Nevada visitor guides are online at the states' respective websites.

Opening hours

Standard office hours are 0900–1700, Mon–Fri. Some tourist offices are open weekends. Most banks are open Mon–Thu 1000–1600, Fri 1000–1800, Sat 0900–1300. ATMs are open 24 hours.

Shopping malls usually open at 0900 or 1000 and close between 2000 and 2200, with shorter hours on Sun. Many restaurants, theatres and museums are closed Mon or Tue, but cinemas and most tourist attractions are open seven days a week.

Opening times and services in missions and places of worship vary widely. Call before visiting if possible.

Climate

Expect sunshine in Southern California, fog along the coast, and heat inland, but uneven terrain creates a patchwork of weather patterns which cannot be explained. Summer fog can hang heavy or burn away to reveal deep blue skies and a blistering sun. Winter temperatures generally drop with altitude and the further north you go, with snow above 1800m. In summer, look for increasing heat inland and to the south.

For national park, monument and seashore information, contact **National Park Service, Pacific West,** *Regional Office, 1111 Jackson St, Ste 700, Oakland CA 94607; tel: (510) 817-1300; www.nps.gov*

For California State Parks and Beaches, contact **State of California Department of Parks and Recreation,** *1416 9th St, Sacramento CA 95814 or PO Box 942896, Sacramento CA 94296; tel: (916) 653-6995 or (800) 777-0369; www.parks.ca.gov. For state park camping reservations, first check www.parks.ca.gov for current regulations, then contact* **Reserve America CA***; tel: (800) 444-7275; www.reserveamerica.com*

For Nevada State Parks, contact **Nevada Division of State Parks,** *901 S Stewart St, Ste 5005, Carson City NV 89701-5248; tel: (775) 684-2770; www.parks.nv.gov*

Packing

Take half as many clothes and twice as much money as you expect to need. Anything you can imagine is sold in California, plus some items you never thought of. Apart from a few restaurants which require business attire, dress is casual and informal, particularly in Southern California. It is a good idea to dress in layers as temperatures can change dramatically during the day, especially in the mountains and near the ocean.

Postal services

Every town has at least one post office. Most are open Mon–Fri 0900–1700 and may operate Sat morning, closed Sun. For stamps, consult the telephone book blue government pages under US Postal Service. Some hotels and supermarkets also sell them. Letters or parcels sent abroad should go airmail to avoid delays. Domestic letters should arrive in three to seven days.

Public holidays

The following public holidays are observed in California and Nevada: New Year (1 Jan); Martin Luther King Jr Day (third Mon in Jan); Lincoln's Birthday (12 Feb); Presidents' Day (third Mon in Feb); Easter (Sun in Mar/Apr); Cesar Chavez Day (31 Mar in California); Memorial Day (last Mon in May); Independence Day (4 Jul); Labor Day (first Mon in Sep); Columbus Day (second Mon in Oct); Veterans Day (11 Nov); Thanksgiving Day (last Thu in Nov); Nevada Day (fourth Fri in Nov); and Christmas (25 Dec).

Unofficial holidays such as the lunar Chinese New Year and Cinco de Mayo (5 May, Mexican victory against French troops) are celebrated with as much gusto as official days off.

Post offices and government offices close on public holidays, as do some businesses. Department stores hold huge holiday sales. Tourist

Right
Giant redwoods in Sequoia
National Park

attractions frequently have longer holiday hours. Accommodation is heavily booked in advance except for Easter, Thanksgiving and Christmas, which are usually celebrated at home.

Reading

- *Adventuring in the California Desert*, by Lynne Foster, 1997, Sierra Club Books, San Francisco.
- *California Historical Landmarks*, edited by McDonald and Carol Cullens, 1997, California Department of Parks and Recreation.
- *California Wildlife Viewing Guide*, by Jeanne Clark, 1996, Globe Pequot/Falcon, Guilford, CT.
- *The Complete Nevada Traveler*, by David W. Toll, 2002, Gold Hill Publishing Co, Virginia City, NV.

Tipping

Tipping is standard except in the very rare restaurant where a service charge is added and a tip may still be expected! Servers expect 15–20 per cent of the food and drink charge; bartenders at least $1 per drink. The traditional reward for poor service is two pennies.

Hotel porters get $1 per bag and the bellperson who shows you to your room several dollars more. Expect to pay $1–$5 for valet parking each time your car is delivered. Don't tip ushers in cinemas, theatres and similar establishments.

Casino employees depend on tips for survival. If you win, be generous with the dealer, croupier or slot machine change person. They can't help you beat the odds, but the dealer's attitude makes the difference between a good time and simply losing money.

For casino shows without reserved seating, $5–$20 to the maître d' usually gets better seats. If you want to change, ask discreetly, bill in hand, before sitting down. Showroom servers get $5–$10 per couple for a cocktail show, $10–$20 for a dinner show.

- *Moon California Hiking,* by Tom Stienstra and Ann Marie Brown, 2008, Avalon Travel Publishing, Emeryville, CA.
- *The Grapes of Wrath,* by John Steinbeck, multiple editions.
- *Haunted Houses of California: A Ghostly Guide to Haunted Houses and Wandering Spirits,* by Antoinette May, 2006, World Wide Publishing/Tetra, San Carlos, CA.
- *Humbugs and Heroes,* by Richard Dillon, 2003, James Stevenson Publisher, Fairfield, CA.
- *The Mountains of California,* by John Muir, 1997, multiple editions.
- *The Painted Ladies Guide to Victorian California,* by Elizabeth Pomada and Michael Larsen, 1991, Dutton Studio Books, New York.
- *Roughing It,* by Mark Twain, multiple editions.
- *Two Years Before the Mast,* Richard Henry Dana, multiple editions.
- *The Ultimate Hollywood Tour Book,* by William A. Gordon, 2007, North Ridge Books, El Toro, CA.

Recreational vehicles

Recreational vehicles, or RVs (camper vans and caravans), are an increasingly popular way to travel. The higher cost of hiring and operating an RV is offset by savings on accommodation and meals and the convenience of not packing and unpacking at every stop. RVs are cramped, and savings evaporate if you give in to the temptation of high-priced hotels and fancy restaurant meals.

Get operating manuals and a full demonstration for *all* systems before leaving the hire lot. Buy a pair of sturdy rubber washing gloves to handle daily sewer chores. Pack old clothes to wear while crawling beneath the vehicle to hook up and disconnect at each stop.

For RV information, contact **Recreation Vehicle Industry Association**, *1896 Preston White Dr., Reston VA 2019; tel: (703) 620-6003; www.rvia.org* or *www.gorving.com,* and/or **Recreational Vehicle Rental Association**, *3930 University Dr., Fairfax, VA 22030-2515; tel: (703) 591-7130; www.rvra.org*

Safety and security

Dial 911 on any telephone for free emergency assistance from police, fire and medical authorities. Use normal common-sense precautions.

Safe travelling

Never discuss travel plans or valuables in public. Use the same caution in rural areas as in cities, driving, parking and walking only in well-lit areas. Don't wear expensive jewellery when walking about. A wallet in a back pocket or an open handbag are invitations to theft. Take precautions – carry bags and camera cases across your chest and keep them between your feet or on your lap in restaurants.

Above
Embarcadero Center, San
Francisco

Stores

Major department store
chains: Bloomingdales, JC
Penney, Macy's, Mervyn's,
Neiman Marcus,
Nordstrom, Saks Fifth
Avenue and Sears.
Discount chains: Ross,
Target and Wal-Mart. For
the best prices, check the
Sunday newspapers.

Time

California and Nevada are
on Pacific Standard Time
(PST), GMT −8. Both
states jump ahead to
Pacific Daylight Time
(PDT), GMT −7, from the
second Sun in Mar until
the first Sun in Nov.

Insurance

Travel insurance should
cover your belongings and
your holiday investment.
Buy cover for delayed or
cancelled flights as well as
weather problems and
evacuation in case of
medical emergencies.

Unwatched luggage can vanish in an instant. Some airports and bus or train stations have lockers; guard the key and memorise the locker number. Hotel bell staff may keep guest luggage for a few days, but always get receipts.

If attacked, hand over your bag or money. Resistance is likely to provoke physical harm. Report incidents to local police immediately, if only to get a report for your insurance company.

Safe driving

Car-hire counter personnel should recommend a safe, direct route on a clear map. Lock all valuables and luggage in the boot or glove box. Keep car doors and windows locked. Don't drive into unlit areas or neighbourhoods that seem unsafe. If told by a passing motorist or pedestrian that something is wrong with your car, *do not stop*. If you must stop, wait for a well-lit or populated area, even if your car is hit by another vehicle.

If your car breaks down, turn on the flashing emergency lights, raise the bonnet and wait inside the vehicle. Lights on emergency vehicles are red or red and blue; never stop for flashing white lights.

Have your keys out to unlock car doors before entering a car park. Check the surrounding area and inside the vehicle before entering.

Don't pick up hitchhikers or leave the car with the engine running.

Safe sleeping

Lock room doors, windows and sliding glass doors from the inside. Ground-floor rooms are convenient but easier to break into. When leaving the room at night, leave a light on to deter prowlers.

When someone knocks at the door, use the peephole to see who it is. If someone claims to be on the hotel staff, check with the front desk. Money, cheques, credit cards, passports and keys should be with you or in the hotel safe-deposit box.

Safe documents

Photocopy the important pages of your passport, visas and tickets. Carry the copies and extra passport photos separately from the documents themselves. If you are robbed, you will have identification and a head start on replacing crucial documents. To replace a passport, apply to your nearest consulate, probably in Los Angeles or San Francisco.

Shopping

Souvenirs include local wines; almonds, walnuts, dates and other dried fruits; sourdough French bread; and prepared mustards, oils and condiments. Clothing is a bargain, especially at discount stores and

National and State Parks

State Parks charge daily entry fees, National Parks charge by the week. Camping fees are extra. If visiting several national parks, national wildlife refuges, Bureau of Land Management lands, and national forests, it would be economical to purchase a National Parks and Federal Recreational and Lands Annual Pass. *Tel: (888)-ASK-USGS (press 1); http://store.usgs.gov/pass.* California's **Annual Day Use Pass** is $125. *Tel: (866) 417-2757; www.store.parks.ca.gov/passes.aspx*

Festivals

California celebrates everything from independence (from England, Jul 4) to garlic (Gilroy Garlic Festival, Aug) and homosexuality (Gay Pride Week, San Francisco and other cities, Jun). California Tourism lists major festivals, or check with local visitor bureaux. Street fairs and Farmers' Markets thrive on sunny weekends.

Above
The entrance to Zion National Park (Utah)

factory outlets. California state sales tax is 7.25 per cent, applicable to all purchases except food and pharmaceuticals. Local taxes can add up to 1.5 per cent.

Sport

San Francisco, Los Angeles and San Diego have professional sports teams. Baseball, football, basketball, hockey and soccer are major draws. Cities like Anaheim, Oakland, Sacramento and San Jose also have pro teams. Tickets may be available at short notice; ask at your hotel. Tickets for training games (late summer for football, spring for baseball) are considerably cheaper than regular season tickets. Better still are small-town minor league baseball games. The minor leagues (called Triple A or farm teams) let you see tomorrow's stars at reasonable prices in small stadiums and a relaxed atmosphere.

Telephones

Public telephones (pay phones), becoming rare in the mobile phone era, are usually marked by a white telephone on a blue background. Dialling instructions are posted on the telephone or in the telephone directory. Most pay phones do not accept incoming or return calls. Local calls generally cost 50¢; toll-free (800, 866, 877 and 888 area codes) and 911 (emergency) calls are free. To talk to an operator, dial 0. To locate local numbers, dial 411. For long-distance information, dial 1–(area code)–555-1212. There is a charge for all information calls. Some areas require a 1 before dialling, even for local calls.

Many hotels and motels add steep surcharges to the cost of phone calls from rooms; use a pay phone in the lobby. Few phone cards or calling cards issued outside the US are accepted by US phone companies, but prepaid calling cards are widely available at supermarkets, post offices, convenience stores and tourist offices.

For international enquiries or assistance, dial 00. For international calls, dial 011 (access code) + country code + city code (omit the first zero if there is one) + local number. To call inner London, for example, dial 011-44-207-local number. If your call does not connect, check the three-digit area code in the telephone directory White Pages, or dial an information telephone operator.

Fax numbers are being used less and less in this technology-savvy area. Internet cafés are widely available in urban areas and around colleges and universities. Yet so many people have or travel with computers, it may be easier to travel with your own computer or with a locally compatible, web-enabled cell phone. Many public areas, including coffee shops, airports, hotels and convention centres – even some cities – have wireless remote connections.

Driver's guide

Automobile clubs

There are no reciprocal agreements between the AA and RAC, and the equivalent AAA in the United States. You should ensure that you purchase sufficient insurance when you hire a car.

Autoroutes & bridges

California has several toll roads, the 17-Mile Drive (Monterey-Carmel area) and two in Orange County in Southern California. Most bridges charge a toll in one direction, although a carpool may use a special toll-free non-stop lane. Cash is fine, but no credit cards or traveller's cheques can be used. California has a FasTrak pass system for commuters that deducts the toll automatically when an enrolled car passes through the tollbooth area.

Documents

A national driving licence is valid in California. It must be in your possession at all times. The minimum driving age, with driver training, is 16, or 18 years of age without training. Provisional licences are not valid. Car rental companies require that all drivers be

Accidents

You must STOP after any accident. You can be in serious trouble if you don't. *Never* leave the site of the accident before contacting the required authorities and exchanging information on who is involved, addresses, telephone numbers, automobile make, licence number and registration, and insurance details. Safeguard against a secondary accident. Hazard lights, warning triangles or red emergency flares signal to other traffic that there is a problem. Call the California Highway Patrol (CHP) or local police if there are injuries or obvious damage to any vehicle. The universal emergency number is 911 to alert the police authorities or to call an Ambulance or the Fire Department. On some freeways, free emergency roadside telephones are located at approximately one-mile intervals. Show police your driving licence, vehicle registration, proof of insurance and contact information, and exchange the same details with the other driver(s). Get the names of any witnesses. Note as many details as you can – photographs can be helpful later. Death or injury must be reported to the police or the CHP within 24 hours of the accident. Collisions in California resulting in death, injury or property damage over $750 must be reported – whether or not you caused the accident – to the California Department of Motor Vehicles (DMV) within ten days on California Accident Report Form SR1. DMV offices are listed in the telephone book blue government pages under California Government. In Nevada, report collisions resulting in death, injury or over $750 in property damage to police or the Nevada Highway Patrol and to the Nevada Department of Motor Vehicles within ten days.

If your vehicle collides with a parked vehicle, leave a note with your name and contact information securely affixed to the other vehicle. For a collision with an animal, do not try to move it, but call the nearest humane society, animal control department or police. With any accident, inform your insurers as soon as possible.

Breakdowns

If you have a breakdown, stop your vehicle on the hard shoulder, getting it as far to the right as possible. On ordinary roads, consider using the verge but beware of roadside ditches. Turn hazard lights on and raise the bonnet. Place one or more reflective warning triangles where they can be seen by other drivers travelling in the same direction. (Remember, it can be very dangerous to walk on the hard

at least age 25. The vehicle registration, proof of liability and collision insurance cover, with any rental care contracts, must be in the car and accessible at all times.

Drinking and driving

DUI, driving under the influence of alcohol (or any other drug), is illegal. The blood alcohol concentration (limit) is not to exceed .08 per cent (.01 per cent if under 21 years of age), and is strictly enforced. Drivers suspected of drunk driving have a choice of a breath, blood or urine test; police are also likely to ask any suspect to get out of the vehicle and walk in a straight line. Refusing a test is an admission of guilt. Penalties include imprisonment for 48 hours to six months, a large fine and the vehicle may be impounded for six months. The law requires attendance at a DUI programme and fees for insurance and other documents.

Police establish random checkpoints, sometimes in unmarked vehicles and sometimes parked in less obvious places. Roads near winery tasting rooms and popular roadside restaurants are closely monitored.

Essentials

You should travel with three red reflective warning triangles, road flares, a torch, a first-aid kit and a jack for tyre repair. If the vehicle has a spare tyre, make sure that it is properly inflated.

shoulder of any freeway or highway.) You and your passengers may be safer out of the vehicle and well up the verge away from the traffic, but for security, stay in the locked car if you are in an isolated area, it is night-time, or it is hard to see for any reason.

If you need assistance on a freeway you may use one of the free roadside telephones to connect you with the police. You may ring for a breakdown lorry, called a tow truck, which is usually dispatched from a local petrol (gas) station. Breakdown insurance is strongly recommended and one phone call is all it takes to hand the whole problem over to an operator who is expert in sorting things out. Your insurance company may call a towing service it has under contract for emergency roadside assistance repairs or towing to a repair garage. You are responsible for payment or for signing the form that affirms to your insurance company that you have had the service. Most car-hire companies either pay for repairs directly or reimburse the cost shown on repair receipts. If a hire car is going to be out of service for more than a few hours, ask the hire company for a replacement vehicle.

Caravans and campervans (trailers and RVs)

RVs are a popular way to move around the countryside and seek the best seasonal weather. Motorhomes are just that – popular year-round with retired people, and may be ideal for holidaymakers with families on a budget, planning to have some meals in or not wanting to change lodging every night. The cost of petrol (gas) may be a consideration.

California permits motorhomes up to 45 feet long on most roads and the United States has a fairly extensive system of private RV parks. Woodall's (*www.woodalls.com*) is *the* reference for 15,000 camping spots, and publishes a comprehensive guide to US facilities. Most state and national parks and national forests have RV or trailer pitches (spaces) that should be reserved as far in advance as possible. Pitches may include a small barbecue grill and a picnic table with benches. Unless otherwise marked, it is generally legal to *park* an RV or trailer along the side of a road or on city streets (although not necessarily to stay in it), but the vehicle must always be pulled off the roadway and should only be parked in a safe, preferably well-lit place in view of passers-by. Thefts and break-ins are not unknown. Official California highway rest stops permit stays of up to eight hours, but overnighting is illegal and may be dangerous. Depending on local laws, it may *not be legal to occupy a vehicle parked overnight on the side of the road or on a city street.* Check in advance with local tourism offices or the police authorities. It is always safest to spend the night in an RV park or booked camping pitch.

Maintenance takes time and attention away from touring, but it must be done. Check the RV inside and out for its condition and understand its driving controls and systems maintenance before leaving the rental lot. For sanitary and environmental reasons, California requires that sewage system disposal be done at authorised dump stations.

Fines

Drivers can be fined for moving violations like speeding, illegal turns or other infractions, for parking violations, and for DUI, Driving Under the Influence (of alcohol or illegal drugs). Police authorities or the highway patrol will issue a citation, commonly called a ticket, on the spot. The citation specifies the police authority, jurisdiction (city, town, county, state), legal code reference number, a short description of the violation, the vehicle reference, the police officer's badge number (identification) and name, your information if it is a moving violation, and where and how the ticket can be paid or challenged.

On-the-spot fine payments are *never* made, and anyone offering to pay a fine when cited may be assumed to be offering a bribe to a police officer, an extremely serious offence.

Citations are registered in a computer database by car licence that is linked to the vehicle identification number. The car or RV rental company will be notified of any citations issued to its vehicles.

Lights

All traffic must use headlights in rain, fog, snow, or when visibility is poor or unclear, i.e., less than 1000 feet ahead. Lights must be on from one-half hour after sunset to one-half hour before sunrise. Lights on are always sensible on small

Motorhomes, towed vehicles and any vehicle with more than two axles pay more for bridge tolls. RVs and trailers are legally considered trucks and must observe truck speed limits and other road directions, including warnings on road declines and inclines.

RVs are blown about by wind more than cars and are more subject to rollover. Taller and wider dimensions can create hazards at gas stations, tollbooths, car parks, and with low-hanging trees and signs.

Driving in California

Sightseers take to the roads on public holidays and during the Jun–Aug school summer break.

The US has several common types of road: highways (that can be Interstate Highways or within the state); freeways (designed to speed traffic flow, although in urban areas like Los Angeles or the San Francisco Bay Area, freeways do anything but); state routes (fewer traffic lanes than highways or freeways and often a more scenic way to transit between areas); rural routes (which seldom have tourist attractions), and city streets. In large cities, expect one-way streets in downtown areas.

Generally, roads are numbered, with odd numbers running north–south and even numbers going east–west. In the Los Angeles area, some freeways, though numbered, are referred to by names like the Hollywood Freeway (Hwy 101 in the Los Angeles region) or San Diego Freeway (I-405).

Interstate 5 (I-5) starts in San Diego, goes through Orange County and Los Angeles, and continues north up California's Central Valley to Oregon and beyond, an efficient route without much scenic value. I-8 from San Diego roughly follows the Mexican border. I-10, east of LA, is the way to Palm Springs and Phoenix, Arizona. From San Diego, I-15 heads north before turning northeast to wind through the desert to Las Vegas. I-80 connects San Francisco, Sacramento and Reno.

Highway 1 is the coast route; the narrow lanes and twisting coast along Big Sur may be California's most famed scenic route. Hwy 101, the old Spanish El Camino that connected the string of 21 missions, follows some coast, but winds inland, too, for a variety of scenery from Hollywood to Crescent City. Hwy 49 serpentines through California's Gold Country.

California has almost every difficult driving condition imaginable outside the tropics. For desert travel, the air conditioner and heater should be in perfect condition. Carry extra water, food, warm clothing and a torch. Rare desert rains can cause flash floods, turning dry riverbeds into churning torrents in seconds. A sand or snow storm can reduce visibility to zero; if caught, pull off the road to a high spot and wait it out. Many passes over the Sierra Nevada mountains are closed Nov–Jun. Open highways in snow country post signs indicating when chains must be used. The petrol tank should always be half full, and

country or mountain roads. Driving only with parking lights is illegal. Most motorcycles will have headlights on at all times, and most cyclists will wear reflectors or have them on the bike; wearing a helmet is compulsory for both.

Mobile phones

Mobile or cell(ular) phone use while driving is illegal in California. A hands-free device is legal. A mobile phone can be useful to call for breakdown assistance, or 911 in an emergency.

Road information

For California road conditions, including closures, call Caltrans, *tel: (800) 427-7623* for recorded information keyed to highway numbers, or check *www.dot.ca.gov/hq/roadinfo.* In some regions, such as in the San Francisco Bay Area, *tel: 511; www.5ll.org,* for travel information. For Nevada Department of Transportation Road Information, *tel: 511* or *(877) 687-6237* or check *http://safetravelusa.com/nv.* Local radio stations broadcast weather and driving information.

Seat belts

The driver and all passengers must wear seat belts. Children under the age of 6 or weighing less than 60 pounds must ride in National Highway Traffic Safety Administration-approved child safety seats. Infants up to 20 pounds or

winter travellers should carry warm clothing, food and water in case of traffic delays. Fog and dust storms cause massive chain-reaction collisions in the Central Valley each year. Slow down and turn the headlamps on low beam for better visibility.

Driving rules

Traffic drives on the right in the United States. Where streets meet and vehicles arrive at close to the same time, priority belongs to the vehicle on the right, and proceeds anti-clockwise. Traffic already in a roundabout (traffic circle or rotary) has the right of way, and those waiting launch in whenever they can. Unless otherwise posted, in California, a vehicle can turn right from the right-hand lane. Before turning, the driver signals the intended direction, although in practice, many drivers don't bother. Horns are seldom used.

Interstate highways, highways and freeway entrances are clearly marked with green and white signs. Heavily used freeways will have a signal light to control traffic flow onto the roadway. In populous areas, the left-hand freeway lane will be marked with a white diamond for HOV (high occupancy vehicle) and accommodate carpools, groups of 2, 3 or more in a vehicle, as signposted by that fast flow lane.

On city streets and occasionally on country roads, bicycle paths are marked as a separate lane on the right where bikes have the right of way. Buses stopping at the right side of the road and pulling out into traffic go first. A school bus stopped with flashing lights and lights at a railway crossing stops traffic as long as the lights flash.

Roadways are marked with a solid white line for 'do not pass', and with a broken line where passing is permitted. Blind curves are not infrequent, dictating slower speeds and no passing on curves.

Police use radar, lasers and aeroplanes to track, stop and cite speeding drivers. In California, pedestrians always have the right of way.

Fuel

Petrol (and diesel) is sold at gas stations in US gallons (about four litres per gallon). Most vehicles take unleaded gas that comes in regular, premium and super grades. Buy regular unless the car rental company or the vehicle operation manual specifies otherwise. Most gas stations are self-service, although some offer a higher-priced full-service alternative. Pump prices include all taxes. Gas stations generally accept cash, credit cards, debit cards and $20 traveller's cheques. Due to counterfeiting and safety concerns, gas station clerks will not accept $50 or $100 bills. Fuel is cheapest at budget chains and at some discount stores (usually not in tourist areas), and there is some competition, so prices can vary. Prices are reasonable off highways exits and highest in the cities where traffic flow is high and stations are scarce. The cost is always shown with .9 at the end of the number,

one year should have the safety seat secured to the back seat and be facing the rear of the vehicle. Safety seats can be hired with the car or purchased for under $100 at a discount store. In an RV, passengers riding behind the driver's seat need not wear belts, but should be safely seated when the vehicle is in motion.

Speed limits

California and the rest of the United States choose miles over metric. Kilometres appear alongside mileage on occasional highway and National Park signs.

Interstate Highways – 60, 65 or 75mph (as posted)

Highways and Freeways – 65mph (55mph for RVs and trailers)

In cities or towns – 25mph unless posted otherwise

Poor driving conditions – keep to a safe speed.

Road signs

European-style road signs are widely used, but not universally. *Red* signs indicate 'stop', 'do not enter', or 'wrong way'. *Yellow* signs are warnings or direction indicators. *Orange* means road repairs (roadworks) or detours (diversions). *White* shows speed limits and distances, almost always in miles. *Brown* indicates parks, camping and other recreation opportunities. *Blue* gives non-driving information such as services in a nearby town.

as $439.9 or $398.9. Chain gas stations stay open long hours daily, and in urban areas may operate 24 hours.

Information

The AAA has the widest map coverage in the USA, though local auto club map designs mean that maps are not consistent between areas. Rand McNally also publishes map series. Local Chambers of Commerce or Convention and Visitors Bureaux will have local maps of varying quality and detail for free or for a small charge.

Parking

Street parking in downtown areas can be scarce; San Francisco has only a fraction of parking spaces per resident, and that does not include workers who commute into the city centre. Multi-storey car parks, called 'garages', indicated by a white P on a blue background, are one choice in downtown areas but can be exorbitant in major cities, as much as $20 per hour. Prices are posted at the car park entrance.

Kerbside parking time is usually limited, either by posted signs or coin-operated parking meters. Kerbs may be colour-coded: *red* means no stopping or parking at any time; *white* is for passenger loading/unloading only; *green* is limited parking, usually 10 minutes; *yellow* is a commercial loading zone; and *blue* is disabled parking. Parking is not allowed within 15 feet of a fire hydrant, within 3 feet of a disabled kerb ramp, in bus stops, zebra crossings (crosswalks), on pavements (sidewalks) or on freeways. Fines vary from a few dollars to several hundred, depending on the infraction and jurisdiction. No police authority accepts cash on the spot to take care of the fine. Fines levied against rental cars are charged against the hirer's credit card.

Security

Sensible care should be taken, particularly where vehicles are left for long periods in vulnerable places such as tourist site car parks. Do not leave items on view inside the car. Even if you know they are of little or no value, a potential thief does not. Park in well-lit areas and double check that the vehicle is locked.

In the large cities, it is wise to keep car doors locked and windows up. If hot weather means you must have the window open, be sure that handbags, wallets, cameras, etc. are well out of sight and reach and, above all, never on a passenger's lap. Check for intruders before getting in, especially at night and in an RV any time. Never leave the vehicle engine running when the driver isn't behind the wheel.

Should you have the misfortune to become a victim of crime, your insurers will require you to report the circumstances to the police and obtain a police report that you have done so.

TYPICAL ROAD SIGNS IN CALIFORNIA

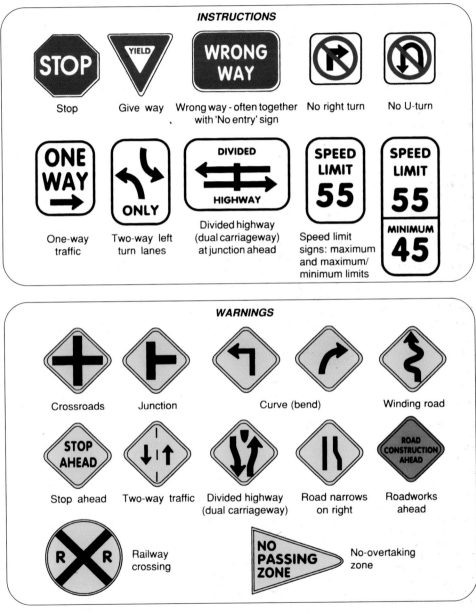

INSTRUCTIONS

Stop

Give way

Wrong way - often together with 'No entry' sign

No right turn

No U-turn

One-way traffic

Two-way left turn lanes

Divided highway (dual carriageway) at junction ahead

Speed limit signs: maximum and maximum/minimum limits

WARNINGS

Crossroads

Junction

Curve (bend)

Winding road

Stop ahead

Two-way traffic

Divided highway (dual carriageway)

Road narrows on right

Roadworks ahead

Railway crossing

No-overtaking zone

Getting to California

Right
The place to unwind after a
long flight

Unless you already live within driving distance of California, flying is the most practicable way to get there. Transcontinental train and motor coach travel is slow, cramped and unpredictable, although AMTRAK operates popular coastal services from San Diego to Seattle, Washington (*www.amtrak.com*). Air travel is even more cramped, but travel time is counted in hours rather than days.

Don't undertake a full day's touring after a long flight. Los Angeles and San Francisco may be only 10–12 air hours from much of Europe and 12–14 hours from Asia, but jet lag intensifies the effects of long-distance air travel. Expect to arrive fatigued, disorientated, short-tempered and otherwise *not* ready to drive.

Night-time flights are attractive because they seem to offer an extra day of sightseeing upon arrival. Resist the temptation. Most travellers do better by timing their flights to arrive in the late afternoon or early evening, then getting a good night's sleep before tackling the sights. Since many airport-area hotels and motels offer free shuttle service to and from the airport, you can take a shuttle to the hotel, recover from the flight and pick up your rental car the next morning at no additional cost.

Many fly-drive programmes offer what looks like an easy first-day drive, ie Los Angeles International Airport to the Disneyland area in Anaheim. It's a 45-minute jaunt that can stretch to hours in heavy rush-hour traffic. Better to rest the first night and hit the road refreshed in the morning – especially if you are not accustomed to urban traffic or driving on the right side of the road.

The reverse is equally true. Don't plan a tight schedule that gets you into Los Angeles or San Francisco and to the airport the requisite three hours before an international departure. Unexpected traffic can leave you stranded on a freeway as your plane takes off overhead. Check current security and luggage requirements with your airline before departure, and verify document requirements again, before travelling. Airlines won't hold an entire flight for a carload of passengers flying on non-refundable bargain fares. Allow a safety margin by spending your last night in California near the departure airport, or at least in the same city.

Luggage trolleys are free in the international arrivals area; in domestic terminals, a major credit card like Visa or Access/MasterCard will hire a trolley.

Currency exchange facilities will be obvious upon arrival in international airport terminals, though numerous ATMs offer the best currency exchange rates and never close. Star and Circus are the most common international ATM networks. US dollar traveller's cheques from Thomas Cook and other major issuers are accepted almost everywhere, but traveller's cheques in other currencies must generally be cashed at a bank. Personal cheques drawn on banks outside the United States are usually not accepted. Major hotel registration desk staff will usually exchange major currencies with unfavourable rates – convenient only as a last resort.

California airports don't have duty-free shopping for incoming travellers. Prices for alcohol and other duty-free items are almost always lower in California supermarkets and discount stores than in duty-free shops. The same goes for other goods. Airport prices are higher than in similar shops nearby and the selection is smaller. Airport fast-food outlets are comparable to chain outlets anywhere, but airport restaurants are generally higher in price and vary in quality, although some are memorably good.

A few car-hire companies have desks located near airport luggage claim areas, but nearly all require that you take a coach to an off-airport facility to pick up your car. Follow terminal signs for Rental Cars to the proper coach or van loading area.

Once at the car-hire location, have your booking number, passport, credit card and driving licence ready. Everyone who might drive the vehicle must show his or her driving licence and be listed on the rental contract. Drivers must generally be at least 25 years old, although some companies allow younger drivers for an additional fee.

Setting the scene

Above
Lake Helen, in Lassen Volcanic National Park

The lure of California is as much mythical as real, but even the reality of the place borders on the unbelievable. The state, a bent rectangle 900 miles long by 200 miles wide, holds every climatic zone on earth except tropical rainforest and arctic wastes. The highest point in North America, Mount Whitney (14,491ft), and the lowest, Death Valley (282ft below sea level), are just 60 miles apart in southeastern California, but the winding 120-mile road trip between the two can take most of the day.

The state is a patchwork of awkward but awesome terrain, formed by tens of millions of years of earthquakes that have rent the landscape into a mosaic of mountains and fault lines. The biggest patch of flat land, the **Central Valley**, is 400 miles long by 50 miles wide. Nearly everything else is vertical.

California's entire coastline of 1264 corrugated miles is hemmed in by the **Coast Range**. Southern slopes are cloaked in explosively flammable brush, northern mountains by dense forests. **San Francisco Bay** is the only break in this natural wall.

The eastern side of the state is guarded by the **Sierra Nevada Mountains**, which rise gently from the Central Valley through the rolling hills of **Gold Country** to drop precipitously down eastern slopes into the Nevada deserts. A series of east–west ranges connects the Coast Range with the Sierra, making north–south travel a slow and tortuous task before the advent of modern roads. Fifty feet and more of snow blankets the Sierra every winter, closing most mountain passes from November until June. Each spring, the runoff roars through canyons up to 5000ft deep.

The climate is officially Mediterranean, even though the winter rain/summer drought pattern more resembles North Africa than Greece or Italy. Annual rainfall varies from less than an inch in the southeast deserts to more than 100ins in the northwest. Coastal redwood forests drip with accumulated mist while the deserts wither under scorching sun and some of the highest temperatures on earth.

In the beginning

The veil of myth and hyperbole that colours California was first woven in Spain. A 1510 Spanish romantic novel created Queen Califa, ruler of an island somewhere to the west of Europe, a land filled with black Amazons who rode griffins into battle and fought with weapons of pure gold. A few years later, Spanish conquistadores ventured north after subduing Native empires in Central and South America, hoping for more conquests, more gold and more glory.

Above
Joshua Tree National Park is named after these striking trees, so-called because they resemble Joshua raising his arms to heaven

What they found instead was the peninsula of lower, or Baja, California. The locals were hostile, the landscape barren and gold nowhere to be found. The would-be conquerors named the unpromising peninsula 'California', hoping that fiction would serve better than truth.

The first European to see Alta, or upper, California, died there. **Juan Rodríquez Cabrillo** landed at San Diego in 1542, then broke his leg on San Miguel Island, now part of **Channel Islands National Park**, and died there, probably of gangrene. His crew sailed north as far as Oregon, then retreated back to Mexico. Spain called Cabrillo's voyage a failed and futile expedition.

Francis Drake, English privateer and later admiral, was the first European to make his fortune in California. Like many who followed, his scheme was not entirely legal but eminently successful.

Drake hunted Manila galleons, the lumbering Spanish treasure ships that sailed east from Manila each year laden with the plunder of Asia and the Philippines. The galleons sailed east to California, then turned south to Mexico and safety. Those that survived the trip were unloaded in Acapulco and other Mexican ports, their treasures transhipped to the east coast of Mexico, then sent through the Caribbean and on to Spain. Drake found the lightly armed galleons such easy prey that his ship, the *Golden Hinde*, was soon splitting from the weight of Spanish booty.

In 1579, he beached the *Hinde* for repairs, probably landing at Drakes Bay, now part of **Point Reyes National Seashore**, just north of San Francisco. Drake and his crew left a few undeniably English silver pennies behind for modern archaeologists. An engraved copper plaque claiming the land for Queen Elizabeth may or may not be authentic. Drake then sailed home to a knighthood while Spain ignored California for another 200 years.

Spain's neglect was a final reprieve for California's Native American population. Rugged terrain limited travel, but the climate was mild and food plentiful. Acorns were the staple, usually made into porridge or bread. Deer and small game were abundant. Rivers and bays were so rich in shellfish that coastal clans left heaps of discarded shells 30ft high. When the Spanish arrived in 1769, the Native American world quickly collapsed beneath the combined weight of disease, slavery and Christianity.

Gaspar de Portola and a Franciscan friar, **Junípero Serra**, led an expedition from Baja California north to San Diego. Serra stayed in San Diego to tend the sick and establish the first of 21 missions that stretched north to Sonoma. Portola explored north along what would become **El Camino Real**, 'the King's Highway', better known today as Hwy 101. The Spanish Empire had come to California.

An advance party climbed a ridge between today's cities of Pacifica and Millbrae and found their way blocked by an immense bay. Portola gave up and turned south again. Juan Crespi, a monk, recorded in his diary the sighting of a bay big enough to hold all the fleets of Europe. It was the first recorded description of **San Francisco Bay**.

Portola later sailed north with Serra from San Diego to Monterey, supposedly a fine harbour. Portola built a *presidio*, or fort; Serra built another mission. More missions were founded, including San Francisco in 1776, the year the United States declared independence from England.

Spain's empire declined during the early 19th century, but the California missions prospered. Vineyards, orchards, herds and maize fields flourished. Buildings began to assume a familiar form: whitewashed stone or brick churches topped by red clay tiles and bordered by arched colonnades. Fountains cooled lush central gardens.

Right
Mission Carmel: San Carlos Borromeo del Rio Carmelo mission church

Above
Trail riders in Grand Canyon
National Park

Californios

Ecclesiastical prosperity was short-lived. Mexico gained independence from Spain in 1821. Thirteen years later, Mexico secularised and sold the vast Mission estates to cattle ranchers (*Californios*). The Church's loss was California's gain.

The *rancho*, or ranch, became the basic social, cultural and economic unit. This gave California a rose-tinted heritage of dashing *caballeros*, gentlemen landowners, and swirling *señoritas*, glamorous young women. They created one of the largest and most prosperous pastoral societies the world has ever seen.

Californios sold 75,000 cattle hides yearly at $2 each to Yankee traders. With no enforceable taxes, plentiful food supplies and no need for armies, everything went to luxury imports. The *caballeros* raised cattle and bought them back as Boston-made boots. *Señoritas* slipped into fine Cantonese silk gowns to dance on floors of packed dirt. English and American merchants, most of them former sailors who had jumped ship, managed the trade.

The foreigners also managed the fur and whaling trade. New Englanders hunted whales migrating between Alaska and Baja California, nearly destroying every species of whale in the Pacific Ocean, while Russians hunted sea otters to the brink of extinction from their base at **Fort Ross**, north of San Francisco.

Furs lured English and American adventurers overland, and the Hudson's Bay Company began California operations in 1829. In 1832, mountain man **Christopher 'Kit' Carson** helped map a trail from Santa Fe, New Mexico, to a lawless, dusty village called **Los Angeles**.

The first American overland immigrants arrived in 1841, the first wagon train in 1844. Then came the Donner Party, which had the misfortune to follow a guidebook written by an explorer who had never actually been to California. The party were snowbound in the Sierra near Donner Summit, on what is now I-80, from November 1846 to February 1847. Forty of the 87 would-be pioneers survived by eating their livestock and their comrades.

Donner survivors arrived to find a new flag. Earlier settlers had been unhappy with a succession of weak Mexican governors, and when American Captain John Frémont 'happened' to appear in 1846 with a troop of 68 heavily armed soldiers, California's foreign population revolted. The rebels raised a flag over Sonoma carrying a star and a bear (which contemporaries said looked more like a pig) and declared the California Republic. Their new republic lasted one month.

The US declared war on Mexico in May; by July, naval units had occupied every California port and taken control of what little provincial government existed. The transition to American rule proceeded smoothly. *Californios* still ruled society and local government, foreign merchants ran the economy and there was land to spare for immigrants.

The Gold Rush

The discovery of gold in January 1848 changed California forever. The population mushroomed from 10,000 to 100,000 in two years. San Francisco metamorphosed from a windy, flea-bitten village into a city of 25,000. Gold, the first significant supply the world had seen since Spain had looted the Aztec, Inca and Maya empires in the 16th century, gave California the economic muscle to escape exploitation by New York and London financiers. The land nurtured its own collection of robber barons and a reputation as a place of eternal opportunity.

Above
Re-enacting the Gold Rush at Columbia State Historic Park

Americans of the era seized upon California gold as evidence of Divine favour and their right to rule the continent. After all, Spain and Mexico, the world's most experienced mining countries, had owned California for 300 years without finding significant deposits of the precious metal. American James Marshall spotted nuggets in a water-wheel raceway just days before America paid Mexico $18.25 million for the entire southwestern quadrant of the continent. Miners pulled more than 30 times that much gold from California alone in less than a decade.

Most of the **49ers** sought their fortunes in what is now called Gold Country, the Sierra Nevada foothills along Hwy 49. When military officials called a constitutional convention in 1849, delegates split along regional lines. The south opposed joining the United States, rightly fearing that land, not mines, would be taxed. The north wanted statehood in order to assure a stable gold market. The northern faction won and California became a state in 1850.

The Gold Rush brought fortune to lucky miners and merchants who supplied the mines. The influx of miners from around the globe created shortages in everything from tea to tin. The American majority discriminated openly and violently against Chinese, Roman Catholics, Mexicans, Indians and anyone else who had the misfortune to be both non-American and successful.

Gold also destroyed the *Californios*. Inflation ravaged their finances as drought devastated their herds. Newly arrived Americans demanded title to the millions of hectares owned by a few hundred *Californio* families. Dubious land commissions awarded most acreage to American claimants whose best arguments were their nationality and ability to speak English.

The California Dream never faltered. As the goldfields played out, a tide of silver from Nevada brought new riches. The Comstock Lode beneath **Virginia City** produced $400 million for San Francisco mining companies before deposits were mined out in the 1880s.

Railroads were even better moneyspinners. **Mark Hopkins, Collis Huntington, Leland Stanford** and **Charles Crocker**, Sacramento merchants who backed the 1863 transcontinental railroad, became The Big Four. The quartet built fortunes on marginal land schemes and outright fraud, but California boomed. San Francisco ruled a commercial empire that stretched from China to Utah and Alaska to Mexico.

Even the weather contributed. As gold and silver lost their lustre, farmers realised that California was the one part of North America where rain fell only in winter. Agriculture flourished, from the vegetable farms that fed the cities to the vineyards that kept them drunk. With later irrigation schemes, the pattern of summer drought and winter water made the state an agricultural powerhouse in everything from apples and cotton to potatoes and marijuana.

In the 1880s, the railroad, by then called 'The Octopus' for its many-tendrilled influence in state and local politics, decided that California needed more people. Transcontinental fares fell to $1 per person just as farmers, real-estate developers and the city of Los Angeles began extolling the virtues of sunny Southern California. Nature provided the sunshine, but California business designed the message, complete with alluring 'California Girl' posters.

The advent of the automobile and the fortuitous discovery of oil made the move west even easier. The burgeoning population demanded water, particularly in the desert that was most of Southern California. In 1913, Los Angeles built an aqueduct to pull water from the Owens Valley, east of the Sierra Nevada Mountains, to the parched city. The scheme was ridden with unscrupulous behaviour, corruption and scandal, as depicted in the film *Chinatown* which was produced half a century later, but Los Angeles had the water it needed to continue growing.

Agricultural interests saw the same future in irrigation; aqueducts carried water from the Colorado River to Southern California and the Central Valley. The Great Depression of the 1930s brought waves of migrant farmers into California from dusty, drought-plagued Oklahoma and Arkansas. Many joined indigenous Mexican farmworkers who migrated to harvest seasonal crops from Southern California to the Canadian border.

When World War II erupted, California became a wartime induction and shipping centre. Thousands of men passed through San Francisco, Los Angeles and San Diego on the way to battlefields in the Pacific, while naval operations brought an influx of military personnel and support services that remained through the 1990s.

After the war

With the war over, soldiers and sailors returned in droves to settle in California's alluring coastal cities. The GI Bill provided free university education for veterans, many of whom attended the University of California in Berkeley, where much of America's atomic bomb research had been conducted. The new life and easy climate helped breed a new movement of artistic protest as beatniks flocked to the coffee houses in San Francisco's **North Beach**.

The protest movement that the Beats began spread to other segments of the population. By the early 1960s, agricultural workers, most of them originally from Mexico, began to organise against backbreaking working conditions, while university students in Berkeley began demanding more freedom of speech.

By the mid-1960s, the first post-war generation was coming of age. Higher education received state funding and was no longer the reserve of the élite. Free thinking, free speech, free sex, free drugs, free everything came together in the hippie movement, while tie-dyed clothing, flowers, beads, incense, bare feet and jeans became the trademarks of a generation. Marijuana was the popular choice of drug, eclipsing the traditional favourites – alcohol and tobacco. Music recording studios in London suddenly had to contend with serious competition from Los Angeles and San Francisco.

Escalation of America's war in Vietnam in the late 1960s again brought thousands of soldiers pouring through California. Antiwar protesters from campuses state-wide took to the streets to demonstrate against the war even as the state's aerospace, communications and electronics industries grew wealthy from military spending.

The end of the Vietnam conflict in 1973 brought yet another wave of immigration, this time from Indochina. Political turmoil in Central and South America sent new waves of Hispanic immigrants heading toward California.

Above
Golden Gate Bridge – San Francisco's world-famous engineering masterpiece

Political turmoil at home created its own refugees. In 1978, California voters approved a ballot initiative, Proposition 13, which sharply cut taxes on homes and other real estate. Government revenues plummeted. Some mental sanatoriums were emptied, homeless shelters were reduced in size or closed and funding for education, libraries, museums and other public services was slashed. Government spending was brought into line, but the number of homeless people living on California streets skyrocketed.

The decline of the Cold War in the late 1980s and early 1990s brought stagnation and economic contraction to once-booming aerospace companies, but technology firms emerged to take their place. A bucolic agricultural area near San Jose, south of San Francisco, gradually lost its old name, 'Valley of Heart's Delight'. The name by which it is now known, **Silicon Valley** (which has started to appear on maps), comes from the time when the area was home to a large number of silicon chip innovators and manufacturers. Today it is the centre of the high-tech world, as the computer revolution that began in a Palo Alto garage continues to ricochet around the globe.

Home to a vibrant electronics industry since the early 20th century, Silicon Valley is now home to many companies, including Google and eBay, featured in the Fortune 1000 – the list of America's largest companies in terms of revenue alone. Right at the heart of the valley, in Cupertino, is Apple Inc., famous for its Macintosh computers, iPod portable media players and, more recently, its iPhone.

The same combination of university research, entrepreneurial drive, venture capital, and willingness to succeed that brought Silicon Valley to life also ignited other business booms: the biotechnology sector was born when an ambitious businessman, Robert Swanson, and a biology researcher, Herbert Boyer, came together to found South San Francisco's Genentech in 1976.

California corporate upstarts have emerged to challenge the likes of IBM and Microsoft. Los Angeles-based automobile designers have helped Volkswagen, Nissan and Toyota knock some of the wind out of the sails of America's own car manufacturers in Detroit.

In the real world, there's no way to know just how long the string of successes and superlatives can continue. In the half-real, half-mythical allure of California, almost no one bothers to wonder, at least not in public.

California's population has nearly doubled every generation since the Gold Rush. The reasons to come change from one generation to the next – gold, silver, farms, oil, jobs – but the hopeful waves of immigrants keep coming, certain that the California Dream will come true for them too, as it did for Austrian-born, ex-actor governor, Arnold Schwarzenegger.

Highlights

One of the best experiences of travel is tailoring an itinerary to match your own interests and tastes. Here are some suggestions for itineraries that will show you different aspects of California, depending on how much time you have at your disposal.

The top 10 sights

Not the top 10 places currently receiving the most visitors, but the 10 that we recommend not to miss.

Anza-Borrego Desert State Park *(page 90)*
California's most accessible desert.
Big Sur Coast *(page 214)*
Spectacular drive along golden, surf-baptised cliffs.
Grand Canyon National Park *(page 277)*
After the IMAX®, feast your imagination on the real place.
Hearst Castle *(page 218)*
Megalomania unhampered by good taste.
Las Vegas *(page 264)*
The ultimate theme park where the casino *always* wins.
Napa/Sonoma Wine Country *(page 154)*
Scenic home to some of the world's best wines.
The Redwoods *(page 196)*
The biggest living things on earth (Sequoia National Park) and the tallest (Redwoods National and State Park).
San Diego Zoo's Wild Animal Park *(page 59)*
The best place in California to see exotic animals.
San Francisco *(page 134)*
Everybody's favourite city.
Yosemite National Park *(page 234)*
Mountain scenery so stunning it overawes you.

The best of California

These two circular tours start and end in Los Angeles, but you can reverse them or pick them up in San Francisco or elsewhere. Suggested overnight stops are in **bold type**.

Two weeks
Marathon driving in 14 days!
Day 1: Arrive in **Los Angeles**.
Day 2: LA to Barstow, Baker, Shoshone and **Death Valley**.
Day 3: Death Valley to Lone Pine, Whitney Portal and **Bishop**.
Day 4: Bishop to Lee Vining, Mono Lake and **Yosemite National Park** (Hwy 120 to Yosemite closed in winter).
Day 5: **Yosemite**
Day 6: Yosemite to Gold Country (Mariposa, Sonora, Columbia) and **South Lake Tahoe**.
Day 7: Loop to Genoa, Carson City, Virginia City, Reno and **South Lake Tahoe**.
Day 8: Squaw Valley, Tahoe City, Sacramento and **San Francisco**.
Day 9: **San Francisco**.
Day 10: Loop to Muir Woods, Point Reyes, Jenner, Guerneville, Healdsburg and **San Francisco**.
Day 11: San Francisco to Monterey, Carmel, Hearst Castle (advance tour booking needed) and **San Luis Obispo**.
Day 12: San Luis Obispo to Santa Maria, Solvang and **Santa Barbara**.
Day 13: Santa Barbara to Ojai, Malibu and **Los Angeles**.
Day 14: Home.

Three weeks
See most of California, Grand Canyon National Park and Las Vegas in 21 fast-paced days.

Day 1: Arrive in **Los Angeles**.
Day 2: **Los Angeles**.
Day 3: Los Angeles to **Palm Springs**.
Day 4: Palm Springs to Blythe and **Prescott, Arizona**.
Day 5: Prescott to Sedona, Flagstaff and **Grand Canyon National Park**.
Day 6: Grand Canyon to Cameron, Marble Canyon, Kanab and **Bryce Canyon National Park, Utah**.
Day 7: Bryce to **Zion National Park** (the road into Zion Canyon, Zion Canyon Scenic Drive, is closed to private traffic but accessible by free Shuttle from April to October).
Day 8: Zion to St George and **Las Vegas, Nevada**.
Day 9: Las Vegas to Pahrump and **Death Valley National Park**.
Day 10: Death Valley to Lone Pine and **Bishop**.
Day 11: Bishop to Lee Vining, Mono Lake and **Yosemite National Park** (Hwy 120 to Yosemite closed in winter).
Day 12: **Yosemite**.
Day 13: Yosemite to Gold Country (Mariposa, Sonora, Columbia) and **South Lake Tahoe**.
Day 14: Loop to Genoa, Carson City, Virginia City, Reno and **South Lake Tahoe**.
Day 15: Squaw Valley, Tahoe City, Sacramento and **San Francisco**.
Day 16: **San Francisco**.
Day 17: Loop to Muir Woods, Point Reyes, Jenner, Guerneville, Healdsburg and **San Francisco**.
Day 18: San Francisco to Monterey, Carmel, Hearst Castle (advance tour booking needed) and **San Luis Obispo**.
Day 19: San Luis Obispo to Santa Maria, Solvang and **Santa Barbara**.
Day 20: Santa Barbara to Ojai, Malibu and **Los Angeles**.
Day 21: Home.

Wine country

California has produced wine since Spanish Mission days, and with Napa Valley marketing and world-judged quality in many wine regions, California is second to none in tasting-room accessibility. Microclimates produce distinctive bouquets in a vintage appellation system of AVAs (American Viticultural Areas).

San Francisco is the gateway to the **Napa Valley** and the multiple valley **Sonoma Wine Region**, and to **Mendocino**'s wineries, a further two hours' drive north. South of **San Francisco, Monterey** and **Santa Cruz** wineries can be found amid redwoods and coastal mountains. The **Sierra Foothills, Amador** and **El Dorado**, off Hwy 49 in Gold Country, produce rich, dry wines from volcanic soil and winter snow.

An east-west mountain range funnels fog and ocean breezes far inland to create a long, cool-climate growing season for Southern California's best vintages from **Santa Barbara** wineries, north of Santa Barbara via Hwy 154 and 246 in the Santa Ynez Valley, and the **Santa Maria Valley**, north on Hwy 101. **Edna Valley** white wines, south of **San Luis Obispo**, and **Paso Robles**' heady reds and rich dessert wines, north of San Luis Obispo, create the flavour of summer heat in California's Central Coast region. **Temecula**, 60 miles north of San Diego, provides easy access to wine-tasting rooms amid rugged mountains enshrouded with morning fog, but gets congested at weekends.

Los Angeles

Ratings	
Art	●●●●●
Museums	●●●●●
Shopping	●●●●●
Food and drink	●●●●○
Nightlife	●●●●○
Architecture	●●●○○
Children	●●●○○
Historic sights	●●●○○

As your plane approaches Los Angeles International Airport, the flat sprawl which houses 10.3 million souls within Los Angeles County ends only at the great Pacific Ocean.

The denizens of the amorphous neighbourhoods, urban villages, slums, beach towns and creative colonies coexisting as Angelinos are an upbeat, eternally optimistic mix. Forty-seven per cent are Hispanic, many from Mexico; 8.8 per cent are African-American; and 13 per cent have an Asian or Pacific Island heritage.

Los Angeles has a relentless beat, a constant music of car horns, computer keys tapping away in cafés, thrumming generators, beeping signs, the whoosh of espresso coffee machines, mechanised leafblowers, and the hiss of water wastefully washing sidewalks in this desert. Angelinos call their home El-Lay, short, snappy, abbreviated, sassy, an entertaining name, like themselves. Often faintly visible through 'haze', Los Angeles's mountains rise startlingly to the north and east. (*For Long Beach, Santa Monica and the beach cities between, see Route 4, pages 70–77.*)

Getting there and getting around

Metro *Tel: (800) 266-6883; http:// metro.net. One-day Metro pass $5; www.metro.net/ riding_metro/riders_guide/ paying_fare-01.htm*

ⓘ **LA, Inc., The Convention and Visitors Bureau** *www.discoverlosangeles.com* **Downtown Los Angeles Visitor Information Center** *685 S. Figueroa St between Wilshire Blvd and 7th St; tel: (213) 689-8822. Open Mon–Fri 0830–1700.*

Los Angeles International Airport (LAX); *tel: (310) 646-5252; www.lawa.org/lax*, is 17 miles southwest of downtown. Taxi to downtown, fare for up to eight passengers, is $40. All outbound transport is on the Lower Level/Arrivals islands outside arrival baggage carousels. LAX to downtown door-to-door van service is about $16 (single). The non-stop FlyAway (bus; *www.lawa.org/lax/LAXflyAway.cfm*) from LAX to Downtown Union Station, Westwood and Van Nuys (San Fernando Valley) is $4, cash only. There are free shuttles to car-hire locations and airport hotels.

Amtrak (*tel: (800) 872-7245; www.amtrak.com*) trains pull into Union Station, where **Metrolink** (*tel: (800) 371-5465; www.metrolinktrains. com*) has weekday commuter train routes north to Oxnard, south into San Diego County, Irvine in Orange County, Riverside, San Bernardino and the San Fernando Valley. For Los Angeles County transportation, there's **Metro**.

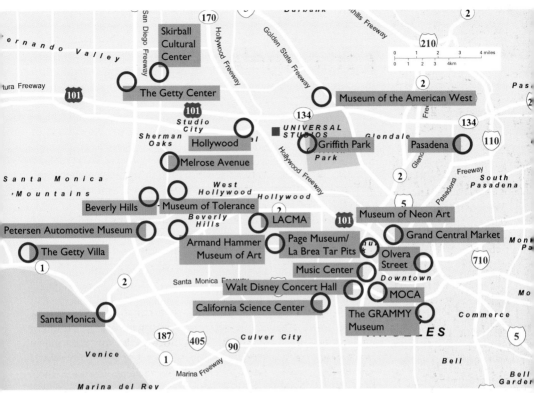

Skirball Cultural Center

The Getty Center

Museum of the American West

Studio City

Sherman Oaks

Hollywood

UNIVERSAL STUDIOS

Griffith Park

Glendale

Pasadena

South Pasadena

Melrose Avenue

West Hollywood

Hollywood

Santa Monica Mountains

Beverly Hills

Museum of Tolerance

Beverly Hills

LACMA

Museum of Neon Art

Petersen Automotive Museum

Armand Hammer Museum of Art

Page Museum/ La Brea Tar Pits

Grand Central Market

The Getty Villa

Music Center

Olvera Street

Downtown

Walt Disney Concert Hall

California Science Center

MOCA

Santa Monica

The GRAMMY Museum

Commerce

Venice

Culver City

Bell

Marina del Rey

Bell Garder

Parking

Parking meters are widely available, take change, and can be a good bargain if parking for less than one or two hours. Hourly restrictions are posted on detailed signs on the kerb and expired parking meters garner hefty fines. Downtown and in posh areas, car parks may charge several dollars per hour. For dining in any popular area, especially at night, valet parking is *de rigueur*, and costs from $5–$20.

Driving

Traffic flows slowly during rush hour on most LA area freeways, so it may be more efficient to take major surface streets (arterials) in the direction desired.

While much of the LA region is served by the **Metro** bus system including the five-line Metro Rail light rail and subway, not all routes are convenient for visitors; most journeys take several hours. The $0.25 **DASH** (*www.ladottransit.com/dash*) bus routes make frequent stops around Downtown LA, a terrific bargain for sightseeing – one DASH shuttle goes to the Griffith Park Observatory.

Listen to local radio stations for traffic reports, especially in the morning and evening rush hours. You will also get regular weather checks, including air pollution reports.

 Hollywood Visitor Information Center 6801 Hollywood Blvd, Hollywood and Highland complex; tel: (323) 467-6412. Open Mon–Sat 1000–2200, Sun 1000–1900.

Port of Los Angeles Visitor Information Center Berth 92, Pacific Cruise Ship Terminal, San Pedro; tel: (310) 514-9484. Visitor Information Centers sell tickets to Universal Studios Hollywood; half-price theatre tickets, Hollywood CityPass®, and more.

Go Los Angeles™ Card $$ Tel: (866) 652-3053 or (617) 671-1001; www. golosangelescard.com discounts admission to approximately 40 attractions.

Sights

 CityPass® $$ Tel: (888) 330-5008 or (208) 787-4300; www.citypass.com offer booklets of discounted attractions for Southern California and Hollywood.

Bradbury Building 304 S. Broadway; tel: (213) 626-1893. Open to 1st landing 0900–1800.

Armand Hammer Museum of Art $ 10899 Wilshire Blvd; tel: (310) 443-7000; www.hammer.ucla.edu. Open Tue, Wed, Fri, Sat 1100–1900, Thu 1100–2100, Sun 1100–1700; free Thu.

Downtown

Whimsical design and classic elegance got lost for decades before Downtown Los Angeles underwent extensive redevelopment and a clean-up. Once shunned as dingy and crime-ridden, today's civic centre has soaring skyscrapers, a pillar-like City Hall, a restored railway station, and a wealth of architecture. **The Los Angeles Conservancy** $ (tel: (213) 623-2489; www.laconservancy.org) offers tours of the notable monoliths, bank buildings and fine art deco, marble and terracotta architecture.

Stroll through the ornate Spanish Renaissance-style lobby of the three-tower 1923 **Millennium Biltmore Hotel** (506 S. Grand Ave; tel: (213) 624-1011), across from Pershing Square's geometric sculptures and fountain. Stop at the **Bradbury Building**, five skylit levels of graceful, intricate ironwork and an exposed lift accented by marble, tilework and polished wood. This fanciful $500,000, 1893 masterpiece is a frequent film location; Harrison Ford and androids battled here in *Blade Runner* (1982).

Shimmering white **City Hall** (200 N. Spring St) served as Superman's Daily Planet Building. The 1939 Spanish Mission exterior of **Union Station** (800 N. Alameda St; tel: (213) 683-6875) encloses the cavernous marble mosaic-lined hallway of a railway station with LAX and regional transportation connections. The **Cathedral of Our Lady of the Angels** $ (555 W. Temple St; tel: (213) 680-5200; www.olacathedral.org) is a spare, minimalist entry on the architectural scene, with free organ concerts on Wednesdays. Architect Frank O. Gehry designed the curving, sweeping, stainless steel-panelled walls of downtown's most obvious landmark, the **Walt Disney Concert Hall** (111 S. Grand Ave; www.disneyconcerthall.com/wdch/home.html), the home of the Los Angeles Philharmonic (www.laphil.com). The Los Angeles Opera (www.losangelesopera.com) performs at the Dorothy Chandler Pavilion (135 N Grand Ave).

Armand Hammer Museum of Art

Dwarfed by the Occidental Petroleum Building, the museum houses the late entrepreneur-philanthropist's third art collection: Old Masters, Impressionist and Post-Impressionist paintings, Dürer watercolours, satirist Daumier's lithographs, and special exhibitions. The museum opens into the heart of Westwood, the **University of California, Los Angeles (UCLA)** shopping and entertainment area.

Beverly Hills

Beverly Hills is a town and a state of mind, doing business within the aptly named Golden Triangle, an area bordered by N. Crescent Dr. and Wilshire and Santa Monica Blvds. **Rodeo Drive's** three blocks of ultra-posh boutiques, where there are more tourists than shoppers, drip with sophistication. **2 Rodeo's** winding street of designer stores and quaint streetlamps offers a microcosm of *la crème de la crème*.

🎬 **The Paley Center for Media $$$**
465 N. Beverly Dr.;
tel: (310) 786-1000;
www.paleycenter.org. Open
Wed–Sun 1200–1700.

California Science Center
(Exposition Park) 700
Exposition Park Dr.; tel:
(323) 724-3623;
www.californiasciencecenter.
org. Open daily 1000–1700.
Free except for a couple of
special rides.

🏷️ **LA Fashion District** (Downtown)
7th St to I-10 (Santa Monica
Fwy), Spring and Main Sts,
and San Pedro; tel: (213)
488-1153;
www.fashiondistrict.org

The film *Pretty Woman* (1990) put the **Four Seasons Beverly Wilshire Beverly Hills Hotel** (*9500 Wilshire Blvd; tel: (310) 275-5200*) on the must-see map. **The Paley Center for Media** is the best spot outside of the museum's New York City venue to view classic films and hear current television casts and entertainers talk about their lives and work.

California Science Center

The **California Science Center** and adjacent IMAX® theatre are in Exposition Park, south of Downtown Los Angeles, within walking distance of the **LA Memorial Coliseum**, central site for the 1932 and 1984 Olympiad, the **California African American Museum** (*tel: (213) 744-7432; www.caamuseum.org*) and the **Natural History Museum of Los Angeles County** (*tel: (250) 763-3466; www.nhm.org*). At the **California Science Center**, magenta light bathes a multi-storey entry pavilion hung with 1578 gold-leaf and palladium globes. You can balance on a bicycle suspended on a highwire, or tackle the Cave Climb climbing wall. Check out the inner workings and appropriate sound effects of Body Works, featuring a 50ft-long anatomically correct female body model, named 'Tess', who discusses teenage physical strains.

LA Fashion District

Vendors of everything to do with clothing and accessories sell wholesale to the trade and retail to the public. The many shops in this 90-block district offer a peek into a $24 billion industry. Merchants and designers operating from posh upper-floor shopfronts or street-level outlets, employ local residents, many immigrants, to design, pattern, sew, display and sell garments, buttons, zippers, coats, dresses, scarves, bolts of cloth and almost anything that can be used to adorn the body or decorate a house. **California Market Center** (*110 E 9th St; tel: (800) 225-6278* or *(213) 630-3600; www.californiamarketcenter.com*)

Below
The California Science Center

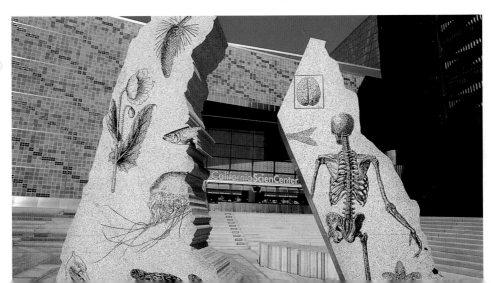

The Getty Center
*1200 Getty Center Dr.,
exit from I-405; tel: (310)
440-7300; www.getty.edu.
Open Tue–Thu, Sun 1000–
1800, Fri–Sat 1000–2100.
Free. Parking $8.*

The Getty Villa
*17985 Pacific Coast Hwy,
Pacific Palisades (Malibu);
tel: (310) 440-7300;
www.getty.edu. Open
Thu–Mon 1000–1700.
Advance, timed individual
tickets required. Free.
Parking $8.*

The GRAMMY Museum
*$ Corner of Olympic Blvd
and Figueroa St at L.A. LIVE;
tel: (213) 765-6800;
www.grammymuseum.org.
Call for hours.*

**Grand Central
Market** *(Downtown)
317 S. Broadway; tel: (213)
624-2378; www.grandcentral
square.com. Open daily
0900–1800. One hour free
parking with a $10
purchase.*

Griffith Park *(Griffith
Park Ranger Visitor
Center), 4730 Crystal Springs
Dr.; tel: (323) 913-4688;
www.laparks.org/dos/parks/
griffithpk/gp_info.htm*

Griffith Observatory
*(Griffith Park) 2800 E
Observatory Rd; tel: (213)
473-0800; www.griffithobs.
org. Weekend shuttle from
downtown – see website.
Free. Admission for shows
in the Leonard Nimoy Event
Horizon theatre and the
Samuel Oschin Planetarium
$$.*

offers wide variety, as does the morning-only **LA Flower Market** (*Wall St between 7th and 8th St; tel: (213) 627-3696; http://laflowerdistrict.com*), the country's largest. Mannequins lurch surreally into the walkway of **Santee Alley** (*between Santee St and Maple Ave, Olympic Blvd–11th St*). The best day to find bargains is Saturday, but some wholesalers also sell samples on the last Friday of the month.

The Getty Center
Dazzling white amongst the brown mountains above Los Angeles, this $1 billion art museum is free and has a pleasant tram ride up, a shimmering pool in the courtyard, a stream through a central garden, inexpensive dining and an eclectic collection ranging from photographs to illuminated medieval manuscripts, Van Gogh to 17th-century French paintings and decorative arts, covering 12 centuries of Western art. A one-hour, quick-tour brochure outlines a 'best of' overview.

The Getty Villa
Classical Greek, Roman and Etruscan art is arranged in a Greek-style villa and surrounding formal gardens above the Pacific Ocean in Malibu. Advance reservations for a free visit to see 1,200 of the collection's 44,000 antiquities from 6,500 BC – AD 400 are required.

The GRAMMY Museum
The GRAMMY Museum is part of the L.A. LIVE entertainment, shopping, and hotel complex near the Los Angeles Convention Center that includes the NOKIA Theatre and Staples Center (L.A. Lakers basketball venue). Four floors of music-related exhibits tout music technology and the winners of GRAMMY Awards.

Grand Central Market
Since 1917, Angelinos have shopped here for Mexican, Thai, Japanese, Chinese, Vietnamese, Armenian and Italian ingredients for their kitchens at home, finding exotic spices, candy and pastries, grains, rice and pastas, meat, fish, tortillas and other produce among 50 shops, restaurants and juice bars which wrap or dish up the freshest staples of ethnic life. Look for the bronze pig heads at the Broadway entrance.

Griffith Park
More than 4000 acres of green space in the Santa Monica Mountains above Hollywood are devoted to recreation and serious culture: cowboy-style at the **Museum of the American West** (*see oppposite*); or pop/folk music-style at the outdoor **Greek Theatre** (*Griffith Park, 2700 N. Vermont Canyon; tel: (323) 665-5857; http://greektheatrela.com; $$$*). There is free science and splendid sunset-watching above the Los Angeles sprawl at the expanded, copper-domed **Griffith Observatory**. The equestrian trail paradise is augmented by the 77-acre **Los Angeles Zoo** (*5333 Zoo Dr.; tel: (323) 644-4200; www.lazoo.org; $$*), and

**Travel Town
Transportation
Museum** 5200 W Zoo Dr.;
tel: (323) 662-5874;
www.laparks.org/grifmet/tt.
Open Mon–Fri 1000–1600,
Sat–Sun 1000–1700 (1800
in summer). Free.

**Los Angeles County
Museum of Art
(LACMA) $$** 5905
Wilshire Blvd; tel: (323) 857-
6000; www.lacma.org. Open
Mon, Tue & Thu 1200–2000,
Fri 1200–2100, Sat–Sun
1100–2000. Free after 1700.

LACMA West $$ 6867
Wilshire Blvd. LACMA West
is undergoing renovation and
will house the Boone
Children's Gallery. Call for
status. Online catalogue:
http://collectionsonline.lacma.
org

**Museum of the
American West $$**
(Griffith Park Campus) 4700
Western Heritage Way;
tel: (323) 667-2000;
www.autrynationalcenter.org.
Open Tue–Sun 1000–1700;
Thu to 2000. Closed Mon.

fascinating railway carriages, equipment and firefighting gear at the free **Travel Town Transportation Museum**. Golf courses and a merry-go-round top off the mix in this urban park.

Hollywood

This district, its name emblazoned across the dry hills, always evokes the magic of film. Stars of film, television, radio, music and the stage have been celebrated with more than 2500 pink **Hollywood Boulevard Walk of Fame** stars, embedded in the pavement from La Brea Ave to Vine St. Bright murals, neon lights and colourful, risqué shop windows brighten the neighbourhood and add a touch of whimsy to the sidewalk clutter. Hand and footprints lure visitors to try out the stars' autographed imprints before the exotic pagoda façade of **Grauman's Chinese Theatre** (6925 Hollywood Blvd). (See Route to the Stars, page 62, for more on Hollywood.)

Los Angeles County Museum of Art (LACMA)

The Western US's largest art museum always has an outstanding special exhibition. A redesign by architect Renzo Piano created an airy atrium and added the **Broad** (pronounced 'Brode') **Contemporary Art Museum (BCAM)** wing, easy to spot on Wilshire Blvd with 202 elegant lampposts installed by artist Chris Burden. LACMA shares a huge block with the **Page Museum** and **La Brea Tar Pits** (see page 49). Amongst LACMA's powerhouse collections are Textiles and Costumes, a world-renowned Indian and Southeast Asian Art Collection, one of the most significant Islamic art collections, and the Japanese Pavilion, two levels of galleries which include magnificent Japanese scrolls in a building designed in the shape of a pagoda. Large outdoor sculptures whet the appetite for what's inside.

LACMA West, a transformed department store building that is undergoing renovation, is a fine example of the 1930s Steamline Moderne deco architecture for which the Wilshire Blvd **Miracle Mile** is known. More than 70,000 artefacts are catalogued online.

Melrose Avenue

A decade of ultra-cool restaurants and Generation X boutique shopping has worn slightly thin around the edges of this punk-hair, black-garbed area between La Brea and Fairfax Aves. Evening dining means posh prices and handsome valets to park your auto – unless you opt for the ubiquitous American fast-food chains. Business façades sport half-sphere mirrors, shocking pink and aqua colours and flowerpot shards.

Museum of the American West

This Griffith Park museum offers a vibrant, honestly captioned collection of Western US art, artefacts and cowboy film memorabilia. Film star Gene Autry, 'The Singing Cowboy', amassed an extensive collection of cinema props, saddles, posters, cowboy costumes, boots,

🏛 **Southwest Museum of the American Indian**
(Mt. Washington) 234 Museum Drive; www.autrynationalcenter.org. Galleries closed for renovation.

Museum of Contemporary Art (MOCA) $$ *250 S. Grand Avenue and* **The Geffen Contemporary at MOCA** $$ *152 N. Central Ave; tel: (213) 626-6222; www.moca-la.org. Open Mon and Fri 1100–1700, Thu to 2000. Sat–Sun 1100–1800.* **MOCA Pacific Design Center** *8687 Melrose Ave, West Hollywood. Free. Open Tue–Wed and Fri 1100–1700, to 2000 Thu, Sat–Sun 1100–1800. All MOCA venues free Thu 1700–2000.*

Museum of Neon Art $$ *136 W. 4th St; tel: (213) 489-9918; www.neonmona.org. Open Thu–Sat 1200–1900, Sun to 1700.*

Museum of Tolerance $$ *9786 W. Pico Blvd; tel: (310) 553-8403; www.museumof tolerance.com. Advance admission required: tel: (310) 772-2504. Open Mon–Fri 1000–1700 (closes Nov–Mar Fri at 1500); Sun 1100–1700. Closed Sat, Jewish and public holidays.*

spurs and related 1950s-era outfits and toys for children. From the first Spanish conquerors to American wagon train expansion West, the museum doesn't shrink from the violence implied by the roomful of Colt firearms, the narrative diorama of the 'Shootout at the O.K. Corral', or descriptions of the decimation of Native Americans and buffalo. The **Southwest Museum of the American Indian**, part of the Autry National Center but closed for renovations (to be completed by 2010), has fine collections of indigenous peoples' artefacts amassed over 90 years that represent cultures from Alaska to South America.

Museum of Contemporary Art (MOCA)

MOCA Grand Avenue downtown venue at California Plaza (*250 S. Grand Ave*) presents an overview of the last 60 years of modern art. Large sculpture, abstract paintings, prints, multimedia and video presentations are in lower level-galleries. The cheerful brick-red building entrance is flanked by an arch. The museum's second venue, **The Geffen Contemporary at MOCA** (*152 N. Central Ave*) in a warehouse-like converted garage, is accessible from **Little Tokyo**, the heart of Los Angeles' Japanese-American community. **MOCA Pacific Design Center** (*8687 Melrose Ave, W. Hollywood*) is MOCA's most recent venue.

Museum of Neon Art

The Museum of Neon Art has exhibited neon tube illumination for several decades, while rescuing and restoring signs around Los Angeles. The museum also offers bus tour 'cruises' ($$) of neon art around the city and Las Vegas.

Museum of Tolerance

The museum is a gripping introduction to – or reminder of – the effects of racism and intolerance. The World War II Holocaust is the final presentation after graphic interactive exhibits of Bosnian and

Right
MOCA on Bunker Hill

Music Center
(Downtown) 135 N. Grand Ave/717 W. Temple St; tel: (213) 972-7211; www.musiccenter.org. Free guided tours; tel: (213) 972-4399.

El Pueblo de Los Angeles Historical Monument *Tel: (213) 485-6855; www.cityofla.org/ELP/. Open daily 1000–1900. Sepulveda House Visitors Center open Mon–Fri 0900–1600. Avila Adobe open Wed–Sun 1000–1500. Plaza Fire House Museum open Tue–Fri 1000–1500. Los Angelinas del Pueblo, 130 Paseo de la Plaza, tel: (213) 628-1274; www.lasangelitas.org/freetours.htm, offers free walking tours of the park Tue–Sat 1000, 1100, 1200.*

Chinese American Museum *$ 425 N. Los Angeles St; tel: (213) 485-8567; www.camla.org. Open Wed–Sat 1000–1500.*

Page Museum/La Brea Tar Pits *$$ 5801 Wilshire Blvd; tel: (323) 934-7243; www.tarpits.org. Open Mon–Fri 0930–1700, Sat–Sun 1000–1700. Free, first Tue of the month.*

Rwandan ethnic cleansing and the closer-to-home 'Final Solution' to the Jews' extermination.

Music Center

The performing arts centre is in the heart of downtown. The **Dorothy Chandler Pavilion** hosts dance companies and the Los Angeles Opera (*www.laopera.com*) while Center Theater Group cutting-edge theatre is presented in the **Mark Taper Forum** along with Broadway plays and mainstream theatre performed at the **Ahmanson Theater**. A Jacques Lipchitz 'Peace' fountain in the courtyard constantly varies its water flow, creating the illusion of an erratic brook in the city centre. The Los Angeles Philharmonic (*www.laphil.org*) is ensconced in the modernistic, white Frank Gehry-designed **Walt Disney Concert Hall**.

Olvera Street

The pedestrian street at the heart of downtown is the centrepiece of the **El Pueblo de Los Angeles Historical Monument**, where the first Spanish settlers arrived in 1781. Among the park's 27 buildings is LA's oldest, the 1818 **Avila Adobe**, perfectly restored and furnished as an 1850s *rancho*, and the Plaza Fire House Museum. A Mexican-style **open-air shopping arcade** has well-crafted leather goods and Mexican tourist trinkets. Restaurants serve modest, authentic Mexican food. The **Chinese American Museum**, in the only surviving structure (1890 Garnier Building) from Los Angeles' original Chinatown, is Southern California's only museum with Chinese history, settlement and ethnic exhibits.

Page Museum/La Brea Tar Pits

This Hancock Park museum belies the feeling of late 20th-century construction that characterises LA. Ice Age fossils around 40,000 years old have been found in bubbling tar pits once mined for natural

asphalt. After the Age of Dinosaurs, giant ground sloths, sabre-toothed cats, wolves, and at least one human, La Brea Woman, roamed the once lush, rich land. More than 1.5 million bones and several million more plant and invertebrate fossils have been recovered just outside the museum building; visible excavations of Pit 91 are ongoing in summer. A bas-relief around the building exterior depicts the world of gigantic birds, sloths, cats and mammoths. Inside, exhibits surround a garden planted with ferns and simple Ice Age-era

Right
La Brea Tar Pits

ⓘ **Pasadena
Convention &
Visitors Bureau** 171 S.
Los Robles Ave, Pasadena, CA
91101; tel: (800) 307-7977
or (626) 795-9311;
www.pasadenacal.com. Open
Mon–Fri 0800–1700, Sat
1000–1600.

ⓖ **Gamble House $$**
4 Westmoreland Pl.,
Pasadena; tel: (626) 793-
3334; www.gamblehouse.org.
Open Thu–Sun 1200–1500,
for tours.

**Norton Simon Museum
$** 411 W. Colorado Blvd,
Pasadena; tel: (626) 449-
6840; www.nortonsimon.org.
Open Wed–Mon
1200–1800, Fri to 2100.

**Huntington Library,
Art Collections and
Botanical Gardens $$$**
1151 Oxford Rd, San
Marino; tel: (626) 405-
2100; www.huntington.org.
Open Mon and Wed–Fri
1200–1630, Sat–Sun
1030–1630, Memorial
Day–Labor Day Wed–Mon
1030–1630. Free first Thu
of month.

**Petersen Automotive
Museum $$** 6060 Wilshire
Blvd; tel: (323) 930-2277;
www.petersen.org. Open
Tue–Sun 1000–1800.

**Skirball Cultural
Center $$** 2701 N.
Sepulveda Blvd; tel: (310)
440-4500; www.skirball.org.
Open Tue–Fri 1200–1700,
Sat–Sun 1000–1700.
Advance, timed-entry tickets
required for Noah's Ark at
the Skirball; check website
for procedure.

flora. The current work of the palaeontology laboratory scientists is on view year-round.

Pasadena

Pasadena, northeast of Downtown LA (on the Metro Gold Line), is beamed into millions of homes on New Year's Day with the televised **Rose Parade** (*tel: (626) 449-4100; www.tournamentofroses.com*) which precedes the Rose Bowl football game.

Wealthy Midwestern settlers spent the early 20th century building mansions in the balmy, orange-blossom-scented climate. The perfectly proportioned **Gamble House**, designed with dark woods and stained glass, is Craftsman architecture at its finest. This style of architecture, popularised by Gustav Stickley (1858–1941), represents a conscious departure from the excessive ornamentation of the Victorian era, and is characterised by large porches, straight lines and dark interior woods. The 1927 **Pasadena City Hall** (*100 N. Garfield Ave*) would look at home in Spain. Find designer wear and casual dining at **One Colorado** complex (*Colorado Blvd and Fair Oaks Ave; tel: (626) 564-1066; www.onecolorado.net*), one block of 22 in Old Pasadena.

The **Norton Simon Museum**, with its wealth of collections ranging from Picasso masterpieces to Hindu and Buddhist statues from India, Tibet and Nepal, is the marriage of a millionaire's exquisite taste with gallery display. In San Marino, close by, the **Huntington Library, Art Collections and Botanical Gardens** showcases fine art, medieval manuscripts, lovely gardens, a conservatory and Liu Fang Yuan (the Garden of Flowing Fragrance), a classic Chinese garden.

Petersen Automotive Museum

One of the most complete car museums chronicles LA's love affair and dependence upon the automobile. Cars of the stars, hot rods, sports cars, roadside cafés, service stations – it's all here.

Skirball Cultural Center

Known as the Skirball, this Jewish cultural centre has museum exhibits, music, film showings, live theatre, and a popular café. The indoor-outdoor wooden **Noah's Ark at the Skirball** takes children and families through the biblical flood story with puppets and other depictions of 186 animal species made from recycled material.

Accommodation and food

Rooms can be found everywhere in this world metropolis. The LACVB (*see page 42*) lists a hotel reservations service but does not make bookings. To conserve time and energy, base yourself close to attractions you intend to see. Downtown, the Westside (Bel Air, Beverly Hills, West Hollywood) and Santa Monica are pricey; some

Hollywood area hotels and motels, and those in less touristic neighbourhoods, are more moderate. Always ask for secure parking.

If there's a cuisine you haven't tried, LA has a restaurant that prepares it. Local newspapers and the free monthly *Where Los Angeles* magazine (*http://wherela.com*) list restaurants and review trendy newcomers.

Mel's Drive-in $ *8585 Sunset Blvd; tel: (310) 854-7201; www.melsdrive-in.com.* Serves quintessential American diner food along Hollywood's Sunset Strip 24 hours a day.

Original Pantry Café $ *877 S. Figueroa St.; tel: (213) 972-9279; www.pantrycafe.com.* A downtown LA old-timer with traditional American comfort food at good prices is open 24 hours.

Chan Dara $$ *11940 W. Pico Blvd, West LA and other locations; tel: (310) 479-4461; http://chandarawestla.com.* Scrumptious Thai food – especially pad Thai noodles.

Entertainment

The Entertainment Capital of the World is rich with amusements, from high culture to schlock to pornography. Look in the free weekly newspapers – *LA Weekly* (*www.laweekly.com*), *Los Angeles Independent* (*www.laindependent.com*), *Los Angeles Downtown News* (*www.downtownnews.com*), *Entertainment Today* (*www.entertainmenttoday.net*) and *Los Angeles CityBeat* (*www.lacitybeat.com*) for the hip crowd – and the mainstream *Los Angeles Times* (*www.latimes.com*), *The Guide* (*http://theguide.latimes.com*) (Sun) and *Weekend* (Thu) sections for listings. Pick a neighbourhood, refer to the listings and gamble that it will be good; many of the world's best and most industrious actors, artists, musicians, comedians and creative people live in the Los Angeles area to be where the action is.

Right
Hollywood Boulevard

Above
Walt Disney Concert Hall,
Los Angeles

LA Stage Alliance offers half-price theatre tickets up to seven days in advance for performances around the region. See what's available and purchase tickets at *www.lastagetix.com*

Sunset Strip, Sunset Blvd in trendy West Hollywood, still offers **Whisky A Go Go** (*8901 Sunset Blvd; tel: (310) 652-4202; www.whiskyagogo.com*), with other star-making (Bruce Springsteen, Bob Marley) music venues such as **Roxy** (*9009 W. Sunset Blvd; tel: (310) 278-9457; http://theroxyonsunset.com*) or American roots music at the **House of Blues® Sunset Strip** (*8430 Sunset Blvd; tel: (323) 848-5100; www.hob.com/venues/clubvenues/sunsetstrip*). Gay clubs are a few blocks south in West Hollywood along Santa Monica Blvd. Most comedians learn to swim upstream to live audiences in LA clubs such as **The Laugh Factory** (*8001 Sunset Blvd; tel: (323) 656-1336; www.laughfactory.com*), **The Improv** (*8162 Melrose Ave; tel: (323) 651-2583; www.symfonee.com/improv/hollywood/home/index.aspx*) and **The Comedy Store** (*8433 W Sunset Blvd; tel: (323) 650-6268; www.thecomedystore.com*). Like the district, Hollywood clubs can be a little raw, attracting an audience of after-work slummers and devotees who seldom see daylight.

One of LA's best bargains is free tickets to live tapings of major television network talk shows and dramas. It's best to book ahead with **Audiences Unlimited** (*tel: (818) 753-3470; www.tvtickets.com*). Occasionally, location film shoots will permit visitors to watch, or filming may take place on city streets. **Warner Bros VIP Studio Tour $$** (*3400 Riverside Dr., Burbank; tel: (818) 972-8687; www2.warnerbros.com/vipstudiotour*) and **Universal Studios Hollywood Studio Tour $$$** (*tel: (800) 864-8377; www.universalstudioshollywood.com/st_info.html*) offer behind-the-scenes tours.

Shopping

If it's made anywhere in the world, you can find it in Greater LA.

Dressing down and casual is almost a science. **Rodeo Drive** or the **Beverly Center** (*Beverly Blvd between La Cienega and San Vicente Blvds; www.beverlycenter.com*) in Beverly Hills are starting places for posh-conservative with touches of Academy Award gown thrown in. Other Westside hotspots are **The Grove** (*www.thegrovela.com*) and the old-fashioned, but ever-hip, produce, flower and food market with café dining, the **Farmers' Market** (*www.farmersmarketla.com*). For the raw materials, visit the **LA Fashion District** (*see pages 45–46*).

For art and books on cowboys and the West, the **Museum of the American West** (*see pages 47–48*) is unparalleled. **Melrose Avenue** is where the trendoids shop to be 'bad'. **Robertson Boulevard** is a hip place to shop. In Venice, **Abbot Kinney Boulevard** stocks boutiques with vintage clothing and one-of-a-kind togs. Hollywood Blvd at Wilcox Ave is the centre for costumes, exotic shoes, and costume and film poster shops. Peruse 'in' furniture along La Brea Ave south of Sunset Blvd and search out antiques in **Old Pasadena**. The Downtown **Toy District** (*Third, Fifth, Los Angeles and San Pedro Streets*) is crammed with toys, costume jewellery, silk flowers, DVDs and other 'finds'. Also Downtown, the **Arts District** (*7th Pl., Alameda, Hwy 101, and the Los Angeles River*), best enjoyed in daylight for safety, is filled with warehouses and lofts, some converted into galleries, furniture and fashion designer studios, and eateries. Join the galleries' **Downtown Art Walk** (*www.downtownartwalk.com; second Thu of the month 1200–2100*). **Third Street Promenade** in **Santa Monica** has upmarket shops and a Farmers' Market patronised by film stars incognito within whiffing distance of the Pacific Ocean.

Suggested tours

Downtown, the **Los Angeles Conservancy Tours $** (*523 W. 6th St, Suite 826; tel: (213) 623-2489; http://laconservancy.org*) cover Art Deco, Biltmore Hotel, Broadway Movie Theatres, City Hall, Little Tokyo (Japantown), Union Station and local architecture on guided walking tours.

Drive-by tours of the stars' homes are on offer via limousine or open-top double-decker bus.

Right
Shops in Olvera Street,
El Pueblo de Los Angeles

Southern California Theme Parks

If optimism and fantasy are Southern California's forte, the upbeat attitude is nowhere more evident than at amusement parks, lands of wonder for children of all ages. The secret is not to choose a park because it's famous, but because its attractions fit your interests.

Theme parks are geared for children. Disneyland® Resort, Knott's Berry Farm® and Universal Studios® Hollywood have oversized cartoon, television and film personalities strolling around the park to greet children, pose for pictures and give 'character' autographs. Baby buggies are ubiquitous, drinking fountains and other facilities are built to accommodate younger visitors, and some rides have safety in mind with posted size restrictions. Jurassic Park exists, but only as a water-soaked, high-spirited roller-coaster ride at Universal Studios® Hollywood. San Diego Zoo's Wild Animal Park is more an entertaining wildlife refuge than a traditional theme park à la Disneyland®, the Granddaddy of them all.

DISNEYLAND® RESORT

Disneyland® Resort
$$$ *1313 Harbor Blvd, Anaheim*;
tel: (714) 781-4565;
www.disneyland.com, is a 30-minute drive southwest of Downtown Los Angeles. Check the website for driving and parking instructions.

Theme parks are would-be kingdoms; most conduct mandatory bag checks for security to ensure that outside food and beverages are not consumed inside.

In 1955, Walt Disney took his flair for cinematic animation and dogged entrepreneurship beyond the Mickey Mouse film empire. Vast orange groves in Anaheim were turned into Uncle Walt's rosy-coloured concept of nostalgia, patriotism, innovation, fairytale and adventure. More than half a century on, the original Disneyland® has grown into the Disneyland® Resort, combining two theme parks, Disneyland® and Disney's California Adventure®; a public entertainment-shopping-dining area, Downtown Disney®; and a collection of hotels.

Disneyland®
Just beyond the Main Entrance lies **Main Street, U.S.A.®**, an idealised version of small-town America from the early 20th century. Disney's first Mickey Mouse cartoon, the 1928 *Steamboat Willie*, plays at the **Main Street Cinema**. The steam locomotive-powered **Disneyland® Railroad** circles the park areas, offering a 20-minute park preview.

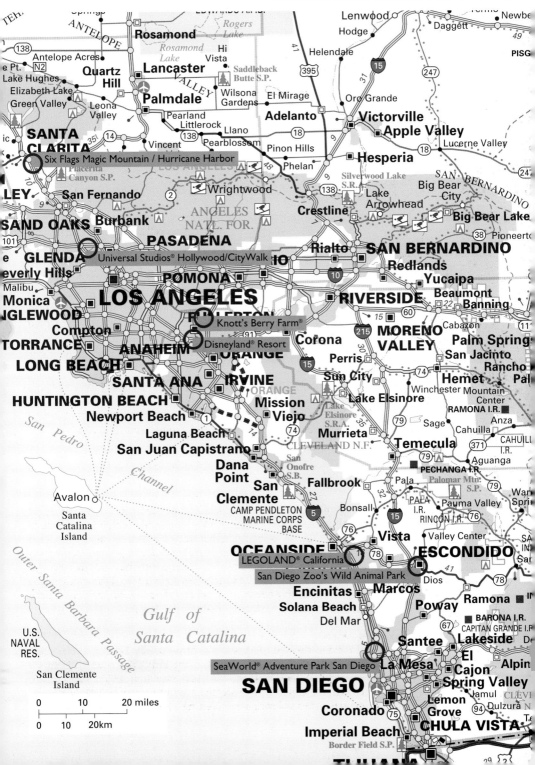

Coping with queues

Summer is a hot, crowded time to visit a Southern California theme park, with long queues for rides, attractions, theme park restaurants, refreshment stands and souvenir shops. Pack for an outing in the country or an imaginary safari, with comfortable shoes, sunhats, sunblock and a large closed bag for your camera and souvenirs. Most parks discourage or forbid outside food or drink; non-alcoholic drinks are widely available in concession to the desert-like climate and cement construction.

Adventureland stars the **Indiana Jones™ Adventure**, a spin-off from the Steven Spielberg films, that features a rough ride through an archaeological temple dig protected by the malevolent Eye of Mara – it's hard not to gulp when a boulder heads straight for your car. The **Jungle Cruise** offers a nostalgic glimpse of 1950s technology with mechanical hippos and elephants.

Fantasyland is the fairy tales come to life, anchored by Disney's signature **Sleeping Beauty Castle**. **Peter Pan's Flight**, **Mad (Hatter's) Tea Party** and **Pinocchio's Daring Journey** vie with dolls cavorting to the theme music of 'it's a small world'. **Frontierland** evokes the 19th century of Mark Twain with the paddlewheel **Mark Twain Riverboat**, rafts to **Tom Sawyer Island** where children can run around, and the replica sailing ship *Columbia*.

Mickey's Toontown has attractions for the youngest. Weasels chase the macho hero bunny in **Roger Rabbit's Car Toon Spin**. **New Orleans Square** is a small land with the ghostly, old-fashioned humorous horrors of the **Haunted Mansion** and the ever so politically correct **Pirates of the Caribbean** town invasion.

Tomorrowland was rebuilt in 1998 with a retro-future look beneath an imposing Leonardo da Vinci astrolabe design transformed into a moving sculpture. **Space Mountain**, an enduring indoor coaster, **Star Tours**, Star Wars misadventures through interstellar space, and **Finding Nemo Submarine Voyage**, a yellow submarine descent into the Tomorrowland Lagoon, are the most popular attractions.

Evening parades down Main Street with fireworks over Sleeping Beauty Castle are worth waiting for, but find a vantage point early.

Disney's California Adventure®

This Disney park is based on California, from the Golden Gate Bridge spanning the entrance to a make-believe beachfront boardwalk.

Golden Gateway is a life-sized picture-postcard entrance with California's most famous landmarks. The **Golden Dreams** show re-creates the dramas and romance of California with help from cinema star Whoopi Goldberg. **Soarin' Over California** puts you in a hang-glider soaring from the giant redwood forests of Northern California to the deserts of Palm Springs. On hot days, crowds head for **Grizzly River Run**, a white-water river raft ride that no one escapes dry.

a bug's land includes a popular 3D production, *It's Tough to Be a Bug*, with rides and activities for younger children.

Paradise Pier idolises the amusement arcades that once framed beaches from San Diego to Santa Cruz. The visual icon of Disney's California Adventure is the 168-foot **Sun Wheel**, a giant Ferris wheel with a sun in the centre. **Maliboomer**, a 180-foot free-fall ride, and **California Screamin'**, a wooden roller coaster that blasts from a standstill to freeway speeds in under 4 seconds, provide the adrenalin rush. Narrated by film characters, the **Toy Story Mania** ride below the coaster's Mickey Mouse silhouette pairs competitors to interactively take on 3D targets.

Hollywood Pictures Backlot offers a classic Hollywood entrance beneath gilded elephants, à la D.W. Griffith, and 1940s-style streetscapes. Eighty-odd cartoon characters cavort across the façade of **Disney Animation**, at its most effective under night-time lighting. Three attractions display the art and artistry of animation. **Disney's Aladdin – A Musical Spectacular** is 40 minutes of cheerful singing and fast-paced dancing.

Arrive early near the Pacific Wharf area for the night-time Electrical Parade with Disney characters.

The Twilight Zone Tower of Terror™ is a thrill ride with weird apparitions who may have died in a violent storm that hit a Hollywood hotel decades ago, temperature effects, narration by the original *Twilight Zone* narrator Rod Serling, and a lurching ride up and down 13 storeys in a simulated elevator (lift) shaft.

Downtown Disney District

Disney's entertainment, shopping and dining arcade is open to the public. The winding promenade separates Disneyland from DCA and links three Disney hotels. **East Garden** is devoted to café dining and shopping. The **Wine Bar District** is filled with outdoor bar and restaurant seating. **Center Plaza** throbs with music and food from Cuba, New Orleans and Italy. **West Side Garden** features a multiplex cinema, sports bar and more cafés.

Accommodation and food in Disneyland

Disney presents a complete vacation package with hotel and special park passes (*tel: (714) 520-7070; www.disneyland.com*). A variety of lodging offers choices, but the trade-off for not staying at one of three official Disneyland® Resort Hotels, the **Disneyland® Hotel $$$**, **Disney's Paradise Pier® Hotel $$$** and **Disney's Grand Californian Hotel® $$$** (*tel: (714) 956-6425*), may be a long wait in traffic to access the park area. Hotel chains and Disney packages abound. Ask for all available discounts upon arrival.

The 'no outside food or drink' policy virtually mandates dining on pricey park fare. All lands except Toontown have at least one vegetarian outlet. The official hotels offer children **Character Dining $$$**, including **Breakfast with Minnie & Friends**.

KNOTT'S BERRY FARM®

Knott's Berry Farm® $$
8039 Beach Blvd, Buena Park; tel: (714) 220-5200; www.knotts.com

America's first theme park started as a 1930s move by a berry farm family to survive the Great Depression. Chicken dinners with all the trimmings and pies are still served – more than 1.1 million annually, in a park well stocked with adrenalin-charged roller coasters, Americana and some history education. Knott's Berry Farm® includes

---

Disneyland's own hotels are close to the park, reflected in higher lodging prices. It may be better value to pay more for accommodation to avoid traffic congestion close to park entrances.

Parks charge $10 and up for parking, usually in covered car parks. Note your vehicle's location in the car park; it's easy to get disorientated after a long park visit. Most parks have kennel arrangements to keep pets cool and safe while their families enjoy the park.

Above
One of the rides at
Knott's Berry Farm

Making the most

The cost of park admission, food, drink and souvenirs may range from $40–$60 per person a day. It pays to research discounts on multiple-day or multiple-park passes, family discounts, senior/pensioner discounts or auto touring club rates in advance. Various programmes include: Southern California **CityPass**® www.citypass.com for Southern California covers a combined 30 per cent discount on admission to Disneyland, Disney's California Adventure, Universal Studios Hollywood, SeaWorld Adventure Park, and a choice of the San Diego Zoo or San Diego Wild Animal Park, over 14 days. If time or energy is limited, enquire if the park of your choice has guided VIP tours, a higher-priced admission which allows access to major attractions without queuing up. Behind-the-scenes views of attractions, entertainment studios, live filming and other pampering may be included.

Soak City, a Spring–Autumn (Fall) water park, a shopping and eating area called Knott's MarketPlace, and a replica of Independence Hall, where the US Declaration of Independence was signed in 1776.

Knott's Berry Farm® has six areas. **Ghost Town** puts visitors in the Wild West, or at least a west with cowboys, gold panning, stage-coaches and *bandito* hold-ups of the **Ghost Town Calico Railroad**. The **Pony Express** coaster with a horse team theme reaches 38mph in three seconds. A 50-ft plunge down a waterfall climaxes **Timber Mountain Log Ride**. GhostRider®, one of the longest and tallest wooden roller coasters in the world, drops 108ft over 4530ft of track.

Wild Water Wilderness area's **Bigfoot Rapids** is a damp whitewater river ride adjacent to a **Nature Center** which delves into Bigfoot/Sasquatch lore. First Nations people present a narrative of magic and origins at **Mystery Lodge**®.

Fiesta Village has the twisting Mayan/Aztec **Jaguar**® roller coaster and **Montezooma's Revenge**®, accelerating to 60mph in less than 4 seconds. The South of the Border theme includes sombrero dances.

The Boardwalk Theme Park at Knott's has a roller coaster called **Boomerang** that launches riders back and forth along a half-sphere path. The biggest adrenalin charge is **Supreme Scream**®, where strapped-in riders rise 254ft skyward, then plunge to earth in 3 seconds. At 50mph, **Perilous Plunge** is a wet boat ride down a water chute. XCELERATOR™ rockets 205ft high in 2.3 seconds, then twists 90° to drop back to earth. The Charles M. Schulz Theatre capitalises on the comic-strip artist's characters with a Snoopy ice show and other flash productions.

The little ones have Peanuts characters in **Camp Snoopy**. Animals and tamer rides are reassuring, even the mini-Supreme Scream, **Woodstock's Airmail**, a 19-ft rise with an air-cushioned return.

Accommodation and food at Knott's Berry Farm®

Lodging abounds because of Disneyland's proximity and Anaheim's numerous conventions. The **Anaheim/Orange County Visitor and Convention Bureau** *800 W. Katella Ave, Anaheim; tel: (714) 765-8888* or *(888) 598-3200; www.anaheimoc.org,* has an accommodation booking service, *tel: (800) 901-9655.*

Mrs. Knott's Chicken Dinner Restaurant $ is a park institution, the place to try fried chicken, broiled chicken, barbecued beef ribs or chicken-fried steak, veggies, rhubarb, mashed potatoes, salad or soup, endless rolls and the obligatory boysenberry pie. A steakhouse, barbecue spot, Mexican restaurant and a diner, serving pizzas and snacks, are sit-down dining alternatives.

Knott's Berry Farm Resort Hotel $$ (*7675 Crescent Ave, Buena Park; tel: (866) 752-2444* or *(714) 995-1111; www.knottshotel.com*) is within the resort.

LEGOLAND® California

LEGOLAND® California $$$
Near I-5 and Cannon Rd interchange, Carlsbad; tel: (877) 534-6526 or (760) 918-5346; www. legoland.com/california.htm

The Danish plastic brick LEGO® Company's theme park is specifically for children aged 2 to 12. More than 30 million LEGO® bricks decorate the Carlsbad site, a beach town famed for exclusive spas and colourful flower fields. Among the main attractions are **Miniland USA**, with miniaturised versions of Cape Canaveral and the Daytona International Speedway, Washington, D.C., New Orleans, New York, San Francisco and the California coast; **Imagination Zone**, a LEGO® block, technology rides and play area; **Castle Hill** with **The Dragon**, a medieval-themed roller coaster, and simulated jousting and gem-panning; and child-size cars, boats and helicopters in **Fun Town**, including a Volvo Driving School. **Dino Island's Coastersaurus** twists around dino models at 20mph – perfect for an introduction to roller coasters! **Pirate Shores** has a **Splash Battle** and a water drenching. Nineteen-twenties Egypt with a LEGO® Pharaoh and camel is the **Land of Adventure** theme, with lasers blasting in **Lost Kingdom Adventure**. A separate admission **SEA LIFE™ Aquarium $$$** with 72 LEGO® models amid exhibits displays water residents from the Sierra Nevada to local coastal waters, including seahorses and a bay of rays.

San Diego Zoo's Wild Animal Park

San Diego Zoo's Wild Animal Park $$ 15500 San Pasqual Valley Rd, Escondido; tel: (760) 747-8702; www. sandiegozoo.org/wap. Open-top, safari-style **Photo Caravan tours** tel: (619) 718-3000, get within a few feet of animals, a superb photographic experience for an additional charge.

When to come

Check on opening hours. Some parks, such as Six Flags Magic Mountain, close for most of the winter season; occasionally parks are hired for private groups. Weekdays are less crowded than weekends. Arrive when the park opens to avoid long queues and ask for a park map for each member of your party. Head instantly for the most popular attractions.

In the midst of rugged, rocky mountains 30 miles north of San Diego, lush savannah vegetation creates a scenario of blooming plants where African and Asian wildlife and birds live, relatively uncaged. Careful landscaping and the lack of obvious bars make this 1800-acre wildlife preserve a fascinating experience on foot. See the panorama in a tethered Balloon Safari.

The 30-minute **Journey Into Africa Tour** is an excellent introduction before setting out for a gentle hike around the park. Shows include elephants, birds and rare species. Extensive botanical gardens with fuschia, epiphyllum, succulents, bonsai, native plants and conifers are connected by paths centred around the **Kupanda Falls Botanical Pavilion** at the north end.

A large pond area shelters pink Chilean flamingos, African and other exotic birds. Gibbons, lowland gorillas, meerkats and red-ruffed lemurs have their own enclosures. The 2-mile **Kilimanjaro Safari Walk** features elephants, rhinos and other African species.

At the entrance to the stunningly accurate **Heart of Africa savannah**, pick up the brochure, a challenging guide to identification of species appearing along the route down to the main area. This is not a walk for the squeamish – fresh animal kills are consumed in front of gawking park visitors. The twisting path ends near the

Above
Grazing giraffe at San Diego Zoo's Wild Animal Park

Okavango Outpost, where cheetahs loll as giraffes and other exotic species wander nearby. The **Lion Camp** savanna puts the big cats, antelope and giraffe on one side and pedestrians on the other side of a 40-ft long glass panel for mutual viewing. **Condor Ridge** shows how North America's largest bird has been saved from extinction.

SeaWorld® Adventure Park San Diego

SeaWorld® Adventure Park San Diego $$$
Mission Bay, San Diego; tel: (800) 257-4268; www.seaworld.com. SeaWorld® organises a hands-on, in the water, **Wild Arctic Interaction and Dolphin Interaction program** for an additional fee; *tel: (800) 257-4268.*

Denizens of the oceans are in residence here, anchored by the orca (killer whale) **Believe** show, with special effects to enhance performances by Shamu and crew. **Journey to Atlantis** is a 6-minute ride through the lost-continent myth, eight storeys up without any sense of displacement, while accompanied by the vocalisations of a dolphin spirit guide. At the end, protected black and white Commerson's dolphins from the tip of South America are on view. On **Wild Arctic,** a simulated helicopter takes off in San Diego and lands in a North Pole scenario with polar bears, beluga whales and walruses going about their business. Florida's gentle herbivores are being rehabilitated in **Manatee Rescue,** a 215,000-gallon freshwater tank with viewing of the sea cows from above and below. A plastic viewing tube protects visitors from the inhabitants of **Shark Encounter.** Bottlenose dolphins, pilot whales, sea lions, river otters and large birds perform routines, and aquariums introduce less tractable species.

Six Flags Magic Mountain/Hurricane Harbor

Six Flags Magic Mountain $$$, Six Flags Hurricane Harbor $ *Both via I–5, Magic Mountain Parkway, Valencia; tel: (661) 255-4100; www.sixflags.com.* Ask for combo tickets if visiting both parks and check for economical online specials.

These adjacent parks offer roller coasters and a water park in the Santa Clarita Valley, a half hour's drive north of downtown Los Angeles, but are open daily only in summer, some weekends the rest of the year.

Magic Mountain's themes include Warner Bros Superheroes and Looney Tunes cartoon characters. Want weightlessness and G force? Try **Superman: The Escape's** 7-second acceleration to 100mph. The **Viper** loops three times vertically, flips riders over seven times, corkscrews, and drops. Six Flags' thrills include **X2,** a roller coaster with

Right
Pacific ray touch tank

wing-shaped cars that spin 360° as riders loop and rocket through fire, fog and sound effects on a massive 3-D maze of tracks and girders, and **Déjà Vu**, which sends riders forward and backwards along a twisted, looping inverted steel track – not recommended for the queasy. **Scream!** is another coaster with seven 360° turns, with a claim to fame that its cars are floorless. TATSU speeds at 62mph over 3600ft of track, looping all around the park. For a breather in summer, try the **Hurricane Harbor**'s raft rides, water slides, tubing and pools.

UNIVERSAL STUDIOS® HOLLYWOOD/CITYWALK

Universal Studios® Hollywood $$$
100 Universal City Plaza, Universal City; tel: (800) 864-8377; www. universalstudioshollywood.com

Metro Red Line (www.metro.net) rail service extends from downtown Los Angeles via Hollywood to Universal City. $1.25.

One of the world's oldest film studios is surrounded by a cinema-themed amusement park, and, unique in the Western US, offers an extensive **Studio Tour** narrated by Whoopi Goldberg. Don't miss the perfect singing and showmanship of **The Blues Brothers® Show** concert from which the stars depart in a siren-wailing cop car.

The Simpsons™ Ride six-minute motion simulator plunge through Krusty the Clown's Krustyland theme park is a 3-D everything-goes-wrong takeoff from the animated television show. Dinosaurs run amok in **Jurassic Park® – The Ride**; prepare to get soaked when an enormous *Tyrannosaurus rex* dunks the ride's car. **Fear Factor Live** pits audience members against each other, unscripted. **Backdraft** re-creates the heat and fright of a raging fire. **Terminator 2® 3-D** offers a stunning integration of stunt actors, film and special effects to save the human race from cyborg imperialism. **Shrek 4-D™**, in OgreVision, is a fun, wide-coverage glasses show full of wild movements by the beloved characters of the ogre, his princess, Fiona, and the ever-talking sassy Donkey. **Revenge of the Mummy – the Ride** uses the modern *Mummy* movies' creepy villain, the Egyptian priest Imhotep, and his tomb as the theme for lots of back and forth on the indoor roller coaster, darkness, and 450-lb mummies in simulated freefall almost dropping onto riders.

Universal CityWalk $$
Tel: (818) 622-4455; www.citywalkhollywood.com. Some clubs have a cover charge.

Outside the park entrance gate is the free (with parking) **CityWalk**, a pedestrian walking, shopping, dining and entertainment complex and a multiplex cinema area. **Café Tu Tu Tango $$** serves an all-starter menu while painters and sculptors work at their newest creations. If it catches your eye, look for the price tag – every piece of art on display is for sale. The **Hard Rock Café Hollywood $$** green and white guitar looms near the domed white restaurant building close to the car park entrance. The **Saddle Ranch Chop House $$** serves up steaks, a dance floor, live music, an outdoor patio for barbecuing, and 100 screens for viewing the latest sports matches. The car park fee may be refundable with purchase of a cinema ticket. **Gibson Amphitheatre** (*tel: (818) 622-4440*) is the place to take in top pop bands and headliners.

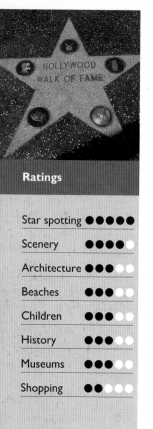

Route to the Stars

S tar-struck! Hollywood conjures up images of sleek blonde starlets in form-fitting satin gowns wearing enormous sunglasses, impossibly handsome actors in evening wear, tyrannical directors, champagne, red convertibles and black limousines, Oscars, larger-than-life heroes and an industry that conveys eternal life upon the chosen. Hollywood, the place, can be shockingly unkempt.

The film (and television) industry has never been physically limited to Hollywood; it has worked, lived and played all over Southern California. The chances of seeing a 'movie' star are best at a location shoot in the Greater Los Angeles area, and probably worst during the popular guided tours of the Homes of the Stars. Like everyone else, stars like to eat, drink and dance at trendy restaurants and clubs, shop for bargains, stroll in supermarkets and walk in parks. Most tolerate autograph seekers only when they are 'on', made up and dressed to meet their fans and satisfy the needs of a publicity circus to promote their careers. Don't overlook luck and chance – a star may run through the airport to catch a flight or go flower-shopping at a local farmers' market – providing you with your personal sighting and a unique story to take home.

Ratings

Star spotting	●●●●●
Scenery	●●●●○
Architecture	●●●○○
Beaches	●●●○○
Children	●●●○○
History	●●●○○
Museums	●●●○○
Shopping	●●○○○

BEVERLY HILLS

ⓘ **City of Beverly Hills**
www.beverlyhills.org

Beverly Hills Conference & Visitors Bureau 239 S. Beverly Dr., Beverly Hills, CA 90212; tel: (800) 345-2210; www.beverlyhillsbehere.com

L.A. Westside Tourism Partnership (Beverly Hills, Marina del Ray, Santa Monica, West Hollywood)
www.westla.com

Beverly Hills has mansions, shopping and an aura of luxury few communities can match (*see Los Angeles, pages 44–5*). **The Paley Center for Media** (*495 N. Beverly Dr.; tel: (310) 786-1000; www. paleycenter.org*) covers the television and live performance industry, but star buffs will enjoy the **Polo Lounge** at the **Beverly Hills Hotel** (*9641 Sunset Blvd; tel: (310) 276-2251; www.thebeverlyhillshotel.com*) for the feeling of *luxe* and the power of moneymen doing deals for films. The **Four Seasons Beverly Wilshire Beverly Hills Hotel** (*9500 Wilshire Blvd; tel: (310) 275-5200*) was the setting for *Pretty Woman*.

Rodeo Drive Shops have back doors for stars' privacy, but hotel spas and hair salons cater to everyone, guests, patrons and celebrities alike. Well-heeled and celebrity shoppers find vintage designer clothing used by stars for the Academy Awards ceremony from **Lily et Cie** (*9044 Burton Way; tel: (310) 724-5757*).

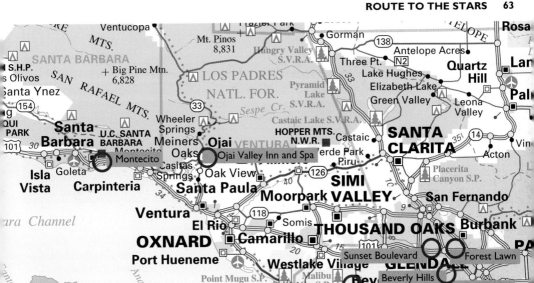

Westwood Village Memorial Park and Mortuary (*1218 Glendon Ave at Wilshire Blvd, behind a car park, Westwood; tel: (310) 474-1579*) is a peaceful cemetery where Marilyn Monroe and other stars are interred.

FOREST LAWN AND HOLLYWOOD FOREVER

Forest Lawn Memorial Park Hollywood Hills 6300 Forest Lawn Dr., Los Angeles; tel: (800) 204-3131. Open 0800–1700.

Hollywood Forever 6000 Santa Monica Blvd, Hollywood; tel: (323) 469-1181; www.hollywoodforever.com

Forest Lawn Memorial Park Hollywood Hills is another spot to see the stars, or rather their memorial tablets and a few opulent crypts. Bette Davis's (*Courts of Remembrance*) white marble maiden belies the crusty epitaph, 'She Did It The Hard Way'.

Hollywood Forever cemetery has buried entertainment industry folk for more than a century, including Rudolph Valentino, Cecil B. DeMille, Douglas Fairbanks, Sr. and Jayne Mansfield.

HOLLYWOOD

Metro Red Line (www.metro.net) rail service extends from downtown Los Angeles via Hollywood to Universal City.

Tinseltown's glitter still shines a little, but much of Hollywood's magnetism as a place where stars hung out on corners like Hollywood (Blvd) and Vine (St) is gone. Politicos, businesspeople and developers have begun pouring money into Hollywood as a spot where history

● **Holly Trolley**
(www.ladottransit/other/
trolley) designed for Hollywood
clubbing, operates Thu–Sat
1830–0230. $1.

ⓘ **LA, Inc., The
Convention &
Visitors Bureau**
Tel: (800) 228-2452;
www.discoverlosangeles.com
**Hollywood Visitor
Information Center**
6801 Hollywood Blvd,
Hollywood and Highland
complex, Hollywood;
tel: (323) 467-6412.
Open Mon–Sat 1000–2200,
Sun 1000–1900.

**Hollywood Chamber of
Commerce** 7018
Hollywood Blvd, Hollywood;
tel: (323) 469-8311;
www.hollywoodchamber.net

**L.A. Westside Tourism
Partnership (Beverly
Hills, Marina del Rey,
Santa Monica, West
Hollywood)**
www.westla.com

🏛 **Frederick's of
Hollywood Lingerie
Museum** 6751 Hollywood
Blvd; tel: (323) 957-5953.
Open daily, call for opening
times. Free.

and image can be exploited for tourist dollars spent on more than thin T-shirts, Maps of the Stars' Homes and a bus-bound whirl outside the gates of purported stars' mansions. Several historic art deco theatres have been restored and reopened as film palaces; Hollywood history-related museums supplement the oddity carnivals presented by Guinness, Ripley's and the inevitable wax museum.

The **Capitol Records Building** (*1750 Vine St*) is a 1954 landmark, 11 storeys piled like long-playing records on a turntable. It has gold records on display in the lobby, but offers no tours.

The **Egyptian Theatre** (*6712 Hollywood Blvd; tel: (323) 466-3456; www.egyptiantheatre.com; tours tel: (323) 461-2020*) was Hollywood's original 1922 art deco movie palace, taking fanciful advantage of interest in the Near East in the year Howard Carter discovered King Tutankhamen's tomb. American Cinematheque's two film theatres show avant-garde, career tribute, foreign and independent films. The Egyptian hosted Hollywood's first film premieres. Filmgoers can admire the elaborate Egyptian décor until portable acoustic walls move into place as films begin. *Forever Hollywood*, a documentary film, is screened sporadically, usually at weekends.

El Capitan Theater (*6838 Hollywood Blvd; tel: (800) 347-6396; http://.disney.go.com/disneypictures/el_capitan*), restored by Disney to its original 1926 art deco splendour, is where Orson Welles's 1941 *Citizen Kane* premiered.

Frederick's of Hollywood Lingerie Museum, a part of the retail store, is a free, cheerful voyage into the world of unmentionables worn by film stars, from Elizabeth Taylor and Mae West to Madonna's *bustier* and Cher's strapless bra.

Hollywood Boulevard Walk of Fame (*Hollywood Blvd, from La Brea Ave–Vine St; Vine St from Yucca St–Sunset Blvd*), a 1960s marketing gimmick to stud the pavements with stars, has turned into an enduring icon. More than 2500 pink terrazzo stars honour stars of film, stage, television, radio, music and a few odd choices such as the Apollo XI astronauts. Caution: tourists searching for stars can wander off kerbs!

Popular stars include:
Charlie Chaplin,   *6751 Hollywood Blvd;*

Hollywood Entertainment District Tel: (323) 463-6767; www.hollywoodentertainmentdistrict.com, has a Visitors Guide and Map.

Hollywood Bowl Museum 2301 N. Highland Ave; tel: (323) 850-2058; www.hollywoodbowl.com/about/museum.cfm. Open Tue–Sun (summer), Tue–Fri (rest of year). Call for hours. Free.

The Hollywood Museum $$$ 1660 N. Highland Ave; tel: (323) 464-7776; www.thehollywoodmuseum.com. Open Thu–Sun 1000–1700.

Hollywood Wax Museum $$ 6767 Hollywood Blvd; tel: (323) 462-8860; www.hollywoodwax.com. Open daily 1000–2400.

Hollywood and Highland 6801 Hollywood Blvd at Highland; tel: (323) 467-6412; www.hollywoodandhighland.com

The **L.A Inc., The Convention and Visitors Bureau Hollywood Visitor Information Center** is in the complex.

John Lennon,	1750 Vine St;
Marilyn Monroe,	6644 Hollywood Blvd;
Mickey Mouse,	6925 Hollywood Blvd;
Elvis Presley,	6777 Hollywood Blvd; and
Jackie Chan,	6834 Hollywood Blvd.

Hollywood Bowl Museum showcases the music and performing arts in the **Hollywood Bowl** (*www.hollywoodbowl.com*), Tinseltown's quarter-sphere outdoor concert hall, with recordings of performances.

The Hollywood Museum uses the old 1935 art deco Max Factor make-up studios building to display costumes, props, posters and film-making equipment illustrating Hollywood eras from silent film to technological wizardry.

Hollywood Forever (Cemetery) (*6000 Santa Monica Blvd; tel: (323) 469-1181; www.hollywoodforever.com*), adjacent to Paramount Studios, is the resting place for director Cecil B. DeMille, heart-throb Rudolph Valentino, and others who never went far away after making it big. LifeStories using touch-screen technology are for visitors dying to know more about those interred recently.

The first venue for the Academy Awards in 1929, **Hollywood Roosevelt Hotel** (*7000 Hollywood Blvd; tel: (323) 466-7000 or (800) 950-7667; www.hollywoodroosevelt.com*) is so rich with Hollywoodiana, it's haunted, allegedly, by Montgomery Clift playing a bugle in Room 928 where he practised when filming *From Here to Eternity*. Refurbishment has again transformed the one-time haunt of Clark Gable, Carole Lombard and Marilyn Monroe into a trendy scene, with poolside cabanas around a David Hockney pool.

The **Hollywood Sign** (*Mount Lee, Griffith Park; www.hollywoodsign.org/history.html*), seen from many Hollywood streets, is closed to visits from the public. Real-estate developers created a 'Hollywoodland' sign in 1923 with 4000 light bulbs to promote a new housing estate; the decrepit sign was restored to its current 50-ft height in 1978, having lost the 'land' early on.

Hollywood Heritage Museum $ (*2100 N. Highland Ave, across from the Hollywood Bowl; tel: (323) 874-4005; www.hollywoodheritage.org. Open Thu–Sun 1200–1600*), devoted to the silent film era, is in Hollywood's first major film studio, the Lasky-DeMille Barn.

Hollywood Wax Museum shows how stars like Sean Connery and Johnny Depp, crooners like Elvis and legends like Marilyn would look if eternally preserved in paraffin.

Hollywood and Highland complex hosts the Academy Awards® ceremony in the Kodak Theatre. The entertainment complex also includes a shopping mall, cinema, bowling, restaurants and clubs.

Grauman's Chinese Theater (*6925 Hollywood Blvd; tel: (323) 464-8111*), Hollywood's best-known building, premiered Cecil B. De Mille's *King of Kings* when it opened in 1927. The fanciful red and green pagoda tower presides over a courtyard of hands, feet and other

Ripley's Believe It or Not! Hollywood
$$ 6780 Hollywood Blvd;
tel: (323) 466 6335;
www.ripleys.com

body parts (such as Betty Grable's leg) imprinted in cement; (see *www.manntheatres.com/chinese/forecourt.htm* for a map of impressions). Original owner Sid Grauman is the target of many inscriptions, some suggestive, a few lewd, most laudatory. The cinema shows first-run films; **VIP Backstage Tours** are conducted daily (*tel: (323) 463-9576*).

Pantages Theatre (*6233 Hollywood Blvd near Vine St; tel: (323) 468-1770; www.pantages-theater.com*), an ornate 1930 art deco film palace, now presents Broadway musicals. A dinosaur and clock mark **Ripley's Believe It or Not! Hollywood** collection of curiosities, including a portrait of John Wayne rendered in laundry lint.

Small, 1.9 square-mile **West Hollywood** claims pride of place with Southern California's largest gay/lesbian population, and many services, hotels, eateries and clubs found on *www.gogaywesthollywood.com*

West Hollywood Marketing and Visitors Bureau *8687 Melrose Ave, Ste M-38, West Hollywood, CA 90069; tel: (800) 368-6020* or *(310) 289-2525; www.visitwesthollywood.com*

Suggested tours

Getting close to the stars and the action is the name of the game. The film industry has increased security for its stars and productions, somewhat curtailing spectators' chance of seeing the magic of filming.

Occasionally, location film shoots will permit visitors to watch, filming may take place on city streets, or another alternative, with no guarantee of a star sighting, is a film studio tour or live tapings of major network television shows (*see page 52*).

Where is a better spot to attend a film festival but where the industry lives and breathes? Major film festivals include:
Los Angeles, Italia Film, Fashion & Art Fest *www.losangelesitalia.com*, pays homage to the Italian version of film-making in February.
Indian Film Festival in Los Angeles *tel: (310) 364-4403; www.indianfilmfestival.org*, brings the subcontinent to LA in April.
Los Angeles Film Festival *tel: (866) 345-6337; www.lafilmfest.com*, hosts 40,000 film folk and aficionados in June.
Los Angeles Latino International Film Festival *tel: (323) 469-9066; www.latinofilm.org*, is on in September.
OUTFEST (Los Angeles Gay and Lesbian Film Festival) *tel: (213) 480-7088; www.outfest.org*, has its major screenings in July, with year-round events in the area.
Los Angeles International Short Film Festival [LA Shorts Fest] *tel: (323) 461-4400; http://lashortsfest.com*, has shown films as short as 58 seconds long, in mid-September.
AFI (American Film Institute) Fest *tel: (866) 234-3378; www.afi.com/onscreen/afifest*, has been a powerhouse venue in November since 1971.

Below
Universal Studios, Hollywood

MALIBU

ⓘ **Malibu Chamber
of Commerce**
*23805 Stuart Ranch Rd,
Suite 100, Malibu; tel: (310)
456-9025; www.malibu.org*

Eighteen miles of beaches, stars' homes and pricey restaurants along Hwy 1, the Pacific Coast Highway (PCH), are flooded every few years. Despite the instability of homes built on stilts, stars have flocked here since 1926, when PCH's opening led a developer to create a stars' hideaway. Those $2600 beach cottages are now worth millions.

Adamson House (*23200 PCH, Malibu Lagoon State Beach; tel: (818) 880-0350; www.parks.ca.gov*) incorporates locally made, late 1920s decorative tiles. In the Adamson House, the **Malibu Lagoon Museum** covers Native American, Malibu Colony and tile history with guided house tours, *tel: (310) 456-8432, Wed–Sat 1100–1400*. Just south near the pier is the **Malibu Surfrider Beach**. **Leo Carrillo State Park** (*Mulholland Hwy at Hwy 1; tel: (818) 880-0363*) is named after a comic sidekick actor who was great-grandson of California's last Mexican governor.

Point Dume State Beach (*access via Westward Beach Rd*), with **Paradise Cove** nearby, is a rugged landscape of golden sands and black rock cliffs close to largely concealed stars' homes. A trail climbs 250ft above the beaches for a 32-mile view of Santa Monica Bay to Palos Verdes and California gray whale migration December to March. Just west is the long strand of **Zuma Beach**. **Broad Beach**, 5 miles north, is celebrity row, well-guarded, but accessible on a public footpath at 31346 Broad Beach. For more Malibu attractions, see Los Angeles (*page 46*).

MONTECITO

Montecito is where stars, directors and technicians get away from the industry, or retire to semitropical foliage, nurseries, oak groves, flowering vines and horse trails. Watch for stars as spectators in Santa Barbara at **Paseo Nuevo** (*www.centerstagetheater.org*) or the 1931 **Arlington Theatre** (*1317 State St; tel: (805) 963-4408*), a film palace decorated as a Mexican village with a ceiling of painted stars that also hosts music concerts and a University of California, Santa Barbara lecture series.

OJAI

ⓘ **Ojai Valley
Chamber of
Commerce** *201 S. Signal
St, Ojai, CA 93023;
tel: (805) 646-8126;
www.ojaichamber.org.
Call for hours.*

Director Frank Capra saw sunset pink on the Los Padres Mountains around Ojai, and captured it as Shangri-la in the 1937 film, *Lost Horizon*. Stars, writers and artists have liked this mountain town, 15 miles and a world away from the Pacific Ocean, as a getaway since the 1920s. **Spa Ojai** at the **Ojai Valley Inn & Spa** (*Country Club Rd; tel: (805) 646-1111* or *(888) 697-8780; www.ojairesort.com*) enhances a smart golf resort famed since that era, and mimics the white Spanish architecture so copied by the stars of silent and early talking motion pictures.

SUNSET BOULEVARD

Also known as **Sunset Strip**, this line of clubs and hot spots stretches from 7800–9200 Sunset Blvd in West Hollywood. The atmospheric, celebrity-heavy **Viper Room** (*8852 Sunset Blvd; tel: (310) 358-1880; www.viperroom.com*), and **The Roxy** (*9009 Sunset Blvd; tel: (310) 278-9457; http://theroxyonsunset.com*) are other over-the-top music joints. Check the scene for the latest in chic slumming or clubbing. **Melrose Ave** (*see Los Angeles, page 47*) is half a mile south. In between is the gay/lesbian mecca along Santa Monica Blvd. Posh **Chateau Marmont** (*8221 Sunset Blvd; tel: (323) 656-1010; www.chateaumarmont.com*) has hosted legions of stars, from Monroe and Garbo to Mick Jagger.

WILL ROGERS STATE HISTORIC PARK

Will Rogers State Historic Park (*1501 Will Rogers Park Rd, Pacific Palisades; tel: (310) 454-8212*) shows the good taste, 1924–35 home, stables and polo field of the beloved humorist, broadcaster and actor, Will Rogers. Ranch House tours are offered *Tue–Sun 1100, 1300 and 1400 (tel: (310) 454-8212 ext 103)*, and the Will Rogers Polo Club plays *Apr–Oct weekends*. The heavily used park has easy-to-rugged hiking trails in the Santa Monica Mountains, many with fine views to downtown Los Angeles and Santa Monica Bay. Will Rogers is also remembered at **Will Rogers State Beach** (*Pacific Palisades/Santa Monica boundary; tel: (310) 305-9503*) and as Beverly Hills' first mayor at **Will Rogers Memorial Park** (*across Sunset Blvd from the Beverly Hills Hotel*).

Suggested tour

Total distance: 125 miles.

Time: 4 hours non-stop, but a stop in Ojai is less frantic.

Links: Los Angeles (*see page 42*). At Pacific Palisades, turn south on Hwy 1 to Santa Monica (*see Southern California Beaches, page 70*). Go north at Santa Barbara for **Big Sur/Central Coast** (*see page 214*).

Route: Take Hollywood Blvd west at Vine St to **La Brea Ave ❶**, turn left two blocks, then right on Sunset Blvd to Pacific Palisades. Go right on Hwy 1, **Pacific Coast Hwy ❷**, past Malibu beaches and **celebrity houses ❸** and inland to **Oxnard ❹**. Go west on Hwy 101 at **Montalvo/Ventura ❺**. Take the Hwy 33 exit to **Ojai ❻**. Return 3 miles west on Hwy 33, then take Hwy 150 past **Lake Casitas ❼**. Continue northwest on Hwy 192, the scenic back road via **Montecito ❽** to **Santa Barbara ❾**.

Also worth exploring

Mulholland Drive/Mulholland Hwy (with one detour at Encino to Hwy 101 going west; exit Hwy 101 at Topanga Canyon Blvd to rejoin the **Mulholland Scenic Drive**) winds west for 55 miles over the spine of the Santa Monica Mountains from Hwy 101 at Cahuenga Pass (Mulholland Dr. exit) to **Leo Carrillo State Beach** in Malibu (*see page 67*). Clear blue skies, rugged rocky mountains, creeks, ranches, canyons and unique mansions reflect the area chosen by many stars for their homes. State and regional parks, along with exclusive housing estates and an occasional golf course, make for an incongruous mix of scenery and recreation enjoyed on foot, horse or bicycle.

Several major routes from the coast bisect the long, west–east stretch of Los Angeles' approximation of a national park, the **Santa Monica Mountains National Recreation Area (Visitors Center,** *401 W. Hillcrest Dr., Thousand Oaks, CA 91360; tel: (805) 370-2301; www.nps.gov/samo; open daily 0900–1700*). **Topanga Canyon Blvd, Malibu Canyon Rd/Las Virgenes Rd** and **Kanan-Dume Rd** all offer vistas as they approach their summits before plunging northward into the San Fernando and Conejo Valleys to Hwy 101.

Paramount Ranch, set up in 1927 as a Western filmset, is still used for many television productions. False building façades are boarded up between productions, with each of several blocks having a complete saloon, marshal's office, general store and livery stables, for flexibility.

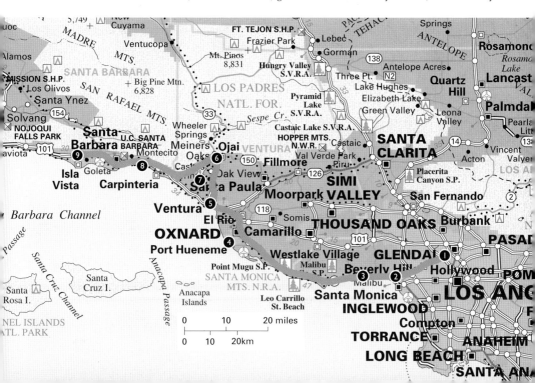

Southern California Beaches

I n Hollywood mythology, life is a beach, and nowhere on earth has as much beach as Southern California. From the heart-throb days of the Annette Funichello and Frankie Avalon *Gidget* beach films to the feel-good bounce of the Beach Boys, Southern California has been associated with broad sandy crescents, curling waves and a carefree life where problems are as ephemeral as tomorrow's sandcastle.

But Southern California is *not* all beaches. Cliffs intrude, providing spectacular viewpoints to watch the coast, migrating whales and surfers. Piers and harbours break up the coastline, sheltering massive ocean freighters as well as solitary sailboats. Offshore oil wells and natural oil seeps dribble bits of petroleum that wash up as tar, sticking to feet and bodies.

None of which matters. For residents as well as visitors, life in Southern California really is a beach. It doesn't matter that beaches can be crowded, the water cold, the parking impossible or the sunburn painful. The sand is waiting, the surf is up and true love could be just over the next crest.

Ratings

Amusements	●●●●●
Beaches	●●●●●
Children	●●●●○
Scenery	●●●●○
Sport	●●●●○
Food and drink	●●●○○
Wildlife	●●●○○
Museums	●●○○○

CARLSBAD

ⓘ Carlsbad Convention & Visitors Bureau 400 Carlsbad Village Dr., Carlsbad, CA 92008; tel: (760) 434-6093 or (800) 227-5722; www.visitcarlsbad.com. Open Mon–Fri 0900–1700, Sat 1000–1600, Sun 1000–1500.

ⓜ Museum of Making Music $ 5790 Armada Dr.; tel: (760) 438-5996 or (877) 551-9976; www.museumofmakingmusic. org. Open Tue–Sun 1000–1700.

Carlsbad is known mostly for the commercial Flower Fields® at **Carlsbad Ranch $$** (*east of 1–5, Palomar, Airport Rd and Paseo del Norte; tel: (760) 431-0352; www.theflowerfields.com. Open daily 0900–1800 March–mid-May*) that burst into colour between February and May, when the 50 acres of ranunculus flowers are in bloom. One of Carlsbad's major attractions is a Southern California theme park, **LEGOLAND® California** (*see page 59*). The CVB publishes self-guided maps of historical landmark buildings and extensive collections of public art. The **Museum of Making Music** has changing exhibits on the history and making of musical instruments and an assortment of real instruments – many electrified – to test your musical skills.

Surfers and scuba divers congregate off **South Carlsbad State Beach** (*tel: (760) 438-3143*). Watch the action from the bluffs above the beach.

Further south is **Batiquitos Lagoon** (*Batiquitos Dr., tel: (760) 931-0800; www.batiquitosfoundation.org*), an extensive wetlands restoration project. A 1.6-mile trail departs from the Nature Center.

LEY

Canyon S.P.

San Fernando

Wrightwood

Crestline

Silverwood Lake
S.R.A.

Lake
Arrowhead

B

SAND OAKS

Burbank

ANGELES
NATL. FOR.

GLENDALE

everly Hills

PASADENA

ONTARIO

Rialto

SAN BE

Redla

Malibu

Santa Monica

Venice Beach

POMONA

LOS ANGELES

RIVERSIDE

NGLEWO

Marina del Rey

FULLERTON

Corona

MORE

VALLE

Compton

Perris

TORRANCE

ANAHEIM

ORANGE

Sun City

Wi

LONG BE

Long Beach

SANTA ANA

IRVINE

ORANGE

Lake Elsinore

HUNTINGTO

Huntington Beach

Mission

Viejo

Lake
Elsinore
S.R.A.

Murrieta

Tem

Newpo

Newport Beach

CLEVELAND N.F.

Lagun

Laguna Beach

San Juan Capistrano

San
Onofre
S.B.

Fallbrook

Pala

PA.
I.R.
R

San Pedro

Dana
Point

San
Clemente

Santa Catalina Island

Channel

Avalon

Santa
Catalina
Island

CAMP PENDLETON
MARINE CORPS
BASE

Bonsall

Vista

E

Oceanside

OCEANSI

Carlsbad

Carlsbad

San
Marcos

Del D

Outer Santa Barbara Passage

Enci

Encinitas

Solana Beach

Del Mar

P

U.S.
NAVAL
RES.

Gulf of
Santa Catalina

San Clemente
Island

La Jolla

Sant

La Mes

SAN DIEGO

0   10   20 miles

0   10   20km

Coronado

Imperial Beach

Border Field S.P.

TIJUANA

Opposite
La Jolla beach, sculpted by the waves

Food in Carlsbad

Tip Top Meats $ *6118 Paseo Del Norte; tel: (760) 438-2620; open daily 0600–2000*, is a popular local breakfast and lunch stop with good picnic supplies and, of course, meat!

ENCINITAS

ℹ **Encinitas Chamber of Commerce Visitor Center**
859 2nd St, Encinitas, CA 92024; tel: (760) 753-6041 or (800) 953-6041; www.encinitaschamber.com. Open Mon–Fri 0900–1700, Sat–Sun 1000–1600.

Lux Art Institute $$
1550 S. El Camino Real; tel: (760) 436-6611; www.luxartinstitute.org. Open Thu–Fri 1300–1700, Sat 1100–1700.

The town of Encinitas is a flower-growing centre, filled with commercial nurseries and spectacular private gardens. **The Paul Ecke Ranch**, which produces 50 per cent of the world's poinsettias, put Encinitas on the map. **Quail Botanical Gardens $$** (*230 Quail Gardens Dr.; tel: (760) 436-3036; www.qbgardens.org; open daily*) are 30 acres planted with exotics from around the world, including some quite local: native plants once used by Kumeyaay indigenous people living in the region.

Encinitas' serenity convinced the **Self-Realisation Fellowship** (*215 K St and First Ave; tel: (760) 753-2888; www.yogananda-srf.org*) to set up an ashram, with quiet cliffside **Meditation Gardens** (*216 K St*) just around the corner. The popular surfing beach below, one of eleven in Encinitas, is called 'Swami's'. Scuba divers can explore the East Marine Life Refuge, off Swami's. The **Lux Art Institute**, in the Encinitas hills, hosts one artist-in-residence at a time to display finished work and while working on a commissioned piece for permanent installation at the facility.

HUNTINGTON BEACH

ℹ **Huntington Beach Conference and Visitors Bureau**
301 Main St, Ste 208, Huntington Beach, CA 92648; tel: (714) 969-3492 or (800) 729-6232; www.surfcityusa.com. Open Mon–Fri 0900–1700.

Nicknamed 'Surf City' by 1950s surfers, Huntington Beach is also one of the largest cities in Orange County. The beach stretches 8½ miles, backed by a paved cycling, skating and walking path. Hwy 1, usually called **PCH, Pacific Coast Highway**, is lined with parking meters.

A favourite local surfing spot is just south of the concrete pier. The **International Surfing Museum** (*411 Olive Ave; tel: (714) 960-3483; www.surfingmuseum.org; open daily*) is filled with photos and old-time surfing gear. Main St is lined with outdoor cafés and coffee houses. Little Saigon has many Vietnamese restaurants, shops and businesses.

Bolsa Chica (*tours, tel: (714) 840-1575; www.amigosdebolsachica.org*), north of Huntington Beach, is a salt marsh and home to endangered bird species. There are over 300 species using these restored wetlands.

LA JOLLA

ℹ **Promote La Jolla**
1150 Silverado St, Ste 221, La Jolla, CA 92037; tel: (858) 454-5718; www.lajollabythesea.com

This upmarket San Diego neighbourhood is a mosaic of coves and cliffs battered by the surf. Most of the coastline is protected in public parks

ℹ **La Jolla Visitor Information Center**
7966 Herschel Ave., Suite A (at Prospect);
tel: (619) 236-1212;
www.sandiego.org. Open winter Thu–Tue 1000–1700; summer daily 1000–1900.

🏪 **La Jolla Cave Store**
$ 1325 Coast Blvd;
tel: (858) 459-0746;
www.cavestore.com. Call for hours.

Salk Institute 10010 N. Torrey Pines Rd; tel: (858) 453-4100 ext. 1287;
www.salk.edu. Guided architectural tours Mon–Fri 1200 by reservation. Free.

Museum of Contemporary Art San Diego $$ 700 Prospect St;
tel: (858) 454-3541;
www.mcasd.org. Open Thu–Tue 1100–1700, Thu to 1900; closed Wed. (MCASD also has a downtown location 1100 and 1001 Kettner Blvd, San Diego.)

Torrey Pines Gliderport
2800 Torrey Pines Scenic Dr.;
tel: (858) 452-9858;
www.flytorrey.com

and beaches, popular with seals and human visitors. Art galleries cluster along **Prospect St**; new exhibitions usually open on Fri evenings.

La Jolla Cove, just off Prospect St, is popular with snorkellers; **Scripps Park**, beside the cove, attracts sun-worshippers and artists trying to capture views along the cliffs. Just north are seven caves; **Sunny Jim Cave** is accessible through **La Jolla Cave Store**.

The **Salk Institute for Biological Studies** is housed in a spectacular pair of buildings overlooking the Pacific Ocean.

Museum of Contemporary Art San Diego (MCASD La Jolla) was built as the palatial Scripps family home in 1916. The museum specialises in emerging California artists, with an outdoor sculpture garden.

Birch Aquarium at Scripps $$ (*Scripps Institution of Oceanography, 2300 Expedition Way; tel: (858) 534-3474; www.aquarium.ucsd.ecu; open 0900–1700 daily*) features ocean life from the entire Pacific Ocean. **Torrey Pines State Natural Reserve** (*N. Torrey Pines Rd, tel: (858) 755-2063; www.torreypine.org; open daily*) protects the only surviving mainland forest of Torrey pines (*Pinus torreyana*) on an isolated bluff fringed by multicoloured sandstone cliffs popular with paragliders. The **University of California, San Diego** (*9500 Gilman Dr.; tel: (858) 534-2117; http://stuartcollection.ucsd.edu*) has the **Stuart Collection of Sculpture** scattered about the campus. Don't miss *Vices and Virtues*, flashing neon around the top of the Charles Lee Powell Structural Systems Laboratory; Niki de Saint Phalle's *Sun God*, a colourful bird near the car park opposite Peterson Hall; and Alexis Smith's *Snake Path*, a 560-ft-long path tiled to resemble a snake, best seen from the **Central Library** upper floors.

LAGUNA BEACH

ℹ **Laguna Beach Visitors Center** 252 Broadway, Laguna Beach, CA 92651; tel: (949) 497-9229 or (800) 877-1115;
www.lagunabeachinfo.org

🎭 **Festival of Arts** $$ 650 Laguna Cyn Rd, Laguna Beach, CA 92651; tel: (949) 494-1145 or (800) 487-3378; www.foapom.com

Laguna Beach spawned one of California's first artistic organisations, the Laguna Beach Art Association. Most of the artists are long gone, but their heritage remains with some 90 galleries and studios and three annual art festivals. The Jul–Aug **Festival of Arts** draws 200,000 visitors, most to see the 'Pageant of the Masters', live tableaux reproducing famous classical paintings.

The coastline is scalloped with beaches separated by rugged cliffs. **Crescent Bay Point Park** (*off Crescent Dr.*) offers striking views across the bay and cliffs to the town centre. **Heisler Park** (*north of the Art Museum*) is the beginning of a pleasant path to **Main Beach** (*foot of Broadway*), the town's largest and most popular beach. The **Laguna Art Museum** $$ (*307 Cliff Dr.; tel: (949) 494-8971; http://lagunaartmuseum.org*) specialises in American art, particularly modern art in California.

LONG BEACH

ⓘ Long Beach Area Convention & Visitors Bureau
One World Trade Center, Ste 300, Long Beach, CA 98031; tel: (800) 452-7829 or (562) 436-3645; www.visitlongbeach.com. Open Mon–Fri 0800–1700.

The **Metro Blue Line** (www.metro.net) runs from Los Angeles to Long Beach.

Ⓗ Aquarium of the Pacific $$$
100 Aquarium Way; tel: (562) 590-3100 or (888) 826-7257; www.aquariumofpacific.org. Open daily 0900–1800. A combined same-day ticket package with the Queen Mary is cheaper.

Once a tawdry military town, Long Beach, America's largest container port, has 6 miles of uncluttered sandy beach stretching south from Rainbow Harbor. The easiest way to explore the waterfront attractions is by **AquaBus** water taxi, or AquaLink catamaran to Alamitos Bay (*www.lbtransit.com/Services/Aquabus.aspx*). For downtown attractions, hop on the free Passport shuttle.

The incredibly clear tanks of the **Aquarium of the Pacific** re-create local temperate waters, the subarctic Bering Sea and coral lagoons from Micronesia. Don't miss the outdoor touch tanks, Shark Lagoon or the Lorikeet Forest aviary.

Belmont Shore (*along Second St, south of downtown*) is a restored 1920s district, with boutiques, galleries, bookstores and restaurants. **Pine Street**, Long Beach's restored city centre, lined with early architecture, restaurants and boutiques, is great for people-watching.

The former luxury liner the **Queen Mary $$$** (*1126 Queens Hwy; tel: (562) 435-3511; www.queenmary.com; open daily 1000–1800*) is moored across Queensway Bay from the **Aquarium of the Pacific**. It has been fitted out as a hotel, with many of the elegant first-class areas refurbished for tours. A Russian **Foxtrot submarine $$$**, next to the Queen Mary, is also open for tours, 1000–1800.

Shoreline Village (*fronting on Rainbow Harbor; tel: (562) 435-2668; www.shorelinevillage.com*) has waterfront shopping and entertainment.

MARINA DEL REY

ⓘ Marina Del Rey Convention and Visitors Bureau Visitor Information Center
4701 Admiralty Way; tel: (310) 305-9545; www.visitmarina.com. Open daily.

This immense marina north of LAX is lined with expensive restaurants known mostly for their harbour views. **Fisherman's Village** (*13755 Fiji Way; tel: (310) 823-5411*), a New England-style shopping and entertainment area, has boutiques, eating places, sport equipment rentals and harbour cruises.

NEWPORT BEACH

Above
Volleyball on Laguna Beach

Six miles of beaches line **Balboa Peninsula**. **Balboa Pavilion** (*400 Main St; tel: (800) 830-7744; www.balboapavilion.com*) was once the terminus for a tourist trolley line from Los Angeles and now has fishing charters, dining, and the *Catalina Flyer* (*tel: (949) 675-1905 or (800) 830-7744; www.catalinainfo.com*) to Santa Catalina Island (*see opposite*). The **Fun Zone** (*www.thebalboafunzone.com*) has a Ferris wheel, carousel, shops and restaurants. Have a Balboa Bar, chocolate-dipped square vanilla ice cream on a stick garnished with candy or nuts. The **Newport Harbor Nautical Museum $** (*600 E. Bay Ave, Balboa Fun Zone; tel: (949) 675-8915; www.*

ⓘ Newport Beach Conference & Visitors Bureau *1200 Newport Center Drive, Suite 120, Newport Beach, CA 92660; tel: (949) 719-6100 or (800) 942-6278; www.visitnewportbeach.com. Open Mon–Fri 0800–1700.*

nhnm.org; open Wed–Mon 1000–1800) has a superb collection of ship models and an ocean creature touch tank.

Marinas along Newport Bay boast one of the largest concentrations of pleasure boats in America, while **Upper Newport Bay Ecological Reserve and Nature Preserve** (*tel: (949) 640-6746; www.newportbay.org*) is at the bay's north end. Body surfers head for The Wedge (beach). Early risers shop at the Newport Pier where Dory fishers sell their fresh catch.

OCEANSIDE

ⓘ Oceanside Visitor Information Center *928 N. Coast Hwy, Oceanside, CA 92054; tel: (760) 722-1534; www.oceansidechamber. com.* Also a **California Welcome Center**, *tel: (800) 350-7873 or (760) 721-1101. Open daily 0900–1700.*

Oceanside hosts several national surfing competitions each year. The free **California Surf Museum** (*223 N. Coast Hwy; tel: (760) 721-6876; www.surfmuseum.org; open daily 1000–1600*) displays vintage surf boards, just up from the **Oceanside Pier**, which stretches more than 900ft into the Pacific. The **Buena Vista Audubon Nature Center** (*2202 S. Coast Hwy; tel: (760) 439-2473; www.bvaudubon.org; call for hours*) explores the mouth of the San Luis Rey River. **Mission San Luis Rey** (*see page 262*) is 4 miles inland.

SANTA CATALINA ISLAND

ⓘ Catalina Island Chamber of Commerce *1 Green Pier, Avalon, CA 90704; tel: (310) 510-1520; www.catalina.com or www.visitcatalinaisland. com. Open daily, hours vary.*

ⓝ Casino *1 Casino Way, Avalon, CA 90704; tel: (310) 510-7400; www.catalina.com or www.visitcatalinaisland.com. Open daily.*

Twenty-one miles off the coast from Long Beach, Catalina Island is a vision of Southern California before LA. Nearly 90 per cent of the island is undeveloped, a mix of sandy beaches and crumbling cliffs. Organised tours take in the interior, Pacific Ocean views, underwater fish from glass-bottom boats or semi-submersibles, flying fish at night, and the Avalon Casino.

The art deco **Casino** overlooking the harbour in Avalon, Catalina's one real town, was a summer escape for Hollywood stars during the 1930s and 1940s; the interior murals are stunning.

Access Catalina by water from Dana Point, Long Beach, Marina del Rey, Newport Beach or San Pedro.

SANTA MONICA

ⓟ Tide Ride *www.bigbluebus.com/ miniblue/tide.html, is Santa Monica's inexpensive downtown public transit bus.*

A walking pier, carousel, upmarket mall, palm-lined beachfront park and youthful style make Santa Monica an oceanside version of what Hollywood would like to be. Santa Monica has a notable British population that patronises British pubs and eateries. **Montana Avenue** (*7th–17th Sts; www.montanaave.com*) is a trendy shopping area sporting everything from baby clothing to racy lingerie and trendy restaurants to wear it in. **Palisades Park** (*clifftop along Ocean Ave*) provides convenient benches to watch the sunset.

ⓘ Santa Monica
Visitor Center *1920*
Main St, Ste B, Santa Monica,
CA 90405; tel: (800) 544-
5319 or (310) 393-7593.
Open daily 0900–1800.

Palisades Park Santa
Monica Visitor Kiosk,
1400 Ocean Ave; tel: (310)
393-7593. Open daily,
summer 0900–1700, winter
1000–1600.

Santa Monica Third
Street Promenade
Visitor Information Cart
Between Arizona Ave and
Santa Monica Blvd. Open
daily 1100–1700;
www.santamonica.com

Santa Monica Pier *(end of Colorado Ave; tel: (310) 458-8900; www.santamonicapier.org)* features a carousel, arcades, restaurants, an amusement park and the **Santa Monica Pier Aquarium $** *(1600 Ocean Front Walk; tel: (310) 393-6149; www.healthebay.org/smpa).*

Third Street Promenade *(Third St, Wilshire Blvd–Broadway; http://thirdstreetpromenade.org)* is an outdoor pedestrian mall with fountains, dinosaur topiary and cafés.

Santa Monica has many farmers' markets *(www.smgov.net/farmers_market)*; top locations are **Arizona between Second and Third Sts** *(Wed, Sat 0830–1300)*, **Pico at the Santa Monica Airport** *(Sat 0800–1300)* and **Main St at Ocean Park Blvd** *(Sun 0930–1300).*

The **Ocean Park** area in south Santa Monica by Venice is anchored by the popular galleries, coffeehouses and eateries on **Main Street**. **Bergamot Station** *(2525 Michigan Ave; www.bergamotstation.com)* in east Santa Monica is renowned for its galleries and exhibitions.

VENICE

ⓘ LA, Inc., the
Convention and
Visitors Bureau
685 S. Figueroa St (between
Wilshire Blvd and 7th St),
Los Angeles, CA 90017;
tel: (800) 228-2452 or
(213) 689-8822;
www.discoverlosangeles.com

Venice was laid out as a romantic replica of the Italian city. It became run-down, but bounced back as a trendy beach town. The beach scene revolves around **Venice Boardwalk**, a winding path packed with an ever-changing crowd of exhibitionists, jugglers, fire-eaters, musicians and magicians. **Muscle Beach** *(south of Windward Ave at 19th Ave)* is a legendary outdoor body-building studio. **Albert Kinney Boulevard**, a few blocks east, is a trendy but down-to-earth shopping and dining strip.

Suggested tour

Total distance: 250 miles.

Time: One long day, or 3–4 days with stops in Carlsbad/Oceanside, Laguna Beach and Santa Monica Bay.

Links: San Diego to the south, LA to the north, and Route to the Stars.

Route: From **LA JOLLA ❶**, follow La Jolla Blvd north to Hwy S21 north of the **Salk Institute ❷** and through **Torrey Pines State Reserve ❸** to **CARLSBAD ❹**, **OCEANSIDE ❺** and I-5. Continue north through **Camp Pendleton ❻** to **San Clemente ❼**.

Take the Hwy 1/El Camino Real/Pacific Coast Highway exit from I-5. Drive north through **Orange County ❽** to **LAGUNA BEACH ❾**, **NEWPORT BEACH ❿** and **HUNTINGTON BEACH ⓫**. Follow Hwy 1 through to **LONG BEACH ⓬** and **Santa Monica Bay ⓭**. Hwy 1 turns inland through **Los Angeles International Airport (LAX) ⓮** to skirt **MARINA DEL REY ⓯** and **VENICE ⓰**, then continues north to **SANTA MONICA ⓱**.

Below
Toning up at the Muscle Beach
Gym in Venice

Ratings

Museums	●●●●●
Architecture	●●●●
History	●●●●
Art	●●●
Children	●●●
Food and drink	●●●
Shopping	●●●
Beaches	●●

San Diego

San Diego is as tropical as California gets. Bright sun and ocean breezes combine with the influence of Mexico, 20 miles south, to concoct a casual, easy-going atmosphere in California's second-largest city. Visually, San Diego is uncongested; homes and businesses do not pile above or against one another.

East over the mountains is desert; north along the coast are round, eroded cliffs and golden sand beaches. Coronado Island offers resort dining and shopping a few minutes from Downtown San Diego. Mission Bay has beaches, SeaWorld San Diego and marinas filled with pleasure boats. Downtown bustles with business, gracefully proportioned high-rises lining the waterfront. Ten inches of annual rainfall encourage alfresco dining most of the year.

While San Diego thrives on tourism and manufacturing, a military presence still defines the city. California's first city was founded in 1769 by soldiers seeking to settle this little-explored area to thwart economic incursions by Russian fur traders – while Spanish Franciscan friars simultaneously Christianised the local native peoples. Mexico ruled from 1821 until 1847, when the United States took over.

Getting there and getting around

San Diego Convention & Visitors Bureau
2215 India St,
San Diego, CA 92101;
tel: (619) 236-1212;
www.sandiego.org

International Visitor Information Centers
Downtown: 1040 1/3 West Broadway at Harbor Dr. across from the Cruise Ship Terminal. Open daily Jun–Sep 0900–1700; Oct–May 0900–1600. La Jolla: 7966 Herschel Ave at Prospect. Call for hours.

San Diego is 120 miles south of Los Angeles; allow three hours to drive from downtown to downtown, more during rush hour. For information on traffic hotspots tune into a local radio station.

San Diego International Airport, Lindbergh Field (SAN) (*tel: (619) 400-2400; www.san.org*), is 3 miles north of downtown. Taxi to downtown $10. San Diego 511 (*for bus, trolley, Coaster tel: 511; www.511sd.com*) bus No 992 'The Flyer,' runs every 10 minutes, $2.25. Hotels' and other shuttles also operate from between Terminals 1 and 2. Pick up car-hire shuttle vans from via a skybridge to ground transportation islands outside arriving baggage areas.

Parking
Downtown meters are inexpensive. Horton Plaza offers three hours' free parking with any mall purchase, an alternative to valet parking at trendy 5th Ave restaurants. Seaport Village has two-hour validation.

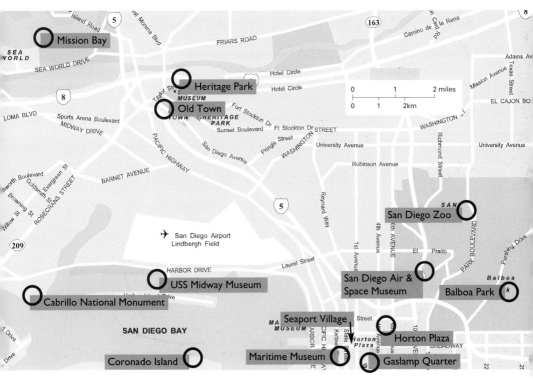

Driving

Freeways can clog abysmally at rush hour. I-5 parallels the coast from Capistrano Beach south to San Diego. Hwy S21 is the much slower scenic route on the coast from Carlsbad to Mission Bay/Mission Beach. I-8 goes east from Old Town, past Mission Valley lodging, to East San Diego County. Around downtown, many streets are one-way; follow directional signs to attractions.

San Diego's transportation is a good alternative to city driving. The **San Diego 511** (*tel: 511; www.511sd.com*) co-ordinates the **North County Coaster** train (*tel: (800) 262-7837; www.gonctd.com. Operates Mon–Sat*), buses and the **San Diego Trolley**.

Naval San Diego

By 1917, US expansionism dictated a Southern California base for naval operations. San Diego remains an important operations centre for the Pacific Fleet. North Island (Coronado) houses the US Naval Air Station. Aerospace companies thrived from the 1920s until aerospace and naval downsizing shocked the region in the 1970s.

The response? San Diego restored its historic downtown, built a convention centre, accommodated cruise ships, revamped the waterfront, and capitalised on the presence of the hi-tech industry stimulated by the La Jolla-based Scripps Institution of Oceanography, Salk Institute for Biological Studies and a large University of California, San Diego campus.

Sights

ℹ️ **Balboa Park**
Visitors Center in the
House of Hospitality,
1549 El Prado, Suite 1;
tel: (619) 239-0512;
www.balboapark.org.
Open daily 0930–1630,
longer in summer.

🏛 **Botanical Building**
Look for the Lily Pond.
Open Fri–Wed 1000–1600.
Free.

Marston House $
3525 7th Ave, northwest
corner of Balboa Park; tel:
(619) 298-3142;
www.sandiegohistory.org/
marston_house.html. Open
Fri–Sun. Call for hours.

**Mingei International
Museum $** 1439 El Prado;
tel: (619) 239-0003;
www.mingei.org. Open
Tue–Sun 1000–1600.

Museum of Man $
1350 El Prado;
tel: (619) 239-2001;
www.museumofman.org.
Open 1000–1630.

**Reuben H Fleet
Science Center $$**
1875 El Prado; tel: (619)
238-1233; www.rhfleet.org.
Open daily, call for hours.

**San Diego Automotive
Museum $$**
2080 Pan American Plaza;
tel: (619) 231-2886;
www.sdautomuseum.org.
Open 1000–1700.

**San Diego Model
Railroad Museum $$**
1649 El Prado, Lower Level;
tel: (619) 696-0199;
www.sdmodelrailroadm.com.
Open Tue–Fri 1100–1600,
Sat–Sun to 1700.

Balboa Park

Balboa Park, the 1200 acres of greenery north of Downtown San Diego, is *the* city park. The collection of plants, trees, California-Spanish baroque architecture, a collection of museums called the Smithsonian of the West, and the world-renowned **San Diego Zoo** (*see page 85*) have rendered its original 1868 chaparral and cacti desertscape unrecognisable outside the sculptured **Desert Garden** (*Park Blvd, east side*). Many of the Spanish baroque buildings were installed for the 1915 Panama-California Exposition.

A free **Balboa Park Tram** from the Inspiration Point car park makes a circuit of 11 stops. The 7-day, 13-museum **Passport to Balboa Park or Zoo/Passport Combo** provides bargain admission; many museums are free on one Tue each month. The park is full of interesting museums, botanical displays, artists' studios and performing arts venues.

Alcazar Garden, behind the Mingei International Museum, is a formal garden enclosed by arcades with a postcard view of California Tower's tile dome.

The plain name of the **Botanical Building** disguises the beautiful orchids and heliconia which bloom amid exotic palms.

The elegant façade of **Casa del Prado Theater** (*tel: (619) 239-1311; www.juniortheatre.com*) would not be out of place in Spain. Enjoy youth productions of ballet, theatre and dance.

Marston House is a Craftsman-style (*see page 50*) mansion with lovely landscaped English-style gardens.

Mingei International Museum (*House of Charm building*) displays worldwide folk arts.

The **Museum of Man** is an eclectic, fun collection of ethnic artefacts from all over – don't miss the mummies, tortilla-making and Mexican Oaxacan weaving.

The **Museum of Photographic Arts $$** (MoPA) (*1649 El Prado, Casa de Balboa; tel: (619) 238-7559; www.mopa.org; open Tue–Sun 1000–1700, Thu to 2100 in summer*) offers changing exhibitions. It is renowned for the largest photography-oriented bookstore in the US.

The **Old Globe Theatre** (*tel: (619) 234-5623; www.oldglobe.org*), a reproduction of the London original, presents Shakespeare plays and more contemporary works on several stages.

Reuben H Fleet Science Center offers hands-on exhibits and an IMAX® Dome Theater.

San Diego Air & Space Museum (*see page 85*).

San Diego Automotive Museum rotates exhibits of Southern California's *raison d'être* from a fine collection of historic vehicles.

San Diego Model Railroad Museum is heaven for train buffs, where scale-model and mini-gauge trains circle, enhanced by realistic sound effects.

San Diego Museum of Art (SDMA) combines contemporary California art with Chinese, Japanese and 15th- to 18th-century European works, supplemented by the outdoor Waters Café @ SDMA in the Sculpture Garden Café.

Spanish Village Art Center, with its wide, colourful courtyard, offers 37 studios where artists work, display and sell sculpture, jewellery, paintings and other arts.

Spreckels Organ Pavilion has 4445 organ pipes which thrill music lovers with free outdoor Sun afternoon concerts (and Mon eve, mid-Jun–Aug).

The European art collections at the **Timken Museum of Art** include magnificent Russian icons.

San Diego Museum of Art $$
1450 El Prado, Plaza de Panama; tel: (619) 232-7931; www.sdmart. org. Open Tue–Sun 1000–1800, Thu to 2100 in summer.

Spanish Village Art Center
Tel: (619) 233-9050; www.spanishvillageart.com. Open 1100–1600.

Spreckels Organ Pavilion Tel: (619) 702-8138; www.sosorgan.com. Organ concerts 1400 Sun, 1930 Mon mid-Jun–Aug.

Timken Museum of Art
1500 El Prado, Plaza de Panama; Tel: (619) 239-5548; www.timkenmuseum.org. Open Tue–Sat 1000–1630, Sun 1330–1630.

Right
Sculptors' studios in Balboa Park's Spanish Village Art Center

Cabrillo National Monument $
Hwy 209 to 1800 Cabrillo Memorial Dr.;
tel: (619) 557-5450;
www.nps.gov/cabr. Open daily 0900–1700.

Monument, visitor centre and Old Point Loma Lighthouse
Open daily 0900–1700.

Cabrillo National Monument

In 1542, three Spanish ships under Portuguese commander Juan Rodriguez Cabrillo found a 'closed and very good port' and Kumeyaay Indians. The explorers landed, claimed 'San Miguel' for the Catholic Majesties, then sailed north to the Channel Islands. The **Cabrillo National Monument**, atop cliffs at the end of Point Loma peninsula sheltering San Diego Bay, is a majestic, oversized white statue of the explorer flanked by cross, crown and the Spanish coat of arms. Cabrillo's head faces east, above the sweep of the bay channel, Coronado Island and Downtown San Diego to the mountains flanking the border with Mexico. Below the statue, an observation area offers stunning vistas of sailboat regattas and the to and fro of US Naval traffic, comprising vessels of the Pacific Fleet.

Old Point Loma Lighthouse, a 5-minute walk from the monument, sits 422ft above the Pacific. Operational from 1855 to 1891, the light tower sits in the middle of the house, furnished as it was for the last keeper's posting. A 2-mile return **Bayside Trail** passes through a mix of prickly pear and succulents with black sage and chaparral as it descends 300ft. A well-marked path close to the monument entrance gives on to accessible **tide-pools**, and the **Whale Overlook** is a prime spot for **California gray whale** spotting from mid-December to March. Below Point Loma, the eroded **Sunset Cliffs** are a popular rendezvous for photographers and lovers at sundown.

Coronado Island

Coronado Visitor Center *1100 Orange Ave (lobby, Museum of History and Art); tel: (619) 437-8788; www. coronadovisitorcenter.com. Open Mon–Fri 0900–1700, Sat–Sun 1000–1700.*

In the 1880s, the arrival of railways in San Diego cried out for a resort – and the **Hotel del Coronado** (*1500 Orange Ave; tel: (619) 435-6611 or (800) 468-3533; www.hoteldel.com*), just a short ferry ride across the beautiful San Diego Bay, met the need. The white Victorian building with its bright red roof and towers still stands as a luxury landmark.

The **San Diego-Coronado Bay Bridge** arcs gracefully over the bay, a lovely drive except at rush hour. The **San Diego-Coronado Ferry** (*tel: (800) 442-7847; www.sdhe.com/san-diego-bay-ferry.html*) transports passengers and bicycles between Broadway Pier and Ferry Landing Marketplace. There is a pricey but fast **water taxi** (*tel: (800) 442-7847 or (619) 235-8294; www.sdhe.com/san-diego-water-taxi.html*) service between Coronado, downtown Shelter Island and Harbor Island, and, during baseball season, the water taxi to PETCO Park. Romantics can step aboard a **Venetian gondola** (*$$*) (*tel: (619) 429-6317; www.gondolacompany.com*) at Loews Coronado Bay Resort.

Ocean Blvd northwest of the Hotel del Coronado is a superb spot for sunsets. North-side shops and restaurants centre around **Coronado Ferry Landing** (*1201 1st St and B Ave; tel: (619) 234-4111; and Ferry Landing Marketplace; tel: (619) 435-8895; www.beachcalifornia.com/ coronado-ferry-landing.html*) which, with its four parks 1½ miles west, has fine views of the afternoon sun glowing on downtown high-rises, while **Orange Ave**, near the **Hotel del Coronado**, is a trendy area to shop,

ⓘ Gaslamp Quarter Association *614 5th Ave, Suite E; tel: (619) 233-5227; www.gaslamp.org.*
Gaslamp Quarter Historical Foundation *William Heath Davis House, 410 Island Ave; tel: (619) 233-4692; www.gaslampquarter.org, offer district tours Sat at 1100 $$.*

ⓘ Heritage Park *2454 Heritage Park Row, Old Town San Diego; tel: (619) 291-9784; www.co.san-diego.ca.us/parks/heritage_park.html*

⌂ Horton Plaza *Broadway-G St, 1st–4th Aves; tel: (619) 239-8180; www.westfield.com/hortonplaza. Shops open 1000, Sun at 1100.*

dine, browse art galleries and people-watch. The **Coronado Museum of History and Art** (*1100 Orange Ave; tel: (619) 435-7242 or (619) 437-8788; www.coronadohistory.org*) has four galleries, offers Hotel del Coronado, tree, and architectural walking tours, and the Coronado Visitor Center.

Gaslamp Quarter

Opulent late-Victorian architecture and streetlamps grace downtown San Diego's 16-block Gaslamp Quarter (*Broadway and Harbor Dr., 4th and 6th Aves*), the trendy shopping, dining and entertainment area. Alone among California's major cities, this civic and business centre has remained visually intact since its beginnings as 'New Town' in 1887, when San Francisco merchant Alonzo E. Horton bought up the waterfront and moved the action from Old Town. The 1850s **William Heath Davis House Museum $** (*410 Island Ave; tel: (619) 233-4692; open Tue–Sat 1000–1800, Sun 0900–1500*) was an early merchant-developer's residence.

Through the next century, the boom town catered to lawman Wyatt Earp's three gambling halls, bordello patrons, sailors and homeless men, evolving into an infamous 'skid row' as the population and businesses shifted north and east. Some homeless missions remain, but the Gaslamp Quarter's 1970s restoration is cemented by great music clubs, fine dining and a cheerful ambience of rediscovery. **Horton Plaza** (*see below*), a multi-level shopping mall with excellent fast food, theatres and a cinema, anchors the district on the north side.

Heritage Park

On the edge of Old Town San Diego, **Heritage Park** (*access Heritage Park Row from Juan and Harney Sts;*) preserves six Victorian mansions and a Jewish synagogue arranged along a pedestrian walk. All of the buildings are still in use: look for wedding parties on weekends. The turret marks the **Heritage Park Inn** in the 1889 Queen Anne **Christian House**, and there are Victorian-style souvenirs in the 1893 Classic Revival **Burton House**. The 1893 **Temple Beth Israel**'s clean Classic Revival lines appealed to Christian congregations, who used the building before they had permanent sites for their churches.

Horton Plaza

Geometric wedges, odd angles, tilework, the eagle-topped Jessops 'San Diego Time' Clock and 41 cheerful colours make this chic downtown shopping mall a destination for San Diegans. **Horton Plaza**, at the north edge of the Gaslamp Quarter, has nearly 200 shops, including a San Diego City Store and Nordstrom and Macy's department stores. The **Lyceum Theatre at Horton Plaza** (*tel: (619) 231-3586*) has comic and classic performances by the San Diego Repertory Theatre (*tel: (619) 544-1000; www.sandiegorep.com*). The restored 1924 **Balboa Theatre** (*868 Fourth Ave; tel: (619) 570-1100; www.sandiegotheatres.org*) is a performing arts centre.

ⓜ Mission San Diego de Alcalá $
10818 San Diego Mission Rd; tel: (619) 281-8449; www.missionsandiego.com. Museum open daily 0900–1645.

New Children's Museum $$ *200 W. Island Ave; tel: (619) 233-8792; www.thinkplaycreate.org. Open Thu–Tue 0900–1600.*

Old Town San Diego State Historic Park *2645 San Diego Ave; tel: (619) 220-5422; www.parks.ca.gov/default.asp ?page_id=663. Open daily 1000–1700. Free. For a self-guided walking tour, purchase an Old Town San Diego State Historic Park Tour Guide & Brief History, $2 at Seeley Stables, or take a ranger-led tour.*

Old Town San Diego Chamber of Commerce *2383 San Diego Ave; tel: (619) 291-4903; www.oldtownsandiego.org*

Mormon Battalion Memorial *2510 Juan St; tel: (619) 298-3317. Open 0900–2100. Free.*

Junipero Serra Museum and Tower Gallery $ *2727 Presidio Dr., Presidio Park; tel: (619) 297-3258; www.sandiegohistory.org/ serra_museum.html. Open daily, call for hours.*

San Diego Air & Space Museum $$ *2001 Pan American Plaza, Balboa Park; tel: (619) 234-8291; www.aerospacemuseum.org. Open 1000–1630, to 1730 Memorial Day–Labor Day.*

Mission Bay

Mission Bay sprang from the imagination when mud dredged from San Diego Harbor created a huge waterside parkland, with beaches on the bay and Pacific Ocean. The best-known attraction is **SeaWorld Adventure Park San Diego** (*see page 60*). The sheltered bay offers hotels, restaurants, children's playgrounds, jet skiing, fishing, sailing, boardsailing, jogging, tennis and golf – even camping.

Mission San Diego de Alcalá, California's first mission (*see page 260*), seems strangely isolated 7 miles from the coast or downtown, but its white façade and lush front gardens are exactly the austere and imposing image the Spanish Church and Empire wished to project. A small museum displays vestments and manuscripts written by California Missions' founder Fra Junípero Serra.

The **New Children's Museum** skews towards the arts with hands-on creations by young museum visitors and a guest artist in a separate teens' studio space. The museum building is across from a park with playgrounds, not far from the convention center.

Old Town San Diego

Old Town San Diego State Historic Park, northwest of downtown, anchors a larger area of motels, restaurants and shops which serve the tourist trade visiting the city's 19th-century settlement. Three original family adobes, **La Casa de Estudillo, Machado y Stewart** and **Machado y Silvas**, are excellently restored house museums. On weekends, volunteers dressed in mid-19th-century military uniforms are inspected in front of the **Robinson-Rose House Visitor Centre**, then drill on the green and parade around the park. A blacksmith demonstrates his skills near **Seeley Stables Museum**; carriages and stagecoaches are on display inside, supplemented by a film on transport in California. The **First San Diego Courthouse**, the first **San Diego Union** (newspaper) building, a school and a dental museum offer insights into daily life, while the **Wells Fargo Museum** in the reconstructed **Colorado House** explains the economics of stagecoaches and the Gold Rush in California. See *www.sandiegohistory.org/links/oldtown.htm*

San Diegans visit Old Town to enjoy margaritas and warm tortillas at good restaurants, including **Casa Guadalajara** (*tel: (619) 295-5111*) along the courtyard of **Bazaar del Mundo**'s (*tel: (619) 296-3161; www.bazaardelmundo.com*) hibiscus-entwined shopping arcade, complete with dancers and mariachi bands.

The **Old Town Trolley Tour** begins on Twiggs St. The **Mormon Battalion Memorial**, celebrating the 1847 arrival of Latter Day Saints troops to support American troops in the fight against Mexico, is between Old Town and Heritage Park. North of Old Town, **Presidio Park** was the site of the original 1769 fort and mission. The artefacts and scale models in the **Junípero Serra Museum and Tower Gallery** explain San Diego's pre-American history.

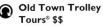 **USS Midway Museum** $$$ *910 N. Harbor Dr., alongside Navy Pier 11A; tel: (619) 544-9600; www.midway.org. Open daily 1000–1700.*

Maritime Museum of San Diego $$ *1492 N. Harbor Dr.; tel: (619) 234-9153; www.sdmaritime.com. Open 0900-2000, to 2100 in summer.*

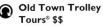 **Old Town Trolley Tours®** $$ *tel: (800) 213-2474; www.trustedtours.com. Operate daily 2-hour, 10-stop tours 0900–1600, to 1700 in summer.*

San Diego Zoo $$$ *2920 Zoo Dr., Balboa Park; tel: (619) 234-3153; www.sandiegozoo.org. Open 0900–1600.*

Below
Victorian houses in San Diego's Heritage Park

San Diego Air & Space Museum

Aviation fans flock to the **San Diego Air & Space Museum**. The combined influence of naval aviation and the aerospace industry in San Diego makes the aircraft on display in the doughnut-shaped Ford Building one of the best history lessons of airborne flight.

USS Midway Museum

San Diego's waterfront has a naval aviation museum on the aircraft carrier that was the Persian Gulf flagship in the 1991 Desert Storm campaign. The *Midway*, as this museum is known, served for 47 years and was the first carrier based in a foreign country, Japan, where it served for 18 years. Restored aircraft are displayed.

Maritime Museum of San Diego

San Diego's embarcadero **Maritime Museum** is dominated by the majesty of the square rigging of the *Star of India*. One of several ships open for touring, this, the oldest merchant vessel still afloat, has been restored to the condition of her launch from the Isle of Man in 1863. The replica *Californian* is the state's official tall ship, enjoyed on 3-hour sails. The 1898 *Berkeley* ferry boat is the sister ship of the *Eureka*, displayed along the Hyde Park Pier of the National Maritime Museum in San Francisco. Both ferries plied San Francisco Bay. The 1904 steamer *Medea*, a Scots-built luxury yacht, is tied up alongside. The HMS *Surprise* is a replica 18th-century Royal Navy frigate, in dramatic contrast to the B-39 Foxtrot class Soviet attack submarine.

San Diego Zoo

The **San Diego Zoo** was among the first to pioneer habitats for 4000 animals and hundreds of birds, freeing them from traditional caged confinement. On several levels of jungle-type vegetation, the zoo wanders through Cat and Bear Canyons and Horn and Hoof Mesa. Guided (double-decker) bus tours see most of the zoo; **Express Bus Tours** has five drop-off points. **Skyfari Aerial Tram** provides a gondola overview with a quick hop to the other side of the park. Queue up early for the **Panda Research Station** for a glimpse of pandas on loan from China. The **Polar Bear Plunge** is happily incongruous in the balmy climate, but **Gorilla Tropics** and the South African klipspringer habitat feel like authentic exotic locales. Rare and endangered species prowl and swing through the Asian and African tropical forests of the **Monkey Trails** habitat at the zoo centre.

Below
The tall-masted *Star of India*
lies at anchor at the Maritime
Museum of San Diego

Seaport Village

Seaport Village has nautical theme shopping and dining near the San Diego Convention Center. A bayside boardwalk at the south end of the embarcadero offers year-round outdoor music, fashion shows and mimes. Take a spin on the new carousel that replaced the 1890 Looff **Broadway Flying Horses Carousel**, or try the **Village Café** (*tel: (619) 544-9444*) for a wide assortment for breakfast and other fare for a cheerful wake-up. **Wyland Galleries** (*tel: (619) 544-9995*) have the famous artist's whale paintings and marine art. If you're looking for a gift for those back home, the **San Diego City Store** (*tel: (619) 234-2489*) has local-name souvenirs and T-shirts.

Entertainment

Local newspapers including the *San Diego Union–Tribune* (*www.signonsandiego.com*) and the free *San Diego Reader* (*www.sdreader.com*) list clubs, nightlife and restaurants. Hopping jazz, blues and rock clubs are attached to Gaslamp Quarter restaurants along 5th Ave, south of Horton Plaza. The **San Diego Performing Arts League** (*tel: (619) 238-0700; www.sandiegoperforms.com*) has bi-monthly listings in its free *What's Playing in San Diego Guide*.

One of the most venerable companies in the country, the **Old Globe Theatre** (*see page 80*) in Balboa Park fills three theatres with productions every year. **ARTS TIX** (*northeast corner of Horton Plaza; www.sandiegoperforms.com/ARTSTIX*) offers on-the-spot, half-price tickets for theatre, dance or concert performances on the day. The proximity of UC San Diego draws big-name music groups to the area.

San Diegans love sports: the **Padres** (*http://sandiego.padres.mlb.com*) play baseball Apr–Oct at PETCO Park and the **Chargers** (*www.chargers.com*) play NFL football Oct–Dec/Jan at QUALCOMM Stadium. Weather encourages outdoor sports with numerous golf courses and tennis courts.

Shopping

Perhaps because of the pleasant climate, it's easy to shop in the San Diego area. **Horton Plaza** (*see page 83*) has restaurants, shops, stores and theatres, and validated parking makes a Gaslamp Quarter exploration a bargain. Shops in the whimsical-coloured shopping hub include the **Sports Fantasy** for genuine US sports team clothing and accessories.

Fashion Valley Mall (*7007 Friars Rd; tel: (619) 688-9113; www.simon.com/mall/default.aspx?ID=765*) in Mission Valley is filled with more than 200 clothing, cosmetic and home furnishing shops, a food court and a multi-screen cinema. Shop for nautical souvenirs at **Seaport Village**, Mexican at Old Town's **Bazaar del Mundo**, or search for unexpected bargains at **Kobey's Swap Meet** (*3350 Sports Arena Blvd; tel: (619) 226-0650; www.kobeyswap.com; Fri–Sun 0700–1500*).

Accommodation and food

San Diego's interest in attracting convention-goers keeps hotel/motel rooms available at reasonable cost almost all the time. Coronado, Mission Bay, coast and downtown hotels are pricey, although prices drop 15–40 per cent from November to March; look for easy freeway access from I-8 in Mission Valley's Hotel Circle, a 15-minute drive to downtown.

The *San Diego CVB Official Visitors Planning Guide* and website (*www.sandiego.org*) lists accommodation by area and makes bookings online or *tel: (800) 350-6205*. **San Diego Visitor Information Center** *2668 E. Mission Bay Dr., San Diego, CA 92109; tel: (800) 827-9188; www.infosandiego.com* can also book accommodation area-wide.

Horton Grand Hotel $$ *311 Island Ave; tel: (800) 542-1886 or (619) 544-1886; www.hortongrand.com*, combines two restored Victorian-era buildings, furnished with period antiques in the heart of the Gaslamp District.

Britt Scripps Inn $$$ *406 Maple St; tel: (888) 881-1991; www.brittscripps.com,* is a 9-room luxury Queen Anne Victorian adjacent to Balboa Park.

Harbor Vacation Club $$$ *1800 Harbor Island Dr., G Dock; tel: (877) 477-7368; www.resortime.com/resorts/profile.asp?resortid=30,* offers overnight accommodation in a yacht or power cruiser with a veranda or deck for sunset watching or sunning.

Heritage Park Inn $$$ *2470 Heritage Park Row; tel: (619) 299-6832 or (800) 995-2470; www.heritageparkinn.com,* is Victorian cosseting two blocks from **Old Town State Historic Park** (*see page 84*).

Hotel del Coronado $$$ *1500 Orange Ave, Coronado; tel: (800) 468-3533; www.hoteldel.com,* is the *grande dame*, picture-postcard resort hotel, complete with ghosts.

Omni San Diego Hotel $$$ *675 L Street; tel: (619) 231-6664; www.omnihotels.com,* near the convention centre, is connected to PETCO Park by a skybridge.

US Grant $$$ *326 Broadway; tel: (800) 237-5029, (866) 837-4270, or (619) 232-3121; www.usgrant.net,* is a luxury landmark hotel named after US civil war hero and later president, Ulysses S Grant.

San Diego's proximity to Mexico makes it easy to find a variety of Mexican food, from bland to chilli-pepper spicy, especially in **Old Town**. San Diego is also getting a reputation for 'fusion cuisines', mixing California's fresh produce with delicate recipes, sauces and presentation from Asia. The **Gaslamp Quarter** has a good choice of restaurants, from moderate to pricey, many with live music in the evening.

Café Coyote $–$$ *2461 San Diego Ave; tel: (619) 291-4695; www.cafecoyoteoldtown.com,* has margaritas, mariachis and fresh-made tortillas in Old Town.

Anthony's Fish Grotto on the Bay $$ *1360 N. Harbor Dr.; tel: (619) 232-5103; www.gofishanthonys.com,* has been serving seafood for more than six decades.

Aubergine Grille $$ *500 4th Ave; tel: (619) 232-8100; www.aubergineon4th.com,* has a fusion of flavours, live music and DJ spins and a dress-to-be-seen single's club.

Chopahn $$ *750 6th Ave; tel: (619) 236-9236; www.chopahnrestaurant. com,* has Afghani specialities with lamb *sabsi challaw* and heavenly *kadu*, sautéed pumpkin with yogurt and meat sauce.

Croce's $$ *5th Ave and F St; tel: (619) 233-4355; www.croces.com,* has all-American cuisine with live jazz at **Croce's Jazz Bar**.

The Prado $$ *1549 El Prado; tel: (619) 557-9441; www.cohnrestaurants.com,* has a Latin and Italian fusion menu in Balboa Park's House of Hospitality.

Sogno DiVino $$ *1607 India Street; tel: (619) 531-8887; www.sogno-divino.com*, is a wine bar with delicious appetisers (starters).

Dakota Grill & Spirits $$$ *901 5th Ave; tel: (619) 234-5554; www.cohnrestaurants.com*, is a low-key Gaslamp Quarter steakhouse.

Dussini Mediterranean Bistro $$$ *275 5th Ave; tel: (619) 233-4323; www.dussini.com*, has superb mussels – go for the small plates to make a meal.

Island Prime $$$ *880 Harbor Island Dr.; tel: (619) 298-6802; www.cohnrestaurants.com*, is a steakhouse with superb bay and skyline views.

Stingaree $$$ *454 6th Ave; tel: (619) 544-9500; www.stingsandiego.com*, is a three-level nightclub scene with a waterfall near the Gaslamp Quarter.

Suggested tours

Below
San Diego's old Point-Loma Lighthouse

San Diego's **59-Mile Scenic Drive** (*www.sandiego.org/article/visitors/338*) signs have a flying white seagull on a blue and yellow field. The half-day circuit begins at the foot of Broadway near the Santa Fe Depot (Amtrak/Coaster), and includes La Jolla and Coronado. The orange and green motorised trams of **Old Town Trolley Tours** (*tel: (800) 213-2474*) can be boarded from Old Town or any of nine other stops for a 2-hour narrated circuit, or reboarded after spending some time in each area.

Have a passport and (for non-US citizens or resident aliens) a multiple-entry visa or visa waiver to hand on the **San Diego Trolley** if you want to make a day trip to the border and walk to **Tijuana** in Mexico.

San Diego Harbor Excursions (*tel: (800) 442-7847; www.sdhe.com*) and **Hornblower Cruises** (*tel: (888) 467-6256; www.hornblower.com*) offer 1- and 2-hour San Diego Bay cruises departing from downtown's Broadway Pier. One-hour Venetian gondola cruises of San Diego Bay depart from Coronado Island with The Gondola Company (*tel: (619) 429-6317*).

Barnstorming Adventures $$$ (*Montgomery Field, 3750 John J. Montgomery Dr.; tel: (800) 759-5667; www.barnstorming.com*) offer 'flightseeing' from open cockpit biplanes and other air combat and warplane flights.

Anza-Borrego Desert State Park

Ratings

Geology	●●●●●
Nature	●●●●●
Outdoor activities	●●●●●
Scenery	●●●●○
Historical sights	●●●○○
History	●●●○○
Children	●○○○○

A short journey east of San Diego or south of Palm Springs is true desert, a desert park surrounding a few golf courses, resort hotels and basic services. Anza-Borrego Desert State Park is rugged, more rocky and mountainous than stereotypical sandy dunes, a place for solitude away from the cities of Southern California. The town of Julian, nestled in forests and apple orchards, is a world in between, a popular and historic getaway for San Diegans. Stop there for an alpine respite before venturing on to Anza-Borrego and an overnight stay in Borrego Springs.

ANZA-BORREGO DESERT STATE PARK

ⓘ **Visitor Center**
1½ miles west of Christmas Circle, Borrego Springs. Open daily 0900–1700 Oct–May; weekends and holidays Jun–Sep, call for hours.
Wildflower Hotline for Jan–Mar season; tel: (760) 767-4684. Ask at visitor centre for details of trails.

🅟 **Anza-Borrego Desert State Park** $ *200 Palm Canyon Dr., Borrego Springs, CA 92004; tel: (760) 767-5311; www.parks.ca.gov*

Two-thirds of the 600,000 acres of this largest state park in the contiguous US is wilderness. Thanks to its proximity to the Colorado River, Anza-Borrego Desert State Park (ABDSP) is technically a Colorado Desert section of the Sonoran Desert, with arid, eye-stretching badlands, palm canyons, desert bighorn sheep camouflaged by raw mountain scarps, temperature- and saline-adaptable pupfish, seas of spring wildflowers and fossils of mammoth elephants and sabre-toothed cats.

In a few places, such as the 3-mile return **Borrego Palm Canyon Trail**, native California fan palm trees, North America's largest palms, offer shade against blistering temperatures from June to September, even as the *borrego* (desert bighorn sheep) move down to water at palm-lined waterholes. Elsewhere, the panoramas and vistas are worth a well-provisioned hike into a sere desert – follow established trails, or risk being caught in a rare but potentially fatal flash-flood downpour. Brilliant expanses of **wildflowers**, between late-January and March, are legendary.

Accommodation in Anza-Borrego Desert State Park

Reserve camp pitches for **Borrego Palm Canyon** and **Tamarisk Grove** (*tel: (800) 444-7275; www.reserveamerica.com*). **Bow Willow Camp** has 16 pitches; **Borrego Springs** has standard accommodation.

BORREGO SPRINGS

ⓘ Borrego Springs Chamber of Commerce *786 Palm Canyon Dr., Borrego Springs, CA 92004; tel: (800) 559-5524 or (760) 767-5555; www.borregosprings.org*

Anza-Borrego Desert Natural History Association Borrego Desert Nature Center *652 Palm Canyon Dr.; tel: (760) 767-3098, www.california-desert.org*

Surrounded by Anza-Borrego Desert State Park, and a service point for park visitors, Borrego Springs holds its own as a desert resort centre and citrus fruit producer for worldwide export. Red grapefruit is the best-known local product, though oranges, lemons and limes also grow in north-side groves, now impinged by real-estate development.

Accommodation and food in Borrego Springs

Cooler weather between October and May draws a million tourists a year – book in advance. Accommodation includes ABDSP camping, RV parks, bed and breakfast, motels and five resort hotels. Prices can drop dramatically in summer.

The Palms Hotel: Krazy Coyote Restaurant $$–$$$ 2220 Hoberg Rd; tel: (760) 767-7788; www.thepalmsatindian head.com. On site where 1950s film stars went for a ranch getaway, with a zen garden.

Palm Canyon Resort $$–$$$ *221 Palm Canyon Dr.; tel: (760) 767-5341 or (800) 242-0044; www.pcresort.com,* has a Western theme and is close to the park. There is also an RV park.

La Casa del Zorro Desert Resort Hotel $$$ *3845 Yaqui Pass Rd; tel: (760) 767-5323 or (800) 824-1884; www.lacasadelzorro.com,* offers rooms, individual *casitas* and formal dining.

JULIAN

Julian Chamber of Commerce 2129 Main St; tel: (760) 765-1857; www.julianca.com. Open daily 1000–1600.

Eagle and High Peak Mine $ End of C St; tel: (760) 765-0036. Open year-round, weather permitting, for 1-hour guided mine tours and gold panning. Call for hours.

Californa Wolf Center $ Tel: (619) 234-9653 or (760) 765-0030 (reservations); www.californiawolfcenter.org. Tours Sat 1400. Reservations required.

Cuyamaca Rancho State Park $ 12551 Hwy 79, Descanso, CA 92016; tel: (760) 765-0755; www.parks.ca.gov

Julian's wooden shopfronts and horse-drawn carriage riders evoke the 1869 gold rush which created the town. **The Eagle and High Peak Mine** has guided tours. The town also attracts visitors for its alpine climate, delicious apples served in pies or quaffed as juice, several wineries, art galleries and llama trekking. The **California Wolf Center** conducts tours, including observation of an Alaskan grey wolf pack as education to encourage wolf conservation. **Cuyamaca Rancho State Park**, 17 miles south on Hwy 79, is a good introduction to the region's pine, cedar and oak forests.

Accommodation and food in Julian

The Chamber of Commerce has an accommodation list. The **Julian Bed and Breakfast Guild** *tel: (760) 765-1555; www.julianbnbguild.com,* represents about a dozen bed and breakfast lodgings. Apple pie is easy to find on menus!

Dudley's Bakery *Junction of Hwys 78 and 79, northwest of Julian; tel: (760) 765-0488; www.dudleysbakery.com; open Thu–Sun 0800–1700,* is famous for its jalapeno pepper and potato breads.

**Observer's Inn $$$** *3535 Hwy 89; tel: (760) 765-0088; www.observersinn.com,* adds guided astronomy tours ($) with a powerful telescope to traditional bed and breakfast.

Suggested tour

Total distance: 90 miles.

Time: 3 hours' driving.

Links: From the Erosion Road Auto Tour, Hwy S22, east of Borrego Springs, continue east. Turn left at Hwy 86, the Salton Sea, going 32 miles north to Hwy 111 at Indio at the eastern side of the Coachella Valley to join the Palm Springs Route (*see page 94*). To include San Diego Zoo's Wild Animal Park (*see page 59*), continue west of Julian on Hwy 79 to the Hwy 78 junction, and go southwest for 25 miles on Hwy 78 through Ramona and San Pasqual.

Palomar Observatory

Northwest of Julian and Santa Ysabel Mission, via Hwy 76, right on Hwy S7, then right on Hwy S6; tel: (760) 742-2119; www.astro.caltech.edu/ observatories/palomar. Open daily 0900–1600.

Route: North of downtown **San Diego** ❶, take I-8 east for 38 miles. Turn left (north) on Hwy 79 to **Cuyamaca Rancho State Park** ❷ and **JULIAN** ❸. For the most direct route from Julian to **ANZA-BORREGO DESERT STATE PARK** ❹/**BORREGO SPRINGS** ❺, take Hwy 78 18 miles east, veer left on to Hwy S3 (Yaqui Pass Rd) for 7 miles, then follow Borrego Springs Road to town.

An alternative route to ABDSP continues 18 miles northwest of Julian on Hwy 79 passing **Santa Ysabel Mission** ❻ *tel: (760) 765-0810*, a reconstructed chapel and museum which served as a satellite of Mission San Diego (*see page 260*). Turn east on to Hwy S2/S22 24 miles to **Borrego Springs** ❺.

Also worth exploring

Palomar Observatory ❼ has a museum and video explaining astronomical phenomena sighted using the huge 200-inch Hale Telescope. The white-domed research facility does not offer night visits, but a special platform allows visitors to view the apparatus' works.

The mountains in the **Cleveland National Forest** ❽ are rocky, stark and impressive. Close by the observatory is **Palomar Mountain State Park** ❾ (*2 miles west of the Hwys S6/S7 junction; tel: (760) 742-3462*), with high meadows rivalling the Sierra Nevada Mountains for scenic beauty.

Palm Springs

Surrounded by thousands of square miles of stark desert beauty, Palm Springs is an artificial oasis overrun with the rich, the famous and the star-struck, all joined in the common pursuit of golf, eternal youth and the perfect sun tan. It's California's desert destination for those who *don't* want to get away from it all.

Palm Springs was originally an isolated hot springs among the desert palms, known only to the Agua Caliente band of the Cahuilla Indians and a few health fanatics. In the 1930s, Hollywood discovered the joys of distant desert getaways, with real-estate developers and golf-course designers in close pursuit. Three generations later, the town created for luxury and leisure has become a string of eight resort cities strung along Hwy 111 through the Coachella Valley. The area is noted for being gay and lesbian friendly. The valley remains one of America's richest agricultural areas, though fields and orchards are now disappearing beneath a jigsaw puzzle of interlocking golf courses and malls.

Getting there and getting around

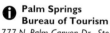 **Palm Springs Bureau of Tourism** *777 N. Palm Canyon Dr., Ste 201, Palm Springs, CA 92262; tel: (760) 778-8415 or (800) 927-7256; www.palm-springs.org* **City of Palm Springs Visitor Center** *2901 N. Palm Canyon Dr. (at Hwy 111); tel: (800) 347-7746 or (760) 778-8418. Open daily 0900–1700.*

Palm Springs is 110 miles from Los Angeles (about 2½ hours) off I-10 on Hwy 111, which becomes North Palm Canyon Dr. From San Diego, follow I-15 north to Hwy 215, then to Hwy 60 and I-10. From Anaheim/Orange County, take Hwy 55 north to Hwy 91. Go east on Hwy to I-10.

Palm Springs International Airport (PSP) *3400 E. Tahquitz Canyon Wy, Palm Springs; tel: (760) 318-3800; www.palmspringsairport.com.* A taxi to Palm Springs is about $10, to Rancho Mirage, $40. Most hotels offer a free or reduced-rate shuttle service.

Traffic can be slow on Palm Canyon Dr. near major shopping malls and in central Palm Springs. There is plenty of parking, almost always free, but watch for golf carts – drivers occasionally swerve without warning or signal as though they were still on the course. Palm Springs is busiest during the winter months, and traffic is heaviest in the evening when crowds come out to shop and drive.

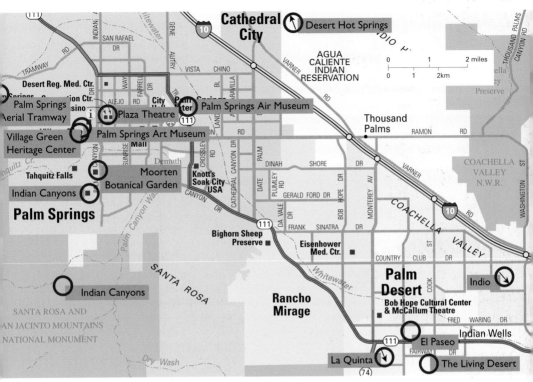

Cities and sights

**❶ Palm Springs
Desert Resort
Communities CVA**
*70–100 Hwy 111, Rancho
Mirage, CA 92270;
tel: (800) 967-3767 or
(760) 770-9000;
www.giveintothedesert.com*
Visitor Center *Open
Mon–Fri 0830–1700.*

The eight cities that make up the Palm Springs resort area tend to blur into each other, especially along Palm Canyon Dr. (Hwy 111), an endless strip of low-rise development.

Cathedral City was named after the rocky spires that are all but hidden behind new sporting complexes and other higher-rise development. The city is family-orientated during the day, but has a bustling gay scene at night, second only to Palm Springs itself.

Desert Hot Springs is noted for the underground wells that supply most of the area's spas and swimming pools. Located north of Palm Springs, it's a convenient location for day trippers to Joshua Tree National Park (*see page 107*) and other desert sights.

Indian Wells became famous as a golf venue thanks to US President Eisenhower's frequent golf holidays here in the 1950s. The town has the valley's largest concentration of grand resorts and private courses.

Indio is the low-key agricultural heart of the Coachella Valley, as well as the commercial, gambling and polo centre.

Palm Desert is mostly a place to shop, relax, play golf and watch wildlife at **The Living Desert** (*see page 97*). The best time to visit is Oct,

Fabulous Palm Springs Follies $$$
Plaza Theater, 128 S. Palm Canyon Dr.; tel: (760) 327-0225; www.psfollies.com. Performances Nov–May.

Indian Canyons $
End of S. Palm Canyon Dr.; tel: (760) 323-6018; www.indian-canyons.com. Open 0800–1700 daily Oct–Jul, rest of year Fri–Sun.

when the growing golfing population stages America's first (and possibly only) golf cart parade.

Palm Springs is where it all began with a primitive mineral hot springs in the 1890s. Most of the city's hotels remain small, a holdover from earlier days.

La Quinta is named after the area's first exclusive resort, which opened in 1927. Hollywood director Frank Capra wrote the script for his Academy Award-winning *It Happened One Night* at the resort and kept coming back with stars such as Clark Gable and Greta Garbo in tow.

Rancho Mirage, the Valley's high-profile neighbourhood, attracts presidents, kings and stars to its golf courses. Golf links share centre stage and newspaper headlines with the Betty Ford Center, California's celebrity health clinic.

Desert Tours
The only way to appreciate the desert is to see it up close and off the main roads. **Desert Adventures Jeep Tours $$$** (*tel: (760) 340-2345 or (888) 440-5337; www.red-jeep.com*) offers a variety of off-road jeep tours through local canyons, over the San Andreas Fault and into nearby mountains with experienced naturalist guides. **Elite Land Tours $$$** (*tel: (800) 514-4866 or (760) 318-1200; www.elitelandtours.com*) does it in a Hummer H2 all-terrain vehicle with an array of outings to the desert at night, Joshua Tree National Park, the Salton Sea, Indian Canyons, and safaris to see wolves or tigers.

Fabulous Palm Springs Follies
The best introduction to Palm Springs' image of itself, this feathers-and-sequins tribute to 1930s and 1940s musicals gives veteran showgirls a chance to strut their stuff – all are over the age of 50. So is the historic **Plaza Theater**, where they perform each winter.

Indian Canyons
The Agua Caliente band of Cahuilla Indians was forced to give up half of the Coachella Valley in the 1890s, but they retained picturesque canyons in the lower slopes of the San Jacinto Mountains south of Palm Springs. Four canyons contain extensive groves of California fan palms (*Washingtonia filifera*), California's only native palm, nourished by year-round streams. Pleasant hiking and equestrian trails climb the canyons from the car park at the head of Palm Canyon. Horses can be hired from Smoke Tree Stables (*tel: (800) 787-3922; www.smoketreeranch.com/ smoketreestables.html*) for individual or guided rides – Western style only.
  Tahquitz Canyon Visitor Center $$$ (*500 W. Mesquite, Palm Springs; tel: (760) 416-7044; www.tahquitzcanyon.com; open Oct–Jul daily 0730–1700, rest of year Fri–Sun*) has a canyon observation deck, cultural presentations, tribal artefacts, and ranger-led tours of rock art, a 60-ft waterfall, flora and fauna.

Palm Canyon shelters about 3,000 palms. Most grow in groves that extend 2 miles up the canyon from below the car park, with shady walking paths through the sandy flats. The trail becomes more difficult and rockier higher in the canyon. **Andreas Canyon** is smaller and equally lush, but an initial section of trail clambers over boulders that have fallen from the canyon rim above.

The trail into **Murray Canyon** passes through a mile of low, unshaded brush before dropping into a shady grove of palms in the stream bed. It's a pleasant walk in winter, but beware the sun in summer.

The Living Desert

The Living Desert is a 1200-acre botanical garden with rare plants and animals from arid climes around the world. The core of the reserve represents the main deserts of North America, including the Upper Colorado, Yuman and Baja California. Animals include bighorn sheep, Arabian oryx, gazelles, zebras, Bactrian wapiti and giraffes, many of them endangered or already extinct in the wild. **Village WaTuTu** is a 3-acre African trading village area. There are model trains on a railway track to perfect scale.

Below
Shaggy giants in Palm Springs

Moorten Botanical Garden $ *1701 S. Palm Canyon Dr.; tel: (760) 327-6555. Open Thu–Sat, Mon–Tue 0900–1630, Sun 1000–1600.*

Santa Rosa and San Jacinto Mountains National Monument Visitors Center *51–500 Highway 74, Palm Desert, CA 92260; tel: (760) 862-9984; www.blm.gov/ca/st/en/fo/palmsprings/santarosa.html. Open daily 0900–1600. Free.*

Moorten Botanical Garden

This private garden and plant store displays more than 3,000 varieties of desert plants from around the world, often in whimsical, seemingly haphazard displays. Though technically a nursery, few specimens are actually for sale.

San Jacinto Mountain

Fifty-four miles of trails at the crest of Mount San Jacinto (pronounced 'ha-seen-toe') are Palm Spring's escape from itself. In summer, altitude tempers the blazing desert temperatures while conifer forests provide welcome shade. The endangered Peninsular Ranges bighorn sheep makes its home here.

Agua Caliente

US Government survey reports originally dismissed the Coachella Valley as 'an immense waste of uninhabited country', but it was neither waste nor uninhabited to the Agua Caliente Band of Cahuilla Indians. The band hunted and harvested the valley floor in winter and retreated up the canyons to cooler country as summer temperatures climbed towards 120°F (49°C).

Early White settlers appropriated what land and water sources they pleased with little regard to traditional Agua Caliente uses. In the 1890s, railway developers took half the valley for real-estate development, forcing the band to accept a chequerboard pattern of alternative square-mile blocks. The Agua Caliente lost control of their land, but financially, at least, they got the last laugh.

Rather than evicting settlers, the band began charging rent. The group owns 6700 acres, nearly 10¼ square miles, of Palm Springs itself, plus similar sections across the Valley. The Agua Caliente have long been amongst the most prosperous Native American groups in the country. With legal changes that effectively open Native lands to unrestricted gambling and casino operations, with two casinos and downtown Palm Springs development, the Agua Caliente have been the biggest winners in Palm Spring's steady explosion of popularity.

Ⓗ **Palm Springs Aerial Tramway $$$** *One Tramway Rd; tel: (760) 325-1391 or (888) 515-8726; www.pstramway.com. Open Mon–Fri 1000–2145, Sat–Sun 0800–2145.*

Palm Springs Air Museum $$ *745 N. Gene Autry Trail; tel: (760) 778-6262; www.air-museum.org. Open daily 1000–1700.*

Palm Springs Art Museum $$ *101 Museum Dr.; tel: (760) 322-4800; www.psmuseum.org. Open Oct–May Tue–Wed, Fri–Sun 1000–1700, Thu 1200–2000; Jun–Sep Wed, Fri–Sun 1000–1700, Thu 1200–2000.*

Village Green Heritage Center $ *221 S. Palm Canyon Dr.; tel: (760) 323-8297; http://palmsprings.com/history. Open mid-Oct–May Wed and Sun 1200–1500, Thu–Sat 1000–1600.*

Opposite
Desert Adventures Jeep Tour

Palm Springs Aerial Tramway
The **Palm Springs Aerial Tramway** rotating tramcars float 2½ miles from the valley floor to San Jacinto Mountain (8516ft) in 10 minutes. The views up (or down) are breathtaking, stretching from the San Jacinto Mountains east to the highlands of **Joshua Tree National Park** (*see page 107*). Be prepared for a 40°F (22°C)-plus temperature change between top and bottom, including deep snow in winter.

Palm Springs Air Museum
World War II is the focus for the Air Museum. Ageing air buffs (and occasionally their grandchildren) slaver over 30 restored aircraft, including a Curtiss P-40 Warhawk, a P-51 Mustang and a Boeing B-17 Flying Fortress.

Palm Springs Art Museum
The museum art collection focuses on the 20th century and California artists, and there are also Native American and Mesoamerican collections.

Village Green Heritage Center
The **Village Green Heritage Center** contains Palm Springs' first two permanent buildings, a hotel and adobe home, both now used as museums by the Palm Springs Historical Society.

Wind Farms
It's impossible to miss the ranks of windmills off I-10 at the San Gorgonio Pass just before Palm Springs. Look for the spreading groves of more than 4000 wind turbines, their steel blades glinting in the desert sun. Steady breezes blow through the pass nearly every day of

Windmill Tours $$
I-10 and 62-950 Indian Ave, N. Palm Springs; tel: (760) 251-1997; www.windmilltours.com

Golf
The Coachella Valley boasts 115 golf courses, some with up to 54 holes. Most of the world's best-known course designers have at least one Palm Springs course to their credit. But regardless of the designer, nearly every Palm Springs course incorporates the almost jarring juxtaposition of rolling emerald green fairways with dusky cacti and stark rock formations leading to mountain heights. The scenery can be as hazardous as any sand trap or hidden lake.

Most courses are open for public play, but tee times can be difficult to obtain on short notice, especially the much sought-after early morning slots in winter. Major resorts can arrange tee times to match guest hotel bookings, but public courses generally only accept tee reservations between one and seven days in advance. Several local companies guarantee tee times up to six months in advance, but demand full prepayment of course fees. Decorated golf carts create a carnival atmosphere in Palm Desert each Oct; tel: (760) 346-6111; www.golfcartparade.com

the year (carrying Los Angeles smog into the desert in the process), generating enough electricity to power a small city. The way to see the turbines up close is with **Windmill Tours**, driving among the whirling generators in electric-powered carts. The visitor centre has an ever-changing collection of unusual electric vehicles.

Shopping

Shopping in Palm Springs has become entertainment, a way to see, to be seen and confirm one's place in the world of conspicuous consumption. Most shops and boutiques open by mid-morning, but serious shoppers restrain themselves until after lunch. That's when the crowds begin to trawl the pavements along **North Palm Canyon Drive** in Palm Springs.

All of the famous brand names are represented, usually at full price, as well as the requisite number of T-shirt shops, souvenir stands and Southwestern art that ranges from the exquisite to exquisitely painful. Best bet is the Thursday evening Village Fest **street fair** which features a collection of stands hawking anything from tawdry souvenirs to artful jewellery.

Serious shoppers make a pilgrimage to **Palm Desert**, just down Hwy 111, and **El Paseo**, a 2-mile strip of trendy boutiques that can match anything on offer along LA's Rodeo Drive. The slightly younger set heads for the nearby **Gardens on El Paseo**, which bills itself as Palm Springs' first development for shoppers in their 20s, 30s and 40s, touting prices more in line with Los Angeles than Beverly Hills.

Accommodation and food

Palm Springs was built for the rich and famous. Luxury resorts abound, especially in Indian Wells, La Quinta and Rancho Mirage. Rates can be exorbitant in winter, but look for summer discounts of up to 70 per cent at major resorts and 20–30 per cent at smaller hotels. The Palm Springs Desert Resort Communities CVA has information on accommodation, golf and other activities.

La Quinta Resort & Club $$$ *49499 Eisenhower Dr., La Quinta; tel: (760) 564-4111 or (800) 598-3828; www.laquintaresort.com.* La Quinta is 'Old Palm Springs', the Coachella Valley's original 1920s resort. It's still one of Palm Spring's most attractive, a collection of flower-bedecked *casitas* at the foot of the Santa Rosa Mountains, surrounded by the PGA West Stadium Golf® Course and four others.

Spa Resort Casino $$$ *100 N. Indian Canyon Dr., Palm Springs; tel: (888) 999-1995; www.sparesortcasino.com.* The spa is built around mineral hot springs long used by the Agua Caliente band for healing; the elegant buildings, hotel and casino are more recent (and more profitable) additions.

The Coachella Valley made its first fortune on farming, watered by an immense Ice Age aquifer that lies beneath the sands. Early immigrants who saw the physical and climatic resemblance to North Africa and the Middle East planted groves of date trees. A number of growers remain, most notably **Shields Date Gardens** *80225 Hwy 111, Indio; tel: (760) 347-7768; http://shieldsdategarden.com.* Built in the 1920s, Shields produce the best date milkshakes in the Valley, the perfect accompaniment to its tongue-in-cheek film, *The Romance and Sex Life of the Date.* Free entry.

Two Bunch Palms Resort and Spa $$$ *67-425 Two Bunch Palms Trail; Desert Hot Springs; tel: (760) 329-8791* or *(800) 472-4334; www.twobunchpalms.com.* Two Bunch was the area's original resort escape, a favourite with gangster Al Capone as well as Hollywood celebs of the 1930s. It's still Palm Springs' most sybaritic, private and star-ridden resort – and no sightseers allowed.

All of the major resorts have much-advertised restaurants, most offering Californian or Southwestern fusion cuisine at top prices. Other Palm Springs possibilities:

Kaiser Grille $$ *205 S. Palm Canyon Dr.; tel: (760) 568-2144* or *(760) 323-1003; www.kaisergrille.com.* A local favourite in the heart of Palm Springs serves seafood, steaks and pasta.

Las Casuelas Terraza $$ *222 S. Palm Canyon Dr.; tel: (760) 325-2794; www.lascasuelas.com,* is the original of a string of family-owned Mexican restaurants (and most popular with locals).

Sherman's Deli & Bakery $$ *401 E. Tahquitz Canyon Way; tel: (760) 325-1199; www.shermansdeli.com,* is Palm Springs' only Kosher deli and bakery.

Below
La Quinta Resort & Club

Desert Parks

Ratings

Scenery	●●●●●
Children	●●●●○
Geology	●●●●○
History	●●●●○
Outdoor activities	●●●○○
Food and drink	●●○○○
Museums	●●○○○
Architecture	●○○○○

California's desert parks include the lowest and the hottest corners of the western hemisphere. To the uninitiated, desert is dry and dangerous, at best an empty quarter to be skirted or transited as quickly as possible. On closer look, it's a delicate balance of extremes between too hot and too cold, too dry and too wet, stark, twisted and irresistibly alluring.

The harsh midday sun seems to bleach all colour and texture from desert landscapes, leaving neither shade nor relief from the ceaseless glare. But the softer light of morning and afternoon reveals a rugged grace, a palette of colours and shapes that change almost by the second. Far from the crowds, the pollution and the enveloping vegetation of the coast, the desert is California in its finest and most unabashed grandeur.

DEATH VALLEY JUNCTION

Amargosa Opera House & Hotel $$
PO Box 8, Death Valley Junction, CA 92328; tel: (760) 852-4441; www.amargosa-opera-house.com

Once a railway junction town, Death Valley Junction is little more than the **Amargosa Opera House**. Owner Marta Becket produces and performs mime-ballets on winter Saturdays; call for schedule and required advance bookings. The Opera House also has 14 air-conditioned rooms.

DEATH VALLEY NATIONAL PARK

Death Valley National Park $$
Box 579, Death Valley, CA 92328; tel: (760) 786-3200; www.nps.gov/deva

Roughly 140 miles long and 10 miles across, Death Valley offers the nation's most dramatically desolate scenery. America's hottest temperature, 134°F (56°C), was recorded in Death Valley in 1913; average summer days hit 116°F (47°C). The National Park protects vast stretches of mountain and desert surrounding the basin.

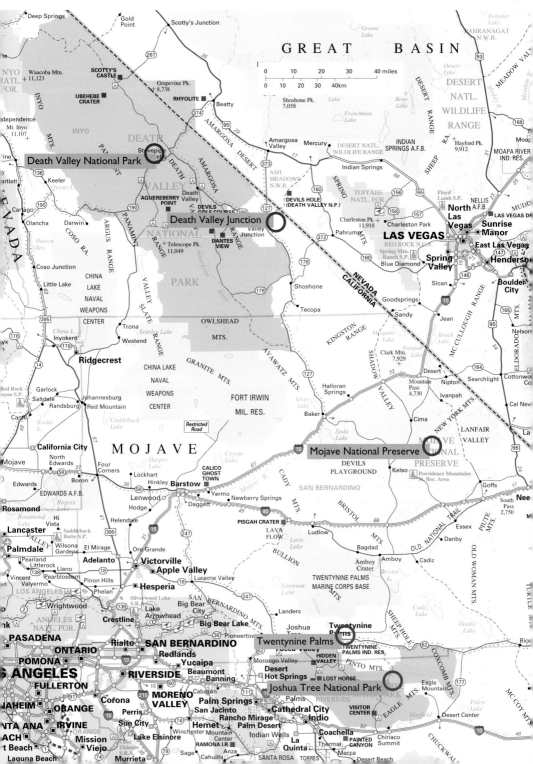

GREAT BASIN

Death Valley National Park

Death Valley Junction

Mojave National Preserve

Twentynine Palms

Joshua Tree National Park

ℹ **Death Valley
Chamber of
Commerce**
118 Hwy 127, Box 157,
Shoshone, CA 92384;
tel: (760) 852-4524; www.
deathvalleychamber.org.
Open daily 0930–1700.

Death Valley was formed as the basin floor subsided, leaving precipitous mountains on all sides. The Sierra Nevada blocks nearly all rainfall; Furnace Creek averages barely 1½in of rain yearly. Climatic changes turned an enormous lake 600ft deep into desert pans cracked into hexagons and piled high with salt crystals. Softer sediments have eroded into vast badlands stained every colour of the rainbow.

Despite its name, Death Valley is anything but dead. Conifers grow on the cooler, wetter heights of the Panamint Mountains. The lower slopes are generally too dry and too salty for cacti, but creosote and other coarse bushes thrive. Even the valley bottom, 282ft *below* sea level, sports unique plants and animals in hot, salty marshes.

Errant immigrants gave Death Valley its name and reputation. Hoping to avoid snowy Sierra Nevada Mountain passes to the north, two bands of gold prospectors stumbled into the valley in 1849. Nearly all survived but were impressed enough by the harsh terrain to call it Death Valley.

There were several abortive mining booms in the 19th century, but only a late-century borax boom brought much permanent change. Millennia of evaporation concentrated boron salts into fluffy

Below
Badwater – nearly as low as you
can get in North America

ⓘ Furnace Creek Visitor Center and Museum Tel: (760) 786-3200. Open daily 0900–1700. Visitor centres at **Scotty's Castle Visitor Center** Tel: (760) 786-2392. Open winter 0830–1700; summer 0900–1630.

Since 1983, the **Furnace Creek 508 Bicycle Race** (www.the508.com) has tested endurance from Santa Clarita north of Los Angeles 508 miles through the desert and Death Valley to Twentynine Palms. The race is held in early October. For sheer difficulty, it is matched in July's heat by the **Badwater Ultramarathon 135 Mile Running Race** (www.badwater.com) from Death Valley to Mount Whitney.

'cottonball' crystals. Workers collected the cottonballs which were processed into borax and used to make fine jewellery, glass and washing powder.

Twenty-mule teams hauled wagons from **Harmony Borax Works** 165 miles to the railway at Mojave. In 1907, a railway (now abandoned) began hauling borax to **Death Valley Junction**. Hoping to stimulate tourism and boost revenues, railway owners built the **Furnace Creek Inn** in 1927. As the inn prospered, less expensive cabins were added at **Furnace Creek Ranch**. Death Valley became a National Monument in 1933 and a National Park in 1994.

Paved roads are passable all year, but most of Death Valley's gravel roads are meant for four-wheel drive. Always check with park rangers before venturing off-road.

Artists Drive (*south of Furnace Creek, off Badwater Rd, vehicles over 25ft prohibited*) is a 9-mile, one-way loop through brightly coloured badlands and alluvial fans. **Artists Palette**, halfway through the drive, displays a startling patchwork of intense red, yellow, orange, green, violet, brown and black tones – most vivid in late afternoon.

Badwater (*south of Furnace Creek*), 279ft below sea level, was long accepted as the nadir of North America. More accurate surveys have found two lower spots, both 282ft below sea level, a few miles away and unmarked. The highly mineralised water isn't poisonous, just a very effective laxative.

Dantes View (*off Hwy 190 east of Furnace Creek*) is one of the most stunning vistas in Death Valley. Located 1 mile directly above Badwater, the view stretches across the basin to **Telescope Peak** (11,049ft) and beyond to **Mount Whitney** (14,491ft), the tallest peak in the continental US. Colours and views are best in early morning.

Devil's Golf Course (*south of Furnace Creek*) is more than 200 square miles of crystalline salt towers sculpted by wind and rain. The salt cracks and groans audibly with temperature changes.

Furnace Creek is an oasis that has become Death Valley's centre for accommodation (Furnace Creek Inn and Ranch) and activities (park visitor centre). The natural spring that watered hay fields in the last century now keeps the world's lowest golf course green. The **Borax Museum** (*Furnace Creek Resort; tel: (760) 786-2345, open daily 0900–1600*) was originally the office and bunkhouse for 20-mule team borax trains. Museum collections include borax mining equipment as well a 20-mule wagon. The Timbisha Shoshone Tribe has land in this area.

Harmony Borax Works (*north of Furnace Creek*) commemorates the 1880s borax boom. A short path passes the refinery ruins and outlying buildings; a 3-mile trail leads to the borax 'cottonballs' labourers collected.

Rhyolite (*35 miles northeast of Furnace Creek, near Beatty, Nevada; www.nps.gov/archive/deva/Rhyolite.htm*) is a stark, imposing collection of stone and concrete ruins from a 1904 boom town. The ruins are haunting at sunset.

Salt Creek (*north of Furnace Creek*) shows the resilience of the inch-long pupfish (*genus Cyprinodon*) which has adapted to the heat, salinity and periodic drought of Death Valley. Related species are found in **Anza-Borrego Desert State Park** (*see page 90*) and other desert watercourses.

Scotty's Castle $$ (*north of Furnace Creek; tel: (760) 786-2392; www.nps.gov/deva/historyculture/scottys-castle.htm. Open daily winter 0830–1700; summer 0900–1630*) represents the extravagant marriage of money (Chicago insurance magnate Albert Johnson) and myth (local cowboy, occasional miner and full-time prevaricator Walter 'Scotty' Scott). 'Scotty' convinced Johnson to build the Spanish-Moorish mansion in 1924 as a restful retreat. Grounds surrounding the $2.4 million extravaganza were never completed, but the interior is elegantly finished with tiles, handcrafted furniture, leather and textiles. The house interior is open by guided tour only ($$) – expect long queues in winter. An Underground Mysteries technology tour is offered daily, from Nov–Apr. The Gas House Museum has Castle artefacts.

Stovepipe Wells (*23 miles northwest of Furnace Creek*) was Death Valley's original settlement; stovepipes driven into the sand to create wells gave it its name. Visitor facilities at Stovepipe Wells Village are a few miles south of the original well, across an immense field of **sand dunes**. The dunes are at their sensuous best in the long shadows near dawn and sunset.

Ubehebe Crater (*west of Scotty's Castle*), 600ft deep and 2600ft wide, was created by an immense volcanic explosion in the last few thousand years. The sides of the cauldron are layered with tones of orange and grey.

Zabriskie Point (*south of Furnace Creek*) overlooks the Golden Canyon badlands from the east. The heavily eroded landscape glows pink in the first few minutes after dawn.

Accommodation and food in Death Valley

Panamint Springs Resort $$ *Hwy 190, 31 miles west of Stovepipe Wells; tel: (775) 482-7680; www.deathvalley.com*, has a motel, restaurant, campground and RV park.

Stovepipe Wells Village $$ *Stovepipe Wells; tel: (760) 786-2387; www.stovepipewells.com*, offers accommodation, supplies, a restaurant, RV park, and information for the northern end of Death Valley.

Furnace Creek Ranch $$–$$$ *Furnace Creek; tel: (760) 786-2345* or *(800) 236-7916; www.furnacecreekresort.com*, is the Inn's motel-like alternative, open year-round with rooms and cabins.

Furnace Creek Inn $$$ *Furnace Creek; tel: (760) 786-2345* or *(800) 236-7916; www.furnacecreekresort.com; open mid-Oct–mid-May*, was built in the 1920s as a vaguely Moorish resort and is still among the poshest accommodation in an American desert park.

All four accommodation locations have restaurants and general stores. Picnic supplies are more reasonable outside the park.

JOSHUA TREE NATIONAL PARK

Joshua Tree National Park $$
74485 National Park Dr., Twentynine Palms, CA 92277; tel: (760) 367-5500; www.nps.gov/jotr

Named after wildly gesticulating trees that are actually lilies, Joshua Tree is an anomaly among national parks. There are no IMAX® theatres, no grand lodges, no biggest-smallest-best-tallest-only-on-earth attractions. In fact, there isn't much of *anything* here except nature – more than 800,000 acres, nearly all of it wilderness.

The park is an eerie, almost mystical landscape. Early and late in the day, long shadows and reddish sunlight seem to animate the bizarre landforms and even stranger plants. Jumbled piles of rounded golden boulders rise from the surface, immense mounds of monzogranite that have been cracked, broken, stacked and eroded into shapes reminiscent of twisted Henry Moore sculptures. Climbers from around the world revere the sheer faces of Wonderland Rocks and 4500 routes.

Namesake Joshua trees (*Yucca brevifolia*) seem to march across the rolling hills, a vast army of stick figures with multiple arms raised to the heavens as though pointing the way to unseen oases fringed with palm trees and willows. Fuzzy cacti that glow like soft velvet in the sun are actually covered with microscopic spines that are nearly impossible to remove.

In spring, the arid hills and canyons disappear beneath carpets of wildflowers. Just weeks later, the same hillsides have become a blazing midday furnace, parched by the sun. In summer, stick to the Joshua tree forests where temperatures top out around 100°F (38°C), a good 25°F (13°C) cooler than the lowlands. In winter, the lowland canyons are a comfortable 75°F (24°C) as the highlands shiver in snow.

The two temperature zones are actually two different deserts, the Mojave and the Colorado. There are few sharp distinctions between the two, no boundary signs to mark the amorphous transition. It's a matter of altitude and, even more, of rainfall, variations.

The lower, hotter and drier Colorado Desert is marked by spindly ocotillo bushes, thorny green sticks dripping scarlet blossoms in spring and practically leafless most of the year. With an average of 3in of rain yearly, double the moisture of Death Valley, the Colorado Desert also supports a varied cactus community. The most common is the

**ⓘ Cottonwood
Visitor Center**
*Cottonwood Spring entrance.
Open daily 0900–1500.*

**Joshua Tree Visitor
Center** *Park Blvd one block
south of Hwy 62, Joshua
Tree Village. Open daily
0800–1700.*

**Black Rock Nature
Center** *Black Rock
Campground. Open
Oct–May Sat–Thu
0800–1600, Fri
1200–2000.*

jumping cholla (pronounced *'choi-yuh'*), named after its proclivity to hook into unwary passers-by.

Life is easier in the higher and moister Mojave Desert. Lying above 3000ft, the Mojave gets nearly 6in of rain annually, enough to support vast groves of Joshua trees. Though they grow up to 60ft tall, Joshua trees aren't proper trees, but yuccas, a lily with woody stems. Clumps of spindly leaves at the end of the branches give the appearance of arms waving wildly against the sky. The trees were named by Mormon immigrants who likened the trees to the biblical prophet Joshua, pointing the way across the desert with raised arms.

One main road bisects the park, from **Cottonwood** in the south, near I-10, to **Twentynine Palms** and Hwy 62 on the north. Another major road runs from the town of **Joshua Tree** south into the park to meet Pinto Basin Rd. Most of the dirt tracks are passable only by four-wheel-drive vehicles; check for current conditions at ranger stations before venturing off the pavement in passenger vehicles. Trailers and RVs are generally not recommended on dirt roads.

Cholla Cactus Garden (*near Pinto Basin Rd*) provides an easy opportunity to see (but *not* to touch) the most common indicator plant of the Colorado Desert. A short, easy trail winds through an especially dense stand of cholla cacti (*Opuntia bigelovii*). Also called 'teddybear cholla' for their soft, fuzzy appearance, 'jumping cholla' is more painfully accurate. Chunks of cactus seem to leap out, propelled by microscopic spines which snag skin, clothing and almost anything else that brushes past. The large piles of dead cholla are nests built by packrats, which use the prickly pads to protect their dwellings, usually built at the base of a creosote bush.

Just south along Pinto Basin Rd is the **Ocotillo Patch**, the park's most accessible ocotillo thicket. This spiny shrub, noted for its brilliant crimson flowers, is the Colorado Desert's other indicator plant. It's also called Jacob's staff, candlewood, coachwhip and vine cactus, a testament to the thorns along the limber, nearly leafless branches.

Cottonwood Spring (*south entrance, off I-10*) is a pleasant oasis one mile east of the visitor centre. The springs are natural, the palms a human addition much used by birds and other wildlife.

Desert Queen Mine (*off a dirt road running north opposite Geology Tour Rd*) lies ¾-mile along an easy trail, a collection of rusting mine machinery. The mine shafts and tunnels are extremely dangerous. A more strenuous half-day walk leads to the **Lost Horse Mine** and the remains of a ten-stamp mill (stamps are blocks for crushing ore).

Keys' Desert Queen Ranch (*open by guided walking tour only, tel: (760) 367-5555, $, Oct–May Sat–Sun 1000, 1300 (other tours occasionally scheduled)*) is a one-family ghost town that died in 1969. The ranch includes an adobe barn from the 1880s, a schoolhouse, junked cars, a

windmill, antique mining equipment and ranch fittings crafted from Joshua tree wood.

Fortynine Palms Oasis (*off Canyon Rd, 4 miles west of Twentynine Palms*) is the best area for spring wildflowers. Desert annuals carpet the ground, barrel cacti explode with blooms and the canyon pool is rimmed with native fan palms. The 3-mile return hike is moderately strenuous; the trail may be closed during late summer against fire danger.

General Patton Memorial Museum contains World War II memorabilia, with special displays of tanks and artillery used by Patton's training camps in Joshua Tree and ten other southwestern desert camps. A West Coast Vietnam Veterans' Wall here honours veterans.

Geology Tour Road (*from Queen Valley, check road conditions at the visitor centre before setting out*) is an 18-mile gravel loop (*sometimes* passable by passenger cars) through some of the park's most spectacular geological features. Great alluvial fans spill toward the road and massive monzogranite heaps tower over the Joshua trees surrounding a desert *playa*, or dry lake bed. Visitor centres sell an excellent road guide.

Keys View (*20 miles south of Joshua Tree town, via Quail Springs and Keys View Rds*) offers the most spectacular panoramas in the park, from atop the San Bernardino Mountains (5185ft) across the Coachella Valley to the San Jacinto Range and south to the Salton Sea.

Oasis of Mara (*Oasis Visitor Center, Twentynine Palms*) was the original oasis of 29 palms first recorded in an 1855 survey. The name *mara* means 'little water' in the language of the Chemehuevi people who occupied the area before white prospectors and settlers arrived. The oasis once held an open pool of water, but years of overdrafting have lowered the water table. An easy ½-mile trail leads from the visitor centre to the oasis.

Queen Valley (*Pinto Valley Rd, centre of the park*) has the park's largest and healthiest stands of Joshua trees, thousands of them marching toward the horizon in every direction. **Jumbo Rocks Campground** offers fine vistas with Joshua trees set against soaring monzogranite towers and spires.

Accommodation and food in Joshua Tree National Park

There are a number of campgrounds in the park, but no accommodation or restaurants. The Palm Springs area (*see page 94*) has the best variety near the park, although Twentynine Palms is (*see page 112*) the closest centre.

ⓘ **Oasis Visitor Center** *Utah Trail at National Park Dr., Twentynine Palms; tel: (760) 367-5500. Open daily 0800–1700.*

ⓟ **General Patton Memorial Museum** $ *Off I-10, 4½ miles east of Cottonwood Spring Rd, 2 Chiriaco Rd, Chiriaco Summit, CA 92201; tel: (760) 227-3483; www.generalpattonmuseum.com. Open daily 0930–1630.*

Above
Eroded boulders in Joshua Tree National Park

MOJAVE NATIONAL PRESERVE

Above
Joshua trees thrive even in the hot dry desert

🅤 **Mojave National Preserve**
(headquarters) 2701 Barstow Rd, Barstow; tel: (760) 252-6100; www.nps.gov/moja. Open Mon–Fri 0800–1630.

Kelso Depot Visitor Center *35 miles south of Baker or 22 miles north of I-40 on Kelbaker Rd; tel: (760) 252-6108. Open daily 0900–1700.*

Hole-in-the-Wall Information Center *Essex and Black Canyon Rds, 20 miles north of I-40, tel: (760) 928-2572. Open Oct–Apr Wed–Sun 0900–1600; May–Sep Fri–Sun same hours.*

This 'Lonesome Triangle' of Mojave Desert between I-40, I-15 and the Nevada border is more mountain than sand and combines Great Basin, Sonora and Mojave desert ecosystems. The vast expanse (1.6 million acres) is accented by cinder cones, sand dunes, caverns, precipitous mountains and lava mesas. Joshua tree forests thrive in the upper elevations; the lower slopes are threadbare beneath a sparse carpet of creosote brush.

Though desolate in human terms, this rugged triangle is home to 700 species of plants and 300 different kinds of animals. It's also an historic thoroughfare. Native Americans have been traversing the region for at least 10,000 years, trading Coastal California goods as far east as Central Mexico. Spanish explorers followed in the 1770s, then American explorers, ranchers, railway lines and highways.

But except for scattered ranches and mines, there has been little permanent settlement. The Eastern Mojave has been a land where anything goes and no one much minded so long as it was safely out of sight. Growing recreational use has changed the government's traditional hands-off policies. The area became a National Preserve in 1994 over fierce local opposition. Ranchers, miners, off-road vehicle users and landowners still object to stricter controls over what many see as *their* land, by right of use if not of ownership.

Signs of human use are never far away, from abandoned mine sites to shot-out Preserve signs, rusted railway tracks and decrepit buildings, but the desert has managed to preserve its expansive emptiness. Without four-wheel drive, stick to the main roads. Rutted side-tracks often disappear into fields of sand or boulders bounded by steep cliffs.

The tiny town of **Amboy** (*www.rt66roys.com*), south of **Mojave National Preserve**, was once an important stop for the transcontinental railway service and auto traffic on Route 66, America's first transcontinental highway. More modern routes have since bypassed Amboy, and its volcanic cone.

Cima Dome (*off Cima Rd, south of Valley Wells*) is best seen from a distance. The almost perfectly formed white batholith (molten magma that solidified before reaching the surface) rises 1500ft above the surrounding plain, but the gentle rise is difficult to see up close. The 75-square-mile dome is cloaked in Joshua trees. The tiny town of **Cima** originated as a railway siding.

Cinder Cones Natural National Landmark (*off Kelbaker Rd, north of Kelso*) is a collection of young (1000–10 million-year-old) cinder cones.

ℹ **California Welcome Center**
2796 Tanger Way, Ste 106 (Tanger® Outlets), Barstow, CA 92311; tel: (760) 253-4782. Open daily.

ℹ **Mitchell Caverns Providence Mountains State Recreation Area**
Box 1, Essex, CA 92332; tel: (760) 928-2586; www.parks.ca.gov/?page_id=615. Caverns open by guided tour ($), daily. Call in advance for reservation forms.

Hole-in-the-Wall Campground (*Essex Rd, off I-40*) is named after the wall of rhyolite lava, filled with holes like rocky Swiss cheese.

Kelso Depot The main Preserve Visitor Center was a railway stop for the Lost Angeles and Salt Lake Railroad from 1924–1962. After many years of neglect, the restored depot, at a convenient stopping point at Preserve crossroads, has exhibits, information and a fine art gallery.

Kelso Dunes (*near Kelso, centre of the Preserve*) are among the tallest sand dunes in California, 600–700ft at the crest fanning out across 45 square miles. The golden rose quartz sand has blown in from the Mojave Sink, to the northwest. Allow about 2 hours to walk to the dune crest and back, plus time to play. The dunes 'sing' as sand slides from the crest, reverberations that sound like a whispering Tibetian gong. Best times to visit are early or late in the day, preferably sunrise/sunset, when long shadows highlight the undulating dune ridges.

Mitchell Caverns (*Essex Rd off I-40*) are the only caves in Southern California developed for tourism. Water-borne deposits have created a wonderland of limestone curtains, stalactites, stalagmites and other rocky formations, all accessible by stairs and walkways. The cave is open for guided tours only. The easy **Mary Beal Nature Trail** offers a scenic introduction to the surrounding **Providence Mountains State Recreation Area**.

Shoshone is a small supply town for Death Valley at the junction of Hwy 178 (the route from Pahrump and Las Vegas, Nevada) and Hwy 127 from Baker.

Zzyzx (*Zzyzx Rd, off I-10 west of Baker*) is the remains of a 60-room spa, hotel, church, castle and radio station built in the 1940s by self-proclaimed minister/healer Curtis Springer. Springer invented the name (pronounced 'zye-zix', to rhyme with 'size six') to be the last entry in the telephone book. The spa was closed in 1974 when Springer was convicted on tax, health and drug charges; the facility is now a California State University Desert Studies Center.

Researchers are usually more than happy to be interrupted. If the station is unstaffed (as it usually is), signboards describe local natural history and the endangered Mojave chub (a desert fish). On a shoreside walk, the old bathhouse offers good views of Soda Dry Lake and the picturesque mountains beyond.

Accommodation and food in Mojave National Preserve

There is camping, but no accommodation, within the Preserve. Fuel and very limited picnic supplies are available in Cima and Nipton. Pick up supplies before entering the Preserve.

TWENTYNINE PALMS

ⓘ Twentynine Palms Chamber of Commerce 73660 Civic Center, Ste C & D, Twentynine Palms, CA 92277; tel: (760) 367-3445; www.29chamber.com. Open Sep–May Mon–Fri 0900–1700, Sat 0900–1300; Jun–Aug Mon–Fri 0900–1500.

ⓜ Hi-Desert Nature Museum $ Community Center Complex, 57090 Twentynine Palms Hwy, Yucca Valley; tel: (760) 369-7212; www.yucca-valley.org/departments/museum.html. Open Tue–Sun 1000–1700.

ⓜ Edchada's $ 73502 29 Palms Hwy, Twentynine Palms; tel: (760) 367-2131, open for lunch and dinner, serves good Mexican dishes and margaritas.

Named after the palm trees surrounding Mara Oasis (Joshua Tree National Park headquarters), Twentynine Palms has become a busy desert town as headquarters for the Marine Corps Air Ground Combat Center (the US Marine Corps' largest base) and **Joshua Tree National Park** (*see page 107*). Almost two dozen public murals depict area history. **Hi-Desert Nature Museum** covers Southern California flora, fauna and natural history.

Accommodation and food in Twentynine Palms

Circle C Lodge $$ *6340 El Rey Ave; tel: (760) 367-7615 or (800) 545-9696; www.circleclodge.com*, includes Continental breakfast and a swimming pool.

The 29 Palms Inn $$–$$$ *73950 Inn Ave, close to the Visitor Center; tel: (760) 367-3505; www.29Palmsinn.com*, is the closest accommodation to the park. The inn also has the best restaurant ($$) in the area, with steaks, seafood and chicken.

Suggested tour

Total distance: 260 miles.

Time: One gruelling driving day, **Palm Springs ❶** to **Death Valley National Park ❿**; three–five days' touring with overnight stops in **Twentynine Palms ❹** and **Baker ❽**.

Links: Palm Springs to the west, Las Vegas to the east, Anza-Borrego Desert State Park to the south.

Route: From **Palm Springs ❶** take I-10 southeast to **Indio ❷**. Continue east 24 miles on I-10 to Cottonwood Spring Road and **JOSHUA TREE NATIONAL PARK ❸**. Drive north through the park to **TWENTYNINE PALMS ❹**, then east and north to **Amboy ❺** and the **MOJAVE NATIONAL PRESERVE ❻**. Follow Kelbaker Rd through the Preserve to **Kelso ❼**, then continue northwest to **Baker ❽** (at I-15). Take Hwy 127 north to **DEATH VALLEY JUNCTION ❾**, then enter **DEATH VALLEY NATIONAL PARK ❿** on Hwy 190.

Also worth exploring:

Shimmering **Salton Sea** (*www.saltonsea.ca.gov*), south of Palm Springs, was created when a Colorado River aqueduct ruptured in 1905. Measuring 35 miles by 15 miles, it's one of the world's largest inland bodies of salt water, a state recreation area, and excellent for birdwatching at the Salton Sea National Wildlife Refuge.

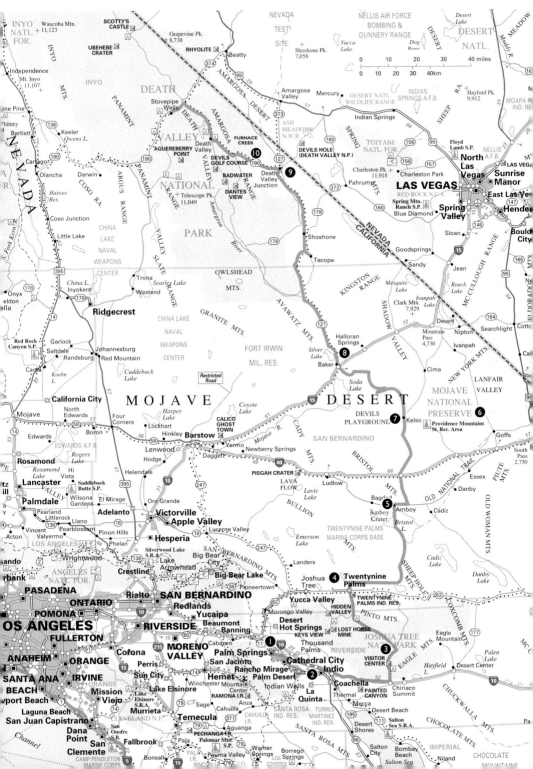

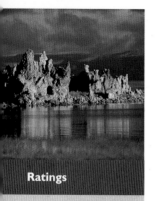

Spine of the Sierra

Ratings

Geology	●●●●○
Outdoor activities	●●●●○
Scenery	●●●●○
Children	●●●○○
History	●●●○○
Wildlife	●●●○○
Food and drink	●●○○○

The eastern slope of the Sierra Nevada is steeper and more dramatic than the gentle foothills leading up from the Central Valley, a mix of serrated peaks, blistering desert, alkaline lakes and rushing streams squeezed into a narrow corridor between snowcapped summits and the Great American Desert in Nevada. It's also an area almost devoid of people – no Interstate highways and no rush hour. Hwy 395 provides easy north–south travel, but heavy snow can close east–west mountain passes south of Hwy 88 from November to May.

BIG PINE

ⓘ Big Pine Chamber of Commerce Visitor Center 128 S. Maine St, Big Pine, CA 93513; tel: (866) 938-2114 or (760) 938-2114; www.bigpine.com

Ⓜ Ancient Bristlecone Pine Forest Off Hwy 168 east of Big Pine. For information: US Forest Service White Mountain Ranger District, 798 N. Main St, Bishop, CA 93514; tel: (760) 873-2500. Open daily May–Oct; Nov–Apr Mon–Fri.

The town of Big Pine is little more than a collection of petrol stations and motels, but it is the gateway to two of the region's top attractions, the **Ancient Bristlecone Pine Forest** (*off Hwy 168; tel: (760) 873-2500*) and **Palisade Glacier** (*Glacier Lodge Rd, west*).

Bristlecone pines (*Pinus longaeva*) are the oldest living things on earth, usually clinging to inaccessible mountain slopes. The world's only drive-up stand of bristlecones is 10,000ft up the White Mountains, east of Big Pine. Bristlecones have been growing on these mountains for at least 4500 years, gnarled branches bleached blonde by centuries of blasting wind, snow and sand beneath a burning sun. The twisted trunks grow only an inch in diameter each century, dead as any chunk of driftwood except for an occasional ribbon of bark leading to a splash of needles and cones on some remote branch.

Schulman Grove $, named after the researcher who first dated the trees in the 1950s, lies at the end of a twisting paved road at 10,000ft.

Look for two self-guiding trails, the 1-mile **Discovery Trail** and the slightly longer **Methuselah Trail**, which passes the 4700-year-old Methuselah Tree and the **visitor center**. **Patriarch Grove**, 12 miles beyond on a gravel road at 11,320ft, offers spectacular views of the Sierra, the Great Basin in Nevada, and the Patriarch Tree, the largest bristlecone. **Palisade** is the southernmost glacier in the US, looming above Big Pine Canyon west of town at the end of Glacier Lodge Rd, 11 miles west from Hwy 395.

BISHOP

ℹ Bishop Chamber of Commerce and Visitors Bureau *690 N. Main St, Bishop, CA 93514; tel: (760) 873-8405 or (888) 395-3952; www.bishopvisitor.com*

Bureau of Land Management (BLM) *351 Pacu Lane, Ste 100; tel: (760) 872-5000; www.ca.blm.gov/ bishop/index.html. Open Mon–Fri 0800–1630.*

Public Lands Information Center *798 N. Main St; tel: (760) 873-2503. Call for hours.*

ℝ Red Rock Canyon Petroglyphs *Off Hwy 6. Stop at the BLM office for free permit and maps.*

Mountain Light Gallery *106 S. Main St; tel: (760) 873-7700; www.mountainlight.com. Open Sun–Thu 1000–1800, Fri–Sat 1000–2000.*

Bishop is the largest town in the Owens Valley, one of the few to survive Los Angeles' insatiable thirst. In 1910, about 4500 people lived between Bishop and Owens Lake, just south of Lone Pine. The valley floor was once a maze of orchards, vineyards and fields of corn, wheat and potatoes, while a steamship plied the waters of **Owens Lake** (now dry).

But Los Angeles, one of California's fastest-growing cities, needed more water. The **Owens Valley** had the bad luck to be the nearest source. LA's Department of Water and Power (DWP) chief engineer William Mulholland and his cronies bought up most of the valley, either through sham corporations or questionable legal tactics. Local officials were bribed or intimidated with the sort of semi-legal real-estate schemes depicted in the 1974 Jack Nicholson film *Chinatown*.

When the Owens Valley Aqueduct opened in 1913, nearly all of the water that once ran through the Owens Valley was diverted to Los Angeles. Steely blue Owens Lake became a pinkish salt flat, and fields and orchards gave way to dunes as the population drifted away.

Bishop, at the head of the valley, survived to become a burst of civilisation surrounded by mountain wilderness that lures anglers (fantastic fly-fishing), hikers, mountain climbers and other outdoor lovers. **Mountain Light Gallery** features photography by the late nature and adventure photographer, Galen Rowell, including images of the nearby High and Eastern Sierra. The most visible signs of Native American history are the **petroglyphs** scattered about the valley. The meaning of the figures pecked into rocks is long lost, but the best place to see them is the **Red Rock Canyon Petroglyphs** (*off Hwy 6*). Most of the images are found at places where water used to be, nearly all of them now dry, courtesy of Los Angeles.

Food in Bishop

Erick Schat's Bakkerÿ $ *763 N. Main St; tel: (760) 873-7156*, has good espresso, light meals and Dutch-style baked goods. **Jack's Restaurant and Bakery** $ *437 N. Main St; tel: (760) 872-7971*, is an institution. **Whiskey Creek** $$ *524 N. Main St; tel: (760) 873-7174*, offers American cuisine and Bishop's liveliest bar.

BRIDGEPORT

ⓘ Bridgeport Chamber of Commerce PO Box 541, Bridgeport, CA 93517; tel: (760) 932-7500; www.bridgeportcalifornia.com

Film buffs might recognize Bridgeport as the village that gave fugitive Robert Mitchum a new start in the 1947 film *Out of the Past*. Mitchum's Mono Motor Service petrol station has disappeared, but the tiny town with its 1880 Mono County Courthouse is otherwise little changed. Those not addicted to the *film noir* genre might look out for the turn-off to **Bodie** (*see page 120*), 6 miles south.

INDEPENDENCE

ⓘ Independence Chamber of Commerce 139 N. Edwards (Hwy 395); tel: (760) 878-0084; www.independence-ca.com. Open Mon–Tue Fri–Sat 0900–1600.

ⓗ Manzanar National Historic Site Tel: (760) 878-2194; www.nps.gov/manz. Site open daily dawn to dusk. Free.

Eastern California Museum 155 N. Grant St; tel: (760) 878-0258; www.countyofinyo.org/ecmuseum. Open Wed–Mon 1000–1700. Admission by donation.

The small town was named after Fort Independence, established in 1862 to protect White settlers from Paiutes angry at the usurpation of their lands. It is better known for the **Manzanar Relocation Camp**, 6 miles south.

Manzanar (the name means 'apple orchard' in Spanish) was a thriving apple- and pear-growing town around the turn of the 20th century that died when Los Angeles diverted its water south. It was reborn during World War II as a desolate internment camp for 10,000 mostly California-born Americans of Japanese ancestry. Considered a threat by military officials, Japanese-Americans were imprisoned until 1944 and their property confiscated.

Most of the internees had owned businesses and homes in coastal California; Manzanar gave them 20sq ft per family in flimsy, paper-covered wooden barracks behind barbed-wire fences, buffeted by freezing winter winds and sweltering summer heat. It took the US government more than 40 years to settle compensation claims and apologise.

All that remains are foundations visible amidst the sagebrush, a pair of ornamental gates, a garage and a cemetery obelisk marking the National Historic Site, and the visitors' centre in a rebuilt former high-school auditorium originally constructed by internees. Rangers lead guided tours, or you can drive the 3.2-mile self-guided auto tour around the site.

The **Eastern California Museum** details the impact of Manzanar on the many children who grew up behind the barbed wire. Other displays cover Owens Valley environments, Paiute and settler artefacts, farming implements and mining equipment.

Just north of town is **Mount Whitney State Fish Hatchery** (*Fish Hatchery Rd; tel: (760) 878-2272*), a stone monastery-style building with a Tudor tower and the ruins of Fort Independence, abandoned in 1877.

LONE PINE

This is a convenient base for exploring the nearby mountains, including 14,491ft **Mount Whitney** and desert areas. It's also the first touch of civilisation west from Death Valley. The best stop is the ℹ **Lone Pine Chamber of Commerce** 120 S. Main St, Lone Pine, CA 93545; tel: (760) 876-4444 or (877) 253-8981; www.lonepinechamber.org. Open Mon–Fri 0830–1630.

🏛 **Beverly & Jim Rogers Museum of Lone Pine Film History** $ Hwy 395, S. end of Main St; tel: (760) 876-9909; www.lonepinefilmhistorymuseum.org. Open Wed–Mon 1000–1600.

Lone Pine Film Festival www.lonepinefilmfestival.org, is in Oct.

Eastern Sierra Interagency Visitor Center (*Hwy 395/136 junction; tel: (760) 876-6222; www.fs.fed.us/r5/inyo; open daily 0800–1700, longer in summer*), which has complete information on Owens Valley attractions as well as routes into Death Valley and a front porch view of Mount Whitney.

If the scenery seems familiar, it probably is. Cowboys, Indians (Native Americans), outlaws, Bengal lancers and space aliens have been parading before cinema cameras in the **Alabama Hills** (*www.ca.blm.gov/pdfs/bishop_pdfs/suv/route2.pdf*) since the early 1920s. Six-mile **Movie Flat Rd** (*Hwy 395 to Whitney Portal Rd*) remains a favourite with film-makers. The gravel road is easily passable by cars and RVs, but unsigned side roads can be rough. Having driven Movie Flat Rd, visit the **Indian Trading Post** (*137 S. Main St; tel: (760) 876-4641*). The souvenir stock is standard, but the front door frame was signed by Gary Cooper, Errol Flynn, John Wayne and other film stars.

The **Beverly & Jim Rogers Museum of Lone Pine Film History** is a private effort to preserve the Eastern Sierra's movie history with posters, photographs and other artefacts of the West and its (film) landscape. The October **Lone Pine Film Festival** screens films from the Westerns' heyday and gives film location tours.

MAMMOTH LAKES

🏛 **Mammoth Lakes Visitors Bureau** Mammoth Lakes; tel: (760) 934-2712 or (888) 466-2666; www.visitmammoth.com

Mammoth Ranger Station and Welcome Center (*Inyo National Forest; www.fs.fed.us/r5/inyo*) Hwy 203; tel: (760) 924-5500. Open daily 0800–1700. The centre dispenses outdoor recreation and camping information, backcountry permits, and directions to the shuttle to Devil's Postpile National Monument, from mid-Jun–Sep.

Originally a short-lived gold-rush town, Mammoth is California's second most popular mountain resort after Lake Tahoe. A major ski centre in winter, more than 50 miles of skiing trails become mountain-bike runs in summer. Either season, the gondola to the top of Mammoth Mountain provides stunning **views** north to Mono Lake. The top of the Sierra Interpretive Center provides an informative preview. **Mammoth Lakes Basin**, just south, is a glacial depression with six scenic lakes as alluring to winter alpine skiers as to summer hikers. **June Lake**, just north, is a quieter alternative with similar scenery.

The Mammoth area's most unusual sight is **Devil's Postpile National Monument**, a wall of basalt columns 60ft tall, rising above the middle fork of the San Joaquin River. The pile was formed about 100,000 years ago as a basalt flow from Mammoth Mountain cooled and cracked into hexagonal and octagonal posts. A glacier cut through the area about 10,000 years ago, exposing the formation.

Right Tufa formations at Mono Lake echo the peaks of the Sierra Nevada Mountains

Devil's Postpile National Monument ($ for road access, not shuttle) tel: (760) 934-2289; www.nps.gov/depo. Open Jun–Oct. In summer, day visitors (but not campers) must take shuttle transport from the Forest Service Adventure Center adjacent to the Mammoth Mountain Inn.

Mammoth Ski Museum 100 College Parkway; tel: (760) 934-6592; www.mammothskimuseum.org. Open Tue–Sun.

The pile is less than a ½-mile by trail from monument headquarters; a second trail leads to the top of the pile, which resembles a tiled floor. The main trail continues 2 miles to **Rainbow Falls**, a 101ft waterfall renowned for rainbows refracted in the spray around midday. A shorter trail leads to the Falls from **Reds Meadow**.

Mammoth is famous for its **hot springs**, which may be the legacy of North America's most destructive volcanic eruption (about 760,000 years ago) or the forerunner of eruptions yet to come. **Hot Creek Geothermal Area** (*Airport/Hot Creek Fish Hatchery Rd, off Hwy 395*) is an icy mountain stream that mixes with near-boiling water from natural vents creating blue pools beautiful to contemplate, but closed as too dangerous for soaking. Don't expect solitude and don't settle too close to heat sources – bathers have been scalded to death by unexpected blasts of superheated water. Skiers search out the Beekley International Collection of Skiing Art and Literature at **Mammoth Ski Museum** to see how the Mammoth resort began and admire skiing pioneers' stories.

Accommodation and food in Mammoth Lakes

Beware of winter weekends, when Los Angeles skiers pour into Mammoth, and summer weekends, nearly as popular with mountain bikers and climbers. Midweek is more reasonable.

The Stove $ *644 Old Mammoth Rd; tel: (760) 934-2821*, is a long-time favourite especially at breakfast for gargantuan portions of American favourites.

Whiskey Creek $$ *Main St and Minaret Rd; tel: (760) 934-2555*, is one of Mammoth's liveliest restaurants and bars and has its own good microbrews.

Mammoth Mountain Inn $$$ *tel: (760) 934-2581* or *(800) 828-8684; www.mammothmountain.com*, is the place to sleep, at the base of the ski lifts, next to the bike park and overlooking the climbing rock.

MONO LAKE

Mono Basin National Forest Scenic Area Visitor Center Hwy 395, 1 mile north of Lee Vining; tel: (760) 647-3044; www.monolake.org/monomap/vc.htm and www.fs.fed.us/r5/inyo/recreation/rec-reports/mono.shtml. Call for hours.

This otherworldly lake, rimmed by salt flats, twisted mineral towers and new-born mountains, may be the oldest lake in North America. It is also the nesting ground for 85 per cent of all California gulls, which feed on the trillions of shrimp and flies that hatch in the salty, alkaline shallows. The towers are made of tufa, limestone deposited underwater when mineral-laden springs bubbled into the alkaline lake. A new aqueduct to Los Angeles that opened in 1941 dropped water levels by more than 40ft, exposing the bizarre towers and nearly destroying the lake. Twenty years of environmental battles forced

ℹ **Mono Lake Committee Information Center/Lee Vining Chamber of Commerce**
Hwy 395 & 3rd St, Lee Vining; tel: (760) 647-6595; www.monolake.org. Open daily 0900–1700, later in summer.

Mono County Tourism has *Motor Touring in the Eastern Sierra-Mono County,* a booklet with suggested tours: *tel: (800) 845-7922; www.monocounty.org/ backroads/index.html*

Inyo County Tourism provides suggested tours in *Motor Touring in the Eastern Sierra and Death Valley: www.inyocounty.us/ InyoMarketing/index.php? page=trip-planning*

🅟 **Mono Lake Tufa State Reserve $**
Tel: (760) 647-6331; www.parks.ca.gov/ ?page_id=514

Mono Basin Bird Chautauqua $
www.birdchautauqua.org, is a fun birding area and hosts a natural history event near the summer solstice. The leading experts on fauna and flora of the Sierra Nevada present hikes, walking tours and talks.

Bodie State Historic Park $ *Hwy 270 (last 3 miles gravel); tel: (760) 647-6445; www.parks.ca.gov/ default.asp?page_id=509. Park open all year, but the road may be closed in winter.*

Opposite
Bodie

LA to cut its water usage and agree to restore Mono Lake to historic levels.

The best place to see the tufa towers is **Mono Lake Tufa State Reserve**, on the south shore. The volcanic cones to the south are the **Mono Craters**, explosion pits, cinder cones and lava flows from California's youngest mountains. A short trail leads up to the rim of **Panum Crater**, about 650 years old. **Lee Vining**, just north, sits next to Hwy 120 east of **Tioga Pass** (summer only) and **Yosemite National Park** (*see page 234*).

Suggested tour

From **Reno**, follow Hwy 395 south to **Carson City**, the twin towns of **Minden** and **Gardnerville** and back into California. The scenic highway continues south over **Devil's Gate Summit** (7519ft) and down to **Bridgeport**, starting point for a detour to **Bodie State Historic Park**. Hwy 395 climbs up over **Conway Summit** (8138ft) before dropping down to **Mono Lake** and **Lee Vining**, then climbing past **June Lake** to **Deadman Summit** (8041ft) and down past **Mammoth Lakes** into the **Owens Valley**, a desert corpse sucked dry to keep Los Angeles green. **Bishop** is the starting point for a side trip to **Laws**. Continue south on Hwy 395 through **Big Pine** and **Independence** to **Lone Pine** and **Mount Whitney**. Take Hwy 136 southeast to **Panamint Springs**, over **Towne Pass** (4956ft) and down into **Death Valley National Park**.

Also worth visiting

Bodie
'Goodbye, God, we are going to Bodie' is how one girl faced the prospect of moving to Bodie in the nineteenth century. In its gold-rush glory during the 1880s, Bodie boasted the widest streets, the meanest men and the most disgusting whisky in the West. A local preacher called the booming town of 10,000 'a sea of sin lashed by tempests of lust and passion'. He probably understated the daily tally of murder and mayhem that wracked California's most remote and lawless outpost. When the gold disappeared, so did the town, along with the churches, saloons, shops, brothels, schools and newspapers. Most people left possessions behind as though they expected to return.

About 170 buildings remain, all in a state of 'arrested decay'. Dusty shop windows are still loaded with merchandise; bedrooms still have tattered lace curtains and sagging mattresses. Pick up a self-guiding brochure for California's official Gold Rush ghost town at the former **Miners' Union Hall**.

Laws Railroad Museum and Historical Site (operated by the Bishop Museum and Historical Society) *Tel: (760) 873-5950; www.lawsmuseum.org.* From Bishop, take Hwy 395 to Hwy 6, drive 4 miles north and east to Silver Canyon Rd. Laws is ½-mile east. *Open daily 1000–1600.* Free.

Laws

The **Laws Railroad Museum and Historical Site** was once a major stop on the narrow-gauge Carson and Colorado Railroad between Carson City, Nevada and Owens Lake. The 11-acre open-air museum preserves the old station, the *Slim Princess*, the last steam locomotive engine to work the line, and other rolling stock. Buildings include a frontier physician's office and dispensary, the station agent's home, Wells Fargo office, library and post office, all furnished with period antiques. The drover's cottage across the road was built for the 1966 Steve McQueen film *Nevada Smith*.

Lake Tahoe and Reno

Ratings

History	●●●●●
Gambling	●●●●○
Scenery	●●●●○
Sport	●●●●○
Children	●●●○○
Lake cruises	●●●○○
Food and drink	●●●○○
Architecture	●○○○○

Lake Tahoe is California Mountain Country at its best, a 12-mile sapphire oval, 6227ft above sea level, more than 1600ft deep and surrounded by snowcapped Sierra peaks laced with hiking, cycling and skiing trails. Although the California–Nevada border divides Lake Tahoe east–west, the real division is north–south. South Shore revolves around Stateline, a miniature Las Vegas just inside Nevada, and the urban clutter of South Lake Tahoe on the California side of the border. North Shore sports a sprinkling of casinos, but the focus is firmly fixed on outdoor activities, from hiking and water-skiing in summer to snowshoeing and snowskiing in winter.

Hwys 28, 50 and 89 link to circle Tahoe, a scenic 72-mile drive that can take 2 hours midweek or most of the day on weekends. The towns of Virginia City, Carson City and Reno, in the historic heart of Nevada, lie just east.

The US National Park Service has *A National Register of Historic Places Travel Itinerary* online for Three Historic Nevada Cities: Carson City, Reno and Virginia City: *www.nps.gov/nr/travel/nevada/nev.htm*

CARSON CITY, NEVADA

ⓘ Carson City CVB Visitors Center
1900 S. Carson St, Ste 100; tel: (775) 687-7410 or (800) 638-2321; www.carson-city.org. Open Mon–Fri 0900–1600, Sat–Sun to 1800.

ⓟ Mormon Station State Historic Park
$ Foothill Rd, Genoa; tel: (775) 782-2590; www.parks.nv.gov/ms.htm. Open daily early May–mid-Oct 1000–1600.

Nevada State Capitol
101 N. Carson St; tel: (775) 687-6800; www.nv.gov/ 2003StateBldgs_Snow.htm.

Ask the Convention & Visitors Bureau for their free self-guided 2½-mile walking and driving maps to the **Kit Carson Trail** historic district, west of Carson St. The tours, narrated on AM radio frequencies, include a home used as a set in John Wayne's final film, *The Shootist* (1976).

Nevada settlement began in 1851 at **Mormon Station State Historic Park**. When silver was discovered beneath what became **Virginia City** (*see page 132*), the Territorial Legislature moved the capitol to **Carson City**, nearer the mines.

The silver-domed **Nevada State Capitol** is open to the public, including the old legislative chambers. **Nevada State Museum** occupies the US Mint where Virginia City silver was turned into legal tender. Exhibits include a mine reproduction, ghost town, minerals, a mint-mark coin collection, guns and a mammoth.

The **Nevada State Railroad Museum $** (*2180 S. Carson St; tel: (775) 687-6953; www.nsrm-friends.org. Open daily 0830–1630. Call to confirm*

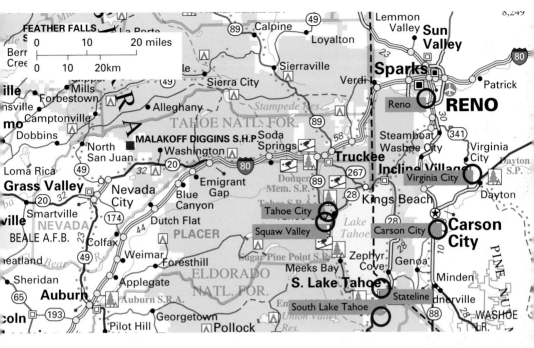

Open during business hours. Free.

Nevada State Museum
$ 600 N. Carson St;
tel: (775) 687-4810;
dmla.clan.lib.nv.us/docs/
museums/cc/carson.htm.
Open daily 0830–1630.

departures for 'steam up' rides) has more than 60 pieces of rolling stock from the Virginia and Truckee Railroad, which ran from Virginia City to Carson City. Historic steam trains and motor cars make short trips in summer.

LAKE TAHOE CIRCUIT

ⓘ **Lake Tahoe
Visitors Authority**
169 Hwy 50, Stateline NV
89449; tel: (775) 588-5900
or (800) 288-2463;
www.bluelaketahoe.com

Most drivers circle Lake Tahoe in a clockwise direction to avoid left turns into car parks. Allow at least a full day for the drive. Must-sees include **Emerald Bay** and **Inspiration Point**, on the southwest shore, and **Cave Rock Tunnel**, **Sand Harbor State Park** and **Zephyr Cove** on the Nevada side. You can request a tailor-made free Visitor Packet from AroundLakeTahoe.com (*www.aroundlaketahoe.com*) from the Lake Tahoe South Shore Chamber of Commerce to give you as much information as you like about Tahoe before travelling.

Tahoe's greatest concentration of hiking trails is on the southwest shore around **Fallen Leaf Lake**. The **Tahoe Rim Trail** circles the lake in 150 ridge-top miles, although parts of the route make pleasant day hikes. The **US Forest Service Visitor Center** (*¾-mile north of Camp Richardson; tel: (530) 543-2674; www.fs.fed.us/r5/ltbmu/recreation. Open daily in summer; call for hours*) offers good recommendations, maps and brochures for everything from easy strolls to high-altitude leg burners.

D L Bliss State Park $ Hwy 89, South Shore; tel: (530) 525-7277; www.parks.ca.gov. Campgrounds open May–Sep.

Emerald Bay State Park $ Hwy 89, South Shore; tel: (530) 541-3030; www.parks.ca.gov. Open daily. **Vikingsholm** $ www.vikingsholm.com. Open daily for guided tours every half-hour 1000–1600 Memorial Day–Sep.

Ed Z'berg-Sugar Pine Point State Park $ 10 miles south of Tahoe City on Hwy 89; tel: (530) 525-7982; www.parks.ca.gov/default.asp?page_id=510. **Hellman-Ehrman Mansion** Open daily for tours Jul–Labor Day, 1100–1600.

For information, ask at the **Lake Tahoe Basin Management Unit Forest Supervisor's Office** (*35 College Dr., South Lake Tahoe; tel: (530) 543-2600. Open Mon–Fri 0800–1630 year-round*). South Shore is dominated by America's only bi-state ski resort, **Heavenly**, with 15 lifts in each state. North Shore has California's greatest concentration of ski resorts. Most ski mountains are open in summer for sightseeing, hiking and mountain biking.

D L Bliss State Park (*South Shore*) has one of Tahoe's most scenic beaches, though the water is icy and the car park fills up early. **Balancing Rock Nature Trail** is a ½-mile loop to a 130-tonne boulder that appears balanced precariously on a granite slab. The **Rubicon Trail** is 4½ miles of spectacular lake views from **Rubicon Point** south to **Emerald Bay**.

Emerald Bay State Park (*South Shore*) surrounds **Emerald Bay**, a shallow, glacier-carved inlet named after its colour. The Bay is best viewed from **Inspiration Point** on Hwy 89. A steep trail (2 miles return) leads from a car park at the north side of the bay down to **Vikingsholm**, a 1929 summer residence built to resemble a 9th-century Nordic castle. Just offshore is **Fanette Island**, with a ruined tea-house. Scuba divers can explore boats and barges in Emerald Bay State Underwater Park.

Ed Z'berg-Sugar Pine Point State Park (*north of Emerald Bay along the west side of Lake Tahoe*) is Lake Tahoe's largest state park. Sugar Pine Point holds several of Tahoe's oldest buildings. **Phipps Cabin** was built in 1872 by early resident William Phipps. The 1903 **Hellman-Ehrman Mansion**, known as the Ehrman (pronounced 'ermine'),

Right
Snowy peaks rise from Emerald Bay

ℹ **Incline Village/
Crystal Bay
Visitors Bureau** 969
Tahoe Blvd, Incline Village,
NV 89451; tel: (775) 832-
1606 or (800) 468-2463;
www.gotahoe.com

**North Lake Tahoe
Visitors & Convention
Bureau** Tahoe City, CA;
tel: (800) 462-5196 or
(530) 581-8703;
www.gotahoenorth.com

**Lake Tahoe-Nevada
State Park** Incline Village
NV; tel: (775) 831-0494;
http://parks.nv.gov/lt.htm

**Nevada Commission
on Tourism** has a
specialised website for ski
resorts, especially those in
Reno and Tahoe, with winter
season information:
http://ski.travelnevada.com

🚌 **Tahoe Rim Trail**
948 Incline Way,
Incline Village, NV 89451;
tel: (775) 298-0012;
www.tahoerimtrail.org

made of local wood and granite quarried from nearby Meeks Bay, is furnished in mid-1930s style. The expansive grounds and the turreted mansion with large sitting porch were used as the opulent Lake Tahoe mansion setting in *Godfather II*.

Incline Village (*North Shore*) is the largest town on Tahoe's Nevada shore, with the closest casinos to Tahoe City and other North Shore hideaways. **Hyatt Regency Lake Tahoe Resort, Spa & Casino $$$** (*Lakeshore & 111 Country Club Dr., Incline Village; tel: (775) 832-1234 or (800) 233-1234; www.laketahoehyatt.com*) is North Shore's most luxurious lakeside hotel and biggest casino.

Lake Tahoe Nevada State Park, a largely undeveloped forest and lakeshore, is dotted with house-sized boulders and occasional patches of sandy beach. **Sand Harbor**, the largest beach, has a small boat dock. Hwy 28 joins Hwy 50 just south of the park to continue around the lake or east toward Carson City.

The 165-mile free **Tahoe Rim Trail** circles Lake Tahoe, offering stunning views of the lake and surrounding countryside. Allow a week to hike the entire trail or spend a few hours walking a short segment. The Tahoe Rim Trail Association arranges shuttle service ($) between several of the more popular trailheads in summer so visitors can walk one way, then get a ride back to their cars.

Hikers, mountain bikers and horses share the trail that was more than 20 years in the making. The trail is narrow – 2ft wide – with varied terrain, track obscured by snow in winter, no predictable source of fresh water and predators like mountain lions (cougars) in their element. Winter hikers and snowshoers carry GPS and quadmaps. The TRT's official summer season begins when snow has melted, in most years from mid-July to late October.

RENO, NEVADA

ℹ **Reno/Sparks
Convention &
Visitors Authority
(RSCVA)** 4001 S. Virginia
St, Reno, NV 89504;
tel: (775) 827-7600 or
(800) 367-7366;
www.visitrenotahoe.com.

 RTC Sierra Spirit
tel: (775) 348-7433;
www.rtcwashoe.com/public-
transportation-11; runs daily
0700–2100 every 10 min and
provides a free yellow bus ride,
with stops from the University
of Nevada campus to
downtown Reno and return.

Reno's slogan, 'The Biggest Little City in the World', blazes from a neon **arch** (*N. Virginia St and Commercial Row*) in the downtown casino district. Reno is also a burgeoning commercial city with a relatively mild winter climate and desert summers made bearable by air-conditioning. Spreading suburbs blend imperceptibly into the town of **Sparks**, which has its own set of casinos along I-80, just east of Reno.

The **National Automobile Museum** is one of America's finest auto collections. Galleries trace the automobile from the 'horseless carriage' of the 1890s through modern and experimental models.

The **Nevada Historical Society Museum** is Nevada's oldest museum. Displays include Native American artefacts, pioneer relics, antique furniture, guns and minerals.

The **Nevada Museum of Art** features touring exhibitions as well as permanent collections of Nevada art and artists. The most striking element in the four-storey museum is the stark black exterior inspired

ⓝ National Automobile Museum $$ *10 S. Lake St; tel: (775) 333-9300; www.automuseum.org. Open Mon–Sat 0930–1730, Sun 1000–1600.*

Nevada Historical Society Museum $ *1650 N. Virginia St; tel: (775) 688-1190; dmla.clan.lib.nv.us/docs/ museums/reno/museum.htm. Open Mon–Sat 1100–1700.*

Nevada Museum of Art $$ *160 W. Liberty St; tel: (775) 329-3333; www.nevadaart.org. Open Tue–Sun 1000–1700, Thu to 2000.*

Great Basin Adventure *Open Memorial Day weekend–early Sep.*

Wilbur D May Center *Rancho San Rafael Regional Park, 1595 N. Sierra St; tel: (775) 785-5961; www.maycenter.com*

by the nearby Black Rock Desert. A Truckee River **Arts District** around the NMA has galleries, coffee houses and restaurants and **River Walk** along the Truckee River.

Pyramid Lake, 30 miles long by 9 miles wide (*36 miles north on Hwy 445*), is the remnant of a prehistoric lake that once covered central Nevada. The sparkling lake, named after a pyramid-shaped formation, is surrounded by sagebrush and brown sandstone mountains, but has some of Nevada's finest trout fishing.

Truckee River Whitewater Park (*Truckee River, Lake St-Idlewild Park*) is a shady riverside park for downtown office workers and casino habitués surrounding a ½-mile river kayak course with Class II and III rapids, 11 drop-pools for manoeuvres, and gates for timed races. Park and course are deserted in winter and thronged on summer weekends.

The **Wilbur D May Center** includes the **Wilbur May Museum**, **Arboretum and Botanical Garden** and **Great Basin Adventure**. The museum is a hodgepodge of tourist trinkets and *objets d'art* collected by department store heir Wilbur D May. The botanical garden re-creates a dozen different eastern Sierra Nevada plant habitats; Great Basin Adventure is a children's park.

Accommodation and food in Reno

Downtown casinos offer good-value accommodation midweek, but prices jump dramatically at the weekend. Special offers appear in the *Datebook* section of the *San Francisco Chronicle* (Sun), or contact the RSCVA.

The local speciality is Basque, thanks to generations of Basque shepherds who have settled across Nevada. The best is **Louis' Basque Corner** *$$ 301 E. Fourth St; tel: (775) 323-7203. Open daily for lunch and dinner.*

Casino buffets (breakfast, lunch or dinner) are barely more expensive than fast food. The best restaurant in town is La Strada $$$ *Eldorado Hotel & Casino; tel: (800) 879-8879; www.eldoradoreno.com, open daily for dinner.* Northern Italian dishes from the owners of the Ferrari-Carrano Winery in California's Dry Creek Valley (*see page 166*).

SOUTH LAKE TAHOE

ⓘ South Lake Tahoe Chamber of Commerce *3066 Lake Tahoe Blvd, South Lake Tahoe; tel: (530) 541-5255; www.tahoeinfo.com*

South Lake Tahoe (*South Shore*) is a collection of hotels, motels, restaurants and businesses sprawling from **The Y**, the junction of Hwys 50 and 89. South Lake Tahoe has the bulk of Tahoe's accommodation, restaurants and other tourist services, and casinos are a free shuttle ride away just across the border in Stateline, Nevada.

Tallac Historic Site is Tahoe's original resort area. The site contains several late 19th- and early 20th-century mansions, when Tahoe was the elegant escape of choice for upper-crust Californians. The grounds are open all year; buildings are open in summer.

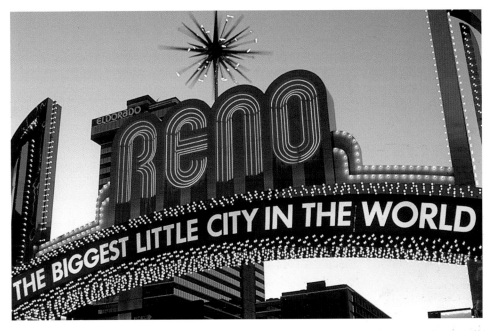

 Taylor Creek US Forest Service Visitor Center
3 miles north of South Lake Tahoe, on the lake side of Hwy 89; tel: (530) 543-2674; www. fs.fed.us/r5/ltbmu/contact. Open daily mid-Jun–Sep.

US Forest Service Headquarters
Lake Tahoe Basin Management Unit, 35 College Dr., South Lake Tahoe, CA 96150-4500; tel: (530) 543-2600; www. fs.fed.us/r5/ltbmu/contact. Open Mon–Fri 0800–1630.

Tallac Historic Site
Hwy 89, 3 miles north of The Y; tel: (530) 541-5227; www.fs.fed.us/r5/ ltbmu/recreation/tallac. Grounds open daily.
Museum $ *Open 1000–1600 Memorial Day–Sep.*

Pope-Tevis Estate is the most lavish of the mansions with tours and living history programmes late June through September. **Valhalla** features wide verandahs and walk-in fireplaces; the interior is open only during special events or cultural performances.

The **US Forest Service Visitor Center** is the best source of information on outdoor activities around Lake Tahoe. Rangers lead nature walks and campfire programmes daily in summer; there are also a number of self-guiding hikes.

Inside the Visitor Center, **Taylor Creek Stream Profile Chamber** offers a glimpse beneath a genuine mountain stream. Bright-red kokanee salmon make their way from Lake Tahoe past the chamber in October to spawning beds farther upstream.

South Lake Tahoe also has a series of fine beaches, though the icy water keeps most people on the sand even in midsummer. The best people-watching is at **Jamison Beach** (*Camp Richardson, 2½ miles north of The Y*), **Nevada Beach** (*Elk Point Rd, 1 mile east of Stateline*) and **El Dorado Beach**, in the centre of town.

The **Heavenly Gondola** provides the best views across Lake Tahoe from the mid-station observation deck, perched 9123ft high on the slopes of Monument Peak. The gondola makes the 2.4-mile run from the base village near Lake Tahoe and the Stateline casinos in 12 minutes. The Carson Valley spreads to the east and the Desolation Wilderness to the west, with the entire expanse of Lake Tahoe directly below. In winter, the gondola provides access to the largest ski resort in California; in summer it provides a lift to miles of scenic hiking trails.

For superb lake photography, visit **The Jon Paul Gallery** (*4000 Lake Tahoe Blvd, Ste C-18; tel: (530) 544-4269; www.jonpaulgallery.com*).

Heavenly Gondola
$$ *Hwy 50, South Lake Tahoe; tel: (775) 586-7000; www.skiheavenly.com. Open daily.*

Lake Tahoe Visitors Authority
Tel: (530) 544-5050 or (800) 288-2463; www.bluelaketahoe.com, handles bookings for the South Shore.

Accommodation and food in South Lake Tahoe

Marriott Timber Lodge Tahoe $$ *4100 Lake Tahoe Blvd; tel: (530) 542-6600 or (888) 236-2427; www.marriott.com,* is next to Heavenly Gondola base.

Embassy Suites Lake Tahoe Resort & Ski $$$ *4130 Lake Tahoe Blvd; tel: (530) 544-5400 or (800) 362-2779; www.embassysuites.com,* is next to Stateline.

Evan's American Gourmet Café $$$ *536 Emerald Bay Rd; tel: (530) 542-1990; www.evanstahoe.com; open daily,* offers an eclectic mix of Italian, Caribbean, Asian and Southwestern dishes and a large wine list. **Scusa! on Ski Run $$** *1142 Ski Run Blvd; tel: (530) 542-0100, open daily,* is Tahoe's top Italian restaurant despite the casino-like lighting. **Sprouts Natural Foods Café $** *3123 Harrison Ave; tel: (530) 541-6969, open daily,* is an easy stop for picnic ingredients.

Marriott Grand Residence Club $$$ *1001 Heavenly Village Way; tel: (530) 542-8400 or (888) 236-2427; www.marriott.com,* is the luxury resort in South Lake Tahoe.

SQUAW VALLEY

Squaw Valley USA & Cable Car $$
Squaw Valley; tel: (530) 583-6985 or (800) 403-0206; www.squaw.com. Open daily, call or check website for hours.

Aerial trams make it easy to explore the near-vertical mountains that lured the 1960 Olympic Winter Games to Squaw Valley. The **Squaw Valley USA Cable Car** climbs 2000ft to **High Camp Bath & Tennis Club,** with ice-skating, swimming, a climbing wall, tennis, restaurants and killer views. Skiing, hiking and mountain biking are among Tahoe's best. Down below, golf courses and hotels have taken over what was one of Tahoe's most tranquil corners.

Accommodation and food in Squaw Valley

River Ranch Lodge $$–$$$ *Hwy 89 and Alpine Meadows Rd; tel: (530) 583-4264 or (866) 991-9912; www.riverranchlodge.com*, is an old-fashioned inn on the Truckee River, midway between Squaw Valley and Alpine Meadows ski areas. **River Ranch Lodge Restaurant $$** *Open daily* for dinner, is a long-time local favourite overlooking the Truckee.

PlumpJack Squaw Valley Inn $$$ *1920 Squaw Valley Rd; tel: (530) 583-1576 or (800) 323-7666; www.plumpjack.com*, has a sophisticated restaurant at its ski resort.

The **Resort at Squaw Creek $$$** *400 Squaw Creek Rd; tel: (530) 583-6300 or (800) 327-3353; www.squawcreek.com*, is Tahoe's most luxurious resort, complete with adult toys like a private golf course and ski lift.

STATELINE, NEVADA

Stateline is the Nevada side of South Lake Tahoe, dominated by the jangling slot machines and flashing neon of **MontBleu Resort Casino & Spa** *(tel: (775) 588-3515 or (888) 829-7630; www.montbleuresort.com)*, **Harrah's** *(tel: (800) 427-7247)*, **Harvey's** *(tel: (800) 427-8397 both on www.harrahs.com)*, **Horizon** *(tel: (800) 648-3322; www.horizoncasino.com)* and a handful of smaller casinos.

Casino accommodation packages can be good value midweek and the buffets are always popular with teenagers and others with gargantuan appetites. Lounges and showrooms offer scaled-down versions of Las Vegas spectacles and the gambling is non-stop. Most restaurants and other services are in South Lake Tahoe.

Left
Pioneer transport

TAHOE CITY

Gatekeeper's Museum $ *130 W. Lake Blvd, William B Layton Park, Tahoe City; tel: (530) 583-1762; www.northtahoemuseums.org. Open mid-Jun–Aug daily 1100–1700; May and Sep Wed–Sun; other times by appointment; call to confirm hours.*

Tahoe City (*North Shore*) is the hub of North Shore. Hwy 89 meets Hwy 28 at the western edge of town and **Fanny Bridge**, named after the view pedestrians present as they peer down at the enormous trout in the Truckee River, which flows from lakeshore gates to Pyramid Lake, in the desert near Reno.

The gates were once opened and closed by a gatekeeper who lived at **Gatekeeper's Museum**, a reconstruction of the original 1910 lodgepole pine cabin. The museum covers pioneer and Native American settlement in the area, with the extensive Marion Steinbach Indian Basket Museum collection.

ⓘ **North Lake Tahoe**
Resort Association
380 N. Lake Blvd,
Tahoe City, CA 96145;
tel: (888) 434-1262 or
(530) 583-3494;
www.gotahoenorth.com

Road conditions
Tel: (800) 427-7623
(California only); www.dot.
ca.gov/hq/roadinfo. For
Nevada highways: tel: 511
or from outside Nevada:
(877) 687-6237;
www.safetravelusa.com/nv

One of the most popular summer pastimes is rafting the Truckee River from Tahoe City to River Ranch Lodge. Whitewater enthusiasts need not apply – the placid 4-mile, 3-hour trip is more suited to inner tubes and air mattresses than crash helmets. Operators provide raft, life jacket, paddle and a lift back to Tahoe City, but arrive before 1100 to avoid the worst of the crowds. Lunch or drinks at the River Ranch Lodge Restaurant is the traditional float finale. The **Truckee River Bike Trail** offers similar scenery from land.

Watson Cabin Curios (*560 N. Lake Blvd, Tahoe City; tel: (530) 583-1762; www.northtahoemuseums.org/watson.aspx*), built in 1908, is the oldest North Shore building still in its original location and is now the Gatekeepers Museum store.

Accommodation and food in Tahoe City

Bridgetender Tavern and Grill $ *65 W. Lake Blvd, Fanny Bridge; tel: (530) 583-3342, lunch and dinner daily*, is Tahoe City's busiest tavern, with fine burgers.

Fire Sign Café $$ *1785 W. Lake Blvd; tel: (530) 583-0871, breakfast and lunch daily*, is a long-time local breakfast favourite, with house-smoked salmon.

Christy Hill $$$ *115 Grove St; tel: (530) 583-8551; www.christyhill.com, dinner only Tue–Sun*, is one of Tahoe's best restaurants with traditional California combinations and sunset views over the lake.

Opposite
Lake Tahoe

Lake Cruises

Traffic and heavy lakeshore development can make the drive around Lake Tahoe disappointing. A more scenic way to tour Tahoe is from the lake itself. Commercial boats ply the lake with breakfast cruises, several trips during the day, and sunset/dinner cruises. Some boats also ferry skiers in winter, and you can parasail above the lake in summer, from Zephyr Cove. Advance bookings are required all year.

MS Dixie II $$ *760 Hwy 50, Zephyr Cove; tel: (888) 896-3830; www.zephyrcove.com.* A replica paddlewheeler sails to Emerald Bay all year.

Tahoe Gal $$ *Lighthouse Marina, 850 N. Lake Blvd, Tahoe City; tel: (800) 218-2464; www.tahoegal.com.* Breakfast, scenic and dinner/dance cruises on the North Shore, *mid-May–Oct.*

Tahoe Queen $$ *Zephyr Cove; tel: (888) 896-3830; www.zephyrcove.com.* This sternwheeler once hauled cotton on the Mississippi River.

Woodwind Sailing Cruises $$ *Camp Richardson and Tahoe Keys Marina; tel: (888) 867-6394; www.sailwoodwind.com.* Yacht and powerboat sailing cruises.

The **North Lake Tahoe Resort Association** (*tel: (888) 434-1262; www.gotahoenorth.com*) makes bookings for the North Shore. Last-minute accommodation *may* be available north of Tahoe City towards the towns of **Tahoe Vista** and **Kings Beach**, but advance bookings are advisable all year and necessary at weekends, holidays and Jun–Aug.

VIRGINIA CITY, NEVADA

ⓘ Virginia City Convention & Tourism Authority
86 South C St, Virginia City, NV 89440; tel: (775) 847-4386 or (800) 718-7587; www.virginiacity-nv.org. Open daily 1000–1700.

Chollar Mine $
S. B St; www.chollarmine.com. See website for more information.

Liberty Engine Company No. 1, The Comstock Firemen's Museum 125 S. C St; tel: (775) 847-0454; www.comstockfiremuseum.com. Open daily 1000–1600.

Julia Bulette Red Light Museum $ 5 N. C St, downstairs from Mandarin Gardens Chinese Restaurant; tel: (775) 847-9288. Open daily 1000–2100.

Ponderosa Saloon Mine Tour $ 106 S. C St; tel: (775) 847-0757. Open daily.

Virginia and Truckee Railroad $ Washington and F Sts; tel: (775) 847-0380; www.virginiatruckee.com. Open daily 1030–1745 May–Oct.

Ⓐ Piper's Opera House $ B and Union Sts; tel: (775) 847-0433. Open daily 1000–1700 mid-May–late Oct for guided tours. Call to verify hours.

Home to 30,000 residents and 110 saloons during the 1860s–1880s Comstock Lode silver-mining boom years, Virginia City nearly died when the mines played out around the turn of the 20th century. Slopes above, beneath and around the town are riddled with hundreds of miles of unmapped mine shafts.

The almost-ghost town resurrected itself as a tourist destination after World War II, building on a reputation laid by former residents Mark Twain and Bret Harte. Twain's novel *Roughing It* recounts his days as a sometime miner, sometime journalist in Virginia City. The best place to see what Twain and company endured is the **Chollar Mine**, an 1861 Comstock Lode mine with original square-set timbers. Wear good walking shoes and expect mud in the tunnel.

Comstock Firemen's Museum displays antique fire wagons and fire-fighting equipment in the original volunteer fire hall. **Julia Bulette Red Light Museum** is all that remains of what was once the biggest and busiest red-light district between Chicago and San Francisco.

Piper's Opera House was the cultural centre of the entire West during the 1880s. Highlights include original 19th-century scenery and furnishings and a floor built on ore cart springs to dampen dynamite blasts in the tunnels deep below. Most of those old tunnels have flooded or collapsed, but the **Ponderosa Saloon** offers guided tours of a small section of mine directly below the building.

The **Storey County Courthouse** (*B St near Union St*) acknowledges the legal realities of the profitable boom years through the 1880s – the statue of Justice that adorns the building façade shows her without her traditional blindfold.

Virginia and Truckee Railroad trains travel part of the railway's original line to Carson City. The V&TR runs through countryside just as rugged, just as dry and just as starkly beautiful as it was when Mark Twain worked the same hills. The entire railway line to Carson City is being restored. Service runs to the town of Gold Hill.

Early-September visitors should be prepared for the crowds and zaniness of the **Virginia City International Camel Races** (*tel: (775) 847-7008*).

Suggested tour

Circle **LAKE TAHOE** ❶ on Hwys 28, 50 and 89 and continue northeast to **CARSON CITY** ❷ on Hwy 50, with awesome desert views snaking down the eastern side of the Sierra Nevada. Take Hwy 395 north to **RENO** ❸, or, for a more scenic route, follow Hwy 50 east to Hwy 341/342 and **VIRGINIA CITY** ❹ before looping north to **RENO** ❸.

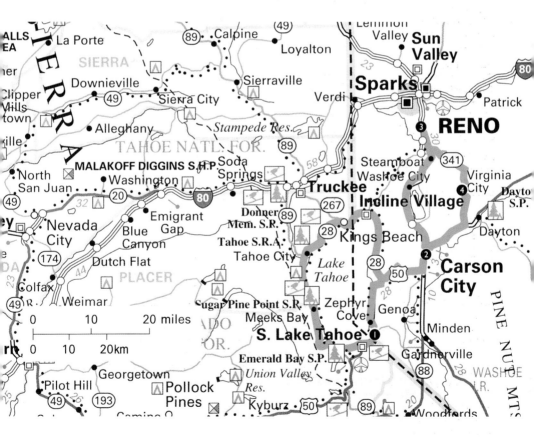

San Francisco

Ratings

Food and drink	●●●●
Nightlife	●●●●
Shopping	●●●●
Architecture	●●●
Art	●●●
Children	●●●
Museums	●●●
Parks	●●●

For those who live here, San Francisco is *never* 'Frisco'; it's *The City*, a refuge of civilisation in an otherwise Wild West. It was, after all, The City the world encountered on the way to Gold Rush riches and The City where the successful few returned to splurge on real estate along the Barbary Coast. After The City was destroyed by earthquake in 1906, it rebuilt itself to host the 1915 Panama-Pacific Exhibition, then rebuilt reality.

The Beatniks of the 1950s shook American society, political demonstrations in the 1960s shook government, the 1967 Summer of Love shook the world and in 2004 Mayor Gavin Newsom shook up the status quo by mandating same-sex unions. Los Angeles may be California's cultural capital, but San Francisco remains its fractious soul, an aggregation of minorities who dislike each other but still manage to live together. Precipitous hills, a sparkling bay, bridges, cable cars, 3000 restaurants and benign tolerance for almost anything short of mayhem are eternal touchstones.

Getting there and getting around

ⓘ San Francisco Convention & Visitors Bureau (SFCVB) *Visitor Information Center, 900 Market St, Hallidie Plaza, Lower Level, corner of Powell and Market Sts; tel: (415) 391-2000; www.onlyinsanfrancisco.com. Open year-round Mon–Fri 0900–1700, weekends 0900–1500 (closed Sun Nov–Apr). 24-hour recorded event information: (415) 391-2001.*

San Francisco International Airport (SFO) *(tel: (800) 435-9736 or (650) 821-8211; www.flysfo.com)*, is 14 miles south on Hwy 101. Taxi to downtown $37. Door-to-door van service $14–$17 single. Free shuttles to car-hire locations and airport hotels.

BART (Bay Area Rapid Transit) *(www.bart.gov)* offers inexpensive public transportation to downtown San Francisco, the East Bay and SFO. For area-wide transportation, *tel: 511 (or (510) 817-1717 outside the area; www.511.org)*.

Parking

Public parking is scarce downtown. Fees range from $2–$20 per hour. Best bets are city-operated garages: **Sutter Stockton Garage** *444 Stockton St, near Union Square*; **Fifth & Mission Garage** *833 Mission St, between Union Square and Yerba Buena Gardens*; **Vallejo Street Garage** *766 Vallejo St*; **Portsmouth Square Garage** *733 Kearny, Clay and Kearny Sts*. Charges are exorbitant at **Fisherman's Wharf** and **Pier 39**.

Municipal ier

Hyde Street Pier

Pier 39 AQUARIUM BY THE BAY

Angel Island

PIER 35

Bay Cruises

Fisherman's Wharf NAL Alcatraz

PIER 33

Aquatic Park

THE CANNERY ANCHORAGE

Jefferson Street

Maritime National Historical Park herman's Wharf

NATIONAL MARITIME MUSEUM

North Point Street

GHIRARDELLI SQUARE

BAY STREET

Palace of the Legion of Honor Street

Golden Gate Park Chestnut Street

Golden Gate Bridge Lombard Street

GGNRA STREET HILL Greenwich Street

Fort Point Filbert Street

Exploratorium UNION STREET

Russian Hill Green Street

Vallejo Street

Lombard Street

COIT TOWER

Filbert Street

THE EMBARCADERO (HERB CAEN WAY)

Washington Square

North Beach ON STREET

Green Street

Davis Street

Front Street

Vallejo Street

Broadway

North Beach

Beach Blanket Babylon Blvd

Columbus Avenue

Broadway

The Beat Museum

Pacific

JACKSON Street SQUARE

Ferry Building

Nob Hill

Pacific Avenue

Jackson Street

Jackson

WASHINGTON STREET

Portsmouth Square

Cable Car Barn

Chinatown

TRANS-AMERICA PYRAMID

Sansome STREET

BATTERY STREET

Front Street

Davis Street

EMBARCADERO CENTER

Van Ness Avenue

Franklin Street

Polk Street

Larkin Street

HYDE STREET

Leavenworth Street

Jones Street

Taylor Street

MASON STREET

Powell Street

STOCKTON STREET

Grant Avenue

Kearney Street

Montgomery Street

M BART/ Muni

SOMA

WASHINGTON STREET

Clay Street

Sacramento Street

CALIFORNIA STREET

GRACE CATHEDRAL

CHINATOWN

Union Square

Financial District

Spear Street

Main Street

BEALE

Pine Street

CROCKER GALLERIA

Bush Street

101

Sutter Street

Union Square

Fremont Street

First Street

STREET

Post Street

M MONTGOMERY ST BART/Muni Metro

GEARY STREET

O'Farrell Street

ST MARY'S CATHEDRAL

Ellis Street

Contemporary Jewish Museum

POWELL ST BART/Muni

Yerba Buena Gardens Complex

Museum of the African Diaspora

Railway Museum

Eddy Street

HALLIDIE PLAZA

SFMOMA

Cartoon Art Museum

80

Turk Street

MARKET STREET

OLD MINT

SAN FRANCISCO SHOPPING CENTRE

COND Street

Golden Gate Avenue

MISSION STREET

FOURTH STREET

South Park

Asian Art Museum

CITY HALL

Civic Center

MISSION STREET

Howard Street

Fifth Street

Folsom Street

M CIVIC CENTER BART/Muni Metro

GROVE STREET

SIXTH STREET

Seventh Street

0   1   2 miles

0   1   2km

EMERGENCY HOSPITAL

Gough Street

Hayes Street

VAN NESS

de Young Museum

California Academy of Sciences

The Castro luni Metro

The Mission

Museum of Craft and Folk Art

EIGHTH

Bryant St

Brannan Street

Street

CALTRANS RAILROAD STATION

01

101

511 *tel: 511* or *(510) 817-1717;* www.511.org; provides area travel and transit information, fares, weather reports and highway construction alerts.

Street parking is nearly impossible in Chinatown, North Beach, Fisherman's Wharf and Union Square, scarce elsewhere. Parking meters accept quarters, dimes and nickels, good for 15–60 mins. Try to park and explore on foot rather than driving, or use the Municipal Railway (MUNI) transport when possible.

Driving

One-way streets, steep hills and lack of parking turn driving into a challenge. Coloured signs point the way to key areas: a green outline of Italy for **North Beach**; a red Chinese lantern for **Chinatown**; an orange crab for **Fisherman's Wharf**; a blue Victorian house for **Union Street** and a white female statue for **Union Square**.

Public transport

The Municipal Railway, or **MUNI** (*tel: (415) 673-6864; www.sfmta.com/cms/home/sfmta.php*), reaches most major tourist attractions, but schedules can be erratic. **Buses** follow numbered routes on city streets. **Metro, light rail and streetcars** follow lettered routes underground in the city centre and on the surface in outlying districts. Historic streetcars from many countries and US cities ply the F-Line along Market Street and the Embarcadero to Fisherman's Wharf. Trolleys are powered by overhead wires. **Cable cars** serve Nob Hill, Fisherman's Wharf, Aquatic Park and California Street. **Muni Passport** (*tel: (415) 923-6050; www.sfmta.com/cms/mfares/passports.htm*) offers one-, three- or seven-day discounts. BART, the Bay Area Rapid Transit (*tel: (415) 989-2278; www.bart.gov*), provides service from SFO and San Francisco beneath the bay to Oakland and other East Bay cities. Fares vary by distance. **San Francisco CityPass $$** (*www.citypass.com*) offers seven days of Muni and Cable Car transit, a Bay Cruise and admission to four museums.

Below
Golden Gate bridge

Ferries

Blue & Gold Fleet (*tel: (415) 705-5555; www.blueandgoldfleet.com*) departs from Pier 39/41 and the Ferry Building, *foot of Market St*, for SBC Park (in Giants' baseball season, Apr, Sept–Oct); the East Bay, Sausalito, Angel Island, Tiburon, Six Flags Marine World (*Vallejo*) and sightseeing cruises. **Red and White Fleet** (*tel: (415) 673-2900; www.redandwhite.com*) has around-the-bay cruises from Pier 431/2. **Alcatraz Cruises** (*tel: (415) 981-7625; www.alcatrazcruises.com*) operates from Pier 33 to Alcatraz Island. **Golden Gate Transit** (*tel: (415) 921-5858; http://goldengateferry.org*) serves Sausalito and Larkspur (Marin County, north of San Francisco) from the Ferry Building.

Sights

Alcatraz Island $$
www.nps.gov/alcatraz.
For tours: tel: (415) 981-
7625; www.alcatrazcruises.
com, departs from Pier 33.

Angel Island State Park
tel: (415) 435-1915;
www.parks.ca.gov/
default.asp?page-id=468;
www.angelisland.org

Asian Art Museum $$$
200 Larkin St, Civic Center
Plaza; tel: (415) 581-3500;
www.asianart.org. Open
Tue–Sun 1000–1700, Thu
1000–2100. Free admission
first Sun of month.

Bay Quackers $$ from
2800 Leavenworth St., The
Anchorage Mall; tel: (415)
431-3825;
www.bayquackers.com

Alcatraz Island

The list of prisoners incarcerated in the infamous federal penitentiary reads like a *Who's Who* of Hollywood celebrity criminals. Al 'Scarface' Capone, Robert 'Bird Man of Alcatraz' Stroud and George 'Machine Gun' Kelly were among the 1554 convicts who spent an average of eight years within sight of San Francisco, yet completely out of touch.

The tiny island is 1½ miles offshore, accessible only by boat. Alcatraz Cruises, with the National Park Service, operates daily self-guided tours of what was once touted as America's only 'escape-proof' prison, as well as a refurbished wardens' wives' garden.

Visitors may wander freely through the former cellblocks, including the 'dark holes' or solitary confinement cells used to punish prisoners. To appreciate fully the dank, depressing atmosphere of Alcatraz, take a **self-guided audio tour** narrated by former prison guards. An evening tour is eerie and evocative. The pervasive security apparently worked. Only 36 prisoners tried to escape: ten were killed in the attempt; 21 captured; and five were never found.

Angel Island

Once the main port of entry from Asia, this was the West Coast equivalent of Ellis Island Immigration Station. The largest island in San Francisco Bay is a rural state park with stunning views of San Francisco, Alcatraz and the Bay Area. Facilities include restored **Angel Island Immigration Station**, with its depiction of the suffering of Chinese immigrants under exclusion laws, picnic grounds, a campground, hiking and cycling trails and a narrated tram ride (*tel: (415) 897-0715, ext 3*) around the island. Access is by private boat or ferry service.

Asian Art Museum

The West's best and most prestigious Asian art collections are in San Francisco's Civic Center. Architect Gae Aulenti, designer of Paris's Musée d'Orsay, took an existing Beaux Arts main library building and revamped the interior with skylights and modern galleries. Of the museum's 13,000 artefacts, 2500 are on permanent display, emphasising Buddhism, trade and regional crafts from most of Asia.

Bay Cruises

The budget version is a commuter ferry ride. Bigger spenders can choose from the official Blue & Gold Fleet tour that circles beneath the **Golden Gate Bridge** and the **San Francisco-Oakland Bay Bridge** with views of **Alcatraz**, **Angel Island**, **Treasure Island** and the **San Francisco waterfront**, as well as luxury yacht cruises and overnight escapes (*see Ferries, page 136*). **Bay Quackers** bright-yellow World War II amphibious vehicle tour drives from Fisherman's Wharf to AT&T

The Beat Museum
*540 Broadway at
Columbus Ave, North Beach;
tel: (800) 537-6822 or
(831) 372-4911;
www.thebeatmuseum.org.
Open daily 1000–2200.*

**Cable Car Barn &
Museum** *1201 Mason St at
Washington St;
tel: (415) 474-1887;
www.cablecarmuseum.org.
Open daily 1000–1700,
1000–1800 Apr–Sep. Free.*

**California Academy of
Sciences** $$ *55 Music
Concourse Dr., Golden Gate
Park; tel: (415) 379-8000;
www.calacademy.org.
Open daily.*

Cartoon Art Museum $
*655 Mission St; tel: (415)
227-8666;
www.cartoonart.org. Open
Tue–Sun 1100–1700. First
Tue of month is 'Pay What
You Wish Day'.*

Cruisin' the Castro $$
*Tel: (415) 225-1821;
www.cruisinthecastro.com.
The Castro District's
must-do tour. Open
Tue–Sat 1000–1200.
Reservations required.*

Park, then launches into San Francisco Bay where game passengers can pilot the 'boat'.

The Beat Museum

Beat artefacts are lovingly displayed in North Beach, Ground Zero for the 1950s beatniks, with correspondence, photographs, books and other personal items that bring the era to life.

Cable Cars

San Francisco's original mechanised public transport still climbs halfway to the stars up **Nob Hill** between the Bay and the turnaround at **Hallidie Plaza** (*Powell and Market Sts*) and along California St. The **Hyde Street Line** runs to **Aquatic Park** (*Beach St between Hyde St and Van Ness Ave*) for easy access to **Fisherman's Wharf**, the historic ships at **Hyde Street Pier** in **San Francisco Maritime National Historical Park** and **Ghirardelli Square**, a former bayside chocolate factory.

Queue up (sometimes for hours) to board at the end of each cablecar line or follow the locals who walk a couple of blocks up the street to climb aboard without waiting. To see how the system works, visit the **Cable Car Barn**. Don't miss the gallery overlooking the 14ft pulleys that haul miles of steel cable beneath city streets to power the cable cars at a constant 9mph. The **Cable Car Museum** in one corner of the Barn displays the history of the system.

California Academy of Sciences

The oldest scientific institution in the Western US (1874) has returned to Golden Gate Park in a new complex with a grass and wildflower-landscaped roof, aquarium, planetarium, natural history exhibits and a domed rainforest.

Cartoon Art Museum

A museum devoted to cartoon art, with 6000 original works and cheerful enthusiasm. Look for comic books, editorial cartoons, cartoon strips, animations, advertisements, greeting cards and the odd video.

Castro District

For a quarter of a century, The Castro (neighbourhood centres around Castro and Market Sts), as it's known, has been a mecca for the gay (and lesbian and transgender) lifestyle, with restaurants, clubs, stores and services sensitively serving a community that has lovingly preserved some of the most beautiful Victorian residences in the city.

Chinatown

What began as a shanty town of Chinese miners expelled from the gold fields around 1850 has become the largest Chinese community outside Asia (*Pine St to North Beach between Kearny and Powell Sts*). Dr

Above
San Francisco Conservatory of flowers

Chinatown
www.sanfranciscochinatown.com

Contemporary Jewish Museum (CJM) $$ *736 Mission St (SOMA); tel: (415) 655-7800; www.thecjm.org. Open Fri–Tue 1100–1730; Thu 1300–2030.*

de Young Museum $$ *50 Hagiwara Tea Garden Dr.; tel: (415) 750-3600; www.famsf.org/deyoung. Open Tue–Sun 0930–1715. Free first Tue of the month.*

Exploratorium $$ *Palace of Fine Arts, 3601 Lyon St at Marina Blvd; tel: (415) 561-0360 (recorded information); www.exploratorium.edu. Open Tue–Sun 1000–1700. Tactile Dome charges additional admission.*

Ferry Building *The Embarcadero at the foot of Market St; tel: (415) 693-0996; www.ferrybuildingmarketplace.com*

Ferry Plaza Farmers' Market *Tel: (415) 291-3276; www.ferryplazafarmersmarket.com. Operates Tue 1000–1400, Sat 0800–1400.*

Sun Yat Sen planned the revolution that became the Chinese Nationalist Republic from a tiny building on Spofford Alley. More recently, Chinatown's Waverly Place featured prominently in San Franciscan Amy Tan's best-selling novel *The Joy Luck Club*. Place names used in the book are as real as the slap of mah jong tiles that can still be heard through neighbourhood doorways.

Grant Ave, Chinatown's official high street, is a tourist trap. Stockton St, one block west, is piled high with vegetables, live fish, smoked ducks and other necessities. *Dim sum* (filled dumplings), noodles and Chinese bakeries are a sure bet for delicious local colour.

Contemporary Jewish Museum

The shimmering blue block in the Yerba Buena Arts District, a section of a refurbished power substation, changes colour with the sky as planned by designer Daniel Libeskind to house exhibitions of commissioned and other work reflecting Jewish culture.

de Young Museum

The copper-clad museum and free (cityscape) observatory tower in Golden Gate Park has 17th- to 20th-century American art, collections from the Americas, the Pacific and Africa, and important textile collections.

Exploratorium and Palace of Fine Arts

This museum of science, art and perception is designed for children, but adults are just as eager to get their hands on 500 do-it-yourself exhibits. The highlight is the **Tactile Dome**, moving by touch through a maze of shapes and textures in pitch blackness. The Exploratorium adjoins the beautiful Palace of Fine Arts, built to resemble a classical ruin for the 1915 **Panama-Pacific Exposition**.

Ferry Building

Say 'Farmers' Market' in this food-loving city and this is the one everyone thinks of – held daily, but crowded with shoppers, foodies and chefs on Tuesday and Saturday mornings. Inside the Ferry Building, restored to 1898 glory, is a food-hall corridor marketplace of 30-odd individual local purveyors of crafted foods. Restaurants offer a spot to dine on Vietnamese (at **The Slanted Door**), and **Book Passage** stocks a selection to browse through while waiting until a ferry is ready to depart to the East Bay.

(H) Fisherman's Wharf
*Jefferson and Taylor
Sts; take a cable car or
historic F-Line Streetcar.
Open daily. Free.*

USS Pampanito $$ *East
side of Pier 45, Fisherman's
Wharf; tel: (415) 775-1943;
www.maritime.org/pamphome.
htm. Open daily, call for
hours.*

**Fort Point National
Historic Site** *Golden Gate
National Recreation Area
(GGNRA); tel: (415) 556-
1693; www.nps.gov/fopo.
Open Fri–Sun 1000–1700.
Free.*

Golden Gate Bridge
*Hwy 101 between San
Francisco and Marin County.
$5 auto toll southbound,
pedestrians and cyclists free.*

**Golden Gate National
Recreation Area**
*Tel: (415) 561-4700;
www.nps.gov/goga. Call for
hours and location of specific
areas of GGNRA. Free.*

Golden Gate Park
*Stanyan St between Fulton St
and Lincoln Ave.*

Japanese Tea Garden $
Hagiwara Tea Garden Drive.

**San Francisco
Botanical Garden at
Strybing Arboretum**
*9th Ave at Lincoln Way,
Golden Gate Park; tel: (415)
661-1316; www.
sfbotanicalgarden.org. Open
Mon–Fri 0800–1630,
Sat–Sun 1000–1700.
Free guided walks daily at
1330. Free.*

**Conservatory of
Flowers $** *JFK Dr.,
Golden Gate Park;
tel: (415) 666-7001; www.
conservatoryofflowers.org.
Open Tue–Sun 0900–1630.*

Fisherman's Wharf

This one-time home to San Francisco's commercial fishing fleet now has more T-shirt and souvenir shops than fishing boats. The USS *Pampanito* submarine is open for tours. Explore on foot between **Pier 39**, **Fisherman's Wharf**, **Aquatic Park** and the **San Francisco Maritime National Historical Park**, **Ghirardelli Square**, **The Cannery** and **Fort Mason**.

Fort Point National Historic Site

The red-brick fort beneath the Golden Gate Bridge was built to defend San Francisco during America's Civil War, 1861–5. Costumed guides re-create life inside the fort with cannon-loading demonstrations, while waves sweeping through the **Golden Gate** blast spray 30ft into the air.

Golden Gate Bridge

The bridge opened in 1937, linking the gap above the tides churning through the Golden Gate, the narrow passage into San Francisco Bay. 'Golden' refers to the Golden Horn in Istanbul, after which adventurer-explorer John Frémont named the entrance in 1846. The bridge is painted orange for better visibility in heavy fog. Park at the San Francisco end to walk or cycle across; drive to the vista point just beyond the north end of the bridge to look back toward San Francisco.

Golden Gate National Recreation Area (GGNRA)

A string of former military bases and coastal defences has become the world's largest urban park, stretching west from **Aquatic Park** and **Fort Mason** along the Bay to the **Presidio**, then south along the Pacific beyond San Francisco. Also included are **Alcatraz** and **Angel Islands**, the **Marin Headlands**, **Muir Woods National Monument**, **Mount Tamalpais** and much of **Tomales Bay** shoreline. Best views can be had from **Crissy Field**, the Golden Gate Bridge to downtown San Francisco; from the **Golden Gate Promenade**; **Baker Beach**, facing the Golden Gate Bridge from the ocean; **Lands End** with the city's most natural landscape and best sunsets; and **upper Fort Mason** for bay vistas.

Golden Gate Park

America's second great urban park (after Central Park in New York), Golden Gate Park is 1000 acres of drifting sand dunes transformed into shady forests, winding drives, lakes surrounded by open glades and museums. Don't miss jasmine tea and fortune cookies in the **Japanese Tea Garden**.

The park is also home to **San Francisco Botanical Garden at Strybing Arboretum**, 9000 plant species arranged in 25 distinct garden habitats and the restored white glass Victorian **Conservatory of Flowers**, with five galleries crammed with tropical plants, including a centenarian *Philodendron* twisting skyward.

🚇 Market Street Railway Museum
77 Steuart St, at the Steuart St F-line stop, Hotel Vitale; tel: (415) 974-1948; www.streetcar.org. Open Wed–Sun 1000–1800.

Museum of the African Diaspora $$ 685 Mission St at 3rd St; tel: (415) 358-7200; www.moadsf.org. Open Wed–Sat 1100–1800, Sun 1200–1700.

Museum of Craft and Folk Art $ 51 Yerba Buena Lane; tel: (415) 227-4888; www.mocfa.org. Open Tue–Fri 1100–1800, Sat–Sun to 1700. Free first Tue of the month.

Coit Tower $
1 Telegraph Hill Blvd; tel: (415) 362-0808. Open daily 1000–1800. Parking is extremely limited; walk up or take bus 39. The hilltop view is free.

Palace of the Legion of Honor $$ 34th Ave & Clement St, Lincoln Park; tel: (415) 750-3600; www.famsf.org/legion. Open Tue–Sun 0930–1715. Free first Tue of the month.

ℹ North Beach Chamber of Commerce Tel: (415) 989-2220; www.sfnorthbeach.org

Market Street Railway Museum

Seen the historic streetcars from all over the world trundling along Market Street and along The Embarcadero? A stop signal marks a collection of lore, history and artifacts gathered by the private streetcar restorers, including a transfer that expired several minutes before the 1906 earthquake.

The Mission (District)

Named after **Mission Dolores** (*17th & Dolores Sts, page 260*), founded in 1776, The Mission is Central and South America come north. Look for brilliant murals blazing messages of equality, ethnic pride and hope, a wide range of Mexican and other Hispanic restaurants, innovative cuisine and lively streets.

Museum of the African Diaspora

The art, music, food, rituals, clothing, photographs, slave history and freedom struggles of people of African origins are catalogued in well-captioned galleries.

Museum of Craft and Folk Art

Sandwiched between the Four Seasons Hotel and Moscone Convention Center, this tiny museum hosts four superb exhibits each year. Shop at its alley-front store for the highest-quality craft art from around the world.

North Beach

Once a northern beach on San Francisco Bay, North Beach (*blocks surrounding Broadway and Columbus Ave*) was settled by Portuguese and Italians. The area has been an entertainment and nightlife district for more than a century. The topless and nude dancing clubs that have spread across America began at **The Condor** (*300 Columbus Ave; tel: (415) 781-8222*) in the 1960s. Sourdough bread is still baked in North Beach.

The Beatnik era survives at poet Lawrence Ferlinghetti's **City Lights Bookstore** (*261 Columbus Ave; tel: (415) 362-8193; www.citylights.com*) and **Vesuvio Café** (*255 Columbus Ave; tel: (415) 362-3370; www.vesuvio.com*). **The Beat Museum** (*see page 138*) is up the block. It's a short, if steep, walk from the coffee houses to the high point of North Beach, tiny **Telegraph Hill**, topped by 212ft **Coit Tower**. The nozzle-shaped tower was built by Lillie Coit, an early City socialite with a notorious fondness for burly firemen. The interior features splendid Depression-era murals.

Palace of the Legion of Honor

This copy of Napoleon's Hôtel de Salm in Paris, usually called the Legion of Honor, displays ancient and European art from 2500 BC to the 20th century, and a large collection of graphic and print artworks. Check for major touring exhibitions and the Rodin sculpture collection.

**🅟 San Francisco
Maritime National
Historic Park $**
*Beach St between Hyde St
and Van Ness Ave; tel: (415)
447-5000; www.nps.gov/safr.
Open daily.* **Visitor Center,**
*corner of Hyde and Jefferson
Streets in the Argonaut Hotel
complex. Open daily
0930–1900, later in summer.*

**San Francisco Museum
of Modern Art
(SFMOMA) $$** *151 Third
St (SOMA); tel: (415) 357-
4000; www.sfmoma.org.
Open Fri–Tue 1100–1745,
Thu 1100–2045; Memorial
Day–Labor Day at 1000.*

Pier 39
One of the state's most popular tourist attractions is an abandoned pier converted to more than 110 retail shops, entertainment and restaurants with fine views of Alcatraz and the bay (*The Embarcadero at Beach St; tel: (415) 981-7437; www.pier39.com, open daily*). The Pier's most famous residents are the barking **sea lions** that have taken over the north side marina. Most Blue & Gold Fleet ferries leave from Pier 41, just west. A **California Welcome Center** (*tel: (415) 981-1280*) is on the second floor.

San Francisco Maritime National Historical Park
The nation's only floating National Park includes the **Maritime Museum** (*reopening after renovations during 2009; call the Visitor Center*), housed in a gleaming white art deco streamline modern building in Aquatic Park and historic ships docked at the **Hyde Street Pier $** (*open 0930–1700, longer in summer*). The square rigger **Balclutha** and the **Eureka**, a former San Francisco Bay ferry, are among the ships open for tours.

San Francisco Museum of Modern Art (SFMOMA)
Northern California's largest collection of modern art is noted for its distinctive architectural design by Mario Botta and the popular Caffé Museo, and is the city's most visited museum.

SOMA
The South of Market (Street) Area (SOMA) was once an industrial haven filled with brick buildings and dark alleyways, but has metamorphosed into a trendy residential, entertainment, art and museum district. Clubs suit every taste from Springsteen to Grunge. AT&T Park (*www.mlb.com/sf/ballpark*), at SOMA's south end, is the waterfront baseball park home of the **San Francisco Giants**.

Union Square
The heart of the shopping and theatre district (*Powell, Post, Stockton and Geary Sts*), the square was renovated in 2002.

Yerba Buena Gardens
A former SOMA slum, Yerba Buena (*north of Moscone Convention Center between 4th, Mission, 3rd and Howard Sts*) has become a lively nexus with SFMOMA, a Performing Arts Center (Yerba Buena Center for the Arts; tel: (415) 978-2700; www.ybca.org), ice-skating rink, Moscone Convention Center, cinemas, shopping, entertainment, hotels, restaurants, a carousel and gardens.

Entertainment

San Francisco has taken entertainment seriously since the days when admiring miners tossed

TIX Bay Area Half-price tickets for theatre, dance and music events on performance day and Muni Passports only (*Powell St side of Union Square; www.theatrebayarea.org*). Full-price advance tickets to area performance events are also sold. *Open Tue–Thu 1100–1800, Fri 1100–1900, Sat 1000–1700, Sun 1100–1500.*

bouquets of roses to touring opera stars and pouches of gold dust to bouncing dance-hall girls. City stages offer the gamut from punk to renowned opera, plus theatre, dance and concerts. The *San Francisco Chronicle* Thursday *96 Hours* section and the *Datebook* section in the *San Francisco Sunday Chronicle* (*www.sfgate.com*) hold the most complete listings for traditional diversions; the *SF Bay Guardian* (*www.sfbg.com*) and *SF Weekly* (*www.sfweekly.com*) concentrate on more avant-garde offerings.

Clubs

Most clubs are in SOMA, catering to every taste from old-line jazz to the latest electronic creations.

Stern Grove Festival *Sigmund Stern Grove, 19th Ave and Sloat Blvd; tel: (415) 252-6252; www.sterngrove.org. Summer Sun afternoons mid-Jun–mid-Aug.* Free outdoor summer classical, opera, popular and jazz.

Street performers

The Cannery (*2801 Leavenworth St; tel: (415) 771-3112*), Del Monte Square Courtyard, Pier 39 and other centres offer stages for buskers, but most jugglers, mimes and musicians set up shop on any convenient patch of pavement. Pier 39's Crystal Geyser Alpine Spring Water Center Stage has a whole street performer schedule.

Audium $$ *1616 Bush St; tel: (415) 771-1616; www.audium.org. Fri–Sat.* Sound sculptures from 136 speakers surround the audience, sitting in a darkened theatre.

Beach Blanket Babylon $$ *Club Fugazi, 678 Beach Blanket Babylon Blvd (Green St, North Beach); tel: (415) 421-4222; www.beachblanketbabylon.com, open Wed–Sun, adults only except Sun afternoon.* Zany cabaret-style musical spoof of popular culture, updated regularly to reflect current and local events.

Grace Cathedral Concerts $$ *1100 California St; tel: (415) 749-6355; www.gracecathedral.org.* Concerts and organ recitals in California's finest Gothic cathedral.

Old First Concerts $$ *Old First Church, Van Ness Ave and 1751 Sacramento St; tel: (415) 474-1608; www.oldfirstconcerts.org. Year-round.* Solo, chamber, choral, jazz and world music concerts.

San Francisco Blues Festival $$ *Great Meadow, Fort Mason; tel: (415) 979-5588; www.sfblues.com. Late Sep.* The oldest blues festival in the nation.

San Francisco Jazz Festival $$ *many venues in San Francisco; tel: (415) 788-7353; www.sfjazz.org. Oct–Nov.* For more than two decades the City by the Bay has attracted the best jazz musicians in the world.

American Conservatory Theater (ACT) $$$ *415 Geary St, Union Sq; tel: (415) 749-2228; www.act-sfbay.org, daily except Mon.* San Francisco's leading repertory theatre company.

The Chinese in California

The Chinese have been part of California since 1848, when the first three immigrants from Guandong Province disembarked in San Francisco. Tens of thousands followed, lured by the promise of untold wealth in *Kum Saan*, or Gold Mountain, as it was known in China. Most early immigrants were men, expecting to work hard for a few years, save a small fortune then return to their ancestral village. Few ever left California and even fewer made their fortunes.

Chinese labourers were systematically exploited, first by agents at home who charged exorbitant fees, then by employers in California who paid them half the going rate for white workers. Those who tried their luck in the gold fields were driven out amid accusations of working too long, too hard and too successfully. Many found work in railway construction, where they were generally given the most dangerous assignments blasting tunnels and chiselling ledges into sheer cliff-faces. The Chinese were easy targets in the days when anyone who wasn't white, Anglo-Saxon and Protestant was suspect.

Anti-Asian sentiment was fanned by Chinese Exclusion laws designed

San Francisco Ballet $$$ *455 Franklin St; tel: (415) 865-2000; www.sfballet.org.* Annual dance season Feb–Apr in the War Memorial Opera House; annual *Nutcracker* performances in Dec.

San Francisco Opera $$$ *War Memorial Opera House, Van Ness Ave and McAllister St; tel: (415) 864-3330; www.sfopera.com. Sep–Dec and Jun.* A world-famous company in an opera palace.

San Francisco Symphony $$$ *Davies Symphony Hall, Van Ness Ave and Grove St; tel: (415) 864-6000; www.sfsymphony.org.* Year-round symphony, summer Pops and holiday programmes.

Shopping

San Francisco is a shopper's dream regardless of budget. The hip, or those who wish to be, gravitate to **Haight St**. The Haight's latest reincarnation is a trendier-than-thou mix of fashion, food and body piercing. **Union Square** is shopping central with Disney and Nike to Saks Fifth Avenue and Tiffany. The **Westfield San Francisco Centre** (*865 Market St at 5th St; tel: (415) 512-6776; http://westfield.com/ sanfrancisco*) is anchored by Nordstrom and Bloomingdale's. **Union Street** caters to the stylishly trendy, offering jewellery, marbled paper, clothing, antiques, furnishings and bric-a-brac from around the world.

Accommodation and food

San Francisco has been famous for high prices since Gold Rush days. It's one of America's most-visited cities, which keeps hotels and restaurants busy all year. *Always* book ahead. The SFCVB (*tel: (800) 637-5196; www.onlyinsanfrancisco.com*) helps with your bookings. **San Francisco Reservations** (*tel: (800) 677-1570; www.hotelres.com*) makes free bookings for more than 225 local hotels. **Union Square** is the best location if you don't have a car, near the main shopping and theatre areas, most major tourist sights and public transport routes. Add $20–$25 per day for parking. Motels along **Lombard St** and **Van Ness Ave** generally offer free parking; ask for a room at the back to minimise street noise. **Fisherman's Wharf** is group-tour territory. Nob Hill is a posh address.

The Galleria Park Hotel $$$ (*191 Sutter St; tel: (800) 792-9639; www.galleriapark.com*) is a refurbished boutique hotel with a rooftop tai chi and Pilates area near Union Square and Chinatown. The ultra-trendy **Hotel Triton $$$** (*342 Grant Ave; tel: (800) 800-1299; www.hoteltriton. com*) is filled with irregular shapes, wavy lines and corners that appear not to meet. The **Palace Hotel $$$** (*2 New Montgomery St; tel: (415) 512-1111; www.sfpalace.com*) is one of the oldest, most historic hotels in San Francisco – and one of the few major buildings to survive the 1906

to keep them out. leading to the indefinite detention of many would-be immigrants at the Angel Island Immigration Station in San Francisco Bay. Local laws banned Chinese (and other Asians) from most occupations; sporadic anti-Chinese riots encouraged them to band together for self-protection. Los Angeles, Sacramento, San Francisco and isolated Delta towns such as Locke gained significant Chinatowns and other Asian neighbourhoods.

Discrimination began to ease after World War II, when the US and China found themselves allied. Immigration opened for refugees fleeing the Chinese Communist government after 1949. By the time quotas were raised again in the 1960s, San Francisco had the largest Chinese population outside Asia – and the Golden Dragon continues an annual New Year Parade dance down Chinatown's Grant Ave that began in the 1860s.

earthquake. The **Garden Court $$$** is a palm-filled restaurant beneath a restored stained-glass dome over the original carriage entrance.

With 3000 eateries, from ultra-luxe to ethnic hole-in-the-wall, San Francisco calls itself the food capital of America, a title justly contested by Los Angeles, New York and New Orleans. The website *www.sfgate.com* offers a selection of current reviews. Local favourites change almost weekly, but **Boulevard $$$** (*1 Mission St; tel: (415) 543-6084*) is a long-term survivor for its French-inspired dishes. **Aqua $$$** (*252 California St; tel: (415) 956-9662*) serves great seafood. **Boudin at the Wharf $** (*160 Jefferson St; tel: (415) 928-1849*) has the best Fisherman's Wharf sandwiches, a demonstration bakery, and a history of sourdough bread museum. **McCormick & Kuleto's Seafood Restaurant $$$** (*900 North Point (Ghirardelli Square); tel: (415) 929-1730* or *(888) 344-6861*) has food to equal the views across Aquatic Park and the Bay. The **Beach Chalet $$** (*1000 Great Highway (Golden Gate Park); tel: (415) 386-8439; www.beachchalet.com*), with its **Park Chalet Garden Restaurant**, is a brewery, restaurant and a Golden Gate Park visitor centre surrounded with 1936 murals. **Yoshi's Jazz Club & Restaurant $$** (*1330 Fillmore St; tel: (415) 655-5600; www.yoshis.com*) is revitalising the Fillmore Jazz District – a musical hotbed after World War II.

Suggested tours

49-Mile Drive
Allow at least a half-day and avoid downtown during rush hours. The drive was created for the 1939 Golden Gate International Exposition. Blue and white seagull signs still mark an outstanding driving circuit. The route is marked on the SFCVB's 49-Mile Scenic Drive map.

Walking tours
San Francisco is best seen on foot. Top guided walking tours: **City Guides** (*tel: (415) 557-4266; www.sfcityguides.org, free*) for culture, history and architecture; **Local Tastes of the City Tours** (*tel: (888) 358-8687* or *(415) 665-0480; www.localtastesofthecitytours.com*) has tours of North Beach, Chinatown, or both on a night tour. **Cruisin' The Castro** (*tel: (415) 255-1821; www.cruisinthecastro.com*) for The City's gay subculture from 1849 to the present; **Wok Wiz Chinatown Tours** (*tel: (650) 355-9657; www.wokwiz.com*) for Chinatown alleys, tea and secrets with chef and author Shirley Fong-Torres; **Mangia! North Beach** (*e-mail: GAW@sbcglobal.net; www.graceannwalden.net*) for Italian food, history and culture with chef and columnist GraceAnn Walden; **Victorian Home Walk** (*tel: (415) 252-9485; www.victorianwalk.com*) for an exploration of San Francisco's Victorian architecture, lifestyle and history.

Do-it-yourselfers can follow plaques on the 3.8-mile **Barbary Coast Trail** (*www.sfhistory.org/bct*) from the Old Mint (SOMA) via Chinatown, Nob Hill and North Beach, to Fisherman's Wharf.

San Francisco Bay Area

Ratings

Art	●●●●○
Food and drink	●●●●○
Scenery	●●●●○
Architecture	●●●○○
Children	●●●○○
History	●●●○○
Nature	●●●○○
Museums	●●○○○

San Francisco has given its name to the Bay Area, but it's hardly the dominant force in a region filled with vibrant cities, each with its own distinctive look and feel. The bay unites a montage of soaring bridges, windswept islands, distant skylines piercing the fog, sailboats and boardsailors weaving past lumbering cargo vessels, Nobel Prize-winners and world-renowned chefs. It's possible to breeze through the entire Bay Area in a day, but more productive to spread the sights over several days. Bridges and freeways can become stop-and-go car parks during rush hours.

BERKELEY

ⓘ **Berkeley Convention & Visitors Bureau Visitor Information Center**
2015 Center St, Berkeley, CA 94704; tel: (800) 847-4823 or (510) 549-7040; www.visitberkeley.com. Open Mon–Fri 0900–1700.

University of California Berkeley Campus Visitor Center
101 University Hall, 2200 University Ave; tel: (510) 642-5215; www.berkeley.edu/visitors. Open Mon–Fri 0830–1630. Walking, online or podcast campus tours are free.

It's hard to separate Berkeley from the **University of California, Berkeley**. The campus, usually called Cal, lends a schizophrenic air to a town already known as 'Berserkely' for its benign loonies and strident politics. It also usually has America's greatest concentration of Nobel laureates.

About 35,000 students make Cal the physical heart and soul of Berkeley. **Sather Tower**, aka **The Campanile**, towers 307ft above them all, slightly shorter than the original in St Mark's Square, Venice. From an observation platform below the 61-bell carillon, views span the bay. On the ground, **Sproul Plaza** (*north of Telegraph Ave and Bancroft Way*) is a non-stop circus, dominated by the student union in **Sproul Hall**.

Campus collections worth seeing are: the **Phoebe A Hearst Museum of Anthropology \$** (*102 Kroeber Hall; tel: (510) 642-3682; hearstmuseum.berkeley.edu; open Wed–Sat 1000–1630, Sun 1200–1600*), with artefacts used by 'Ishi', last survivor of California's Stone Age

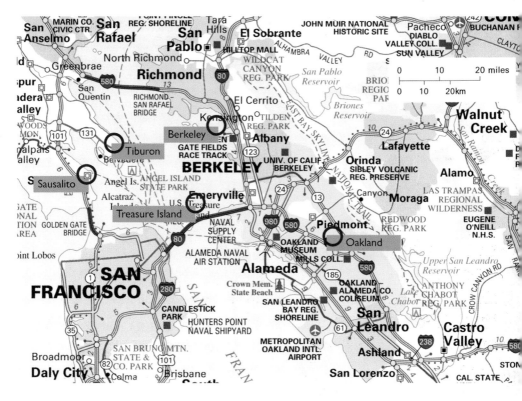

Lawrence Hall of Science $$
Centennial Dr.; tel: (510) 642-5132; www.lhs.berkeley. edu. Open daily 1000–1700.

Museum of Paleontology
Near Oxford St/University Ave, 1101 Valley Life Sciences Bldg; tel: (510) 642-1821; www.ucmp.berkeley.edu. Call for hours. Free.

Judah L Magnes Museum $ 2911 Russell St; tel: (510) 549-6950; www.magnes.org. Open Sun–Wed 1100–1600, Thu 1100–2000.

Yahi aboriginals; modern and contemporary art at the **UC Berkeley Art Museum $$** (2626 Bancroft Way; tel: (510) 642-0808; www.bampfa.berkeley.edu; open Wed–Sun 1100–1700); the **Pacific Film Archive** (2575 Bancroft Way; tel: (510) 642-1124), which screens popular, foreign, independent and avant-garde films; the **Lawrence Hall of Science**, a popular participatory museum with a fine Bay view from the Berkeley Hills; and a few foyer exhibits from the enormous fossil collection at the **Museum of Paleontology**.

The **UC Botanical Garden $** (200 Centennial Dr.; tel: (510) 643-2755; botanicalgarden.berkeley.edu; open 0900–1700, free first Thu of the month) has over 12,000 species from around the world, neatly labelled and divided into regional habitat zones. The rhododendron collection is stunning during the spring bloom. Cacti, a Chinese medicinal herb garden and California native plants are major collections, and views of San Francisco Bay are eye-catching.

Off-campus Berkeley swirls around **Telegraph Ave**, an ever-changing collection of coffee houses, booksellers, street musicians, panhandlers, students and homeless people. The **Judah L Magnes Museum**, the first Jewish museum in the Western US, collects fine art, ceremonial objects and rare books.

The Cheese Board Collective *1504 Shattuck Ave; tel: (510) 549-3183.*

The Cheese Board Pizza Collective *1512 Shattuck; tel: (510) 549-3055; shared website: cheeseboardcollective.coop*

Below
Modelled on St Mark's Campanile in Venice, the Campanile at the Berkeley campus of the University of California

Food in Berkeley

Berkeley takes everything seriously, including food. California cuisine got its start here, the idea that fresh ingredients, cultivated on small plots by happy farmers, are absolutely vital to health, taste, prosperity and peace on earth. To see the raw ingredients, tiny 'baby' vegetables and exotically coloured produce, visit the **Monterey Market** (*1550 Hopkins St; tel: (510) 526-6042; open Mon–Fri 0900–1900, Sat 0830–1800; www.montereymarket.com*) and **Berkeley Bowl Marketplace** (*2020 Oregon St; tel: (510) 843-6929; www.berkeleybowl. com; open Mon–Sat 0900–2000, Sun 1000–1800*).

High temple to the Cult of Cuisine is **Chez Panisse $$$** (*1517 Shattuck Ave; tel: (510) 548-5525; www.chezpanisse.com*), whose reputation exceeds its execution, but upstairs **The Café** (*tel: (510) 548-5049*) offers better value. Both restaurants book tables exactly one month in advance.

The area around Chez Panisse, Shattuck Ave near Cedar and Vine Sts is called **Gourmet Ghetto** for the enormous concentration of fine restaurants. Chez Panisse neighbours include the employee-owned **Cheese Board Collective** with cheeses and on-premises baked goods and its independent adjunct, The **Cheese Board Pizza Collective**, for late-afternoon and dinner pizza pies.

People-watchers head for **Bette's Oceanview Diner $$** (*1807 4th St; tel: (510) 644-3230; www.worldpantry. com/bettes/home.html*), a casual breakfast and lunch-only diner with some of the area's tastiest American traditions: pancakes, French toast, blintzes (thin rolled pancakes filled with cheese or fruit and then baked or fried), sandwiches, soup, meatloaf and to-die-for milk shakes. Grab a **Sketch Ice Cream $** (*1809A 4th St; tel: (510) 665-5650; www. sketchicecream.com*). They both sit in the bustling **Fourth Street Shopping District**, a former warehouse area that has become a lively artistic, shopping, dining and entertainment district.

OAKLAND

ⓘ Oakland Convention & Visitors Bureau (OCVB) 463 11th St, Oakland CA 94607; tel: (510) 839-9000; http://oaklandcvb.com. Open Mon–Fri 0830–1700.

Ⓩ Oakland Int'l Airport (OAK) Tel: (510) 563-3300; www.oaklandairport.com

ⓘ Oakland Public Library Oakland History Room 125 14th St, 2nd floor; tel: (510) 238-3222; www.oaklandlibrary.org. Open Mon, Tue and Sat 1000–1730, Wed–Thu 1200–2000, Fri 1200–1730, Sun 1300–1700.

Pardee Home Museum $ 672 11th St; tel: (510) 444-2187; www.pardeehome.org. Tours Mon–Sat 1000–1600.

Oakland Museum of California $$ 1000 Oak St; tel: (510) 238-2200; www.museumca.org. Open Wed–Sat 1000–1700, Sun 1200–1700, first Fri of month to 2100.

Chabot Space & Science Center $$ 10000 Skyline Blvd; tel: (510) 336-7300; www.chabotspace.org. Hours change seasonally.

Lake Merritt Boating Center $$ Tel: (510) 238-2196. Open daily except rainy days, call for hours.

Oakland traditionally doesn't get much respect. Yet it is a sunny, diverse city with a long cultural, musical and artistic heritage. Jack London, Oakland's first literary light, has his name plastered along the waterfront where he once stole oysters and lobsters for a living.

Jack London Square (*west of downtown; tel: (866) 295-9853; www.jacklondonsquare.com*) is a modern complex of shops, restaurants and museums. The **Oakland Public Library Oakland History Room** and **Jack London State Historic Park** (*see page 174*) have better London collections. The Square's only genuine Londoniana is **Heinold's First and Last Chance Saloon** (*48 Webster St; tel: (510) 839-6761; www.heinoldsfirstandlastchance.com*), where London drank. The **USS Potomac** (*540 Water St; tel: (510) 627-1215; www.usspotomac.org*), FDR's one-time American presidential yacht, is *open Wed, Fri and Sun* for dockside tours $$, and *May–early Nov Thu and Sat* for bay cruises $$$.

The Square's other highlights are a **ferry terminal** with hourly connections to San Francisco, and **Yoshi's** (*510 Embarcadero West; tel: (510) 238-9200; www.yoshis.com*), a Japanese restaurant that is the East Bay's top jazz club.

The best place to see early Oakland is **Preservation Park** (*Martin Luther King Jr Way and 13th St; tel: (510) 874-7580; www.preservationpark.com*), a re-created neighbourhood with restored buildings from 19th-century Victorian to early 20th-century Craftsman. Most are private offices, but **Pardee Home Museum** is open for guided tours. **Old Oakland** (*Broadway, Clay, 8th and 10th Sts; http://oldoakland.org*) is the former commercial district, largely restored as an official historic district. **Chinatown** (*Broadway, Fallon, 6th and 8th Sts*), more Pan-Asian than Chinese, has shops, restaurants and bakeries that are as busy – and far less touristy – than San Francisco, and Oakland Chinatown Streetfest in August (*www.oaklandchinatownstreetfest.com*).

Many of Oakland's grand buildings from the early 20th century survive in the downtown City Center, including **City Hall** (*14th St*) and the **Tribune Tower** (*Franklin St*), former home of the *Oakland Tribune* newspaper. A restored 1920s movie palace, the **Paramount Theatre** (*2025 Broadway; tel: (510) 465-6400; www.paramounttheatre.com*), shows Hollywood classics as well as stage productions and Oakland Symphony.

The stunning **Oakland Museum of California** is California's *de facto* state museum. **Lake Merritt**, the nation's oldest wildlife refuge, has Venetian gondola rides (*Gondola Servizio; tel: (866) 737-8494; www.gondolaservizio.com*). The **Chabot Space & Science Center**, in Oakland's hills, has interactive exhibits, a dome theatre and planetarium, and offers one of the best spots for year-round public telescope perusal of the heavens on clear Friday and Saturday evenings. **Camron-Stanford House** is the last of the elegant Victorian mansions that once lined the lake. Canoes, rowboats, paddleboats, kayaks and sailboats can be hired

⚫ **Children's Fairyland $$$** *Grand & Bellevue Aves; tel: (510) 238-6876; www.fairyland. org. Hours vary by season, closed rainy days.*

🅗 **USS Hornet Museum $$** *Pier 3, Alameda Point, Alameda; tel: (510) 521-8448; www.uss- hornet.org. Open daily 1000–1700 for self-guided tours.*

⚫ **Old Oakland Farmers' Market** *Broadway and 9th St; tel: (510) 745-7100; www.urbanvillageonline.com/ oldoakland. Open Fri 0800–1400.*

from the **Lake Merritt Boating Center. Children's Fairyland** was reputedly the model for Fantasyland in Walt Disney's original Disneyland.

The **USS Hornet Museum** preserves a ship in fit-for-duty state that saw service in World War II Pacific combat, Vietnam, and recovered the first two lunar modules, Apollo 11 and Apollo 12. Painted footsteps on Hangar Bay 2 deck are where Neil Armstrong walked after returning from the first moon walk.

Accommodation and food in Oakland

The white gleam against the hills is the **Claremont Resort & Spa $$$** *Ashby and Domingo Aves; tel: (510) 843-3000 or (800) 551-7266; www.claremontresort.com*

Oakland is filled with colourful eateries, from a rainbow of Asian flavours in Chinatown to Oakland's own Gourmet Ghetto, **Rockridge** (*College Ave between 63rd and Alcatraz Sts*).

Citron $$ *5484 College Ave; tel: (510) 653-5484; www.citronrestaurant. com*, shows distinct French and Italian touches.

Zachary's Pizza $$ *5801 College Ave; tel: (510) 665-6385; www.zacharys.com*, has won awards since 1983 for several-inch-thick pies with layers of ingredients. Prepare to wait for long lines ordering to go or stake out a feast spot at a table. There are also locations in Berkeley and San Ramon.

Bay Wolf $$$ *3853 Piedmont Ave; tel: (510) 655-6004; www.baywolf.com*, avoids Berkeley-like flights of fancy for restrained Mediterranean-California dishes.

SAUSALITO

ℹ️ **Sausalito Chamber of Commerce** *10 Liberty Ship Way, Bay 2, Ste 250, Sausalito CA 94965; tel: (415) 332-0505 or (415) 331-7262; www.sausalito.org. Visitor Center, 780 Bridgeway, open Tue–Sun 1130–1600.*

🅑 **Blue & Gold Fleet (ferry)** *Pier 39, San Francisco; tel: (415) 705-8200; www.blueandgoldfleet.com*

Golden Gate Transit (ferry) *Ferry Bldg, San Francisco; tel: 511 or (415) 455-2000; http://goldengateferry.org*

A small 19th-century summer resort and fishing town expanded as a ship-building centre during World War II, then sank into obscurity as a haven for 1950s artists, poets and Beats. A free-thinking reputation was assured when Sally Stanford, one of San Francisco's infamous bordello madams, retired here, opened a restaurant and became mayor.

Sausalito marinas and houseboats orient the town to the bayfront. Shopping complexes wind and twist like rabbit warrens. Much of the town centre is a National Historic Landmark District, including the **Plaza de Viña del Mar**, with its Spanish-style fountain and elephants from the 1915 Panama-Pacific Exposition. At the north end of Sausalito is the **San Francisco Bay Model**, used to test the impact of development, dredging and clean-up efforts. The best way to see the Bay is a 3-hour guided sea kayak tour from **Sea Trek Ocean Kayaking Center**, a 30-minute **ferry ride** from San Francisco.

San Francisco Bay Model *2100*
Bridgeway; tel: (415) 332-3871; www.spn.usace. army.mil/bmvc. Open Tue–Sat 0900–1600, longer summer hours. Free.

Bay Area Discovery Museum $$
557 McReynolds Rd, East Fort Baker; tel: (415) 339-3900; www.baykidsmuseum. org. Open Tue–Fri 0900–1600, Sat–Sun 1000–1700.

Sea Trek Ocean Kayaking Center
$$ Tel: (415) 488-1000; www.seatrekkayak.com. Open daily, advance booking required.

To go back to Sausalito's roots, stop and watch craftspeople and students at the **Arques School of Traditional Wooden Boatbuilding** (*Spaulding Wooden Boat Center, foot of Gate 5 Road; tel: (415) 332-3179; www.arqueschl.org. Visits are limited, call for current hours*).

Getting out of the car in Sausalito

Sausalito's best bay vistas are from Bridgeway, walking south to Second St, Alexander Ave and Fort Baker Rd to the former military base. It's a 2-mile walk with unexpected views of the **Golden Gate Bridge** to reach the **Bay Area Discovery Museum**, with lively science, art and media exhibits geared to children aged 1 to 10.

Accommodation and food in Sausalito

Casa Madrona Hotel and Spa $$$ *801 Bridgeway; tel: (800) 288-0502 or (415) 332-0502; www.casamadrona.com*, is a collection of cottage rooms, modern spaces and a posh spa stretching up the hillside from Bridgeway to a Victorian mansion.

Cavallo Point – the Lodge at the Golden Gate $$$ *601 Murray Circle, Fort Baker; tel: (415) 339-4700 or (888) 651-2003; www.cavallopoint.com*, is a posh inside-a-national-park remake of historic army officer quarters within sight of the Golden Gate Bridge.

Inn Above Tide $$$ *30 El Portal; tel: (800) 893-8433 or (415) 332-9535; www.innabovetide.com*, is the only hotel built *over* San Francisco Bay.

Scoma's $$$ *588 Bridgeway; tel: (415) 332-9551; www.scomassausalito. com*, has Bay views with seafood.

Spinnaker Restaurant $$$ *100 Spinnaker Ave; tel: (415) 332-1500; www.thespinnaker.com*, has on-the-water views.

TIBURON

Tiburon Chamber of Commerce *96B Main St, Tiburon, CA 94920; tel: (415) 435-5633; www.tiburonchamber.org. Open Mon–Fri 0800–1600. Find a keyed walking map at www. samscafe.com/tourmap.html*

Originally called Punta de Tiburon (Shark Point) by Mexican fishermen, today's town was born in 1884 as the terminus for the San Francisco and North Pacific Railroad ferry to San Francisco. Sweeping bay views, and daily ferries, helped turn Tiburon and neighbouring **Belvedere** into exclusive dormitory communities for San Francisco.

Tiburon's tiny and almost always sunny **waterfront** has become a trendy San Francisco getaway. Restaurants with outdoor decks surround the ferry landing. A long park offers space to run and enjoy views of San Francisco shimmering beyond Angel Island, a few hundred yards offshore. Central Tiburon was once a lagoon dotted with houseboats, or arks, that were eventually placed on pilings. **Ark**

Row has become a popular dining and shopping area. Other sites include **Old St. Hilary's**, a restored Carpenter Gothic church overlooking the town; **Tiburon Uplands Nature Preserve**'s 0.7-mile loop trail; and the **Richardson Bay Audubon Center and Sanctuary**.

Food in Tiburon

Above
Going to Angel Island from Tiburon

Richardson Bay Audubon Center and Sanctuary $
376 Greenwood Beach Rd; tel: (415) 388-2524; www.tiburonaudubon.org; call for opening hours.

Frequent ferry connections make Tiburon an easy restaurant excursion from San Francisco.

Sam's Anchor Cafe $$ *27 Main St; tel: (415) 435-4527; www.samscafe.com*, is noisy, hospitable, busy and worth the wait for simply prepared seafood and burgers. Arrive about an hour early, leave your name with the *maître d'* and go explore.

Guaymas $$$ *5 Main St; tel: (415) 435-6300; www.guaymasrestaurant. com*, Mexican, and **Servino's Ristorante $$$** *9 Main St; tel: (415) 435-2676; www.servino.com*, Italian seafood, have similar views and require reservations.

TREASURE ISLAND

Treasure Island Development Authority (TIDA)
Tel: (415) 274-0660; www.sfgov.org/site/treasureisland_index.asp

Treasure Island Sailing Center $$ Tel: (415) 421-2225; www.tisailing.org, conducts reasonably priced sailing classes at all experience levels.

The tabletop expanse of Treasure Island was created for the 1939 Golden Gate International Exposition, with access via the **San Francisco-Oakland Bay Bridge**. The large art moderne building facing San Francisco was originally the control tower and terminal building for Pan American Airways' flying boat service to Asia.

The island became a Naval base during World War II and reverted to the city of San Francisco 50 years later. Some of the former Navy buildings are now studios and sound stages for cinema and television productions. Part of the island has become a small marina and public park with seldom-visited views of the **San Francisco waterfront**. Best vistas are in the morning and at sunset.

Suggested tour

From San Francisco, follow I-80 east on the **San Francisco-Oakland Bay Bridge ❶** to TREASURE ISLAND ❷, then continue through the toll plaza area. Follow I-580 southbound to OAKLAND ❸. From Oakland, return northbound on I-580 to I-80 eastbound. Take the **University Ave ❹** exit into BERKELEY ❺ toward the **University of California, BERKELEY ❻**.

Return to I-80 eastbound along San Francisco Bay to the **Richmond-San Rafael Bridge 7** to **Marin County 8**. The golden structure just south of the Marin County end of the bridge is **San Quentin Federal Prison 9**. Take Hwy 101 south to Paradise Dr. and the **Tiburon Peninsula 10**. The road becomes narrow, winding and steep, but passengers can expect good bay views.

Continue around the peninsula to **TIBURON 11** and **Belvedere 12**. Follow Tiburon Blvd along the shores of **Richardson Bay 13** to Hwy 101 and turn south to **SAUSALITO 14**. Cross the **Golden Gate Bridge 15** into San Francisco or, for pleasant afternoon views of the bridge, take the last exit before the bridge on to the **Marin Headlands 16** and drive uphill to any of several car parks.

Also worth exploring

Belvedere 12 is Tiburon's smaller and wealthier neighbour. The name means 'beautiful view' in Italian, an assessment of the panorama west toward Sausalito and south across San Francisco Bay. The **SS China Cabin** (*52 Beach Rd; tel: (415) 435-1853; open Apr–Oct, Sun and Wed 1300–1600*) is an elegantly restored Victorian social saloon salvaged from the 1867 steamship SS *China*. The floor is made of oak and walnut; cut-glass floral window panes provide light and the cabin is trimmed in 22-carat gold.

Napa Valley Wine Country

Ratings

Food and drink	●●●●●
Wine	●●●●○
Outdoor activities	●●●○○
Scenery	●●●○○
Shopping	●●●○○
Walking	●●○○○
Wildlife	●●○○○
Children	●○○○○

This 30-mile strip of valley covered with lush vineyards and more than 400 wineries could be a theme park version of Southern France. Some of America's finest wines and extraordinary promotional skills have made Napa the self-proclaimed Capital of California Wine – and turned Hwy 29 into one long traffic jam during the summer and at every weekend. The best time to visit is midweek during the spring and autumn. If you must visit in summer, traffic is less congested on the Silverado Trail, which runs along the eastern side of the valley.

CALISTOGA

ⓘ Calistoga Chamber of Commerce *1506 Lincoln Ave, Calistoga, CA 94515; tel: (707) 942-6333; www.calistogachamber.com. Call for hours.*

ⓜ Sharpsteen Museum $ *1311 Washington St; tel: (707) 942-5911; www.sharpsteen-museum.org. Open daily 1100–1600.*

The town's mud baths and hot springs are better known than its wineries, thanks to Sam Brannan, the entrepreneur who quietly bought up San Francisco's entire supply of picks and shovels before shouting news of James Marshall's gold discovery on the streets of San Francisco in 1848. In 1860, Brannan founded a town he intended to promote as the 'Saratoga of California' after a famed resort town in New York state. What purportedly emerged was the 'Calistoga of Sarifornia'. Brannon's other historic contributions survive at the **Sharpsteen Museum**.

Hot springs, volcanic mud and a relatively low-key atmosphere have come together in California's most relaxed spa town. Treatments run the gamut from simple soaks in hot mineral water to wallows in volcanic mud, herbal wraps and deep tissue massage. **Dr Wilkinson's Hot Springs Resort** caters to the famous and the film stars. **Lavender Hill Spa** caters to couples and is known for its 'unthick' mud baths of volcanic ash mixed with kelp. Ordinary people flock to the down-to-

Lower Lake
Cobb
Dunnigan
Robbins
Knights
Landing
Guinda
Zamora
ale
9
175
37
Geyserville
YOLO
Yolo
Ros
Middletown
NAPA
505
N. High
29
R.L. Stevenson
S.P.
Esparto
in Healdsburg
128
Pope
Valley
Lake
Berryessa
Woodland
West Sacramento
113
17
4
Calistoga
Angwin
Winters
Davis
Windsor
SANTA
ROSA
the-Napa Valley S.P.
St Helena
31
12
Forestville
St Helena
Rutherford
Oakville
Davis
Graton
116
12
oaf Ridge
Yountville
ville
128
Dixon
idental
S.P.
113
Clarksburg
Courtland
Sebastopol
Glen Ellen
121
Vacaville
Fairfield
Rohnert Park
Napa
Napa
Beach
Tomales
101
Sonoma
Napa
TRAVIS A.F.B.
Walnut Grove
116
160
Petaluma
121
SOLANO
12
1
Novato
20
37
680
Rio Vista
Isleton
les Bay S.P.
HORE
Inverness
Reyes Station
muel P. Taylor S.P.
29
11
Brannan I. S.R.A.
160
Termir
Vallejo
Frank
Tract
S.R.A
yes
MARIN
VALLEJO
Benicia
Carquinez Strait
Pittsburg
Antioch
ATE N.R.A.
Fairfax
Martinez
19
4
San Rafael
14
9
CONCORD
Brentw
Mill Valley
Richmond
24
Walnut Creek
4
32
SAN
BERKELEY
OAKLAND
CONTRA
COSTA
L
FRANCISCO
Danville
San Ramon
Trac
SAN FRANCISCO
580
880
Daly City
101
San Leandro
580
Pacifica
Livermore
San Bruno
HAYWARD
Pleasanton
San Mateo
30
ALAMEDA
Redwood City
84
880
FREMONT
Half Moon Bay
SAN MATEO
Milpitas
Palo Alto
1
SUNNYVALE
280
10
20 miles
28
84
SAN JO
Pescadero
Cupertino
Campbell
10
20km
Saratoga
85
SANTA
Butano
Los Gatos
101
CLARA

Dr Wilkinson's Hot Springs Resort
$$ 1507 Lincoln Ave;
tel: (707) 942-4102;
www.drwilkinson.com. Open
0830–1730.

Lavender Hill Spa $$
1015 Foothill Blvd; tel: (707)
942-4495 or (800) 528-
4772; www.lavenderhillspa.
com. Open daily 0900–2100.

Indian Springs $
1712 Lincoln Ave; tel: (707)
942-4913;
www.indianspringscalistoga.
com. Open daily 0900–2000.

Old Faithful Geyser $
1299 Tubbs Ln;
tel: (707) 942-6463;
www.oldfaithfulgeyser.com.
Open 0900–1700, winter;
0900–1800 summer.

Petrified Forest $
4100 Petrified Forest Rd;
tel: (707) 942-6667;
www.petrifiedforest.org.
Open daily 0900–1900
summer; 0900–1700 winter.

Schramsberg $$$
1499 Schramsberg Rd;
Tel: (800) 877-3623 or
(707) 942-4558;
www.schramsberg.com.
Open daily for tours and
tastings by appointment.

**Chateau Montelena
Winery** $$$ 1429 Tubbs
Ln; tel: (707) 942-5105;
www.montelena.com.
Open daily 0930–1600,
tours by appointment.

Cuvaison $$ 4550
Silverado Trail; tel: (707)
942-2468; www.cuvaison.
com. Open 1000–1700.

Sterling Vineyards® $$
1111 Dunaweal Ln;
tel: (800) 726-6136;
www.sterlingvineyards.com.
Open daily 1030–1630.

earth spas along Lincoln Ave. **Indian Springs** is one of the more popular, with a sunbathing pool with a hot spring (geyser water).

Napa's hot underground springs also surface at **Old Faithful Geyser**, which spits boiling water and steam every half hour or so. The geyser was born when an exploratory oil rig drilled into a geothermal source in the 1920s. After numerous failed attempts to cap the regular eruptions, landowners turned the inevitable into a tourist attraction. The source is part of the volcanic plumbing system that gave rise to eruptions at nearby **Mount St Helena** (4344ft) and turned a lush grove of redwood trees into the **Petrified Forest** about three million years ago.

The mountain is protected within **Robert Louis Stevenson State Park** (7 miles north on Hwy 29; tel: (707) 942-4575). A 2½-mile trail leads to the top of the Napa Valley, with spectacular views stretching north to **Mount Shasta** on clear days. The park is named after the Scottish novelist Robert Louis Stevenson, who honeymooned in an abandoned miner's cabin on Mount St Helena in 1880. The cabin is long gone, but a trailside plaque marks the site. The highlight of his stay, Stevenson wrote in *Silverado Squatters*, was sampling 18 different champagnes from wine baron Jacob Schram's nearby **Schramsberg Vineyards**.

Don't miss winery visits around Calistoga. **Chateau Montelena Winery** has a formal Chinese garden with a traditional pagoda-pavilion overlooking a lake with a half-sunken junk. The French château-like architecture is also worth the drive, as is the Cabernet Sauvignon. **Cuvaison** is a winery on the Silverado Trail on the valley's east side, with a picnic area beneath oak trees. **Sterling Vineyards**® sits atop a small hill, an extravagant white Greek island-style mansion accessible by aerial tram. The bells of London's St Dunstan Church (destroyed in World War II) ring every half hour.

Accommodation and food in Calistoga

Rooms in all categories are snapped up quickly at peak periods, so book in advance all year. **Bed and Breakfast Inns of Napa Valley** tel: (707) 944-4444; www.napavalley.com, makes bookings throughout Wine Country.

Bosko's Ristorante $$ 1364 Lincoln Ave; tel: (707) 942-9088; www.boskos.com; open daily 1130–2200, is Calistoga's best Italian choice.

Wappos Bar & Bistro $$ 1226 Washington St; tel: (707) 942-4712; www.wappobar.com, serves variety, from cassoulet and tandoori chicken to Brazilian seafood stew and Singapore noodles.

Wine Way Inn $$ 1019 Foothill Blvd; tel: (707) 942-0680 or (800) 572-0679; www.winewayinn.com, is an historic craftsman-style inn.

Mount View Hotel & Spa $$$ 1457 Lincoln Ave; tel: (707) 942-6877 or (800) 816-6877; www.mountviewhotel.com, is one of Calistoga's oldest spas.

CARQUINEZ STRAIT

Benicia Chamber of Commerce & Visitors Center *601 First St, Ste 100, Benicia, CA 94510; tel: (800) 559-7377 or (707) 745-2120; www.beniciachamber.com. Call for hours.*

Benicia Capitol State Historic Park $ *115 West G St; tel: (707) 745-3385; www.parks.ca.gov. Open Wed–Sun 1000–1700.*

Below
Sterling Vineyards

This narrow channel is the sole outflow for Central Valley rivers draining the Sierra Nevada. The tiny port town of **Crockett** is cut into the hills along the south side of the Straits, dominated by the gigantic C&H Sugar refinery. **Carquinez Strait Scenic Drive** leads 2 miles to the former ferry town of **Port Costa**, which lost its *raison d'être* when the recently rebuilt **Carquinez Bridge** originally was built at Crockett. The town is still a good spot to watch huge freighters sailing to the inland ports of **Sacramento** and **Stockton**.

On the north side of the Straits is **Benicia**, a one-time rival to San Francisco and the state capital for 13 months. **Benicia Capitol State Historic Park** preserves the 1852 Greek Revival capitol building, as well as the **Fischer-Hanlon House**, a renovated Gold Rush-era hotel. The capitol is furnished in the legislative style of the era, complete with polished spittoons. The Chamber of Commerce publishes a free self-guided walking tour map of this Victorian town which is still largely intact. An arts community includes several well-known art-glass artists (*www.beniciachamber.com/guide/arts.html*).

NAPA

ℹ **Napa Valley Conference & Visitors Bureau**
1310 Napa Town Center (off First St), Napa, CA 94559; tel: (707) 226-7459; www.napavalley.com. Open daily 0900–1700.

COPIA $ 500 First St; tel: (888) 512-6742 or (707) 259-1600; www.copia.org. Open daily 1000–1800.

Oxbow Public Market 610 First St; tel: (707) 226-6529; www. oxbowpublicmarket.com. Open daily.

Napa Valley Opera House $$ 1030 Main St; tel: (707) 226-7372; www. napavalleyoperahouse.org

Napa Valley Wine Train $$ 1275 McKinstry St; tel: (707) 253-2111 or (800) 427-4124; www.winetrain. com. Excursions daily.

Domaine Carneros $$ 1240 Duhig Rd (off Hwy 12/121); tel: (800) 716-2788; www.domaine.com. Open daily 1000–1800, call for tour times.

The Hess Collection $ 4411 Redwood Rd; tel: (707) 255-1144; www.hesscollection.com. Open daily 1000–1700, art collection to 1645.

di Rosa Preserve $ 5200 Carneros Hwy; tel: (707) 226-5991; www.dirosapreserve.org. Tours by reservation, call for hours.

Napa River Adventures $$ Tel: (707) 224-9080; www.napariveradventures. com

Napa, the town, is the economic heart of Napa, the valley. The town centre, west of the Napa River, remains a scenic reminder of a less hurried past, filled with Victorian homes, spreading trees and quiet sidewalks. Napa also has the majority of the Valley's hotels, restaurants and tourist facilities. **COPIA**, the **American Center for Wine, Food & the Arts**, is an upscale presentation of Wine Country. Julia's Kitchen restaurant, a tribute to folksy American chef Julia Child, has an open kitchen, making it easy for patrons to watch chefs. Wine-tasting, theatre, wine-oriented shop, art exhibits and superb kitchen gardens complete Napa's showpiece. Nearby, the **Oxbow Public Market** has locally grown fruit and vegetable purveyors, restaurants, wine tasting and sales, a bakery and enough to make a 'sustainable' picnic. The restored **Napa Valley Opera House**, built in 1879, has a wide range of famous-name music, plays, musical theatre, opera and dance productions in the Margrit Biever Mondavi Theatre.

To see (but not to visit more than one) the greatest number of wineries in the shortest possible time, ride the **Napa Valley Wine Train**, an elegantly restored passenger train that makes 3-hour, 36-mile lunch and dinner runs up and down the valley between Napa and St Helena.

Not far away on the highway to Sonoma is **Domaine Carneros**, Taittinger's Napa Valley sparkling winery modelled on the French champagne maker's 18th-century Château de la Marquetterie.

Art lovers should make time to visit at least two collections: **The Hess Collection**, a restored early 20th-century winery and eclectic modern art collection neighbouring a calm Franciscan retreat centre, and the **di Rosa Preserve** with hundreds of contemporary Bay Area artists' work, amassed over 40 years, displayed amidst vineyards and olive trees – look for the cow on the lake!

Napa River Adventures offers narrated cruises, or active holidaymakers can hire a kayak or canoe to navigate the tidal river.

Accommodation and food in Napa

The best way to absorb wine country is to spend a night or two in an inn or bed and breakfast (usually pricey). Contact **Bed and Breakfast.com**® www.bedandbreakfast.com/napa-california.html; www.napavalley.com/lodging or **Napa Valley Reservations Unlimited** tel: (707) 252-1985 or (800) 251-6272; www.napavalleyreservations.com, who can book most rooms.

Alexis Baking Company $ 1517 Third St; tel: (707) 258-1827; www.alexisbakingcompany.com; open Mon–Fri 0630–1600, Sat 0730–1500, Sun 0800–1400, has breakfast and picnic supplies.

High Tech Burrito $ 641 Trancas St: tel: (707) 224-8882; open Mon–Sat 1030–2100, Sun to 2000 offers international versions of burritos.

Downtown Joe's Brewery & Restaurant $$ *902 Main St; tel: (707) 258-2337; www.downtownjoes.com; open daily 0900–2200* is great for California-style bistro dishes, beers and ales.

Julia's Kitchen at COPIA $$$ *500 First St; tel: (707) 265-5700; www.juliaskitchen.org; open Wed–Mon 1130–1500, Wed–Sun 1730–2130 and Sunday brunch*, combines California and French cuisine and the organic garden's produce.

RUTHERFORD/OAKVILLE

Robert Mondavi Winery $–$$
7801 St Helena Hwy, Oakville; tel: (888) 766-6328; www.robertmondaviwinery.com. Open daily 0900–1700.

Mumm Napa $$ *8445 Silverado Trail, Rutherford; tel: (707) 967-7700 or (800) 686-6272; www.mummcuveenapa.com. Open daily 1000–1700, tours hourly 1000–1500.*

Rubicon Estate $$$
1991 St Helena Hwy, Rutherford; tel: (800) 782-4266 or (707) 968-1161; www.rubiconestate.com. Open daily 1000–1700 only for those purchasing wine or touring.

Rutherford Hill Winery $ *200 Rutherford Hill Rd, Rutherford; tel: (707) 963-1871; www.rutherfordhill.com. Open daily 1000–1700. Tours at 1130, 1330, 1530.*

St Supéry Winery $
8440 St Helena Hwy (Hwy 29), Rutherford; tel: (707) 963-4507 or (800) 942-0809; www.stsupery.com. Open daily 1000–1700.

Above
The late Robert Mondavi, standard-bearer for Napa Valley wineries

The tiny hamlets of Rutherford and Oakville, along Hwy 29, are ground zero in the continuing explosion of Napa wineries. **Robert Mondavi Winery** is the standard-bearer for the Napa Valley, the first American winemaker in modern times to commit to the French heresy that wine tastes better if made in small barrels rather than in 40,000-litre vats and that Cabernet Sauvignon demands different vinification than Cabernet Franc or Sauvignon Blanc. Mondavi's tours are among the most informative and the best suited to wine beginners. The downside is that the winery is so well known it attracts enormous crowds. Make tour bookings five days in advance in summer and at holiday weekends. There are a number of other good tours on offer.

Mumm Napa offers sweeping views of the valley, sparkling wine and fine art photography galleries.

Rubicon Estate is an historic château (formerly the Inglenook Estate Winery, now Rubicon Winery) with a pay-to-enter tasting room and Centennial Museum (cinema memorabilia) owned by director Francis Ford Coppola. Book in advance for château and vineyard tours.

Rutherford Hill Winery has an excellent cave tour as well as shady picnic grounds.

St Supéry Winery has the valley's best interactive exhibit, with a 3-D valley map, samples of the varied aromas – 'SmellaVision' – found in fine wines and enormous windows overlooking winery operations.

Food in Rutherford/Oakville

The **Oakville Grocery** *7856 St Helena Hwy, Oakville; tel: (707) 944-8802; www.oakvillegrocery.com; open daily 0800–1800*, has been selling oil, vinegar and barbed wire since 1881, but the valley's oldest mercantile has grown into a gourmet haven. The store is packed with food, wine and – at lunchtime – people queuing for sandwiches. Have lunch or watch the sun set over olive trees and vineyards on the balcony at the **Auberge du Soleil Restaurant** *180 Rutherford Rd; tel: (800) 348-5406; www.aubergedusoleil.com*

St Helena

ℹ St Helena Chamber of Commerce *1010 Main St (Hwy 29), Ste A, St. Helena, CA 94574; tel: (707) 963-4456 or (800) 799-6456; www.sthelena.com. Open Mon–Fri 1000–1700, Sat 1100–1500.*

🏛 Robert Louis Stevenson/ Silverado Museum *1490 Library Ln; tel: (707) 963-3757; www. silveradomuseum.org. Open Tue–Sun 1200–1600. Free.*

Below
The Auberge du Soleil, in Rutherford

St Helena's attractive and lively town centre has the valley's finest collection of historic buildings. The literati should visit the **Robert Louis Stevenson/Silverado Museum**, with more than 8000 items related to Stevenson. The other half of the former library building is occupied by the **Napa Valley Wine Library**, a collection of photographs and newspaper cuttings related to local viticulture. **Ambrose Bierce House** (*1515 Main St; tel: (707) 963-3003; www.ambrosebiercehouse.com*), where the misanthropic author lived for 15 years before disappearing into the Mexican Revolution, is a bed and breakfast with a small collection of Bierce memorabilia.

The town also has two of the valley's better outdoor attractions. **Bale Grist Mill State Historic Park** (*3 miles north on Hwy 29; tel: (707) 942-4575; www.parks.ca.gov*) surrounds an 1846 grist mill. Hiking trails lead to the mill pond and **Bothe-Napa Valley State Park** (*4 miles north on Hwy 29; tel: (707) 942-4575; www.parks.ca.gov*), once home to the Wappo Indians. The park has several fine hiking trails, a swimming pool, camping, and spots to dine on wine, cheese and your own picnic.

Californian Wine

Rules about drinking white wine with fish and red wine with meats seemed sensible enough when both food and wine were predictable. But today's recipes incorporate a wider range of ingredients and flavours – and not just in California. It's more useful to find out what a wine actually tastes like than to look to the colour for guidance, especially as winemakers are now experimenting with lesser-known varietals. Here are the major California grapes and wines, with an important caveat: every wine develops a different taste, depending on where and how the grapes were grown and how they were vinified, or made into wine. No two wines taste precisely the same and no two drinkers experience precisely the same taste from the same bottle. If it doesn't taste good to *you*, it doesn't taste good, no matter how long or loudly the 'experts' declaim. Most California wineries sell their own wine by the bottle or the case. Case purchases usually bring a 10–20 per cent discount off the list price, but it's often cheaper to buy wine at a local supermarket or discount store than at the winery or a wine shop. The disadvantage: smaller wineries have limited distribution, so their wines may be available only at the winery. If in doubt, ask at the winery.

Blanc de Blancs Literally 'white from whites', wine made from white grapes, usually Chardonnay.

Blanc de Noirs 'White from blacks', sparkling white wine made from red grapes, usually Pinot Noir. The skins, which contain most of the colour, are separated from the juice immediately after pressing to preserve the light colour. Blanc de Noirs normally has a richer, fruitier taste than Blanc de Blancs. Both are quite dry in California.

Blush Pink wines, usually white Zinfandels, are somewhere between almost-white and almost-red. The longer the juice is left with the skins after crushing, the darker the colour and the more intense the flavour. Most blush wines are light, sweet and meant to be drunk as young as possible.

Cabernet Sauvignon California 'Cabs' are normally dry, medium to full-bodied, and can be tannic, a less direct way to say astringent. The dominant flavours are berries and cherries.

Chardonnay The white wine of choice for many people. Pick your style: light, with simple flavours like apples, citrus and flowers; rich, with oak, butter and nuts; or steely, with very little taste at all.

Gewürztraminer California winemakers usually opt for a slightly sweet German style, but Gewürz can also be made dry, in the Alsatian style, or as an almost too-rich dessert wine. All three styles taste of spice, flowers and fruit.

Merlot This red is softer than Cabernet, ie, it is less astringent and more 'fruity'. Winemakers traditionally blend Merlot with Cabernet to create a softer, more drinkable wine that requires less ageing.

Petit Sirah A delicate red that is less common in California. Look for it as Syrah in French blends or Shiraz in Australia.

Pinot Noir Usually a silky-smooth light red that leaves a lingering freshness rather than the heaviness more typical of Cabernet and Merlot.

Riesling Germany's other white grape is the classic for sweet dessert wines, but can also be made as a delicate dry wine filled with flower and fruit flavours.

Sauvignon Blanc or **Fumé Blanc** By either name, wines made from this white grape are normally lighter and less pronounced in flavour than Chardonnay.

Sparkling wine California's way around Champagne's legal lock on the name Champagne. Look for 'methode champenoise' or 'fermented in this bottle' for top quality. 'Charmant' is plonk produced in bulk. Most of the major French champagne houses also produce sparkling wine in California.

Viognier Emerging as a staple on Californian wine lists, this dry white varietal is also known for hints of stone fruits and is recommended for hearty dishes or with cream sauces.

Zinfandel This rich red is usually spicy, with a strong hint of berries.

Beringer Vineyards $
2000 Main St;
tel: (707) 967-4412;
www.beringer.com. Open
daily Jun–Oct 1000–1800;
Nov–May 1000–1700;
tel: (707) 963-8989
(ext. 2222) for tours.

Beringer Vineyards, Beringer Vineyards' Rhine House, is the valley's most-photographed building, modelled after an ancestral Gothic German homestead. The winery can be crowded, but it's worth seeing the rich, wood-panelled interior and regal tasting room.

Accommodation and food in St Helena

Cindy's Backstreet Kitchen $$ *1327 Railroad Ave; tel: (707) 963-1200; www.cindysbackstreetkitchen.com*, is famed chef Cindy Pawlcyn's relatively informal eatery, with her favourite, spice-rubbed quails, on the menu, along with meatloaf, pork chops and other locally sourced plates.

Auberge du Soleil $$$ *180 Rutherford Hill Rd, Rutherford; tel: (707) 963-1211* or *(800) 348-5406; www.aubergedusoleil.com*, is a Mediterranean-inspired retreat surrounded by olive groves and valley vistas.

Go Fish $$$ *641 Main St; tel: (707) 963-0700; www.gofishrestaurant.net*, is another Pawlcyn eatery with seafood on the menu.

Meadowood Resort $$$ *900 Meadowood Ln, St Helena; tel: (707) 963-3646* or *(800) 458-8080; www.meadowood.com*, surrounds a private croquet lawn and golf course.

Tra Vigne $$$ *1050 Charter Oak Ave; tel: (707) 963-4444; www.travignerestaurant.com*, specialises in Italian-laced California cuisine, with a separate brick-oven pizzeria and wine bar.

The **Wine Spectator Greystone Restaurant $$$** *2555 Main St; tel: (707) 967-1010; www.ciachef.edu/restaurants/wsgr*, part of the Culinary Institute of America's nearby campus at the former Christian Brothers Winery, has California versions of Mediterranean staples.

Woodhouse Chocolate $$$ *1367 Main St; tel: (800) 966-3468* or *(707) 963-8413; www.woodhousechocolate.com*, is worth a stop for heavenly by-the-piece house-made confections.

VALLEJO

Vallejo Convention & Visitors Bureau
Vallejo Ferry Terminal, 289 Mare Island Way, Vallejo, CA 94590; tel: (707) 642-3653 or (800) 482-5535;
www.visitvallejo.com. Open Mon–Fri 0830–1700, Sat–Sun 0830–1300.

Vallejo was California's first state capital, named after General Mariano Vallejo, one of California's few Mexican leaders who became a successful American politician. Vallejo was also home to a major US Navy repair facility and mothball fleet, the **Mare Island Naval Shipyard**, which closed in 1996. The rusting hulks that once lined the mouth of the Napa River are gone and the **Mare Island Historic Park Foundation** (*tel: (707) 557-1538* or *(707) 644-4746; www.mareislandhpf.org*) offers tours.

Local history is recounted in the **Vallejo Naval and Historical Museum** in the old city hall building. Many of Vallejo's graceful Victorian buildings were replaced or altered beyond recognition

Vallejo Naval & Historical Museum
$ 734 Marin St;
tel: (707) 643-0077;
www.vallejomuseum.org.
Open Tue–Sat 1000–1630.

during the frantic growth and ship building of World War II. Enough historic structures survived to create a small **Architectural Heritage District**, between Georgia, Sutter, Carolina, Monterey and York Sts.

Vallejo's theme park is **Six Flags Discovery Kingdom** (tel: (707) 643-6772; www.sixflags.com/parks/discoverykingdom). The most scenic way to visit is aboard a Blue & Gold Fleet (www.blueandgoldfleet.com) catamaran ferry from San Francisco's Pier 39 (see page 142).

YOUNTVILLE

Yountville Chamber of Commerce
6484 Washington St, Ste F,
Yountville, CA 94599;
tel: (707) 944-0904;
http://yountville.com.
Open daily 1000–1500.

Napa Valley Museum $
55 Presidents Circle;
tel: (707) 944-0500;
http://napavalleymuseum.org.
Open Wed–Mon 1000–1700.

This is the culinary heart of the Napa Valley and the beginning of serious, shoulder-to-shoulder wineries. Art lovers head for the **Napa Valley Museum**, an art gallery, wine museum and cultural centre. **V Marketplace** (6525 Washington St; tel: (707) 944-2451; www.vmarketplace.com) is a one-time winery turned shopping mall.

Domaine Chandon has the valley's most informative sparkling winery tour. Hot-air balloons frequently take off from the winery grounds or nearby.

Food in Yountville

Yountville is Napa's answer to Berkeley's Gourmet Ghetto, with prices to match. Make bookings as far in advance as possible. All are *open daily*. Hours change with the economy.

Californian Wine History

California has been producing wine since Mission friars first planted criolla grapes for sacramental use. In 1857, Hungarian immigrant Agoston Haraszthy planted European *Vinifera* grapes in Sonoma. His successful **Buena Vista Winery** soon attracted competitors **Gundlach-Bundschu** (1858), **Charles Krug** (1861), **Schramsberg** (1862) and a host of other familiar names. By the 1890s, California wines were winning gold medals in every major European competition.

The 1906 San Francisco earthquake and subsequent fire destroyed enormous stocks of wine ageing in San Francisco warehouses as well as wineries up and down Wine Country. By the time the industry was back on its feet, America was plunging into Prohibition. From 1919–33, it was illegal to make or consume wine (or any other alcoholic beverage) except for sacramental, medicinal or family purposes.

A few vineyards hung on, but most switched to fruit trees and other crops or went bankrupt. Robert Mondavi and the few other 1940s and 1950s winemakers who dreamed of re-establishing the glory days were dismissed as dreamers. Today, they're worshipped as saints.

Their dogged vision, plus research from the University of California at Davis, near Sacramento, and technological improvements from bulk winemakers such as Gallo, gave California vintners more control over the art of turning grape juice into wine than any winemakers in the world. When **Stag's Leap** bested Mouton Rothschild in a Paris competition in 1976, the California wine rush was on.

Right
Ballooning over the vineyards
of the Napa Valley

Domaine Chandon $$$ 1 California Dr.; tel: (707) 944-2280; www.chandon.com. Open daily at 1000. Call for tour times.

Above the Wine Country Ballooning Tel: (800) 759-5638 or (707) 538-7359; www.balloontours.com

Balloons Above the Valley Tel: (707) 253-2222 or (800) 464-6824; www.balloonrides.com

Napa Valley Balloons Tel: (707) 994-0228 or (800) 253-2224; www.napavalleyballoons.com

Chef Thomas Keller's **The French Laundry $$$** *6640 Washington St; tel: (707) 944-2380; www.frenchlaundry.com,* is one of the valley's original name eateries with a jacket required to dine, followed by **Mustards Grill $$$** *7399 St Helena Hwy; tel: (707) 944-2424; www.mustardsgrill.com,* **Bistro Jeanty $$** *6510 Washington St; tel: (707) 944-0103; www.bistrojeanty.com,* and a constantly changing constellation of would-be stars.

Wine Country from the air

One of the most common sounds on a Napa morning is the gentle roar of propane burners from hot-air balloons drifting above the vineyards. Balloon tours nearly always lift off near dawn, when breezes are light, just as the night mists burn away to reveal rank upon rank of trellised vines sweeping across valley contours. Plan on landing 90 minutes later to a champagne breakfast.

It's not cheap – about $225 per person – but it's worth the experience. Advance booking is required.

Suggested tour

Take the **San Francisco–Oakland Bay Bridge** ❶ to I-80 eastbound. Cross the **Carquinez Bridge** ❷. Detour through VALLEJO ❸ or continue on I-80 to Hwy 37 then to Hwy 29. Follow Hwy 29 north through NAPA ❹, YOUNTVILLE ❺, OAKVILLE ❻, RUTHERFORD ❼, ST HELENA ❽ and CALISTOGA ❾.

Ratings

Food and drink	●●●●●
Scenery	●●●●●
Wine	●●●●●
Architecture	●●●○○
History	●●●○○
Children	●●○○○
Museums	●●○○○
Wildlife	●●○○○

Sonoma Wine Country

Sonoma is an agglomeration of several wine valleys, one of which is actually called Sonoma. The geographic variety makes Sonoma slower to drive through than neighbouring Napa, but far more rustic and interesting. California's wine industry was born in Sonoma, but the region has been far less aggressive in promoting itself than Napa. For visitors, that makes Sonoma a somewhat less crowded and far more pleasurable experience – and Sonoma wines win at least as many medals as their Napa counterparts.

DRY CREEK VALLEY

ⓘ Sonoma County Tourism Bureau
Tel: (800) 576-6662;
www.sonomacounty.com

Dry Creek, a twisting valley running north from Healdsburg to **Lake Sonoma**, was one of Sonoma's first official wine appellations. **Dry Creek Vineyards** (*3770 Lambert Bridge Rd; tel: (800) 864-9463; www.drycreekvineyard.com; open daily 1030–1630*) is one of its first and most-awarded wineries. **Preston of Dry Creek Winery and Vineyards** (*9282 W. Dry Creek Rd; tel: (800) 305-9707 or (707) 433-3372; www.prestonvineyards.com; open daily 1100–1630*) offers picnic tables and home-made bread to go with rich red wines. **Ferrari-Carano Vineyards & Winery** (*8761 Dry Creek Rd; tel: (800) 831-0381 or (707) 433-6700; www.ferrari-carano.com; open daily 1000–1700*) is an architectural masterpiece with killer Chardonnay.

GEYSERVILLE

The famous film director has begun transformation of a château-inspired winery into **Francis Ford Coppola Presents Rosso & Bianco**

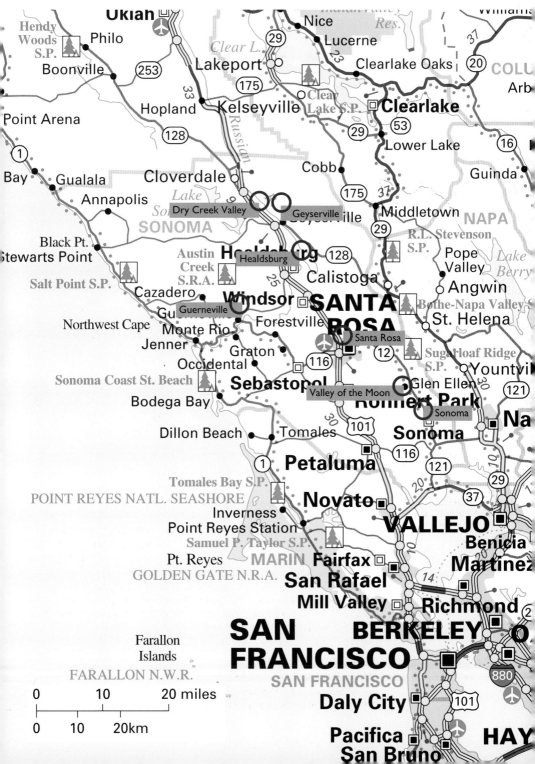

Ukiah
Hendy Woods S.P.
Philo
Boonville
253
33
Point Arena
1
Bay
Gualala
Annapolis
Hopland
128
Cloverdale
Lake So
SONOMA
Black Pt.
Stewarts Point
Salt Point S.P.
Cazadero
Austin Creek S.R.A.
Dry Creek Valley
Healdsburg
Healdsburg
25
128
Windsor
Guerneville
Gu
Northwest Cape
Monte Rio
Jenner
Graton
Occidental
Sonoma Coast St. Beach
Sebastopol
Bodega Bay
Dillon Beach
Tomales
Tomales Bay S.P.
POINT REYES NATL. SEASHORE
Inverness
Point Reyes Station
Samuel P. Taylor S.P.
Pt. Reyes
MARIN
Fairfax
GOLDEN GATE N.R.A.
San Rafael
Mill Valley
Farallon Islands
FARALLON N.W.R.
SAN FRANCISCO
SAN FRANCISCO
Daly City
Pacifica
San Bruno

Nice
Lucerne
Clearlake Oaks
Lakeport
175
29
Clear L.
Clear Lake S.P.
Kelseyville
Russian
Cobb
Cloverdale
Geyserville
ille
Middletown
29
R.L. Stevenson S.P.
Pope Valley
Angwin
Calistoga
Bothe-Napa Valley S
St. Helena
SANTA ROSA
Santa Rosa
116
12
Sugarloaf Ridge S.P.
Yountvi
Forestville
Valley of the Moon
Glen Ellen
121
Rohnert Park
Sonoma
Na
Sonoma
101
116
Petaluma
121
Novato
37
VALLEJO
Benicia
Martinez
14
Richmond
SAN BERKELEY O
FRANCISCO
101
HAY
880

Clearlake
53
Lower Lake
29
175
37
16
Guinda
NAPA
Lake Berry
COLU
Arb
20
Res.
Williams
37

0   10   20 miles
0   10   20km

ⓘ **Geyserville Chamber of Commerce** *Geyserville, CA 95441; tel: (707) 857-3745; www.geyserville.com*

ⓕ **Francis Ford Coppola Presents Rosso & Bianco Winery** *300 Via Archimedes; tel: (877) 767-7624 or (707) 857-1462; www.rossobianco.com. Open 1100–1700.*

Pedroncelli Winery $$ *1220 Canyon Rd; tel: (707) 857-3531 or (800) 836-3894; www.pedroncelli.com. Open daily 1000–1630.*

Trentadue Winery $$ *19170 Geyserville Ave; tel: (707) 433-3104 or (888) 332-3032; www.trentadue.com. Open daily 1000–1700.*

Right
Francis Ford Coppola
Presents Rosso & Bianco
Winery, in Geyserville

Winery. Continue exploring the Alexander Valley at **Pedroncelli Winery**, one of the area's last family-owned wineries, and Tuscan-inspired **Trentadue Winery**, which espouses sustainable agricultural practices.

Accommodation in Geyserville

Victoriana lovers may swoon at **Hope-Merrill House $$** *21253 Geyserville Ave; tel: (800) 825-4233 or (707) 857-3356; www.hope-inns.com*, a three-storey bed-and-breakfast jewel with symmetrical landscaping, extravagant silk-screened wallpaper, carved armchairs and velvet-covered divans.

Hope-Bosworth House $$ *across the street at 21238 Geyserville Ave; tel: (800) 825-4233 or (707) 857-3356; www.hope-inns.com*, is a more cheerful, less formal and less expensive Queen Anne restoration.

GUERNEVILLE

ⓘ Russian River Chamber of Commerce and Visitors Center
16209 First St, Guerneville, CA 95446; tel: (877) 644-9001 or (707) 869-9000; www.russianriver. com. Open Mon–Sat 1000–1700, Sun to 1500.

Korbel Visitor Center
13250 River Rd (in Railroad Station). The Visitor Centers carry an excellent Russian River Wine Road map listing all the wineries along the river. Unlike their more formal counterparts in the Napa and Sonoma valleys, Russian River and nearby wineries seldom charge, or charge less, for tasting.

Ⓗ Armstrong Redwoods State Natural Reserve $
2 miles north of Guerneville, 17020 Armstrong Woods Rd; tel: (707) 869-2015. Open 0800–1 hour after sunset. Visitor Center, tel: (707) 869-2958; www.parks.ca.gov. Open daily 1100–1500.

Korbel Champagne Cellars 13250 River Rd; tel: (707) 824-7000; www.korbel.com. Open daily for wine tasting 0900–1700. Call for hours for winery and rose garden tours.

Russian River Vineyards 5700 Gravenstein Hwy N., Forestville; tel: (707) 887-3344; www.russianrivervineyards. com. Open 1100–1700.

Pronounced *gurnvil*, the biggest settlement in the Russian River Valley began as a logging town in the 1880s, blossomed as a San Francisco summer resort and slipped into the hippie era. Wealthy city escapees have since filtered into the valley, creating an appealing mix of counter-culture, urban sophisticates, gay holidaymakers and local winemakers, none of them in a rush to get anywhere.

Wine touring and lazing about the Russian River are the main activities in Guerneville. **Johnson's Beach**, a placid strand in the centre of town, offers sand, **canoes, paddle boats** and rubber rafts in summer. The beach is also the main stage for the wildly popular **Jazz on the River** (*www.russianriverfestivals.com*), held each September. The river is less benign in winter, when heavy rains produce periodic floods. Many river-front homes and businesses have been raised to the first floor to escape the high waters.

Guerneville's most often-ignored asset is **Armstrong Redwoods State Natural Reserve**, 750 acres of virgin coast redwood groves, hiking trails and primitive camping. Don't stray off the trails as it's easy to get lost in the tangled thickets in the centre of the park. **Armstrong Woods Pack Station** (*tel: (707) 887-2939; www.redwoodhorses.com*) offers half-day tours and overnight forest expeditions on horseback (advance booking required).

The Russian River is lined with vineyards and wineries, most of them upstream (east) from Guerneville. One must-see, even if you are not doing the wineries, is **Korbel Champagne Cellars**, which makes beer, wine, brandy, and yes, champagne-style sparkling wines. The red-brick buildings are swathed in ivy and surrounded by hundreds of varieties of roses with plenty of shaded picnic tables.

Russian River Vineyards produces reds and is one of the river's friendliest wineries in a pleasant forest retreat.

Accommodation and food in Guerneville

The Stumptown Brewery $ *15045 River Rd; tel: (707) 869-0705; www.stumptown.com/brews; open 1200–0200*, has beer, a sense of humour about itself, and ribs, smoked chicken and meat at its **Stumptown Grill** restaurant.

The **Russian River Resort $–$$** *16390 4th St; tel: (800) 417-3767 or (707) 869-0691; www.russianriverresort.com*, has a pool and fine downtown location, popular with gay and lesbian holidaymakers.

Applewood Inn & Restaurant $$$ *13555 Hwy 116; tel: (800) 555-8509; www.applewoodinn.com*, is the Russian River's most luxurious inn and best gourmet restaurant (*www.dineatapplewood.com*) with its own kitchen garden.

HEALDSBURG

Healdsburg Chamber of Commerce & Visitors Bureau *217 Healdsburg Ave, Healdsburg, CA 95448; tel: (707) 433-6935; www.healdsburg.org. Open Mon–Fri 0900–1700, Sat 0900–1500, Sun 1000–1400.*

Gallo Family Vineyards Tasting Room *320 Center St; tel: (707) 433-2458; www.gallosonoma.com. Open daily 1000–1800.*

Kendall-Jackson Healdsburg Tasting Room $ *337 Healdsburg Ave; tel: (707) 433-7102; www.kj.com/visit/healdsburg. asp. Open daily 1000–1700.*

Healdsburg Museum *221 Matheson St; tel: (707) 431-3325; www.healdsburgmuseum.org. Open Thu–Sun 1100–1600. Free.*

Hand Fan Museum $ *327A Healdsburg Ave (Hotel Healdsburg); tel: (707) 431-2500; www.handfanmuseum.com. Open Wed–Sun 1100–1600.*

This is one of the few wine country towns that may have more grape growers and farm workers than tourists. Founded in 1857 by a migrant farmer turned merchant, the tranquil town remains focused on its tree-lined **central Healdsburg Plaza**. Healdsburg straddles an invisible border between the Russian River, Dry Creek and Alexander Valleys, which makes it a popular starting point for wine tours.

If time is short, half a dozen wineries have tasting rooms on or near the plaza, including **Gallo Family Vineyards** and **Kendall-Jackson.** More than 20 wineries are within easy cycling distance of the bed and breakfasts that have sprung up all over town, and dozens lie within a quick drive. And when wine touring gets too much, try **Veterans Memorial Beach Park** *(tel: (707) 433-1625)* on the Russian River, a mile south of the plaza. Canoes and rubber rafts can be hired for a cooling float downstream; the hire company provides the return trip.

The **Healdsburg Museum**, in the 1910 Carnegie Library building, has a collection of Pomo Indian baskets and artefacts from California's Mexican period. Extensive displays explain local history, assisted by one of the area's largest photographic archives. The **Hand Fan Museum** shows off 2500 fans.

Accommodation and food in Healdsburg

Downtown Bakery & Creamery $ *308A Center St; tel: (707) 431-2719; www.downtownbakery.net; open Mon–Fri 0600–1730, Sat 0700–1730, Sun 0700–1600,* and **Flying Goat Coffee Roastery and Cafe** $ *324 Center St; tel: (707) 433-3599; open Mon–Fri 0700–1800, Sat–Sun 0800–1800,* are favourite local breakfast stops.

Belle de Jour Inn $$ *16276 Healdsburg Ave; tel: (707) 431-9777; www.belledejourinn.com,* is a luxurious collection of refreshingly simple cottages and carriage house.

Bistro Ralph $$ *109 Plaza St; tel: (707) 433-1380; open Mon–Sat,* is an intimate bistro and long-term survivor in a turbulent restaurant scene.

Healdsburg Inn on the Plaza $$$ *112 Matheson St; tel: (707) 433-6991 or (800) 431-8663; www.healdsburginn.com,* is the best town-centre choice.

Madrona Manor $$$ *1001 Westside Rd at Dry Creek Rd; tel: (707) 433-4231 or (800) 258-4003; www.madronamanor.com,* is a rambling manor house surrounded by exotic gardens and a citrus orchard amid the vineyards.

Madrona Manor Restaurant $$$ *1001 Westside Rd; tel: (707) 433-4231; www.madronamanor.com,* is one of the most sought-after tables in Healdsburg, known for its ambience, presentation, fresh garden ingredients and one Michelin Star.

Above
Grapes ripening in the
Californian autumn sun

SANTA ROSA

🛈 **Santa Rosa
Convention &
Visitors Bureau**
9 Fourth St, Santa Rosa, CA
95401; tel: (707) 577-8674
or (800) 404-7673;
www.visitsantarosa.com.
Open daily 0900–1700. The
North Coast California
Welcome Center is in the
same location, in Railroad
Square.

Santa Rosa is ringed with shopping malls and plagued by traffic jams. It also has splendid residential neighbourhoods and more than its fair share of quirky museums, gardens and other attractions.

One of the quirkiest is the **Church of One Tree** (*492 Sonoma Ave*), built in 1874 of wood milled from a single redwood tree and filled with objects and papers from the life of native son Robert Ripley, of Ripley's Believe It or Not fame. The **Charles M. Schulz Museum**, named after the late creator of the 'Peanuts' comic strip, has exhibits devoted to his illustration, as well as other comic illustrators. Most novel are the full-scale SNOOPY™ Labyrinth, named after the beloved beagle of the strip, and the 3588 four-panel 'Peanuts' strips which compose a huge wall mural. Another attraction is the **Luther Burbank Home & Gardens**, the long-time home and gardens planted by the horticulturist who created more than 800 new varieties of commercial fruits, flowers, vegetables and other plants.

There are several other traditional museums worth visiting. The **Sonoma County Museum**, in a restored 1909 post office and federal building, spans the eras from Native American habitation through the

 **Charles M. Schulz Museum $$**
2301 Hardies Lane;
tel: (707) 579-4452;
www.schulzmuseum.org.
Open autumn–spring Mon,
Wed–Fri 1100–1700,
Sat–Sun 1000–1700;
summer Mon–Fri
1100–1700, Sat–Sun
1000–1700.

Luther Burbank Home & Gardens $
Santa Rosa & Sonoma Aves;
tel: (707) 524-5445;
www.lutherburbank.org.
Gardens open daily
0800–sunset; building tours
Apr–Oct Tue–Sun
1000–1600.

Sonoma County Museum $ 425 7th St;
tel: (707) 579-1500; www.
sonomacountymuseum.com.
Open Tue–Sun 1100–1700.

Jesse Peter Native American Art Museum
Bussman Hall, Santa Rosa
Junior College, 1501
Mendocino Ave; tel: (707)
527-4479;
www.santarosa.edu/museum.
Open mid-Aug–mid-May, call
for hours. Free.

Kendall-Jackson Wine Center $ 5007 Fulton Rd;
Fulton; tel: (866) 287-9818
or (707) 571-8100;
www.kj.com/visit. Open daily
1000–1700; garden tours
1100, 1300, 1500.

Safari West $$$ 3115
Porter Creek Rd; tel: (800)
616-2695 or (707) 579-
2551; www.safariwest.com.
Open year-round, call for
hours, tour and overnight
safari tent accommodation.

Victorian era. **Jesse Peter Native American Art Museum** displays Native American arts and crafts from across the continent and beyond.

Grapes are only one of many products that have made Sonoma County famous; the area is at least as well known for apples, escargot, berries, salad greens, lamb, goat's milk cheese, duck and other comestibles. The best guide to local farms, seasonal produce and agricultural tours is **Sonoma County Farm Trails** (*tel: (800) 207-9464; www.farmtrails.org*), a free self-guiding tour map available at most wineries and visitor centres and online.

The **Kendall-Jackson Wine Center** has wine tasting, but its wine-sensory and culinary gardens – designed for visitor tasting – are the stunning highlights of this 120-acre winery between Santa Rosa and Healdsburg. Have a craving for Africa in Wine Country? **Safari West** is a 400-acre wildlife preserve with as many animals as acres. It's an eclectic combination of safari tours, winter walking tours, day visits, overnight stays, and occasional educational fund-raisers on an enclave amidst vineyards and ranches, but the stars are endangered species of African animals and birds and two conserved species of extinct-in-the-wild Saharan antelope. Visitor sightings and encounters may take in ostrich, cheetahs, lemurs, giraffes, Cape buffalo and zebras.

Accommodation and food in Santa Rosa

Hotel La Rose $$$ *308 Wilson St; tel: (707) 579-3200* or *(800) 527-6738; www.hotellarose.com*, occupies a historic landmark building. **John Ash & Co $$$** *4350 Barnes Rd; tel: (707) 527-7687; www.vintnersinn.com/dining; open daily*, blends Asian, French, Italian and Southwestern American flavours. **Kenwood Restaurant and Bar $$$** *9900 Hwy 12, Kenwood; tel: (707) 833-6326; www.kenwoodrestaurant.com; open daily Wed–Sun*, is a Wine Country favourite just south of Santa Rosa.

SONOMA

Sonoma Valley Visitors Bureau
453 First St E., Sonoma, CA 95476; tel: (707) 996-1090 or (866) 996-1090; www.sonomavalley.com. Open Mon–Sat 0900–1700, Sun at 1000. The other visitor centre is 23750 Arnold Dr. at Cornerstone Gardens, Hwy 121, south of Sonoma. Open daily.

Sonoma State Historic Park $
363 3rd St W.; tel: (707) 938-5960; www.parks.ca.gov. Open daily 1000–1700.

Buena Vista Winery $
18040 Old Winery Rd; tel: (800) 926-1266; http://buenavistacarneros.com

Gundlach-Bundschu Winery $ 2000 Denmark St; tel: (707) 938-5277 or (707) 939-3015; www.gunbun.com. Open daily 1100–1630.

Sebastiani Vineyards & Winery $ 389 Fourth St E.; tel: (800) 888-5532; www.sebastiani.com. Open daily 1000–1700.

Viansa Winery & Italian Marketplace $$ 25200 Arnold Dr. (Hwy 121); tel: (800) 995-4740; www.viansa.com. Open daily 1000–1700.

Cornerstone Gardens $ 23570 Hwy 121; tel: (707) 933-3010; www.cornerstoneplace.com. Open daily 0900–1700.

Opposite
California poppies in the gardens of the Preston of Dry Creek Winery and Vineyards

Sonoma town retains much of its original Mexican flavour despite years of Wine Country gentrification, thanks in large part to the 8-acre **plaza** designed by General Mariano Vallejo in 1835. The Bear Flag Revolt of 1846 that catapulted California into America began in Sonoma. The revolt, which looms large in California history books, involved about three dozen American settlers who seized control of the unused and unguarded *presidio* at Sonoma. Their chief prisoner was General Vallejo, a long-time supporter of American annexation for California. Both the revolt and the California Republic dissolved a month later when the US Navy sailed into Monterey Bay.

A monument to the revolt sits in the middle of the shady plaza, across from **Sonoma State Historic Park**, which includes **Mission San Francisco Solano de Sonoma** (*tel: (707) 938-9560; tours Fri–Sun 1100, 1200, 1300, 1400*), **Vallejo's Home** (*tel: (707) 938-9559; tours Sat–Sun 1300, 1400, 1500*), and the **Sonoma Barracks** (*tel: (707) 939-9420*), once occupied by a handful of Mexican soldiers. A dozen or so Mission-era buildings surround the plaza, most of them now used as restaurants, shops or boutiques. One of the more interesting is the 1850 **Swiss Hotel** (*18 W. Spain St; tel: (707) 938-2884; www.swisshotelsonoma.com*), a good restaurant and small hotel.

California's modern wine industry was born at **Buena Vista Winery**, a large estate with a stone winery, hillside tunnels, an art gallery and picnic area. **Gundlach-Bundschu Winery** is nearly as scenic with rich, up-to-date vintages. **Sebastiani Vineyards & Winery** has embarked on a second century. Look for the hand-carved casks. **Viansa Winery & Italian Marketplace** has one of Sonoma's best winery shops and a picnic area overlooking a wildlife refuge. Not far down Hwy 121 is Cornerstone Gardens, an eclectic collection of changing garden sculpture, salvaged items as fine arts, galleries and a café.

Accommodation and food in Sonoma

Cafe La Haye $$ *140 E. Napa St; tel: (707) 935-5994; http://cafelahaye.com; open for dinner Tue–Sat*, is a fine American-style choice.

Della Santina's $$$ *133 E. Napa St; tel: (707) 935-0576; www.dellasantinas.com; open daily 1100–1500, 1700–2130*, does Italian.

The Fairmont Sonoma Mission Inn & Spa $$$ *100 Boyes Blvd at 18140 Sonoma Hwy; tel: (707) 938-9000 or (800) 257-7544; www.fairmont.com/sonoma*, is the most elegant and most expensive spa in Sonoma County. The luxurious spa is the main draw, but the inn is a traditional favourite for visiting Hollywood types.

The Swiss Hotel $$$ *18 W. Spain St; tel: (707) 938-2884; www. swisshotelsonoma.com; open daily 1130–1430 and from 1700*, concentrates on modern California cuisine.

VALLEY OF THE MOON

Jack London State Historic Park $
2400 Jack London Ranch Rd, Glen Ellen; tel: (707) 938-5216; www.parks.ca.gov. Museum and park open daily.

Triple Creek Horse Outfit $$
Tel: (707) 887-8700; www.triplecreekhorseoutfit.com

Wine Country Chocolates $$
14301 Arnold Dr. (Jack London Village); tel: (707) 996-1010; www.winecountrychocolates.com has a free tasting bar for heavenly home-made chocolates, 1000–1700 daily. A Sonoma tasting room, 414 1st Street E., is on Sonoma Plaza.

This is the capital of the Jack London cult. The author of *Call of the Wild* and numerous other stories that celebrate nature, manhood and the nobility of suffering in the Great Outdoors named the valley between Santa Rosa and Sonoma after the way the moon seems to appear and disappear behind the surrounding mountain peaks. London and his wife settled at the well-named **Beauty Ranch**, 800 acres that have become **Jack London State Historic Park**. London was the highest-paid writer of his era, which makes more intriguing the collection of rejection letters displayed in his house, now the park museum. A series of trails leads to the ruins of **Wolf House**, built for the couple in 1913 and destroyed by arson just before they moved in. Both are buried on a hilltop above Wolf House. **Triple Creek Horse Outfit** offers guided horseback rides through the state historic park from spring to autumn.

Accommodation and food in Valley of the Moon

Glen Ellen Inn Restaurant $$ *13670 Arnold Dr.; tel: (707) 996-6409; www.glenelleninn.com; call for opening hours,* specialises in using local ingredients.

Saffron $$ *13648 Arnold Dr.; tel: (707) 938-4844; www.saffronrestaurant.com; open Tue–Sat 1700–2100,* serves California cuisine with ingredients from local farms.

Beltane Ranch $$$ *11775 Sonoma Hwy (Hwy 12); tel: (707) 996-6501; www.beltaneranch.com,* is a buttercup-yellow ranch bunkhouse become bed and breakfast.

Gaige House Inn $$$ *13540 Arnold Dr.; tel: (707) 935-0237 or (800) 935-0237; www.gaige.com,* a Victorian house, is very modern inside with an eclectic collection of modern art.

Suggested tour

Follow Hwy 101 north from San Francisco across the **Golden Gate Bridge ❶** through Marin County to **Rohnert Park ❷**, SANTA ROSA **❸** and HEALDSBURG **❹**. Take Healdsburg Ave and Alexander Valley Rd north, then east to **Jimtown ❺** and Hwy 128. Turn south to **Kellog ❻** and Franz Valley Rd to Porter Creek Rd and follow Calistoga Rd to Hwy 12 and **Kenwood ❼**. Take Warm Springs Rd south to **Glen Ellen ❽**. Continue south to **El Verano ❾** and turn east to SONOMA **❿**. Return to San Francisco via the Carneros Hwy and the Napa Valley or take Hwy 121 to Hwy 37 and back to Hwy 101.

Detour: From HEALDSBURG **❹**, take Dry Creek Rd through the **DRY CREEK VALLEY ⓫** to Canyon Rd, then turn east on Canyon Rd to Hwy 101. Either follow Hwy 101 south to Alexander Valley Rd or take Hwy 128 to GEYSERVILLE ⓬ and Jimtown.

Marin Coast

Ratings

Nature	●●●●●
Scenery	●●●●○
Children	●●●○○
Coastal villages	●●●○○
Wildlife	●●●○○
Beaches	●●○○○
Food	●●○○○
Museums	●●○○○

The western edge of Marin County (pronounced 'mah-rinn') offers the most civilised, most accessible and most crowded stretch of Northern California coast. The possibilities run from fine beaches with frigid water to shady, almost dank redwood groves, open pastures, sheer cliffs, windy picnic sites and elegant hideaways.

Marin's scenic bounty is natural, albeit highly modified by early loggers and farmers who stripped the forests from miles of coastal hills. But the style in which the coast is enjoyed, the roads, the parks, the restaurants and country inns, are imports from East Marin, the San Francisco Bay side of the county.

The Bay side of Marin is a striving, style-conscious enclave whose tone has largely been set by 1960s Flower Power survivors. Most have long since traded psychedelic trips for more prosaic journeys by BMW, Mercedes and top-of-the-line mountain bikes, but personal gratification remains central to life in Marin – thousands swarm across the open hillsides, beaches and trails of West Marin and a section of Sonoma County coast just north at weekends to keep bodies and auras well exercised.

BODEGA BAY

ⓘ Marin County Visitors Bureau
1 Mitchell Blvd, Ste B, San Rafael, CA 94903; tel: (866) 925-2060 or (415) 925-2060; www.visitmarin.org

Sonoma Coast Visitors Center
850 Hwy 1, Bodega Bay; tel: (707) 875-3866; www.bodegabay.com. Open daily.

Pomo and Miwok bands lived along the sheltered curve of Bodega Bay when Juan Francisco de la Bodega y Quadra Mollineda stopped by on his way north to British Columbia in 1775. The Native Americans were long gone by the time Alfred Hitchcock portrayed the fishing village as a town under siege from the air in *The Birds* (1963). Squawking hordes of seagulls and other birds still haunt the harbour, but they're far more interested in stealing scraps from fishermen than in dive-bombing tourists and schoolchildren.

Bodega was failing fast as commercial fishing declined in the 1970s, but holidaymakers discovered the town and turned the economic tide. The best walks are over **Bodega Head**, one of the first California sites where local opposition successfully derailed utility schemes to build nuclear power stations along the coast. The **University of California Davis Bodega Bay Marine Laboratory** offers public tours.

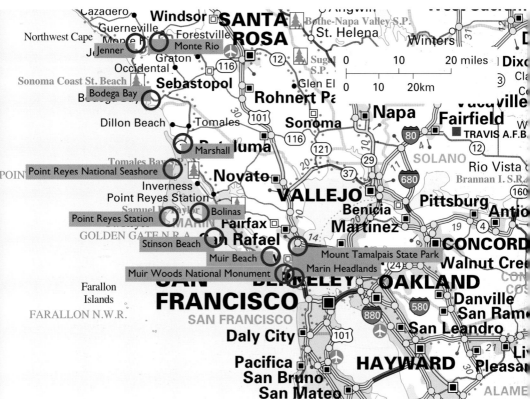

University of California Davis Bodega Bay Marine Laboratory *2099 Westside Rd, Bodega Head; tel: (707) 875-2211; www-bml.ucdavis.edu. Open Fri 1400–1600. Free.*

Sonoma Coast State Park *Beaches along 17 miles from Bodega Head to 4 miles north of Jenner; tel: (707) 875-3483; www.parks.ca.gov*

Sonoma Coast State Park is multiple beaches separated by headlands and bluffs overlooking craggy cliffs and small coves. Views are magnificent, swimming is treacherous, and there is environmental protection of snowy plover breeding grounds.

Accommodation and food in Bodega Bay

Bookings are essential in summer; at weekends all year.

Lucas Wharf Restaurant $$ *595 Hwy 1; tel: (707) 875-3522; www.suncompsvc.com/lucas*, concentrates on more traditional seafood. **Lucas Wharf Deli and Fishmarket**, next door, is the best source for picnic supplies.

Bay View Restaurant $$$ *The Inn at the Tides, 800 Hwy 1; tel: (800) 541-7788 or (707) 875-2751; www.innatthetides.com*, offers monthly 5-course winemaker dinners and continental cuisine *Wed–Sun*.

Bodega Bay Lodge & Spa $$$ *103 Hwy 1 (Doran Beach Rd); tel: (888) 875-2250 or (707) 875-3525; www.woodsidehotels.com/bodega*, is a posh resort.

Bodega Coast Inn & Suites $$$ *521 Hwy 1; tel: (707) 875-2217 or (800) 346-6999; www.bodegacoastinn.com*, has large view rooms.

BOLINAS

Audubon Canyon Ranch Bolinas Lagoon Preserve *4900 Hwy 1, 2 miles north of Stinson Beach; tel: (415) 868-9244; www.egret.org. Open mid-Mar–mid-Jul Sat–Sun 1000–1600.*

Just north of Stinson Beach along Hwy 1 is **Bolinas Lagoon**, a usually sunny resting spot for seabirds and harbour seals that haul out on sandbars. Off the eastern side of the Lagoon is **Audubon Canyon Ranch Bolinas Lagoon Preserve**, the premier place on the entire West Coast to observe majestic great blue herons and great and snowy egrets as well as dozens of other species.

Bolinas is an anti-outsider, though not unfriendly, surfer and beach town west of Bolinas Lagoon. It's worth the short drive off Hwy 1 (look for the unmarked paved road beyond the Lagoon, as there's a long tradition of locals removing signs to discourage visitors) to get picnic supplies from **The People's Store $** (*end of the gravel drive, next to Bolinas Bakery; tel: (415) 868-1433*), a co-operative famous for locally grown produce and sublime service. To find the real Bolinas and denizens, check out the bar and live music on weekends at **Smiley's Schooner Saloon and Hotel $** (*41 Wharf; tel: (415) 868-1311; www.coastalpost.com/smileys*), operating since 1851.

Duxbury Reef Nature Reserve (*end of Elm Rd*) is a rocky shelf with wonderful tide pooling. Keep an eye on the water, especially on a rising tide. Birdwatchers usually opt for the **PRBO Palomarin Field Station and Visitor Center** (*999 Mesa Rd; tel: (415) 868-0655 ext. 395; www.prbo.org; open sunrise to 1700*), which has a self-guided visitor centre and nature trail at one of America's few full-time ornithological research stations.

JENNER

Below
Arcadian countryside around Jenner

The tiny village marks both the mouth of the Russian River and the end of Hwy 116, which follows the river inland to dozens of wineries. The 'logs' on the sand at the mouth of the river are most likely seals warming themselves. Beaches north of Jenner are wild, windy and fabulously popular for hiking, beachcombing and enjoying the scenery.

Accommodation in Jenner

Jenner Inn & Cottages $$$ *Hwy 1; tel: (707) 865-2377 or (800) 732-2377; www.jennerinn. com*, is a collection of several houses and bed-and-breakfast establishments, with 20 rooms 'where the river and ocean meet'.

Timber Cove Inn $$$ *21780 N. Hwy 1; tel: (800) 997-8319 or (707) 847-3231; www. timbercoveinn.com*, has oceanfront lodging.

MARIN HEADLANDS

❶ Marin Headlands Visitor Center
*3 miles west of Alexander exit from Hwy 101;
tel: (415) 331-1540;
www.nps.gov/goga. Open daily 0930–1630.*

❷ Golden Gate National Recreation Area
www.nps.gov/goga. Free.

Nike Missile Site
*Tel: (415) 331-1453;
www.nps.gov/goga/nike-missile-site.htm. Open Wed–Fri 1230–1530 and the first Sat of every month. Free.*

Marine Mammal Center *Tel: (415) 289-7335; www.tmmc.org. Open daily 1000–1600. Free.*

❸ Marin Headlands Hostel $ *Fort Barry;
tel: (888) 464-4872 ext. 168 or (415) 331-2777;
www.norcalhostels.org*

The windswept, nearly naked headlands directly north of the Golden Gate Bridge are the least-changed hillsides in Marin. They have been a military preserve since the US Civil War, when artillery batteries were installed to repel an invasion that never happened. Slopes facing the Pacific Ocean and the Golden Gate were honeycombed with batteries, observation posts and supply bunkers during World War II; anti-aircraft and Nike missile batteries were added during the Cold War years. The demilitarised Headlands is now part of the **Golden Gate National Recreation Area** (*see page 140*).

Most of the old batteries survive as scenic vantage points. Among the best is **Battery Wallace** (*above the southwestern tip*), with nicely framed views of the Pacific and the Golden Gate Bridge. The last surviving **Nike Missile Site SF-88** is complete with decommissioned missiles. **Point Bonita Lighthouse** (*western tip of the Headlands*) is open for visits via a steep hike and a tunnel, Sat–Mon 1230–1530.

Most Headlands activities begin around the Point from the lighthouse turn-off at the **Marin Headlands Visitor Center**. A wide, sandy beach separates the cold Pacific surf from the warmer waters of **Rodeo Lagoon** (no swimming, to protect nesting birds). Nearby is the **Marine Mammal Center**, a rescue and rehabilitation centre for injured and sick marine mammals. The centre is open daily for tours, volunteer staff and workload permitting. Officers' quarters at the former **Fort Barry**, just inland, have been converted into a spacious youth hostel.

MARSHALL

❹ Tomales Bay Oyster Company
*15479 Hwy 1, just south of Marshall; tel: (415) 663-1242;
www.tomalesbayoysters.com.
Open daily 0800–1800.*

Hog Island Oyster Co
20215 Hwy 1; tel: (415) 663-9218; www.hogislandoysters.com. Open daily 0900–1700.

Straus Family Creamery
*Tel: (415) 663-5464;
www.strausmilk.com.
Tours for adults: www.malt.org/hp/hikestours.html;
tours for adults and children:
tel: (415) 663-1158. Free tours spring–autumn.*

Marshall was once a major oyster and fishing port for San Francisco. The fishing is long gone, but the oysters are back, courtesy of the **Tomales Bay Oyster Company** and **Hog Island Oyster Co** which sell oysters fresh from the water. Another reason to stop is **Tony's Seafood Restaurant $** *18863 Hwy 1; tel: (415) 663-1107*, which has specialised in oysters for half a century. Barbecue is the preferred preparation.

Since it became the first certified organic dairy west of the Mississippi River in the 1960s, the **Straus Family Creamery** has been a leader in preserving West Marin County agricultural lands while making superb, flavourful, milk, butter, yoghurt and other dairy products, including award-winning ice cream.

MONTE RIO

ℹ **Monte Rio Chamber of Commerce**
Tel: (707) 865-1533;
www.monterio.org

This Russian River resort town 3 miles west of Guerneville (*see page 169*) is filled with gracefully crumbling Victorian houses and a few more modern resorts. The town is best known as the entrance to the **Bohemian Grove**, a private camp that lets out San Francisco's Bohemian Club for an annual camp-out for the world's biggest boys – former heads of state, bank presidents, media moguls, military leaders, politicos and the like, with neither women nor cameras allowed.

Accommodation in Monte Rio

Huckleberry Springs Mountaintop Inn $$$ *8105 Beedle Rd; tel: (800) 822-2683; www.huckleberrysprings.com*, is a collection of very private cottages surrounded by towering redwoods. The restaurant (guests only) is among the Russian River's best.

Rio Villa Beach Resort $$$ *20292 Hwy 116; tel: (877) 746-8455 or (707) 865-1143; www.riovilla.com*, has pleasant views of the Russian River.

MOUNT TAMALPAIS STATE PARK

🏞 **Mount Tamalpais State Park $**
801 Panoramic Hwy, Mill Valley; tel: (415) 388-2070; www.parks.ca.gov. Open daily 0700 to sunset.

◐ **Mountain Home Inn $$$** *lodging $$ restaurant, 810 Panoramic Hwy, Mill Valley; tel: (415) 381-9000; www.mtnhomeinn.com*

Mount Tamalpais (Mount Tam to locals) dominates the Marin skyline. Ridges leading up to the 2571ft peak neatly divide the county into wild western slopes leading to the Pacific Ocean and suburbanised slopes leading to San Francisco Bay. More than 50 miles of hiking and biking trails wind through the park to connect with another 200 miles in surrounding recreation areas. If fog and smog permit, panoramic views stretch from the Farallon Islands (26 miles west) to the Sierra Nevada (150 miles east). The Panoramic Hwy is the most direct route from Hwy 1 to Muir Woods, but traffic on the winding road can be extremely slow.

MUIR BEACH

Just down the road from **Muir Woods National Monument** (*see opposite*), Muir Beach is one of Marin's prettiest beaches, a deep crescent of sand behind a semicircular cove. It is seldom crowded during the week, but can turn into a zoo (with almost no parking) at weekends and holidays during fine weather. Swimming is not recommended on account of ferocious rip tides.

Accommodation and food in Muir Beach

The **Pelican Inn** **$$$** (*10 Pacific Way; tel: (415) 383-6000; www.pelicaninn.com*) is the creation of a homesick British expatriate, who conjured up a dark and inviting 16th-century Tudor inn. Book as early as possible – the Inn is even more popular for its food, drink and boarding than its romantic atmosphere.

MUIR WOODS NATIONAL MONUMENT

Muir Woods National Monument $
Mill Valley, CA 94941; tel: (415) 388-2595; www.nps.gov/muwo. Open daily 0800–sunset.

Right
A hundred shades of green: Muir Woods National Monument

This 560-acre virgin grove of Coastal redwoods is all that remains of the vast redwood forests that once cloaked Mount Tam and most of the rest of coastal Marin, Sonoma and Mendocino counties – Mill Valley, just over the flank of Mount Tam, was named after the many lumber mills the town once supported. The next significant stand of easily accessible redwoods, in **Redwood National and State Parks** (*see page 203*), is towards the Oregon border.

Muir Woods sits in a steep canyon that was uneconomic for early lumbermen to log. Today, it's a calm and majestic place, with tatters of fog and beams of sunlight filtering through 250ft-tall redwoods to the valley floor carpeted with ferns and laurel.

Paved, self-guided trails circle the flat canyon floor. Unpaved trails climb the canyon walls to connect with Mount Tam and Pacific Ocean routes. The monument was named after pioneer conservationist John Muir in 1908.

Easy access also makes Muir Woods impossibly popular. The small car park fills up early at weekends and holidays and sightseeing coaches from San Francisco clog the road every day. Crowds are smallest midweek and in winter, which is also when salmon and steelhead trout migrate up **Redwood Creek** to spawn. For salmon viewing updates during the Nov–Mar season *tel: (415) 388-2595*.

POINT REYES NATIONAL SEASHORE

Point Reyes National Seashore
Point Reyes Station, CA 94956; tel: (415) 464-5100; www.nps.gov/pore

Point Reyes is a patch of semi-wilderness surrounded by the Pacific Ocean and Tomales Bay. This wing-shaped peninsula of rolling hills, sheer cliffs and drifting fog is a mecca for hikers, cyclists, bird-watchers, backpackers, mountain bikers, sea kayakers, wildflower enthusiasts and just about anyone else who enjoys outdoor activities.

ℹ **Bear Valley Visitor Center** *off Hwy from Olema; tel: (415) 464-5100. Open Mon–Fri 0900–1700, Sat–Sun 0800–1700.*

Kenneth C. Patrick Visitor Center *Drakes Beach; tel: (415) 669-1250. Open Sat–Sun 1000–1700.*

Lighthouse Visitor Center *Above the lighthouse; tel: (415) 669-1534.* **Visitor Center** *open Thu–Mon 1000–1630; lighthouse stairs and exhibits open to 1630, lens room open as staffing permits.*

🅿 **Drake's Bay Oyster Farm** *17171 Sir Francis Drake Blvd; tel: (415) 669-1149; www.drakesbayfamilyfarms.com. Open daily 0800–1630.*

Northern elephant seals (*Mirounga angustirostris*) have returned to the Point Reyes headlands after a century's absence. Volunteers provide tours of the colony of up to 1,800 five-thousand-pound animals during the Dec–Mar pupping and breeding season; tel: (415) 464-5134. Best spots for viewing are: the lighthouse parking lot overlooking South Beach, by the historic Lifeboat Station, and a viewing area about ¼ mile from Chimney Rock parking lot.

It is also the most itinerant piece of California. Five million years ago, Point Reyes was south of San Francisco Bay, about where Monterey now stands. A hundred million or so years earlier, it was part of the Tehachapi Mountains in Southern California. Presuming it hasn't been swamped by erosion and global warming, the whole peninsula will eventually end up in the Gulf of Alaska.

Point Reyes is drifting northwestwards along the San Andreas fault, which produced California's most famous earthquake. The 1906 quake that destroyed San Francisco was centred beneath Point Reyes; the entire peninsula jumped 16ft to the north in the blink of an eye. The only damage was to a few fences, which can be seen along the easy Earthquake Trail from the Bear Valley Visitor Center.

The park, which is adjacent to, but not part of, the Golden Gate National Recreation Area, has several distinct areas.

Bear Valley Visitor Center is the main visitor centre. The huge, barn-shaped building houses exhibits covering local history and ecosystems.

The easy 1-mile **Earthquake Trail** displays some of the more notable effects of the 1906 San Francisco earthquake, which was far stronger at largely uninhabited Point Reyes than it was in San Francisco. Behind the visitor centre stands the **Morgan Horse Ranch**, a working ranch for the Morgan horses used to patrol seashore wilderness areas. **Kule Loklo** is a re-created Miwok village that offers a glimpse of local life before European contact. An easy ½-mile walk with self-guiding exhibits leads from the visitor centre to the village.

Several popular hikes leave from the Bear Valley centre, including an 8-mile return walk to **Arch Rock** on the coast. Check with rangers before setting out; the coast can be dramatically wetter, colder and windier than this protected valley.

Drakes Beach (*off Sir Francis Drake Blvd*) is a calm strand backed by white sandstone cliffs behind the crook of Point Reyes. The beach and **Drakes Estero**, a shallow estuary, designated as a wilderness area that shelters harbour seals and many bird species, are generally accepted as the place Sir France Drake careened the *Golden Hinde* in 1579 during his round-the-world pursuit of Spanish booty. Exhibits in the **Kenneth C. Patrick Visitor Center** focus on 16th-century maritime explorations as well as the local marine environment. Contemporary accounts have Drake remarking upon the white cliffs behind his makeshift shipyard and their resemblance to the white cliffs of Dover. A weathered copper plaque claiming *New Albion* for Queen Elizabeth I was discovered in the 1930s, but it is widely regarded as a forgery. Harder to dismiss are English coins of the era found in Native American encampments as far inland as **Olompali State Historic Park**, off Hwy 101 between **Novato** and Petaluma. As Drake's logbook was burnt in an Admiralty fire, the truth may never be known.

Also on the estero is **Drake's Bay Oyster Farm**, one of several oyster producers in the area selling the bivalves for about half the price of area restaurants.

Sir Francis Drake

Francis Drake was the first English tourist to California, a sometime-pirate, sometime-privateer who found fame, fortune and Point Reyes in the course of 'annoying' King Philip of Spain. Drake was so successful that his tiny *Golden Hinde* was splitting at the seams from the Spanish treasure his crew had captured during 18 months in the Caribbean and the Pacific. In 1579, he put ashore in a place whose physical description matches Drakes Bay for five weeks of rest and repair, then posted a brass plate claiming *Nova Albion* for Queen Elizabeth I before sailing west for Plymouth.

In 1937, University of California archaeologists announced that they had found Drake's plate; x-ray diffraction tests in the 1970s revealed that the plate was made in the 20th century, not the 16th. Silver sixpenny coins found in local Native American encampments support Drake's Bay as Drake's landing place, but this has never been confirmed. Drake's three-year round-the-world voyage earned him a knighthood, but England never tried to capitalise on his claim to *Nova Albion*.

Great Beach (*off Sir Francis Drake Blvd*), sometimes called 'Point Reyes Beach', is more than 10 miles of undeveloped beach, backed by untrammelled dunes and beach grasses. The beach is open to the full force of the Pacific, which makes swimming dangerous (and cold), but the wave action inspires awe, particularly during the winter storm season. Snowy plovers nest north of the north entrance May–Oct.

Limantur Beach (*end of Limantur Rd*) is one of the best swimming beaches in the area, protected from the full force of the Pacific by the Point Reyes headland. The nearby estuary is a good spot for bird-watching.

Mount Vision Overlook (*Mt Vision Rd, off Sir Francis Drake Blvd*), at 1282ft, provides the best panoramic view of the entire Point Reyes Peninsula, especially for colourful sunsets.

One of the oldest and most successful of the many dairy ranches established on the Point Reyes in the 19th century is **Pierce Point Ranch** (*Pierce Point Rd, Tomales; tel: (415) 669-1534*). A short self-guided trail guides visitors through the historic complex.

Point Reyes Light Station (*end of Sir Francis Drake Blvd; tel: (415) 669-1534*) stands 300 weather-whipped steps below the visitor centre at the tip of Point Reyes. Panoramas are stunning on clear days, but the winter whale migration is visible even on many foggy days. The visitor centre is ¼-mile from the car park; on weekends and holidays during winter whale-watching, board a free shuttle. Dress warmly, even on sunny days, as temperatures can drop as precipitously as the cliffs surrounding the lighthouse.

Tomales Point (*off Pierce Point Rd*), the northern end of Point Reyes, protects Tomales Bay, immediately to the east. Herds of dairy cattle and tule elk wander the windy moors.

Tule Elk Reserve (*end of Pierce Point Rd*) protects reintroduced tule elk which once ranged over coastal grasslands throughout Northern and Central California.

Right
The Point Reyes Light Station

POINT REYES STATION

 West Marin Chamber of Commerce *Box 1045, Point Reyes Station, CA 94956; tel: (415) 663-9232; www.pointreyes.org,* has information for Inverness, Marshall, Muir Beach, Olema, Point Reyes, Stinson Beach and Tomales.

Old Point Reyes Schoolhouse $$$ *11559 Hwy 1; tel: (415) 663-1166; www.oldpointreyesschoolhouse. com,* is a compound of hand-restored cottages and the historic schoolhouse, with peaceful gardens.

Cowgirl Creamery *80 4th St, Point Reyes Station; tel: (415) 663-9335; www.cowgirlcreamery.com. Open Wed–Sun 1000–1800. Fri ($) tours at 1130.*

This former ranching town is turning from milking dairy cows to milking tourists, an easier, less odorous and more lucrative task, yet **Cowgirl Creamery** has wide renown for the flavour, quality and variety of the artisan cheeses made in Point Reyes Station. Visitors can watch cheese making and sample the best of the best.

Accommodation and food in Point Reyes Station and Olema

West Marin accommodation is booked out early, especially at weekends and in summer. For help, try the **Inns of Marin** *tel: (415) 663-2000 or (800) 887-2880; www.innsofmarin.com,* or **Point Reyes Lodging Association** *tel: (415) 663-1872 or (800) 539-1872; www.ptreyes.com,* 16 inns and cottages in Inverness, Olema and Point Reyes Stations.

Bovine Bakery $ *11315 Hwy 1, Point Reyes Station; tel: (415) 663-9420,* has heavenly muffins and pastries.

Point Reyes Farmers Market $ *in front of Toby's Feed Barn, Hwy 1, Point Reyes Stations; Sat 0900–1300,* is a super place to sample the locally grown organic produce that attracted Prince Charles and the Duchess of Cornwall in late 2005.

Olema Farm House Restaurant Bar & Deli $$ *10005 Hwy 1, Olema; tel: (415) 663-1264; www.olemafarmhouse.com,* serves local seafood, burgers and local beer in an 1865 building in keeping with the tiny hamlet of Olema.

STINSON BEACH

West Marin Chamber of Commerce *Box 1045, Point Reyes Station, CA 94956; tel: (415) 663-9232; www.pointreyes.org/stinson. html*

Stinson is where Marin teenagers (adults, too) head when they need a taste of sand, Southern California beer-and-bikini-style. Swimming is allowed (there are lifeguards on duty in summer), but the bone-numbing water tends to discourage more than perfunctory dips. For recorded weather and surf conditions *tel: (415) 868-1922.*

Food in Stinson Beach

The Parkside Café $$ *43 Arenal Ave; tel: (415) 868-1272; www. parksidecafe.com,* is a popular neighbourhood café for breakfast and lunch with more complex offerings at dinner. Weather permitting, go for an outdoor table.

Sand Dollar Restaurant $$ *3458 Shoreline Hwy; tel: (415) 868-0434; www.stinsonbeachrestaurant.com,* is a favourite after a hike for tasty food and live music at weekends.

Suggested tours

Total distance: 60 miles.

Time: Half to full day.

Links: San Francisco south, Mendocino Coast north, Sonoma Wine Country east.

Route: From San Francisco, follow Hwy 101 north over the **Golden Gate Bridge ❶** to the Hwy 1 exit at the south end of **Sausalito ❷**. Take Hwy 1 to the Panoramic Hwy; follow Panoramic Hwy through MOUNT TAMALPAIS STATE PARK ❸ to MUIR WOODS NATIONAL MONUMENT ❹ and back to Hwy 1 at **Muir Beach ❺**. Turn north past STINSON BEACH ❻ and BOLINAS LAGOON ❼ along the POINT REYES NATIONAL SEASHORE ❽ to Olema ❾ and POINT REYES STATION ❿. If time allows, follow Sir Francis Drake Blvd west through Point Reyes National Seashore to the **Point Reyes Light Station ⓫**. Otherwise, continue north on Hwy 1 along **Tomales Bay ⓬**, then inland to **Valley Ford ⓭** and back to BODEGA BAY ⓮ and on to **Jenner ⓯**.

Detour: Tired of ocean? From **Valley Ford ⓭**, take Valley Ford Rd north to the Bodega Hwy. Turn east to the Bohemian Highway, then go north through **Camp Meeker ⓰** to the **Russian River ⓱** at MONTE RIO ⓲ and Hwy 116. Take Hwy 116 west along the Russian River to Hwy 1 and rejoin the main route at **Jenner ⓯**.

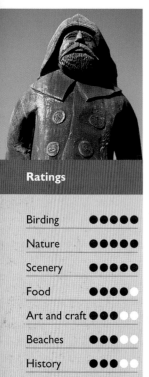

Mendocino Coast

Ratings

Birding	●●●●●
Nature	●●●●●
Scenery	●●●●●
Food	●●●●○
Art and craft	●●●○○
Beaches	●●●○○
History	●●●○○
Outdoor activities	●●●○○

The Mendocino Coast, once a fishing and redwood lumbering centre, has become one of the most sought-after and most pleasant tourist destinations in the United States. This 100-mile stretch of Pacific Coast is legendary for its dramatic cliffs and coves, quaint but artistic towns and varied flora.

It also has a hidden secret which confounds visitors expecting Southern California's sunny strands: thick fog which rolls in year-round, treacherous for fishing boats entering the narrow coves and adding a drippy nip to a climate where forests, rhododendrons, roses and heathers thrive. The fog can be invigorating, inviting exploration of the half-hidden scenery just around the next bend of Hwy 1.

FORT BRAGG

ℹ Mendocino Coast Chamber of Commerce *332 N. Main St, Fort Bragg, CA 95437; tel: (800) 726-2780 or (707) 961-6300; www.mendocinocoast.com. Open Mon–Fri 0900–1700, Sat to 1500. Covers Point Arena–Westport.*

City of Fort Bragg *www.fortbragg.com*

Mendocino Coast Alliance *Tel: (866) 466-3636; www.gomendo.com, has information for all of Mendocino County.*

Fort Bragg is the pragmatic commercial centre between San Francisco and Eureka. Eight miles north of Mendocino, Fort Bragg has an historic railway excursion, a tidy downtown, a commercial fishing harbour and economical accommodation and dining.

Pomo and Coast Yuki Native Americans, permanent residents when Russians settled Fort Ross in 1812, became otter pelt suppliers. By 1855, with the Russians and fur trade gone, the tribes were confined to a reservation, pushed out by Western US settlement. An army base on reservation land marked Fort Bragg's founding in 1857.

Local coast redwoods provided strong, fire-resistant lumber for San Francisco's Gold Rush era construction; by 1869, mills on headlands above every cove were rendering lumber for shipment south. Noyo Harbor, south of the main section of Fort Bragg, was the largest port for over 100 miles, and Fort Bragg's mills were among the largest.

A railway east to Willits was begun to enable shipment of lumber south. Most of Fort Bragg was rebuilt after the 1906 San Francisco

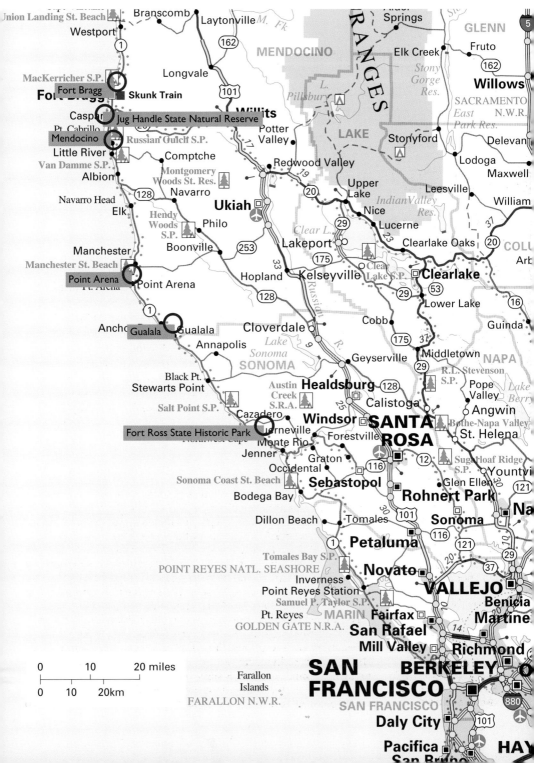

Mendocino Coast Botanical Gardens
$ 18220 N. Hwy 1;
tel: (707) 964-4352;
www.gardenbythesea.org.
Open Mar–Oct 0900–1700;
Nov–Feb 0900–1600.

Skunk Train $$$
Foot of Laurel St;
tel: (800) 866-1690;
www.skunktrain.com. Check
in advance for schedule.

Below
Getting ready to ride the Skunk
Train through the redwood
forests

earthquake levelled it and 1950s redevelopment removed most, but not all, architectural distinctiveness.

Mendocino Coast Botanical Gardens is 47 acres of plants, flowers, landscaping and eroded ocean bluffs where coastal fog and surprisingly mild winter temperatures permit an astounding variety of flora in formal plantings, fern canyons, wetlands and a pioneer cemetery. A nursery sells the gardens' signature rhododendrons and heathers. Bloom schedules include rhododendrons (Feb–May), camellias, flowering plums and Pacific Coast irises (Feb–Mar), wildflowers, heritage roses and cacti (May–Jul), dahlias, fuschias and heathers (Aug–Oct) and winter heathers and mushrooms (Nov–Jan).

Grey whales migrate Dec–Apr, and butterflies swarm in summer. The gardens and Mendocino Coast Audubon Society bird list covers 100 resident species, including hummingbirds, ospreys, pelagic cormorants and black oystercatchers.

California Western Railroad's wonderfully named **Skunk Train** hauls 65,000 holidaymakers a year on a 40-mile route through the redwoods from Fort Bragg to Willits. The all-day return excursion,

**Pacific Star
Winery $$**
*33000 N. Hwy 1, 12 miles
north of Fort Bragg;
tel: (707) 964-1155;
www.pacificstarwinery.com.
Open daily 1100–1700.*

named Skunk for 1920s cars which had an unbearable stench, crosses
31 bridges and manoeuvres 381 curves and two tunnels in a 1740ft
rising journey east. The railway offers fair-weather open cars and
closed passenger carriages pulled by diesel locomotive engines, or by
No 45, a classic 1924 Baldwin Steam Engine. The loud steaming
up whenever No 45 is rolled out is an attraction in its own
right, worth arriving 45 minutes before scheduled departure to see the
spectacle.

Pacific Star Winery, California's westernmost winery, sits just
above the crashing surf. In addition to winery tours, coastal walks
explore caves and bluffs, with fine views of migrating whales in
autumn and late winter.

Accommodation and food in Fort Bragg

Chain and independent motels abound and Fort Bragg has its share of
bed-and-breakfast inns. Book summer and holiday weekends in
advance as reasonable prices make accommodation so close to
Mendocino very popular. Restaurants use fresh, locally grown
ingredients and freshly caught fish.

Harvest Market $ *Hwys 1 and 20, 171 Boatyard Dr., Boatyard Shopping
Center; tel: (707) 964-7000; www.harvestmarket.com, open daily
0500–2300,* is stocked with a huge assortment of picnic provisions,
preserves, fresh produce and local fare.

North Coast Brewing Co $$ *455 N. Main St; tel: (707) 964-2739;
northcoastbrewing.com,* **Tap Room and Grill** restaurant, *open daily from
1200,* is relaxed, with tasty salads, appetisers and entrées, seafood, fine
beer and cheerful service.

Lodge at Noyo River $$$ *500 Casa del Noyo Dr.; tel: (800) 628-1126* or
(707) 964-8045; www.thelodgeatnoyoriver.com, has walking paths and
fine views of the harbour.

FORT ROSS STATE HISTORIC PARK

**Fort Ross State
Historic Park $**
*Hwy 1, 12 miles north of
Jenner; tel: (707) 847-3286;
www.fortrossstatepark.org.
Open 1000–1630.*

Fort Ross's reconstructed wooden stockade beneath rugged hills
encompasses two blockhouses, officials' quarters, two houses, a well
and a chapel. Russian Orthodox services are conducted on Memorial
Day and Fourth of July weekends. Schoolchildren and volunteers can
take part in regular 'Living History Day' events, when the daily life
and dances of California's Russian settlement are re-enacted
throughout the year. You get an idea of life as it was here in the early
19th century, the formal contact between Russians and Mexicans –
who succeeded the Spanish in California – and soldiers and
colonists.

GUALALA

Redwood Coast Chamber of Commerce Tel: (800) 778-5252 or (707) 884-1080, takes enquiries for Hwy 1 communities between Fort Ross and Gualala; www. redwoodcoastchamber.com

'Water-coming-down place' residents can spot visitors to their town, 100 miles north of San Francisco, by how they say the name. *Wah-la-la*, once a lumber centre, now has posh inns, fine restaurants, a pleasant rock-sheltered coast, artists, film stars, musicians and a few metaphysical devotees left from the 1960s.

Accommodation and food in Gualala

Gualala is blessed with accommodation and dining venues good enough to be destinations in their own right.

Pangaea $$ *39165 S. Hwy 1; tel: (707) 884-9669; www.pangaeacafe.com*, uses organic ingredients, most from within 30 miles, for sophisticated dinners.

St Orres $$$ *36601 Hwy 1; tel: (707) 884-3303; www.saintorres.com*, stops traffic with the inn's weathered old redwood and Douglas-fir dome turrets *à la Russe*. Succulent game specialities include wild boar, venison, quail and pheasant. The chef gathers wild mushrooms for the vegetarian tart selection herself.

Whale Watch Inn $$$ *35100 Hwy 1, 5 miles north of Gualala; tel: (800) 942-5342; www.whale-watch.com*, has large rooms and a golden strand of private beach below.

JUG HANDLE STATE NATURAL RESERVE

Jug Handle State Natural Reserve Hwy 1, 5 miles north of Mendocino; tel: (707) 937-5804; www.parks.ca.gov. Free.

Looking at wave action against rocks and cliffs along the Mendocino Coast gives little hint of geological formation at **Jug Handle State Reserve**. The 2.5-mile **Ecological Staircase** takes a path upwards through five successive and distinctive land/vegetation areas, each one 100ft and 100,000 years older than the one before.

A combination of earth crust uplift, repeated cycles of rising seas when retreating glaciers melted and thawed, and layering of gravel and sand upon the terraces that formed have created a natural west-to-east staircase. The path, within a 1-mile-wide strip, crosses Hwy 1. The forests become more dwarfed with each higher terrace, gnarled pygmy forests of Mendocino cypresses, rare Bolander pines and dwarf Fort Bragg manzanita growing in rock-hard soil which has been leeched of nutrients by wind and rain over the ages.

MENDOCINO

Views of the sea in three directions, artists and galleries galore, Victorian buildings, inns, restaurants, saloons, occasional solitude and

ℹ Mendocino Coast Chamber of Commerce
332 N. Main St, Fort Bragg, CA 95437; tel: (800) 726-2780 or (707) 961-6300; www.mendocinocoast.com. Open Mon–Fri 0900–1700, Sat 0900–1500. Covers Point Arena–Westport.

ⓗ Ford House Museum *735 Main St; tel: (707) 937-5397; www.mendoparks.org/ Mendocino-Headlands/ the_mendocino_headlands_ ford_h.HTM. Open daily 1100–1600. Incorporates Mendocino Headlands State Park Visitor Center. Free.*

Kelley House Museum
45007 Albion St; tel: (707) 937-5791; www.mendocinohistory.org. Open Jun–Sep Thu–Tue 1100–1500; Oct–May Fri–Mon 1100–1500.

Below
The scenic coast of Mendocino

the ever-mysterious fog make the town of Mendocino (and its almost indistinguishable southern neighbour, Little River) a mecca for all who can take the time to drive there and can afford it. It's a free-spirited place, where the neat grid of blocks disappears close to the ocean, dogs abound, hikers are determined to get somewhere, seals mimic surfers waiting for waves in the bay, canoeists paddle rivers and honeymooners walk hand-in-hand. Mendocino is also a ready-made film set, often used to represent quaint New England seaside towns, as it did for Angela Lansbury's television series *Murder, She Wrote*.

Ford House Museum is the **Mendocino Headlands State Park Visitors Center,** with a fine museum explaining lumbering, 'doghole port' (*see Point Cabrillo Light Station, page 192*) and schooner history. The restored 1854 home originally had a basement kitchen and dining room, requiring 23-year-old newlywed Martha Hayes Ford to illuminate her house with candles even on sunny days. Rangers maintain a fine herb garden outside, resembling the one cultivated around Mendocino's second house in the 1880s.

Owner Jerome Ford stopped in Mendocino while searching for the valuable Asian cargo carried in the hold of the *Frolic*. What he found were redwoods, a discovery followed by his establishing lumbering operations to supply the heavy demand of newly rich San Franciscans.

Kelley House Museum shows a family home constructed from local redwood which was built by a couple from Prince Edward Island, Canada, in 1861. Restored period rooms display photographs of early coastal shipping and artefacts from the family whose patriarch, William Henry Kelly, once owned most of the Mendocino Headlands, sawmills and lumbering operations for miles around.

Mendocino Headlands State Park *North, west and south of Mendocino town; tel: (707) 937-5804; www.parks.ca.gov*

Point Cabrillo Light Station *At the north side of Russian Gulch State Park; ¾ mile west on foot; tel: (707) 937-6122; www.pointcabrillo.org*

Van Damme State Park *Hwy 1 at Little River, 3 miles south of Mendocino; tel: (707) 937-5804; www.parks.ca.gov. Visitors Center open daily in summer, call for winter hours.*

Lighthouse Inn at Point Cabrillo $$$ *Point Cabrillo; tel: (866) 937-6124 or (707) 937-6124; www.mendocinolighthouse. pointcabrillo.org, offers bed and breakfast in the former head lightkeeper's house, with after-dark docent tours of the premises for inn guests.*

Mendocino Headlands State Park combines the beach and surf at the mouth of the Big River, favoured by surfers and aquatic mammals, grassy headlands, eroded cliffs, nestled coves, bluffs, carpets of wildflowers and prime grey whale-spotting Nov–Apr. The fog rolls over the western headland as a blanket, with nothing to define the horizon; just as suddenly, it retreats.

Point Cabrillo Light Station is a small, well-proportioned 1908 lighthouse with several keeper houses nearby. The walk from the car park to the shore traverses the Point Cabrillo Reserve meadows with grasses and wild blackberries lining the route. Guides conduct exterior tours with winter whale-watch weekends.

Craggy coast broken by narrow, rocky coves offered little protection from shipwreck and weather. These 'dogholes' (inlets only large enough, it was said, to permit a dog to go in, turn around and depart) became ports for lumber schooners plying to San Francisco. Specially designed wharves, chutes and cables from the tops of cliffs transported goods and people back and forth over the water. The invention of a steam engine attached to windjammer-style doghole schooners made for swifter shipping of milled redwood lumber south.

Van Damme State Park is popular for camping. The 1864 lumber mill site on the Little River is now the park recreation hall. The park and **Fern Canyon Trail** extend 5 miles east of the ocean to the **Pygmy Forest. Kayak Mendocino $$** (*tel: (707) 964-7480; www.kayakmendocino.com*) departs from the beach for sea cave tours.

It's easier to drive than hike to the **Pygmy Forest** (*3½ miles east of Hwy 101 on Little River Airport Rd*), a segment of the dwarf species forest formed by the terracing of the ecological staircase along the Mendocino Coast (*see Jug Handle State Natural Reserve, page 190*). Periodic signs for the 10-minute circuit around a boardwalk indicate California huckleberries, Bolander pines, Mendocino cypresses, bordering Bishop pines and red-pink California Rose Bay rhododendrons, five times smaller than relatives in the redwood forest.

Shopping in Mendocino

Mendocino could be the only tourist town in California that boasts more art galleries than T-shirt emporia. The **Mendocino Art Center** (*45200 Little Lake St; tel: (707) 937-5818 or (800) 653-3328; www. mendocinoartcenter.org; open daily*) offers arts and crafts classes with resident artists, exhibitions, and a retail shop with reasonably priced visual art and sculpture by local artists. Visit the artist-owned **Artists' Cooperative of Mendocino** (*45270 Main St; tel: (707) 937-2217; www. artgallerymendocino.com*). Ask at the Chamber of Commerce, galleries or museums for the *Mendocino Gallery Guide,* which lists 20 venues for openings and artists' receptions, *1700–2000 on the second Sat of the month.*

William Zimmer Gallery (*Lansing and Ukiah Sts; tel: (707) 937-5121; www.williamzimmergallery.com*) has an upper-crust attitude with one-of-a-kind *objets d'art,* including glass, wooden furniture and jewellery. **Highlight Gallery** *(45052 Main St; tel: (707) 937-3132; www.thehighlightgallery.com)* joins clothing shops, wine tasting and real-estate brokers on Main Street. **Lark in the Morning** *(45011 Ukiah St; tel: (707) 937-5275; www.larkinam.com)* sells unique musical instruments.

Accommodation and food in Mendocino

Mendocino's attractions and ambience drive prices high and accommodation availability low, especially in summer, at weekends and during holidays. Camping in state parks *(tel: (800) 444-7275)* can be an alternative, but pitches fill quickly. Enough restaurants are deliberately vegetarian to make a full meat, fowl and fish menu a surprise – and most post menus outside. Call ahead to reserve dining and arrive early to ensure a seat.

Cafe Beaujolais $$ *961 Ukiah St; tel: (707) 937-5614; www. cafebeaujolais.com,* known for its fresh ingredients, open for dinner 1745–2100. Gardens offer brick-oven-baked breads from 1100.

Dennen's Victorian Farmhouse $$$ *Little River, 2 miles south of Mendocino; tel: (800) 264-4723 or (707) 937-0697; www.victorianfarmhouse. com,* has quiet country atmosphere and a pet-free, no-barking zone.

MacCallum House Inn & Restaurant $$$ *45020 Albion St; tel: (800) 609-0492 or (707) 937-0289; www.maccallumhouse.com.* The restaurant is an 1882 mansion surrounded by flower gardens.

Stanford Inn By the Sea $$$ *Hwy 1 and Comptche-Ukiah Rd, south of Big River; tel: (707) 937-5615 or (800) 331-8884; www.stanfordinn.com.* The owners have created a luxury inn on the south side of Big River, and, with their resident cats, dogs, llamas and other animals, welcome pets, from dogs and cats to iguanas. An extensive organic produce and herb garden supplies the vegetarian and vegan-accommodating **Ravens' Restaurant $$$** *www.ravensrestaurant.com;* ferns decorate an indoor pool and spa area. The inn offers **Catch a Canoe & Bicycles, Too!** *tel: (707) 937-0273,* for recreation around the area.

Below
The coastline at Point Arena

POINT ARENA

Point Arena Cove *(½ mile west of Point Arena)* is a lovely cove with a fish-packing plant, several restaurants and an inn. It was once a late 19th-century whaling station and lumber boom town.

Point Arena Lighthouse and Museum *(Lighthouse Rd, 2 miles north of Point Arena (town); tel: (877) 725-4448 or (707) 882-2777; www.pointarenalighthouse.com),* a 115ft white beacon, is visible for miles south. The light

Russians in California

Europe was at war over Napoleon when the Russians built Fort Ross in 1812. Distant turmoil mandated extension of Russian imperialism, a direct challenge to the Spanish whose northernmost California outpost was at San Francisco. The lucrative fur trade with China was the impetus to send soldiers and colonists south from the Russian settlement at Sitka, Alaska, to hunt and grow crops in a longer growing season. With the Russians came Aleuts from Alaska, adept with kayak-type ocean craft.

Russian officials had not counted on the coastal fog which limited farming productivity, nor on the colonists' general lack of interest in farming, or the almost total extinction of the fur seals, harbor seals and river otters within three decades. In 1841, the Russians sold the fort to John Sutter (of subsequent Gold Rush fame), and left forever. Fort Ross became a ranch. The 1906 San Francisco earthquake destroyed most traces of the Russian era.

station property is fenced to discourage after-hour visitors. There is a 145-step circular climb to the first-level Fresnel lens. The lighthouse museum and tower ($) are open *daily 1000–1530*. **Vacation rental cottages $$** (*Point Arena Lighthouse Keepers, Inc; tel: (707) 882-2777 or (877) 725-4448*) are on site. **Coast Guard House Historic Inn $$$** *695 Arena Cove; tel: (707) 882-2442; www.coastguardhouse.com*, offers Arts and Crafts Movement décor in a former life-saving station.

Russian Gulch State Park (*Hwy 1, 2 miles north of Mendocino; tel: (707) 937-5804*) offers beautiful views from every angle: the Hwy 1 arch bridge over the gulch near a blowhole, the gulch beach popular with abalone and urchin divers and sea kayakers, the canyon trail with redwoods and Douglas fir, and inland to a waterfall and pygmy forest.

Salt Point State Park (*Hwy 1, 20 miles north of Jenner in Sonoma County; tel: (707) 847-3221; www.parks.ca.gov*) is supplemented by **Kruse Rhododendron State Natural Reserve**, and **Gerstle Cove Marine Reserve** with scuba diving. Damage from a 1993 campfire is obvious, but attractions include the spring wildflowers, abalone diving, ocean fishing and the only state park permitting mushroom hunting for king boletes and chanterelles.

The Sea Ranch (*29 miles north of Jenner*). Unique, skylit, weathered wooden homes, developed in the 1960s to harmonise with landscape and vegetation. Widely copied, these homes along 10 miles of Hwy 1 are exclusive and gated or landscaped away from public areas. An 18-hole golf course provides fine views to the Pacific. Real-estate companies handle rentals (*tel: (888) 732-7262; http://searanchescape.com*), or stay at **Sea Ranch Lodge $$$** (*60 Shore Walk Dr.; tel: (707) 785-2371 or (800) 732-7262; www.searanchlodge.com*).

Suggested tour

Total distance: 100 miles.

Time: 3 hours' driving; speed limits are slow, traffic congested, lanes narrow. There are few restaurants or services between Jenner and Albion except in Gualala. Picnicking overlooking the Pacific Ocean is a local tradition. The 8-mile stretch north from Albion to Mendocino (town) has some of the most popular inns and bed and breakfasts in California.

Links: From Jenner at the beginning of this route, join the Marin Coast Route (*see page 176*). To continue north, for redwoods, Victorian homes and more coastline, join the Coast Redwoods Route (*see page 196*) from Point Bragg. For a Wine Country experience, follow the Anderson Valley Detour from Hwy 1 (via Hwy 128) to Hwy 101, 1 mile north of Cloverdale. Take Hwy 101 south 10 miles, then turn left at Canyon Rd on to the continuation of Hwy 128 to Jimtown and Calistoga (*see Sonoma Wine Country (page 166) and Napa Valley Wine Country, page 154*).

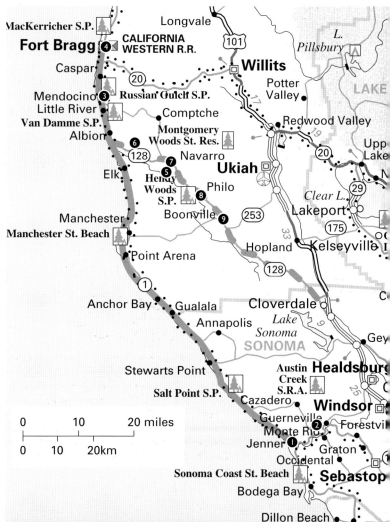

Route: From **Jenner** ❶, at the mouth of the **Russian River** ❷, follow Hwy 1 north to **MENDOCINO** ❸ and **FORT BRAGG** ❹.

Also worth exploring

The **Anderson Valley** ❺ along Hwy 128 between Hwy 1 and Hwy 101 at Cloverdale offers magnificent coast redwoods at **Navarro River Redwoods State Park** ❻, fine wines and sparkling wines around **Navarro** ❼, apples at **Philo** ❽, and **Boonville** ❾, one of the state's quaintest towns. *Boontling*, a locally invented dialect (*www.avbc.com/visit/boontling.html*), has faded with the influx of tourists, but Bucky Walters remain (phone booths named after the cost of early calls – a nickel, or 'bucky').

ℹ Anderson Valley Chamber of Commerce *Boonville; tel: (707) 895-2379; www.andersonvalleychamber.com*

Anderson Valley Winegrowers Association *Box 63, Philo, CA 95466; tel: (707) 895-9463; www.avwincs.com*

⑪ Navarro River Redwoods State Park *11 miles west from Hwy 1 on Hwy 128; tel: (707) 937-5804; www.parks.ca.gov. Free.*

Anderson Valley Brewing Company $ *17700 Hwy 253, Boonville; tel: (800) 207-2337 or (707) 895-2337 for brewery tours; www.avbc.com*

☾ Boonville Hotel $$$ *14050 Hwy 128 and Lambert Lane; tel: (707) 895-2210; www.boonvillehotel.com.* Ten bright, simply furnished rooms and a renowned wood grill restaurant for lunch and dinner.

Highland Guest Ranch $$$ *Philo; tel: (707) 895-3600; www.highlandranch.com,* is all-inclusive, with cabins, meals, horseback riding, hiking, swimming, tennis and occasional yoga retreats.

Coast Redwoods

Ratings

Birding	●●●●●
Nature	●●●●●
Scenery	●●●●●
Architecture	●●●○○
Children	●●●○○
History	●●●○○
Outdoor activities	●●●○○
Walking	●●●○○

Towering forests of coast redwoods, pastoral dairies, historic Victorian towns, lighthouses, sea stacks and rocky bluffs isolate this northwesternmost section of California, while preserving its regional personality. Timber and fishing were Redwood Empire economic mainstays, and much of the region has not recovered financially or emotionally from the diminishment of both.

Coast redwoods are preserved in the Redwood National and State Parks, a series of mixed-use parks and groves along Hwy 101 which are located a few miles south of Garberville. Despite the late President Ronald Reagan's comment that, having seen one redwood, you've seen them all, the clumps and groves differ in character. Second growth allows much more light to penetrate the canopy, but the size and magnitude of one or more old-growth giants, the world's tallest living things, is simply astounding.

Fog clings to this coast much of the year with a mild coolness which stimulates vibrant green ferns, redwood sorrel and surprising numbers of wildflowers twined with mint underneath the redwoods. Roosevelt elk and birds, and even foot-long yellow banana slugs thrive.

ARCATA

ⓘ Arcata Chamber of Commerce/ California Welcome Center *1635 Heindon Rd, Arcata, CA 95521; tel: (707) 822-3619; www.arcatachamber.com. Open daily 0900–1700.* Ask for the excellent Victorian Building/ Architectural Homes walking tour section of the Relocation brochure.

Youth, counterculture, environmentalism, organic produce and vegetarianism are bywords in this youthful enclave by Humboldt State University. Sand dunes and marshy wetlands are within a mile of an urban forest sheltering magnificent redwoods along trails. Bicycles are common, especially by the marshes and estuaries of the Mad River between Arcata Bay and McKinleyville.

Arcata Community Forest/Redwood Park (*east on 14th to Redwood Park Dr.; tel: (707) 822-8184; www.cityofarcata.com*) is this town's answer to timber clear-cutting: the preservation of 622 acres on a slope east of Hwy 101 near Humboldt State University, with 10 miles of trails.

Arcata Marsh and Wildlife Sanctuary (*G-I Sts; tel: (707) 826-2359; www.humboldt.edu/~ere_dept/marsh*) is a birdwatcher's paradise year-round with Marsh tours Sat at 0830. River otters and 200 species of birds are visible from trails and blinds on a flat track by grassy uplands. There is also a freshwater marsh, a tidal slough, a brackish lake and mudflats, and a system designed to purify waste water naturally. A 5½-mile

OREGON
CALIFORNIA

Crescent City

Del Norte Coast Redwoods State Park

Prairie Creek Redwoods State Park

Redwood National and State Parks

Patrick's Point State Park

Trinidad

Arcata

Ferndale

Humboldt Redwoods State Park

Avenue of the Giants

Garberville

Richardson Grove State Park

Hammond Coastal Trail from Mad River Beach in Arcata to Clam Beach near Trinidad (*see page 203*) is a locals' place to hike, bike or jog.

Arcata Plaza (*8th-9th, G-H Sts*) is the town square set aside by original lumber company owners as a park and meeting place. Among well-restored buildings near the plaza are the 1857 **Jacoby's Storehouse** (*8th and H Sts*) with 2ft-thick stone walls sheltering three restaurants; the 1914 **Minor Theatre** (*10th and H Sts; tel: (707) 822-3456*), the oldest operating cinema in the US, enhanced by isinglass door panels; and the 1915 **Hotel Arcata** (*9th and G Sts*).

The **Kinetic Grand Championship** (*Kinetic Universe; tel: (707) 499-0643; www.kineticgrandchampionship.com*), Memorial Day weekend in May, begins at Arcata Plaza, and takes three days for contestants to navigate the 38 or so miles to Ferndale. Whimsical people-powered contraptions, the essence of clever design, ornamentation and wackiness, are in keeping with Arcata's nickname, Ecotopia, and race founder Hobart Brown's belief in a 'New Race, conceived in insanity, and dedicated to the proposition that all mechanical nightmares definitely are not created equal'. The mechanical sculptures are displayed in **Ferndale's Kinetic Sculpture Race Museum** (*see page 201*).

Accommodation and food in Arcata

Chain motels cluster around E. Guintoli Lane. Closer to downtown, a smattering of bed and breakfasts offer Victoriana. Book in advance for Kinetic Grand Championship weekend in May. Vegetarian and vegan is easy to find in this organic-conscious town, but freshness of ingredients is what counts.

North Coast Co-Op $ *811 I St; tel: (707) 822-5947; www.northcoastco-op.com; open 0600–2100*. Socialism applied to food, selling groceries to all.

Wildberries Marketplace $ *747 13th St; tel: (707) 822-0095; www.wildberries.com; open 0700–2300*, is a newer, hipper rival to the Co-Op.

Abruzzi $$ *791 8th St in Jacoby's Storehouse; tel: (707) 826-2345; www.abruzziarcata.com*, offers Italian dinners nightly in an historic building on Arcata Plaza.

Golden Harvest Cafe $$ *1062 G St; tel: (707) 822-8962; www.goldenharvestcafe.com*, has a wide range of mostly vegetarian dishes two blocks north of Arcata Plaza.

Hotel Arcata $$ *708 9th St; tel: (800) 344-1221 or (707) 826-0217; www.hotelarcata.com*, on Arcata Plaza, is a cheerful 1915 former hunting lodge.

Folie Douce $$$ *1551 G St; tel: (707) 822-1042; www.holyfolie.com*, is fine dining with organic and sustainable deeply incorporated into the menu.

AVENUE OF THE GIANTS

Avenue of the Giants Association
PO Box 1957; 3493 Briceland Rd, Redway CA 95560; tel: (707) 923-3727; www.avenueofthegiants.net

Just north of Garberville, coast redwood groves extend for a narrow 31-mile strip along both sides of Hwy 101 from Phillipsville to Pepperwood, cutting left and right over the south fork of the Eel River. Most of the groves are named in tribute to the group of people who, in the early 20th century, worked to save a small number of redwoods before they disappeared. **Humboldt Redwoods State Park** (*www.humboldtredwoods.org*) (*see page 202*) surrounds and helps interpret the long life span and predator-resistant coastal species. Most of the groves have a lay-by to park in so that you can explore the forest.

CRESCENT CITY

Crescent City/Del Norte County Chamber of Commerce 1001 Front St, Crescent City, CA 95531; tel: (707) 464-3174 or (800) 343-8300; www.northerncalifornia.net. Open Mon–Sat 0900–1700, Sun to 1200.

Battery Point Lighthouse West end of Front St; tel: (707) 464-3089; www.cr.nps.gov/maritime/light/battery.htm. Open for guided tours Apr–Sep (tide permitting).

As elsewhere on the north coast, Crescent City, 18 miles south of the Oregon border, was dependent upon fishing and timber. It is also a crossroads for over-the-border traffic and eastward routes to more redwood parks and the Hwy 199 Smith River Wild and Scenic River drive to the Rogue River Region in Oregon.

The city is named after the shape of its bay. A tsunami tidal wave caused by a major Alaskan earthquake in 1964 wiped out the harbour and downtown; a Japanese earthquake in November 2006 caused a tsunami that wiped out docks and caused other waterfront damage. Local activities include fishing, cycling, scuba diving and surfing in frigid waters.

Battery Point Lighthouse, perched since 1856 on well-eroded golden rock, has lovely proportions from any angle and at any time of day or night when it is illuminated around the outside. Check in advance about walking from the beach to a causeway at low tide.

North from Battery Point Lighthouse, scenic **Pebble Beach Drive** looks west to sea stacks and **Castle Rock National Wildlife Refuge** (*tel: (707) 733-5406; www.fws.gov/refuges/profiles/index.cfm?id=81647*), home to huge numbers of seabirds and noisy sea lions. Go left on Washington Blvd to **Point St George** where there are vistas, beaches and trails, with its namesake lighthouse 6 miles offshore.

Below
Battery Point Lighthouse

Accommodation and food in Crescent City

Proximity to Oregon (where prices are lower and there's no state sales tax) keep prices at Crescent City motels to bargain levels. Hwy 101 divides into north (*M St*) and south (*L St*) throughways between Front and 9th Sts; most motels are found here. Others are near the harbour at Anchor Rd.

Dining is basic, but seafood is an excellent choice. Ask for the fresh-caught special of the day.

From Jun–Oct the town turns out at the Del Norte County Fairgrounds for the **Crescent City Certified Farmers Market** fresh produce (*3rd and K Sts; open Sat 0900–1300*).

DEL NORTE COAST REDWOODS STATE PARK

One of the Redwood National and State Parks (*7 miles south of Crescent City; tel: (707) 465-2146; www.parks.ca.gov*), Del Norte Coast Redwood State Park has old-growth forest which includes redwoods with spectacular rocky coast and uncrowded Damnation and Footsteps Rock Trails.

EUREKA

Humboldt County Convention & Visitors Bureau
1034 2nd St, Eureka, CA 95501; tel: (707) 443-5097 or (800) 346-3482; www.redwoods.info. Open Mon–Fri 0900–1700.

No building in far Northern California is more recognisable than the green Victorian **Carson Mansion**, built in 1885 by a lumber baron's employees to fill time. Now a private club, this centrepiece of Eureka's Historic Old Town (*B-I Sts, Waterfront-7th St*) shows the 19th-century value of a good fishing harbour with access to lumber. Galleries, stores, restaurants and bed and breakfasts are found in this area. **Arts Alive** (*tel: (707) 442-9054; first Sat of each month 1800–2100*), Old Town's art walk, shows an art scene comparable to San Francisco or Seattle. Salmon and Dungeness crab are still menu staples, though fisheries are restricted. Catch the **MAKADET $** (*foot of F Street, tel: (707) 445-1910; www.humboldtbaymaritimemuseum.com/makadetcruises.html, operates late May–Sep*), one of seven Humboldt Bay ferries, for a narrated harbour cruise.

Food in Eureka

The **Lost Coast Brewery $** *617 4th St; tel: (707) 445-4480; www. lostcoast.com, open 1100–0100*, with half a dozen brews, is the liveliest place in town beyond a giant string spider guarding its 1892 door.

Samoa Cookhouse $ *Samoa Peninsula in Humboldt Bay; tel: (707) 442-1659; www.samoacookhouse.net; open daily 0700–2100, 2200 in summer*, serves large, family-style portions of stick-to-the-ribs lumberjack fare in keeping with its status as the last surviving lumber camp cookhouse in the west. Prices are low. There is a free logging museum and the **Humboldt Bay Maritime Museum $** *tel: (707) 444-9440; www. humboldtbaymaritimemuseum.com* is next door.

Café Waterfront $$ *102 F St; tel: (707) 443-9190; open daily 0900–2100*, has seafood, salads, sandwiches, a long wooden bar, a stained-glass window, and, most remarkable in the landmark Old Town Eureka building, wall paintings of flowers and natural scenes. Two Victorian-style flats can be rented upstairs.

Below
Carson Mansion, centrepiece of Eureka's Old Town

FERNDALE

❶ Ferndale Chamber of Commerce *PO Box 325, Ferndale, CA 95536; tel: (707) 786-4477; www.victorianferndale. org/chamber*

Ferndale Art & Culture Building Merchants *580 Main St,* have maps and brochures.

Ferndale has trademarked its moniker, 'The Victorian Village', and the entire village is a California Historical Landmark. Settled in 1852, the town's low-lying, lush pastures were perfect for dairy cattle. Prosperity arrived, and by the 1890s dairymen in Cream City were building heavily embellished Victorian mansions called 'Butterfat Palaces'. Two subsequent earthquakes wreaked havoc, but the homes, mansions, churches and Main Street shopfronts were repaired and repainted.

Ferndale is a walker's paradise. **Main Street** is the place for shops, galleries, restaurants, bakeries, a meat market, a pioneer museum and the **Kinetic Museum** (*part of the Ferndale Art & Culture Building, 580 Main St; see also Arcata, page 196*).

Ferndale's *de facto* image is the **Gingerbread Mansion Inn** (*400 Berding St*), an 1899 turreted and gabled froth of Victorian style, with magnificent English formal garden landscaping and a perfect and perfectly incongruous palm tree.

Accommodation in Ferndale

Ferndale is about 5 miles southwest of Hwy 101 from the Fernbridge/ Ferndale exit. Five bed-and-breakfast inns, three motels and a county fairground camping area should be booked in advance, as Ferndale is popular with local tourists from San Francisco and Los Angeles.

The Victorian Inn $$–$$$ *400 Ocean Ave; tel: (888) 589-1808* or *(707) 786-4949; www.a-victorian-inn.com*, offers bed and breakfast in 1880 Victorian splendour.

Gingerbread Mansion Inn $$$ *400 Berding St; tel: (800) 952-4136* or *(707) 786-4000; www.gingerbread-mansion.com*

GARBERVILLE

❶ Garberville Redway Chamber of Commerce *782 Redwood Dr.; Garberville, CA 95542; tel: (800) 923-2613; www.garberville.org. Call for hours.*

Garberville serves as a hub for forestry, for holidaymakers seeking the redwoods, a base for exploring the **Avenue of the Giants** (*see page 199*) and a convenient stopping point for travellers taking Hwy 101 between San Francisco and Eureka/Crescent City. The friction between environment protection and lumbering is notable, while musicians and young counterculture types hang out for the atmosphere.

Accommodation and food in Garberville

As a service hub, Garberville is well supplied with motels.

Sicilitos $ *445 Conger St; tel: (707) 923-2814; www.asis.com/sicilitos*, with old advertising and sports memorabilia around the walls, serves tasty Mexican food and Italian-American fare, made from scratch.

Benbow Inn $$$ *445 Lake Benbow Dr., 1 mile south of Garberville; tel: (707) 923-2124 or (800) 355-3301; www.benbowinn.com*, is a stunning redwoods version of Tudor style, with lovely flower gardens outside and a high-ceilinged lobby and dining room.

HUMBOLDT REDWOODS STATE PARK

ℹ Humboldt Redwoods State Park $ *Tel: (707) 946-2409; www.parks.ca.gov.* **Visitor Center** *2 miles north of Weott on Avenue of the Giants; tel: (707) 946-2263. Open Feb–Mar 1000–1600; Apr–Oct 0900–1700. Find more park information at: www.humboldtredwoods.org*

Most visitors encounter **Humboldt Redwoods State Park** as the **Avenue of the Giants** (*see page 199*), but its 52,000 acres include the awesome trees of **Rockefeller Forest**, estimated to constitute 10 per cent of remaining old-growth redwoods. Stop at the convenient and informative **Visitor Center** (*2 miles north of Weott on Avenue of the Giants*); a short path outside gives a rare opportunity to see all three redwood species side by side: dawn (*Metasequoia glyptostroboides*), coast (*Sequoia sempervirens*) and giant (*Sequoiadendron giganteum*).

PATRICK'S POINT STATE PARK

ℹ Patrick's Point State Park $ *West of Hwy 101, 4150 Patrick's Point Dr., 5 miles north of Trinidad; tel: (707) 677-3570; www.parks.ca.gov*

Patrick's Point State Park has superb views offshore to whale migrations, northward to Agate Beach and Big Lagoon and south to Trinidad Head, a blufftop **Rim Trail** and a **Yurok (Native American)** Sumêg Village, with wooden houses, a sweat house, a dance pit still reserved for use by tribal members, and a Native American Plant Garden.

PRAIRIE CREEK REDWOODS STATE PARK

ℹ Prairie Creek Redwoods State Park $ *West of Hwy 10, 50 miles north of Eureka, tel: (707) 465-7354, (707) 465-7347 or (707) 464-6101 ext 5300; www.parks.ca.gov. Visitors Center open Mar–Oct daily 0900–1700; Nov–Feb Wed–Sun same hours.*

ℂ Elk Meadow Cabins $$$ *(2 miles north of Orick; tel: (866) 733-9637; www.redwoodadventures.com)* are next to elk Prairie's grazing Roosevelt elk and offer interpretive tours in the park, including the tall redwoods.

Prairie Creek is best known for the Roosevelt elk which roam around three areas from Aug–Oct: **Davidson Rd**, **Elk Prairie** and **Gold Bluffs** (remote). These huge animals can cause traffic jams on Hwy 101.

Prairie Creek is rich in redwoods, with connecting trails circling through the major groves. Try **Newton B Drury Scenic Parkway exit** from Hwy 101. The most dramatic redwoods, however, are near the south exit where **Elk Prairie** and the **Prairie Creek Visitor Center** offer previews of what's ahead. Stop and hike to **Big Tree**, 304ft high and 216in in diameter, and to the twined trunks of the **Corkscrew Tree**.

REDWOOD NATIONAL AND STATE PARKS

ℹ **Thomas H. Kuchel Visitor Center** Hwy 101, west of Orick; tel: (707) 465-7765; www.nps.gov/redw. Open daily Mar–Oct 0900–1700; Nov–Feb 0900–1600.

Redwood National and State Parks Information Center 1111 2nd St, Crescent City; tel: (707) 465-7306; www.nps.gov/redw. Open daily Mar–Oct 0900–1700; Nov–Feb 0900–1600.

The jointly managed park, with three state parks: **Prairie Creek Redwoods** (*visitor centre 8 miles north of Orick on Hwy 101, open daily*), **Del Norte Coast Redwoods** and **Jedediah Smith Redwoods** (*east of Crescent City*) protect old-growth (250 years or more) coast redwoods, among the tallest, biggest and oldest natural objects on the planet. The parks are a **World Heritage Site** and an **International Biosphere Reserve**, accessible by vehicle, but much better enjoyed on foot, by bicycle or on a horse (trails are well marked). Dress for frequent fog and rain. While coast redwoods and elk are the focus, the parks conserve coastline, tide-pools, waterfalls, oak woodlands and prairies. As tame as the stately trees look, it's a wild world out there full of ticks, banana slugs, cougars (mountain lions), bears and elk.

RICHARDSON GROVE STATE PARK

Richardson Grove (*tel: (707) 247-3318*), 7 miles south of Garberville, provides services and an early glimpse of stands of coast redwoods on the Hwy 101 route north. Families can swim in the Eel River south fork in summer, while anglers fish for steelhead later in the year.

TRINIDAD

ℹ **Greater Trinidad Chamber of Commerce** PO Box 356; tel: (707) 677-1610; www.trinidadcalif.com

Below
Some of the world's oldest and largest trees

Trinidad qualifies as a hamlet, just south of Patrick's Point State Park (*see opposite*), with more than its share of bed-and-breakfast inns and a fishing fleet. Its symbol is the red-roofed, white replica of an 1871 **Memorial Lighthouse**. **Trinidad State Beach** (*off Trinity St, north of Main St; tel: (707) 677-3570*) is a good spot to watch a dramatic sunset behind jewel-sharp rocks rising from the sea, with diving and swooping black oystercatchers. Trinidad Scenic Drive (*south from Trinity St; parallel to Hwy 101*) provides access to **Luffenholtz Beach County Park**, with clamming and surf fishing, and **Houda Point**. The area is also known for great surfing.

Suggested tours

Total distance: 221 miles.

Time: 6 hours' driving. Allow a day for the main route, two days with **Detour 2**. Add a minimum of three extra days to drive into and hike the Lost Coast (*see Also worth exploring*).

Links: From Fort Bragg, the beginning of this route, connect with the Mendocino Coast (*see page 186*). For direct access from San Francisco, take Hwy 101 180 miles north to Leggett and on to Crescent City.

Route: Take Hwy 1 north from **Fort Bragg ❶**, turning inland north of **Rockport ❷** for a 16-mile drive over the mountains to **Leggett ❸**. Continue north on 101 to **EUREKA ❹**, **ARCATA ❺** and **CRESCENT CITY ❻**.

Detour 1: Weaving in and out of the **Avenue of the Giants ❼** for 31 miles between **Phillipsville ❽** and **Pepperwood ❾** will take 45 minutes longer than going straight through on Hwy 101.

Detour 2: Two miles north of **Weott ❿** at **Dyerville ⓫**, take the Rockefeller Forest exit west from Hwy 101. Follow the **Mattole Rd ⓬** from the redwood groves to **Honeydew ⓭**, a small apple-growing hamlet. Continue northwest on the same road to **Petrolia ⓮** and the coast south of **Cape Mendocino ⓯**. As Mattole Rd turns to rise steeply inland, the road narrows further, with 10mph speed limits to **FERNDALE ⓰**. Add half a day to the driving time for this scenic route.

Also worth exploring

The **Lost Coast ⓱** is little known because of its remoteness from roads and settlements. North of **Rockport ❷** off Hwy 1 on Usal Rd, south from **Honeydew ⓭** from Wilder Ridge/Kings Peak Rd, or west 24 miles from **Redway ⓲** to **Shelter Cove ⓳**, is a barely touched section of coast, with sheer mountain peaks and slate black sand.

The coast, park and conservation areas are not signposted from any highway. Ask rangers or locally for directions, as some north and south roads are unpaved, and can be treacherous from October to March from heavy rainfall when even four-wheel-drive vehicles can get stuck. RVs can't manoeuvre the steep, narrow, rugged roads.

Shelter Cove ⓳, with its working fishing fleet, has recently seen an influx of the rich and celebrated who are building homes on the hills.

South of Shelter Cove, the 7367-acre **Sinkyone Wilderness State Park ⓴**, *PO Box 245, Whitethorn, CA 95589; tel: (707) 986-7711; www.parks.ca.gov*, has a 17-mile trail through the wilderness.

King Range National Conservation Area ㉑ (*Arcata Resource Area, US Bureau of Land Management, 1695 Heindon Rd; Arcata, CA 95521; tel: (707) 825-2300 or (707) 986-5400; www.blm.gov/ca/arcata/kingrange*) has 64,000 acres of rugged hiking and camping.

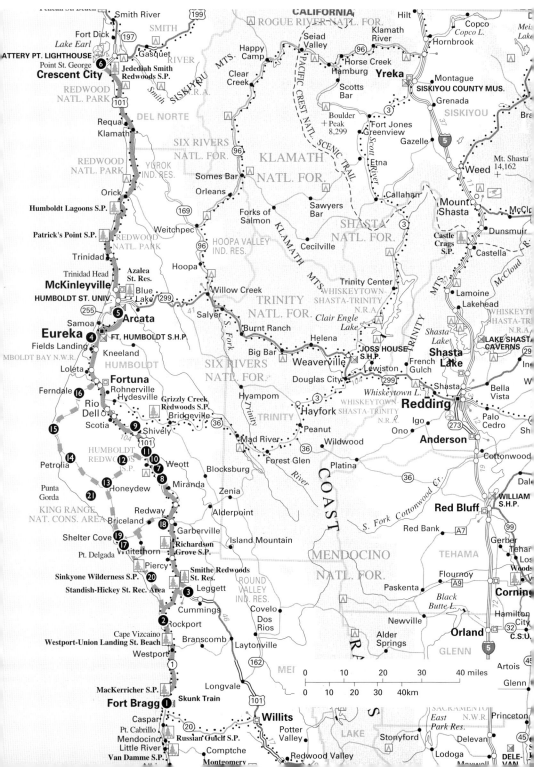

CALIFORNIA

ROGUE RIVER-NATL. FOR.

Pelican St. Beach
Smith River
SMITH
199
Hilt
Copco
Copco L.
Mei
Lake

Fort Dick
Lake Earl
197
Gasquet
RIVER
Happy
Camp
Seiad
Valley
Klamath
River
Hornbrook

ATTERY PT. LIGHTHOUSE
Point St. George
6
Crescent City
Jedediah Smith
Redwoods S.P.
SISKIYOU
Clear
Creek
Horse Creek
Hamburg
Scotts
Bar
Yreka
Montague
SISKIYOU COUNTY MUS.

REDWOOD
NATL. PARK
101
Smith
SISKIYOU
N.R.A.
Boulder
+Peak
8,299
Fort Jones
Greenview
3
Grenada
SISKIYOU
Bra

DEL NORTE
Requa
Klamath
SIX RIVERS
NATL. FOR.
96
KLAMATH
NATL. FOR.
Somes Bar
Orleans
Sawyers
Bar
Gazelle
Callahan
Etna
3
Gulch
Weed
Mt. Shasta
14,162
+

REDWOOD
NATL. PARK
YUROK
IND. RES.
Orick
169
Forks of
Salmon
SHASTA
NATL. FOR.
Mount
Shasta
McClo

Humboldt Lagoons S.P.
Weitchpec
96
HOOPA VALLEY
IND. RES.
Cecilville
Castle
Crags
S.P.
Dunsmuir
Castella

Patrick's Point S.P.
REDWOOD
NATL. PARK
Hoopa
Trinity Center
WHISKEYTOWN-
SHASTA-TRINITY
N.R.A.
Lamoine
Lakehead
WHISKEYTO
SHASTA-TR
N.R.A.

Trinidad
Trinidad Head
Azalea
St. Res.
Blue
Lake
Willow Creek
TRINITY
NATL. FOR.
Clair Engle
Lake
Shasta
Lake
LAKE SHAST
CAVERNS

McKinleyville
HUMBOLDT ST. UNIV.
255
5
Arcata
299
41
Salyer
S. Fork
Burnt Ranch
JOSS HOUSE
S.H.P.
Shasta
Lake
Shasta

Samoa
Eureka
4
FT. HUMBOLDT S.H.P.
Kneeland
SIX RIVERS
NATL. FOR.
Big Bar
Helena
Weaverville
French
Gulch
Lewiston
Shasta
LAKE
Bella
Vista

Fields Landing
MBOLDT BAY N.W.R.
Loleta
HUMBOLDT
Fortuna
Rohnerville
Hydesville
Hyampom
Douglas City
104
299
Whiskeytown L.
Shasta
Redding

Ferndale
16
Rio
Dell
Scotia
Grizzly Creek
Redwoods S.P.
Bridgeville
36
TRINITY
Hayfork
WHISKEYTOWN-
SHASTA-TRINITY
N.R.L.
3
Igo
Ono
Palo
Cedro
Anderson
Sh

15
9
Shively
101
HUMBOLDT
REDWOODS
S.P.
12
11
10
Weott
7
8
Miranda
Blocksburg
Peanut
Wildwood
36
Forest Glen
Platina
36
Cottonwood
Dal

14
Petrolia
13
Honeydew
Redway
Zenia
S. Fork
River
COAST
Red Bluff
WILLIAM
S.H.P.

Punta
Gorda
21
KING RANGE
NAT. CONS. AREA
18
Briceland
Garberville
Island Mountain
Red Bank
A7
99
Gerbe
Tehar
Los
Woods

Shelter Cove
19
17
Pt. Delgada
Whitethorn
Richardson
Grove S.P.
MENDOCINO
NATL. FOR.
Flournoy
A9
Cornin

Sinkyone Wilderness S.P.
Piercy
20
Smithe Redwoods
St. Res.
ROUND
VALLEY
IND. RES.
Covelo
Paskenta
TEHAMA
Black
Butte L.
Orland
C.S.U.

Standish-Hickey St. Rec. Area
3
Leggett
Dos Rios
Newville
Hamilton
City
32

2
Cummings
Rockport
Covelo
Alder
Springs
GLENN
Artois
45

Cape Vizcaino
Branscomb
Laytonville
162
MEI
0   10   20   30   40 miles
0   10   20   30   40km
Glenn

Westport-Union Landing St. Beach
Westport
1
Longvale
101
S
SACRAMENTO
East
N.W.R.
Princeton
45

MacKerricher S.P.
Skunk Train
Willits
LAKE
Stonyford
Delevan
DELE-
VAN

Fort Bragg
1
Caspar
Pt. Cabrillo
Mendocino
Little River
Van Damme S.P.
20
Russian Gulch S.P.
Comptche
Montgomery
Potter
Valley
Redwood Valley
Lodoga
Maxwell

Monterey Peninsula

Ratings

History	●●●●●
Scenery	●●●●●
Food and wine	●●●●○
Children	●●●○○
Coastal villages	●●●○○
Wildlife	●●●○○
Art and craft	●●○○○
Beaches	●●○○○

Highway 1 from San Francisco to the Monterey Peninsula is surrounded by flower fields and vast vegetable farms, fringed by an ever-changing panorama of lighthouses, beaches and crumbling cliffs. Coastal attractions run the gamut from the ponderous mating of elephant seals on the sands of Año Nuevo to the theme-park atmosphere of the Santa Cruz Beach Boardwalk, historic buildings in Monterey and the contrived artistic atmosphere of Carmel.

The whale-watching season runs from November to April, depending on location. Some areas, notably Point Reyes, Gualala and the north Mendocino coast, offer good views of whales passing just offshore. Ports from San Diego to Crescent City offer closer views from whale-watching cruises. Whale-watching boats like those from Monterey aren't allowed to pursue whales, but if a canny captain manages to place his vessel ahead of the pod and a curious whale just happens to surface a few yards away, expect the view of a lifetime.

AÑO NUEVO STATE NATURAL RESERVE

Año Nuevo State Natural Reserve $
Hwy 1, 22 miles north of Santa Cruz; tel: (650) 879-0227; www.parks.ca.gov. Open daily. Advance reservations required for mid-Dec–Mar, tel: (800) 444-4445 or (916) 638-5883 (international reservations). Guided walks.

This state reserve is a 4000-acre promontory of bluffs and beaches with the largest northern elephant seal rookery on the California mainland. There are always a few of these huge aquatic mammals in residence, but the main show is between winter and spring, when immense bulls (up to 2.5 tons) battle for harems, and females give birth. Access is by guided tour only, mid-Dec–Mar, self-guided Apr–Nov.

CARMEL-BY-THE-SEA

This one-time artists' colony has tried to legislate its rustic past. Local ordinances prohibit parking meters, street addresses, postal delivery, high-heeled shoes and digging on the beach unless building a sand castle. Instead of the usual franchise stores and T-shirt shops, the town

Carmel Visitor Center *Above Hog's Breath Inn, San Carlos, between 5th and 6th Sts; tel: (831) 624-2522 or (800) 550-4333; www.carmelcalifornia.org. Open daily 1000–1700.*

Mission Carmel $ *2080 Rio Rd, Carmel; tel: (831) 624-1271; www.carmelmission.org. Open Mon–Sat 0930–1700, Sun 1030–1700.*

Point Lobos State Reserve $ *Hwy 1, 3 miles south of Carmel; tel: (831) 624-4909; www.parks.ca.gov. Open daily. Sea Lion Point Information Station 0900–1600. Diving information: tel: (831) 624-8413.*

Tor House $$ *26304 Ocean View Ave; tel: (831) 624-1813; www.torhouse.org. Open for hourly guided tours Fri–Sat 1000–1500; advance reservation required.*

centre, **Ocean Avenue**, has mock Tudor art galleries, overpriced antique shoppes, traffic congestion and an unending stream of weekend events to keep the tourists coming. Parking is scarce, pavements uneven and prices high. The area from Junipero to the beach, between 5th and 8th Sts, is filled with unique homes, from ersatz adobe to shingled cottages and 'dolls houses' trimmed with Victorian finery.

The emerald-blue cove of **Carmel City Beach** (*foot of Ocean Ave*) is bordered by soft white sand and green cypress trees. Enjoy the sand, but beware, a fierce undertow makes swimming dangerous.

Mission Carmel (Mission San Carlos Borromeo del Rio Carmelo) is the very stereotype of a California Mission (*see page 258*), with golden sandstone walls, Moorish towers and contemplative gardens splashed with scarlet bougainvillaea. Mission founder Fra Junípero Serra is buried beneath the sanctuary of the rebuilt complex. Carmel is also one of the most-visited of the California missions; go early in the day before the crowds arrive. The church is closed during services, but the courtyard and grounds, including a museum, remain open.

Point Lobos State Reserve has 6 miles of jagged shoreline above hidden aquamarine coves favoured by scuba divers, known as much for rolling meadows filled with spring wildflowers as the sea lions, whales, sea otters, seals and flocks of sea birds in permanent residence. Rangers lead nature walks daily, but parking is limited. Arrive early, especially between May and October.

Tor House is Carmel's most imposing residence, a medieval-looking structure built of golden boulders hauled from the beach below by poet Robinson Jeffers. The family still lives in the house.

Accommodation and food in Carmel

Nothing in Carmel is inexpensive. **Hog's Breath Inn $$** *San Carlos and 5th Sts; tel: (831) 625-1044; www.hogsbreathinn.net; open daily 1130–2200*, was once owned by film star Clint Eastwood, and serves lunch and dinner with local specialities like Castroville artichoke soup. The **Tuck Box English Tea Room $$** *Dolores St and Ocean Aves; tel: (831) 624-6365; www.tuckbox.com; open daily 0730–1500*, is kitschy, entertaining and anything but English, tiny and known for scones. **Carmel Valley Ranch $$$** *One Old Ranch Rd, Carmel, CA 93923; tel: (866) 282-4745; www.carmelvalleyranch.com*, escapes the crowds (and coastal fog) in Carmel Valley, a few miles inland. The **Highlands Inn, A Hyatt Hotel $$$** *120 Highlands Dr., Carmel, CA 93921; tel: (831) 620-1234; www.highlandsinn.hyatt.com/hyatt/hotels*, sits above the coast just south of Point Lobos. Golfers gravitate to **Pebble Beach** and **The Inn at Spanish Bay $$$** or **The Lodge at Pebble Beach $$$** *Box 567, Pebble Beach, CA 93953; tel: (800) 654-9300; www.pebble-beach.com*, on the famed 17-Mile Drive.

ELKHORN SLOUGH NATIONAL ESTUARINE RESEARCH RESERVE

Elkhorn Slough National Estuarine Research Reserve $
3 miles north of Castroville; tel: (831) 728-2822; www.elkhornslough.org/vc/htm. Open Wed–Sun 0900–1700.

This is California's largest surviving coastal wetland, teeming with birds, seals, sea otters and fish. Trails ($) provide shoreline access. **Elkhorn Slough Safari Nature Tours $$** *(tel: (831) 633-5555; www. elkhornslough.com)* offers boat tours; **Monterey Bay Kayaks $$$** *(tel: (800) 649-5357; www.montereybaykayaks.com)* offers guided or self-guided kayak tours. Advance bookings required for tours.

HALF MOON BAY

Half Moon Bay Coastside Chamber of Commerce & Visitor Bureau *235 Main St, Half Moon Bay, CA 94019; tel: (650) 726-8380; www.halfmoonbaychamber. org. and tel: (866) 558-6823; www.visithalfmoonbay.org. Open Mon–Fri 0900–1700. Free self-guided walking maps to several of Half Moon Bay's charming Victorian buildings, including one built in 1849.*

Half Moon Bay is part old-fashioned farming town, part artistic community and part surfing destination. Bay and town are named after the half-moon-shaped beach stretching south from **Pillar Point Harbor** (staging point for late Dec–Apr whale-watching tour) and **Princeton-by-the-Sea**. **St Francis Beach** may be the most beautiful local beach; surfers head for **Surfer's Beach** (*El Granada*) and **Mavericks** (off Pillar Point), renowned for enormous and occasionally lethal waves. **Venice Beach** and **Dune Beach** are the least crowded. **San Mateo County Farm Bureau** (*765 Main St; tel: (650) 726-4485; http://sanmateo.cfbf.com*) publishes a free map to vegetable, fruit and flower farms in the area, many of which invite visitors to pick for themselves. October brings the world-renowned **Half Moon Bay Art & Pumpkin Festival** (*tel: (650) 726-9652*).

Accommodation and food in Half Moon Bay

Barbara's Fishtrap $$ *281 Capistrano Rd at Hwy 1; tel: (650) 728-7049, call for hours*. This rustic bayside cash-only diner is a long-time favourite with San Franciscans.

Cetrella Bistro and Café $$$ *845 Main St, Half Moon Bay; tel: (650) 726-4090; www.cetrella.com, call for hours*, serves award-winning Mediterranean cuisine, has jazz in the lighter-fare café and a summertime Farmers' Market in its car park.

Old Thyme Inn $$$ *779 Main St; tel: (650) 726-1616 or (800) 720-4277; www.oldthymeinn.com*, an 1898 Victorian, has an English herb and flower garden.

Pillar Point Inn $$$ *380 Capistrano Rd, Princeton-by-the-Sea; tel: (650) 728-7377 or (800) 400-8281; www.pillarpointinn.com*, is more bed and breakfast than motel.

Ritz-Carlton Hotel Half Moon Bay $$$ *1 Miramontes Point Rd, Half Moon Bay, CA 94019; tel: (650) 712-7000; www.ritzcarlton.com/ resorts/half_moon_bay*, is a sprawling East Coast-style building with two golf courses.

Montara

Fitzgerald Marine Reserve *Off Hwy 1, just north of Pillar Point, California and N. Lake Sts, Moss Beach; tel: (650) 728-3584; www.fitzgeraldreserve.org. Free.*

The coastal hamlet of **Montara** is known primarily for the **Point Montara Lighthouse Hostel** (*16th St at Hwy 1; tel: (650) 728-7177 or (888) 464-4872; www.norcalhostels.org/montara*), a former lighthouse converted to a youth hostel, and **Fitzgerald Marine Reserve**. At high tide, the reserve could be any stretch of rocky coastline, but low tide uncovers broad rocky terraces and innumerable tide pools.

Food in Montara

Moss Beach Distillery $$ *140 Beach Way at Ocean Blvd, Moss Beach; tel: (650) 728-5595; www.mossbeachdistillery.com; open daily 1200–2100.* The 'distillery' was an illicit spirits storehouse and bar/restaurant/brothel during Prohibition and boasts its own Blue Lady ghost. The bar and restaurant remain, one of the better eating spots along the coast and a popular protected vantage point for sunsets.

Monterey

Monterey County Convention & Visitors Bureau *PO Box 1770, Monterey, CA 93942; tel: (877) 666-8379; www.montereyinfo.org.* **Maritime Museum Visitor Center** *5 Custom House Plaza; tel: (888) 221-1010. Open daily 0900–1700.* **Lake El Estero Visitor Center** *Franklin & Camino El Estero. Open daily.* A 'Literary and Film Map' to Monterey County is keyed to locations.

Monterey Bay Aquarium $$$ *886 Cannery Row; tel: (831) 648-4888 or (800) 756-3737; www.mbayaq.org. Open daily 1000–1800, from 0930 in summer.*

Monterey Bay National Marine Sanctuary *299 Foam St; tel: (831) 647-4201; www.mbnms.nos.noaa.gov. Open daily. Free.*

Monterey was the capital of California under Spanish, Mexican and American flags. Overfishing in the 1940s killed the gritty sardine canneries immortalised in John Steinbeck's *Cannery Row*, but the town has been successfully trolling for tourists ever since.

Cannery Row (*west of Fisherman's Wharf; www.canneryrow.com*) lost its last cannery decades ago, but the area has been resurrected as Monterey's main tourist district. The mile-long bayfront street is lined with restaurants, art galleries, shops and similar attractions.

Fisherman's Wharf has a bevy of restaurants, galleries, handicraft shops, sport fishing boats and whale-watching operations.

Built around Monterey's last cannery at the edge of the tide pools, the **Monterey Bay Aquarium** explores the rich and varied sea life of the Monterey Bay National Marine Sanctuary. Time your visit to begin with watching divers clean the three-storey-tall glass of the **Kelp Forest** with interactive diver narration. Check out the cavorting sea otters, African penguins and the Splash Zone. There are sharks and rays from around the world. The aquarium has a superb collection of jellyfish and seahorses moving in tanks. A giant Pacific octopus and wolf eels are in the Deep Reefs Gallery Stroll, a walk-through tunnel beneath tidal action coastal wetlands, and shorebird aviary.

The best way to see the real bay is by kayak; **Monterey Bay Kayaks** (*see page 209*) is the biggest operator. **Monterey Bay National Marine Sanctuary** stretches 276 miles south along the California coast from Marin to Cambria, the largest marine sanctuary in the country. Within its 5322 square miles is a variety of marine habitats, including wetlands, beaches, kelp forests, sunken canyons and open ocean.

⊕ Monterey State Historic Park $ 20
Custom House Plaza; tel: (831) 649-7118 for current tour information; www.park.ca.gov. Open daily 1000–1600. Guided walking tours. Hours vary.

Maritime Museum of Monterey $
5 Custom House Plaza; tel: (831) 372-2608; www.montereyhistory.org/maritime_museum.htm. Open Thu–Tue 1000–1700.

Monterey State Historic Park operates 37 historic buildings, sites and museums detailing Monterey from the 17th to 20th centuries. Daily guided tours begin from the visitor centre at **Pacific House** on **Custom House Plaza**, next to Fisherman's Wharf. A 1½-mile **Path of History** walk connects the sites, most of which are closed except to guided tours. **The Maritime Museum of Monterey** covers seafaring in the Monterey Bay.

Accommodation and food in Monterey

Quock Mui Tea Room $ *774 Wave St; tel: (831) 655-2010; www. wavestreet.biz*, has a warmed stone seating area by a cascading waterfall.

Rappa's Seafood Restaurant $$ *end of Fisherman's Wharf; tel: (831) 372-7562; www.rappas.com*, combines good seafood with great views.

Casa Munras Garden Hotel $$$ *700 Munras Ave; tel: (800) 222-2446; www.hotelcasamunras.com*, incorporates one of the first homes built outside the walls of the original Presidio in 1824. If you absolutely *must* have a harbour view, try the **Monterey Bay Inn $$$** *242 Cannery Row; tel: (800) 424-6242; http://montereybayinn.com*

PACIFIC GROVE

ⓘ Pacific Grove Chamber of Commerce *584 Central Ave, Pacific Grove, CA 93950; tel: (831) 373-3304 or (800) 656-6650; www.pacificgrove.org. Information Center, Central and Forest Aves. Open Mon–Fri 0930–1700, Sat 1000–1500.*

The most scenic way out of Monterey is Pacific Grove, via the **Seventeen Mile Drive** (*see page 213*), but the town has its own attractions. **Monarch Grove Sanctuary** (*Ridge Rd, between Lighthouse Ave and Short St; tel: (831) 648-5716; www.pgmuseum.org*) is winter home to millions of monarch butterflies, which congregate between October and February before migrating north. **Point Piños Lighthouse $**, in operation since 1855, shows how lighthouse keepers lived and worked in the 19th and early 20th centuries (*Asilomar Ave and Lighthouse Ave; tel: (831) 648-5716; www.pgmuseum.org; open Thu–Mon 1300–1600*). **Asilomar Conference Grounds $$** (*800 Asilomar Ave; tel: (866) 654-2878; www.visitasilomar.com*) is on the dunes, with historic buildings and rooms designed in Arts & Crafts architectural style.

PESCADERO

⊕ Duarte's $–$$ *202 Stage Rd; tel: (650) 879-0464; www.duartestavern.com. Open daily 0700–2100, it is one of the most talked-about fish restaurants, with famed home-made pies.*

This former Portuguese fishing and farming town presents a tidy face, but is best known for the 115-foot-high **Pigeon Point Lighthouse** (*Pigeon Point Rd in Pigeon Point Light Station State Historic Park; tel: (650) 879-2120*). A **Pigeon Point Lighthouse Hostel $** (*210 Pigeon Point Rd; tel: (650) 879-0633; www.norcalhostels.org/pigeon*) stay includes a clifftop hot tub. **Año Nuevo State Natural Reserve** (*see page 206*) is nearby.

SANTA CRUZ

ⓘ Santa Cruz County Conference and Visitor Council *1211 Ocean St, Santa Cruz, CA 95060; tel: (831) 425-1234 or (800) 833-3494; www.santacruz.org. Open daily.*

ⓝ Seymour Marine Discovery Center *$ 100 Shaffer Rd; tel: (831) 459-3800; www2.ucsc.edu/ seymourcenter. Open Tue–Sat 1000–1700, Sun 1200–1700.*

Santa Cruz Beach Boardwalk *400 Beach St; tel: (831) 423-5590; http://beachboardwalk.com. Boardwalk free, rides $. Open daily. Check website for details.*

Santa Cruz Surfing Museum *ground floor of the lighthouse, 701 West Cliff Dr.; tel: (831) 420-6289; www. santacruzsurfingmuseum.org. Open Thu–Mon 1200–1600; 4 Jul–mid-Sep Wed–Mon 1000–1700. Free.*

Wilder Ranch State Park *$ Hwy 1, 2 miles north of Santa Cruz; tel: (831) 423-9703 or (831) 426-0505; www.santacruzstateparks.org and www.parks.ca.gov. Open daily 0800–sunset.*

Perched on the north end of Monterey Bay, Santa Cruz began as a Mission town in 1791 and boomed as a beach resort with the coming of the railway. A University of California campus adds one more layer to this hard-working, relaxed, blue-collar, intellectual and artistic surfer city. The city **beach** is one of the widest, warmest, sunniest and busiest strands north of Santa Barbara. **Art galleries and studios** are concentrated in the city centre along **Pacific Ave** (*between Water and Cathcart Sts*), rebuilt following the 1989 earthquake.

Seymour Marine Discovery Center is part of the University of California's Joseph M. Long Marine Laboratory. The museum and guided tours explain current research projects and provide ample time to explore aquaria, touch-tank creatures and marine mammal pools. The lab overlooks **Natural Bridges State Beach** (*tel: (831) 423-4609*) – also the location of the **Monarch Butterfly Natural Preserve** – named after mudstone arches (only one is still standing).

Roaring Camp Railroads (*Box G-1, Felton; tel: (831) 335-4484; www.roaringcamp.com*) is America's last steam-powered railway with a daily, year-round passenger service. Two lines take passengers through the redwood forests near Roaring Camp or between Roaring Camp and the Santa Cruz Beach Boardwalk. Rail buffs will opt for the narrow-gauge steam train to the summit of Bear Mountain, with options to bike around or down from the top, a 1-hour return trip. The beach train takes 3 hours return.

Santa Cruz Beach Boardwalk was California's first beach boardwalk amusement park (1904) and the only one to survive. Top rides are the **Hurricane** roller coaster and the 1924 **Giant Dipper** wooden roller coaster, one of America's Top Ten Coasters. The 1911 Charles Looff **merry-go-round** has its original organ and ring toss. There's also an assortment of lose-your-lunch rides for adrenalin addicts and free on the beach rock 'n' roll concerts Friday nights in summer.

Exhibits hearkening back to 100lb redwood surfboards of the 1930s are on display at the **Santa Cruz Surfing Museum**, which overlooks prime surfing beaches.

Wilder Ranch State Park has 34 miles of coastal hiking, cycling and equestrian trails as well as preserved ranch buildings. Guides in period costume explain the life of early Central Coast ranchers.

Accommodation and food in Santa Cruz

Gabriella Café $$ *910 Cedar St; tel: (831) 457-1667; www.gabriellacafe. com; open daily*, is one of the area's best Northern Italian restaurants. **Casablanca Inn & Motel $$$** *101 Main St; tel: (831) 423-1570; www.casablanca-santacruz.com*, is a converted mansion across from the Beach Boardwalk. **The Dream Inn $$$** *175 W. Cliff Dr.; tel: (831) 426-4330; www.jdvhotels.com/hotels/centralcoast/dream*, with balconies or patios, is Santa Cruz's only beachfront hotel.

SEVENTEEN MILE DRIVE

Seventeen Mile Drive $$ *www. pebblebeach.com/page.asp?id =1373*

This is the scenic coastal route from Monterey (Pacific Grove) to Carmel by way of the coast, Pebble Beach and 21 marked points of interest. Don't miss **The Lone Cypress**, one of California's most-photographed trees clinging to a bare rock (with help from guy wires).

Suggested tour

Total distance: 90 miles.

Time: 2½ hours' driving. Allow a full day or overnight in Santa Cruz, plus a day exploring the Monterey Peninsula.

Links: San Francisco and the Marin Coast to the north, Big Sur and Southern California to the south.

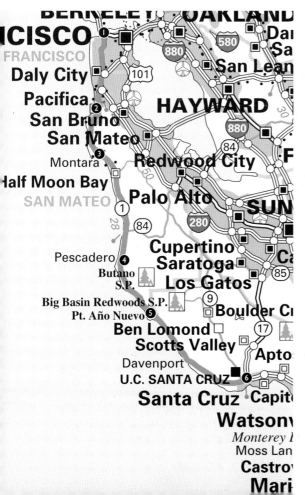

Route: From **San Francisco ❶**, follow Hwy 1 south over the spine of the San Mateo Peninsula to **Pacifica ❷**, the self-proclaimed Fog Capital of California. The road south follows golden cliffs set with small beaches and fronted by rocky reefs and lighthouses at **MONTARA ❸** and **Pigeon Point**. Beach parks at **Pomponio** and **Pescadero ❹** are local favourites. Continue past AÑO NUEVO STATE NATURAL RESERVE **❺** to SANTA CRUZ **❻**. The coastline is pocked with beaches, many accessible only by rough tracks.

Also worth exploring

The **Santa Cruz Mountains**, east of Santa Cruz, produced some of California's finest wines in the last century. For current information on tours and tastings, contact **Santa Cruz Mountain Winegrowers Assn** *7605-A Old Dominion Court, Aptos, CA 95003; tel: (831) 685-8463; www.scmwa.com*

Bonny Doon Vineyard *10 Pine Flat Rd, Santa Cruz; tel: (831) 425-4518; www.bonnydoonvineyard.com, open daily 1100–1700,* is one of California's most colourful (and most awarded) wineries.

Big Sur and the Central Coast

Ratings

Scenery	●●●●●
Nature	●●●●○
Beaches	●●●○○
Children	●●●○○
Sport	●●●○○
Food	●●○○○
History	●●○○○
Architecture	●○○○○

Big Sur is elemental California, undeveloped and seemingly untouched. Hwy 1 is the sole access, a route frequently blocked by winter rains and mud slides and clogged with summer weekend traffic. South of Big Sur, the road becomes wider, straighter and less crowded, but no less scenic for the easier access. The Central Coast, Hearst Castle to Santa Barbara, offers an alluring combination of good weather, easy driving and rolling countryside that invites leisurely exploration.

Big Sur and its series of state parks is one of the most visited parts of California, yet manages to retain an air of isolation, mystery and mysticism. The 90 rugged, craggy miles of Hwy 1 were carved into trackless cliffs by convict labour in the 1930s. Enjoy the ethereal magic of the cobalt and turquoise Pacific Ocean battering soaring mountains cloaked in swirling mists and dense forests.

BIG SUR

ⓘ **Big Sur Chamber of Commerce**
*Box 87, Big Sur, CA 93920;
tel: (831) 667-2100;
www.bigsurcalifornia.org*

Big Sur Ranger Station
½-mile south of Pfeiffer-Big Sur State Park; tel: (831) 667-2315. Open daily 0800–1630.

All **state parks** *found on www.parks.ca.gov*

The best views are south-bound, driving on the ocean side of Hwy 1. The scenery is unendingly stunning, but the winding road demands full driving attention – drivers should wait for the frequent lay-bys before taking in the views. The most complete local guide is the *Big Sur Guide*, free from the Chamber of Commerce online or at ranger stations and shops. The best information stop is the **Big Sur Ranger Station** (*just south of Pfeiffer-Big Sur State Park*). Big Sur ends at **Piedras Blancas Lighthouse**, just north of **Hearst Castle** (*see page 218*).

Andrew Molera State Park (*south of Point Sur Lighthouse; tel: (831) 667-2315*) is the largest and least developed of the Big Sur parks. Miles of trails wander its open beaches, meadows and hilltops.

Big Sur Valley (*25 miles south of Carmel*), the centre for tourist services, stretches for 6 miles along Hwy 1.

Bixby Creek Bridge (*3½ miles south of Garrapata State Park*), a solitary and much-photographed arch, soars high above Bixby Creek. Best **views** are from an overlook at the north end. **Esalen Institute** (*8 miles south of Julia Pfeiffer Burns State Park; tel: (831) 667-3000; www.esalen.org*) is

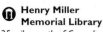 **Henry Miller Memorial Library**
35 miles south of Carmel; tel/fax: (831) 667-2574; www.henrymiller.org. Open Wed–Mon 1100–1800. Free.

Julia Pfeiffer Burns State Park $ *12 miles south of Pfeiffer Big Sur State Park; tel: (831) 667-2315. Open daily dawn–dusk.*

Nepenthe $$ *South of Big Sur Valley; tel: (831) 667-2345; www.nepenthebigsur.com. Open daily for lunch and dinner.*

Point Sur State Historic Park $ *19 miles south of Carmel; tel: (831) 625-4419; www.pointsur.org. Guided tours Sat–Sun 1000, Wed in summer, Thu Jul–Aug.*

America's original New Age retreat. The public are allowed as far as the famed hot springs $$; *tel: (831) 667-3047; www.esalen.org/place/ hot_springs.shtml; open daily 0100–0300.*

Garrapata State Park (*10 miles south of Carmel; tel: (831) 624-4909*) contains 4 miles of undeveloped coast, but has no car parks or other facilities. Park paths from lay-bys around **Soberanes Point** headlands run to beaches, through stands of cacti and into dense redwood groves. **Henry Miller Memorial Library** is a shrine to the infamous writer who lived in Big Sur for 18 years. The library is filled with Miller memorabilia, much of it for sale. The toilet has erotic tiles by local artist Ephraim Doner, and oversized sculptures grace the lawn.

Julia Pfeiffer Burns State Park includes some of Big Sur's best coastline. Don't miss the easy ½-mile return trail to **McWay Waterfall**, which drops from a bluff into the ocean. Follow the Waterfall Overlook Trail for whale-watching in December and January. Another easy ½-mile return trail leads from Hwy 1 to **Partington Point**, overlooking the surging, kelp-filled waters of Partington Cove. **Nepenthe** is a restaurant best known for its **views**. The multi-storey structure, 800ft above the crashing surf, was built by Hollywood director Orson Welles for his bride, Rita Hayworth, in the 1940s. **Café Kevah** has the best views.

Pfeiffer Beach (*no sign; off Sycamore Canyon Rd, the only paved road west off Hwy 1 between the Big Sur Post Office and Pfeiffer-Big Sur State Park*) is Big Sur's best and hardest-to-find beach. The white strand is dominated by a rock hump that changes from brown to fiery orange as the sun sets. Richard Burton and Elizabeth Taylor produced some of their steamier cinematic love scenes here for *The Sandpiper* in 1965. Their beach scenes notwithstanding, a fierce undertow makes swimming extremely hazardous.

Pfeiffer Big Sur State Park (*tel: (831) 667-2315*) sits in the midst of the Big Sur Valley, groves of redwoods, conifers and oaks interspersed with open meadows along the Big Sur River. There are miles of hiking trails and deep, clear river swimming-holes amongst the boulders in

Right
Big Sur's scenic coastline

summer. Pfeiffer-Big Sur is headquarters for all of the Big Sur State Parks, with the best visitor and information centre.

Point Sur State Historic Park contains the **Point Sur Lightstation** in operation since 1889. The light is automated, but the building's interiors are being restored to their turn-of-the-20th-century appearance. The station is open only for guided tours (*www.pointsur.org*) as part of a 2½-mile return hike, with moonlight tours in summer.

Accommodation and food in Big Sur

High demand and low supply tends to keep prices high. Advance bookings are essential. **Deetjen's Big Sur Inn $$** *48865 Hwy 1, tel: (831) 667-2377; www.deetjens.com*, is a rambling, old-fashioned inn popular with long-time visitors. **Deetjen's Big Sur Inn Restaurant $$** serves good Euro-Californian cuisine with larger-than-average portions. **Big Sur Lodge $$–$$$** *Pfeiffer Big Sur State Park; tel: (831) 667-3110 or (800) 424-4787; www.bigsurlodge.com*, is the only non-camping accommodation in the Big Sur state parks, with modern cottages around a swimming pool. **Cielo $$$** (*Ventana Inn – see below*) terrace on a sunny day has 50-mile views. **Post Ranch Inn $$$** *tel: (831) 667-2200 or (800) 527-2200; www.postranchinn.com*, a post-modernist retreat below Hwy 1, has stunning views, rooms and restaurant. **Sierra Mar $$$** *tel: (831) 667-2800* (*Post Ranch Inn – see above*), keeps to cutting-edge California dishes. **Treebones Resort $$$** *71895 Hwy 1; tel: (877) 424-4787; http://treebonesresort.com*, has luxury Mongolian-style yurts. **Ventana Inn & Spa $$$** *tel: (831) 667-2331* or *(800) 628-6500; www.ventanainn.com*, is another posh equivalent above Hwy 1.

GUADALUPE

Rancho Guadalupe Dunes County Park *Hwy 166 west of Guadalupe; tel: (805) 934-6123.*

Guadalupe is a California time capsule, a town that never lost its past. The traditional **Italian Cemetery** at the intersection of Hwys 1 and 166 is filled with ornate funerary monuments; the brick shop fronts lining Main St still display the names of the Italian, Mexican, Chinese and Basque merchants who erected them. **Rancho Guadalupe Dunes County Park** has biking, hiking, fishing and an uncrowded beach.

Food in Guadalupe

Santa Maria Barbecue, a holdover from Californio days, is the best reason to stop here. The **Far Western Tavern $–$$** *899 Guadalupe St; tel: (805) 343-2211; www.farwesterntavern.com; open Mon–Thu 1100–2100, Fri–Sat 1100–2200, Sun 0900–2100*, specialises in thick steaks, grilled with salt, pepper, garlic and olive oil, sliced paper-thin.

HEARST CASTLE

Hearst San Simeon State Historical Monument
$$ *750 Hearst Castle Rd, San Simeon, CA 93452; tel: (805) 927-2020 or (800) 444-4445; international reservations: tel: (916) 414-8400 ext. 4100; www.hearstcastle.org.* Advance bookings essential in summer and recommended all year. Walk-in space may be available midweek mid-Nov–mid-May.

The rolling hills of the Central Coast have long been a magnet for dreamers with money to bring their fantasies to life – none with more extravagance than William Randolph Hearst. Hearst called his 165-room Renaissance-Moorish-Medieval holiday house 'The Ranch'. The official name was *La Cuesta Encantada*, The Enchanted Hill, but the world knew it as **Hearst Castle**.

More estate than castle, *Casa Grande*, the Big House, is surrounded by guesthouses and an outdoor swimming pool complex, the whole set within lush gardens and a private zoo with free-roaming zebras and other exotic creatures.

Hearst, an only child, inherited a failing *San Francisco Examiner* and turned it into a hugely profitable chain of papers. In the euphoria following World War I, America's most famous media personality decided to build America's most famous house. With the help of architect Julia Morgan, Hearst got an eclectic pastiche of European treasures. The grand façade to *Casa Grande* once graced a Spanish cathedral; the ceilings were pulled from European monasteries. No museum of the day could outbid Hearst's buyers, who filled the Castle with priceless treasures.

Never one to underplay his own success, Hearst invited the social and political elite of the world to visit The Ranch for as long as they wished. Charlie Chaplin, Winston Churchill, Greta Garbo, Clark Gable, Charles Lindbergh, George Bernard Shaw and hundreds more accepted. Hearst's 'home movies', seen as part of the tour, show just how carefree life could be at The Ranch; Orson Welles's 1941 film *Citizen Kane* gives an equally accurate – if fictionalised – rendition of Hearst, castle and company.

The property eventually passed to the State of California and became **Hearst San Simeon State Historic Monument** (*tel: (805) 927-2020*), open by guided tour. **Tour One** is an overview of the property. **Tour Two** concentrates on the upper floors of *Casa Grande*, including the art collection and Hearst's library and bedroom suite. **Tour Three** looks at one of the guesthouses in detail. **Tour Four** (Apr–Oct) inspects the grounds and gardens. **Tour Five** (Fri–Sat evenings, spring and autumn) is a living history tour with guides dressed as famous guests and servants from the 1930s. It's possible – but ill-advised – to cram all five tours into a single day. After the first few hours, one baroque tapestry starts looking much like any other. The **Visitor Center** is worth a visit even if tours are fully booked. The free museum provides a good overview of the Castle and architect Julia Morgan's other and far more original work.

The **Coastal Discovery Centre** (*tel: (805) 927-2145*) at San Simeon Bay across Hwy 1 from Hearst Castle has information, live rainbow trout, and a talking tidepool sculpture. Four miles north at **Piedras Blancas** (*www.elephantseal.org*) is a vista point for Northern elephant seal-watching.

Below
Sybaritic luxury – the Neptune Pool at Hearst Castle

LOMPOC

ⓘ Lompoc Valley Chamber of Commerce and Visitors Bureau *111 S. I St, Lompoc, CA 93436; tel: (805) 736-4567 or (800) 240-0999; www.lompoc.com. Open Mon–Fri 0900–1700.*

ⓜ La Purisima Mission State Historic Park $ *2295 Purisima Rd; tel: (805) 733-3713. Tour information, tel: (805) 733-1303; www.parks.ca.gov and www.lapurisimamission.org. Open daily 0900–1700.*

Lompoc Museum $ *200 S. H St; tel: (805) 736-3888; www.lompochistory.org/lompocmuseum.html. Open Tue–Fri 1300–1700, Sat–Sun 1300–1600.*

Right
Commercial flower farms blaze with colour in the Californian summer

Many of the flower seeds sold in America are grown on acres of fields in Lompoc, which blaze with colour between June and August. The town also boasts more than 70 wall murals (*www.lompocmurals.com*), inspired by Chemainus in British Columbia, Canada.

La Purisima Mission State Historic Park (*see page 259*) is the most authentically restored of the 21 California Missions. The park includes ten buildings restored to their 1820s glory, the historic water system, replanted gardens and period barnyard animals. **Lompoc Museum** has a large collection of artefacts from local Native American bands, including the Chumash. **Santa Rita Hills** is a new wine region with open tasting rooms between Lompoc and Buelton.

MORRO BAY

ⓘ Morro Bay Chamber of Commerce & Visitor Center *845 Embarcadero Rd, Suite D, Morro Bay, CA 93442; tel: (805) 772-4467 or (800) 231-0592; www.morrobay.org. Open Mon–Fri 0900–1700, Sat 1000–1600.*

Once a lively port for the area's ranchers, Morro Bay has become a busy fishing port and holiday destination. The town and bay are named after **Morro Rock**, first in a line of volcanic cores stretching south to San Luis Obispo. The sand spit which protects the harbour is accessible only by boat. Kayaking around the protected estuary at the south end of the Bay is popular in all seasons.

The Embarcadero is the town's main tourist and commercial fishing area. Many fishing boats unload directly into restaurant kitchens or sell straight to consumers. **Chablis Cruises'** riverboat *Chablis* passes Morro Rock, the Embarcadero and Moro Back Bay. **Sub Sea Tours $$** (*tel: (805) 772-9463; www.subseatours.com*) offers 45-minute bay tours on a semi-submerged vessel with view windows beneath the waves.

Montaña de Oro State Park, 'Mountain of Gold' in Spanish, was named after the mounds of golden California poppies, wild mustard

Chablis Cruises $$ *Embarcadero; tel: (805) 305-1841; www.chabliscruises.com. One-hour trips – call for cruise times.*

Montaña de Oro State Park $ *End of Los Osos Valley Rd, south of Morro Bay; tel: (805) 528-0513 or (805) 772-7434.*

Morro Bay State Park and Museum of Natural History $ *South end of Morro Bay; tel: (805) 772-2560. Museum, tel: (805) 772-2694, open daily 1000–1700.*

and other wildflowers that bloom each spring. There are more than 50 miles of walking paths in the park; among the most popular is **Hazard Canyon**, ½-mile from gum forests to tide pools.

Morro Bay State Park takes in most of the south end of Morro Bay, including a public golf course. The **Museum of Natural History** covers the Bay's complex ecosystem, including a network of walking paths.

Morro Rock (578ft) has been mined for building materials for nearly four centuries, but still dominates the bay and town. The Rock itself is closed to protect peregrine falcons nesting on the upper slopes. Morro Bay's estuary is a major stopover point for birds on the Pacific flyway, especially in winter. The **Morro Bay Harbor Walk** extends from the Embarcadero to Morro Rock.

Food in Morro Bay

Fish is the obvious best choice in town. **Windows on the Water $$$** *699 Embarcadero; tel: (805) 772-0677; www.windowsonthewater.net, open daily from 1700,* has a wide variety of excellent seafood, an extensive wine list and bay views.

PISMO BEACH

Pismo Beach Chamber of Commerce *581 Doliver St, Pismo Beach, CA 93449; tel: (805) 773-4362 or (800) 443-7778; www.pismochamber.com and www.classiccalifornia.com. Open Mon–Sat 0900–1700, Sun 1000–1600.*

Pismo State Beach $ *2 miles south; tel: (805) 489-1869.*

The town took its name from the Pismo clam, a local mollusc once so plentiful that newspapers talked of 45,000 clams being dug in a single day. Few legal-sized clams survived decades of depredation, though hardware stores hire digging gear and sell the requisite fishing licences. The fishing pier offers excellent views of surfers riding the waves toward shore.

At the **Monarch Butterfly Grove** (*www.monarchbutterfly.org*), in the **Pismo State Beach North Beach Campground** between Pismo Beach and Grover City, the orange and black butterflies hang in great clusters from the gum trees and Monterey pines from November to February.

Pismo Beach, Grover City and Oceano are often lumped together as the **Beach Cities**. The **Nipomo Dunes** begin south of the Beach Cities, a sand sea stretching 18 miles to **Point Sal**. Cecil B. DeMille filmed the original *Ten Commandments* in the dunes beyond West Main St (Hwy 166) in Guadalupe (*see page 217*). Bits of his faux-Egypt set occasionally reappear as the dunes shift.

Food in Pismo Beach

Splash Café $ *197 Pomeroy Ave; tel: (805) 773-4653; www.splashcafe. com; open daily 0800–2000 or 2100,* is famous for clam chowder, its surfing murals inside and out and a surfboard above the entrance.

Below
San Luis Obispo County Park

Cracked Crab $$–$$$ *751 Price St; tel: (805) 773-2722; www.crackedcrab.com*, dumps the bucket of shellfish – among many other fish specialities – on the table with mallet and crab cracker for ultimate dining.

SAN LUIS OBISPO

ⓘ San Luis Obispo Chamber of Commerce Visitor Center *1039 Chorro St, San Luis Obispo, CA 93401; tel: (805) 781-2777; www.VisitSLO.com. Open Sun–Wed 1000–1700, Thu–Sat 1000–1900.*

Ⓖ California Polytechnic University *Tel: (805) 756-5734; www.ess.calpoly. edu/_admiss/visit/guided.htm. Tours Mon–Fri 1110. Free.*

Mission San Luis Obispo de Tolosa, *Chorro at 782 Monterey St; tel: (805) 781-8220; www. missionsanluisobispo.org. Open daily 0900–1700. Free.*

ⓘ San Luis Obispo County Visitors & Conference Bureau *811 El Capitan Way, Ste 200, San Luis Obispo, CA 93401; tel: (800) 634-1414 or (805) 541-8000; www. sanluisobispocounty.com. Open Mon–Fri 0800–1700, for area information.*

Ⓖ San Luis Obispo County Historical Museum $ *696 Monterey St; tel: (805) 543-0638; www.slochs.org. Open Wed–Sun 1000–1600.*

San Luis grew up as a Mission farming community that blossomed when the railway arrived in 1894. The Mission heritage remains, both in the pronunciation (Lou-iss, Spanish-style) and the town's common appellation, SLO, as in 'slow', the relaxed pace of life.

The town centre, **Higuera and Monterey Sts**, contains some of the finest small-town commercial architecture in the state, from adobes to art deco and Frank Lloyd Wright. The **Chamber of Commerce** has free self-guided walking and driving maps, or ride the inexpensive **SLO Trolley** around a circular route covering the main tourist sites, Thu–Sun.

California Polytechnic University, usually called Cal Poly, offers free 80-minute campus tours. Don't miss the **Botanic Garden** or **Poly Canyon**, an outdoor laboratory for experimental architecture and construction.

Generations of teenagers have festooned **Bubblegum Alley** (*between Chorro and Broad Sts*) with graffiti, names and freeform designs, all carefully executed in well-used chewing gum. The oral appliqué changes slightly almost every night. Every Thursday night, Higuera St becomes a pedestrians-only **Farmers' Market** with food and produce stalls, sidewalk restaurants and free entertainment.

Mission San Luis Obispo de Tolosa (*Chorro and Monterey Sts; tel: (805) 781-8220*) pioneered the red-tile roof that became the Mission hallmark – the 1772 Mission needed something more substantial than thatching to withstand fiery attacks by local Native American tribes (*see page 261*). **Mission Plaza**, fronting the Mission, is a shady park sloping down to **San Luis Creek** and the business district. Music wafts through the trees from several restaurant patios that open on to the plaza. **San Luis Obispo County Historical Museum** has a collection of local artefacts in the historic Carnegie Library building.

Accommodation and food in San Luis Obispo

Big Sky Café $$ *1121 Broad St; tel: (805) 545-5401; www.bigskycafe. com*, has fresh seasonal ingredients with cuisine spanning Europe to Morocco.

Madonna Inn $$ *100 Madonna Rd; tel: (805) 543-3000 or (800) 543-9666; www.madonnainn.com*, is a shocking pink temple of kitsch, from the 200-ton boulders in the Jungle Rock Room to the crimson silk Love Nest and equally whimsical décor for the Fabulous 50s, Cave Man and other theme rooms.

Koberl at Blue $$$ *998 Monterey St; tel: (805) 783-1135; www. epkoberl.com*, has fine dining with Wine Country cuisine and finely crafted Martinis.

SANTA BARBARA

ⓘ **Santa Barbara Conference & Visitors Bureau** *1601 Anacapa St, Santa Barbara, CA 93101; tel: (800) 676-1266 or (805) 966-9222; www.santabarbaraca.com*

Santa Barbara Visitor Information Center *1 Garden St, Santa Barbara, CA 93101; tel: (805) 965-3021. Open Mon–Fri 0830–1700.* Visitor information is also available at the **Santa Barbara Harbor Outdoor Visitor Center**, *113 Harbor Way, Waterfront Center 4th Fl; tel: (805) 884-1475.*

ⓟ **El Presidio de Santa Barbara State Historic Park $** *100-200 E. Canon Perdido St; tel: (805) 965-0093. Call for hours.*

Mission Santa Barbara *$ E. Los Olivos at 2201 Laguna St; tel: (805) 682-4149; www.sbmission.org. Open daily 0900–1700.*

Santa Barbara began as a Mission town, but the Mission-look of downtown, red-tile roofs, whitewashed plaster walls and colourful wall tiles, dates from a 1925 earthquake. Faced with rebuilding nearly the entire city centre, authorities opted to create their own historic look with a strict architectural code. The result is one of the most gracious, visually pleasing cities in Southern California. Built on a series of rolling hills between broad beaches and the rugged Santa Ynez Mountains, Santa Barbara happily lives up to the name Lotusland bestowed by an early opera diva who retired here.

El Paseo and State St are centrepieces of the 1920s reconstruction. **El Paseo** is an early shopping arcade, filled with delightfully sunny niches and fountains. **El Paseo Nuevo** is an updated version with the same Mission motif, while **State St** is Santa Barbara's high street.

El Presidio de Santa Barbara State Historic Park is the site of the 1782 Spanish fort that first lured settlers to Santa Barbara. The restored **El Cuartel** is among the oldest structures in California. The padres' quarters, chapel, commandant's office and other buildings are reconstructions.

Mission Santa Barbara (*see page 263*), the 'Queen of the Missions', starred in numerous early cinematic epics. Buildings, gardens and the church interior are beautifully preserved.

Santa Barbara Botanic Garden is devoted to native trees, cacti, shrubs and flowers.

Santa Barbara County Courthouse, in an extravagant take on the Mission style, has tiled corridors, heroic furnishings and a red-tiled roof. The courthouse has a Moorish tower with fine views of city and sea.

Santa Barbara Historical Museum offers local historical exhibits, while the **Santa Barbara Museum of Natural History** specialises in Native American tribal artefacts, as well as local flora and fauna.

Stearns Wharf (*foot of State St; tel: (805) 564-5518; www. stearnswharf.org*), built in 1872, now houses small speciality shops,

(see page 50)

Santa Barbara Botanic Garden $
1212 Mission Canyon Rd;
tel: (805) 682-4726;
www.sbbg.org. Open daily
Mar–Oct 0900–1800;
Nov–Feb 0900–1700.

Santa Barbara County Courthouse 1100 Anacapa
St; tel: (805) 962-6464. Open
Mon–Fri 0800–1700, Sat
1000–1700. Free tours
Mon–Sat 1400 and Mon, Tue,
Fri 1030.

Santa Barbara Historical Museum $ 136 E. De La
Guerra St;
tel: (805) 966-1601; www.
santabarbaramuseum.com.
Open Tue–Sat 1000–1700,
Sun 1200–1700.

Santa Barbara Museum of Natural History $
2559 Puesta del Sol Rd;
tel: (805) 682-4711;
www.sbnature.org. Open daily
1000–1700.

restaurants and the **Ty Warner Sea Center** $ (tel: (805) 962-2526; open daily 1000–1700), a small museum devoted to marine and bird life of the Channel Islands National Marine Sanctuary.

Accommodation and food in Santa Barbara

Santa Barbara's popularity as a quick getaway for Los Angelinos keeps accommodation demand and prices high.

The **Enterprise Fish Co** $$ 225 State St; tel: (805) 962-3313; www.enterprisefishco.com; open Sun–Thu 1130–2200, Fri–Sat to 2300, has great fish.

Wine Cask $$ 813 Anacapa St (El Paseo); tel: (805) 966-9463 or (800) 436-9463; www.winecask.com; open Mon–Fri 1130–1430, Mon–Fri 1730–2100, Sat–Sun to 2200, has one of Santa Barbara's best Central Coast wine lists. Don't miss the five-course tasting menu on request.

Bouchon $$$ 9 W. Victoria St; tel: (805) 730-1160; www.bouchon.net; open daily, combines local farm-to-table ingredients with many Santa Barbara County wines by the glass.

El Encanto Hotel $$$ 1900 Lasuen Rd; tel: (805) 568-1357; www.orient-express.com or www.elencantohotel.com, has sweeping views and a mix of Craftsman (see page 50) and Spanish-style cottages.

The **Hotel Santa Barbara** $$$ 533 State St; tel: (805) 957-9300 or (800) 549-9869; www.hotelsantabarbara.com, is a posh stop in the city centre.

SANTA BARBARA BEACHES

El Capitan, Gaviota and **Refugio State Beaches** (Hwy 101, N. of Santa Barbara; tel: (805) 968-1033) are three of Santa Barbara's most popular beach parks. **El Capitan** has rocky tide pools, a sandy beach and stands of sycamore and oak trees. **Gaviota** boasts a wooden fishing pier. **Refugio** offers palm trees along a small creek. Two luxury resorts have appeared in recent years: **El Capitan Canyon** $$$ 11560 Calle Real, Gaviota; tel: (866) 352-2729; www.elcapitancanyon.com, with cedar cabins, safari tents and spa treatments, and one of California's largest spa resorts, **Bacara Resort & Spa** $$$ 8301 Hollister Ave, Santa Barbara; tel: (877) 422-4245; www.bacararesort.com

SANTA BARBARA WINERIES

Santa Barbara County has three dozen wineries, most of them in the Santa Ynez Valley, off Hwys 154 and 246 near Solvang, or near Foxen Canyon Rd in the **Santa Maria Valley** (tel: (800) 331-3779;

www.santamariawines.com). For information on visits and tasting facilities, contact the **Santa Barbara County Vintners' Assn**, *Santa Ynez, CA 93460; tel: (800) 218-0881* or *(805) 688-0881; www.sbcountywines. com*. The **San Luis Obispo Vintners Association** *tel: (805) 541-5868; www.slowine.com* represents San Luis Obispo, Edna Valley and Arroyo Grande wineries. **Paso Robles Wine Country Alliance** *tel: (805) 239-8463; www.pasowine.com* covers Paso Robles wineries.

Suggested tour

Total distance: 245 miles.

Time: 6 hours' driving. Big Sur deserves at least a day to itself. Allow half a day to tour **Hearst Castle**, with an overnight stop in **Morro Bay** or **San Luis Obispo**.

Links: Monterey Peninsula (north), Southern California (south).

Route: Follow Hwy 1 south from **Monterey ❶/Carmel ❷** past **Point Lobos ❸** into **Big Sur ❹** . **Hearst Castle ❺** marks the start of the San Luis Obispo coast. From **Morro Bay ❻** , Hwy 1 runs inland to join Hwy 101 at **San Luis Obispo ❼** . Hwy 1 returns to the coast at **Pismo Beach ❽** and runs south towards **Guadalupe ❾** and **Lompoc ❿** before rejoining Hwy 101 28 miles north of **Santa Barbara ⓫** .

Also worth exploring

San Luis Obispo to Port San Luis

Take San Luis Bay Rd west from Hwy 101 just south of San Luis Obispo to Avila Beach Dr. **Avila Hot Springs Resort $$** (*250 Avila Beach Dr; tel: (805) 595-2359; www.avilahotsprings.com*) was a favourite party stop for Hollywood stars on their way to Hearst Castle (*see page 218*). Today the resort is a family stop.

Sycamore Mineral Springs $$$ (*1215 Avila Beach Dr.; tel: (805) 595-7302* or *(800) 234-5831; www.sycamoresprings.com*) offers a full-service spa and an excellent restaurant, **The Gardens of Avila $$**.

The fishing village of **Avila Beach** has been dug up and largely rebuilt to remove decades of petroleum pollution and is one of the few beaches on this section of coast known for soft sand and no undertow. **Point San Luis Lighthouse $** (*tel: (805) 541-8735* or *(805) 546-4904; www.sanluislighthouse.org*) has 3½-mile docent-led hikes on the Pecho Coast Trail to the lighthouse on Saturdays. The nearby **Diablo Canyon Nuclear Power Plant** is no longer open for tours. The plant visitor center (*6588 Ontario Rd, San Luis Obispo; tel: (805) 546-5280; open Mon–Fri 0900–1300*) has exhibits and a short film on power plant operations.

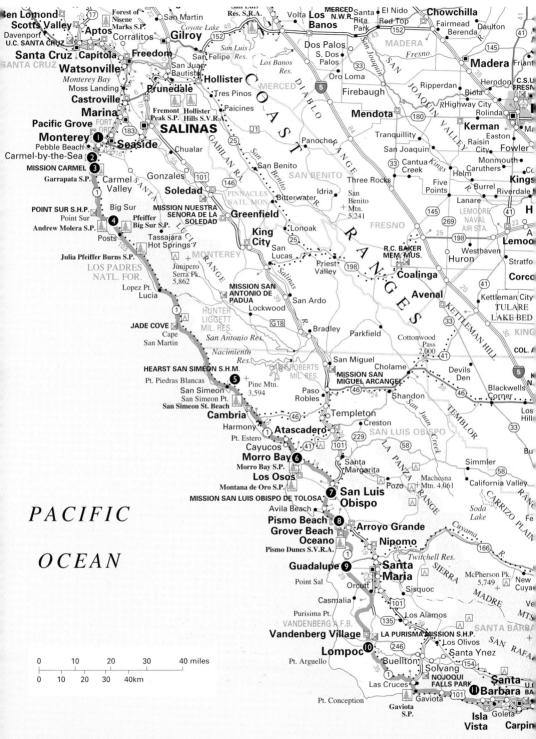

Santa Barbara Channel

Gold Country to Yosemite

Ratings

Scenery	●●●●●
History	●●●●○
Mountains	●●●●○
Children	●●●○○
Food	●●●○○
Museums	●●●○○
Wine	●●○○○
Architecture	●○○○○

The discovery of gold in 1848 catapulted California from backwater to powerhouse and created Sacramento as its capital. Gold Country, the Sierra Nevada foothills from Sierra City south to Mariposa, shaped the California psyche far more dramatically than today's placid landscape would suggest. The rough-and-tumble promise of riches just over the next hill was fulfilled often enough that Californians still embrace calculated risks that many Americans might consider foolhardy. Try to visit in spring or early autumn; winding roads are congested in summer and most attractions are closed Mon–Wed in winter. Yosemite Valley is a summertime city, complete with crowds, traffic, noise and pollution, but the rest of the park is delightfully calm.

ANGELS CAMP

ⓘ Calaveras Visitors Bureau *1192 S. Main St, Angels Camp, CA 95222; tel: (209) 736-0049 or (800) 225-3764; www.gocalaveras.com. Open daily 0900–1700.*

◆ Calaveras County Fair *$ Calaveras County Fairgrounds, 2 miles south; tel: (209) 736-2561; www.frogtown.org*

⬛ Angels Camp Museum & Carriage House *$ 753 Main St; tel: (209) 736-2963; www.angelscamp.gov/museum. htm. Open daily Mar–Dec; weekends Jan–Feb; call for hours.*

A young prospector with literary ambitions heard the story of a jumping frog contest here, and *The Celebrated Jumping Frog of Calaveras County* brought fame and the beginnings of fortune to Mark Twain. Twain may have written the short story in a rebuilt cabin just outside of town. Fans flock to the **Jumping Frog Jubilee** on the third weekend in May at the **Calaveras County Fair** (*tel: (209) 736-2561*). Bring your own frog or hire a jumper on the spot.

Angels Camp Museum & Carriage House has photographs, carriages and relics of gold-mining equipment from the old days, a taste of the romance – and the backbreaking labour – of panning gold by swirling gravel, sand, mud and water in an oversized pie tin to wash away the dross and recover a few flecks of precious metal.

OARS (*tel: (209) 736-4677 or (800) 346-6277; www.oars.com*) offers river trips from local half-day floats to whitewater expeditions. In-shape adventurers hike, climb, crawl and raft through **Gold Cliff Mine** tours (*$$$ tel: (866) 762-2837 or (209) 736-2708; http://caverntours.com/Gold_Cliff.html*). Calaveras winery tours make pleasant terrestrial expeditions (*Calaveras Winegrape Alliance, tel: (866) 806-9463; www.calaveraswines.org*).

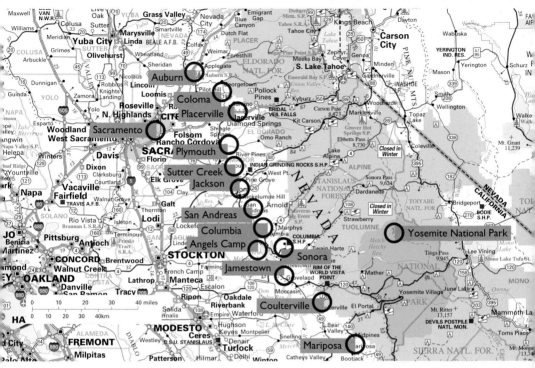

Accommodation and food in Angels Camp

Angels Inn Motel $$ *600 N. Main St.; tel (888) 753-0226 or (209) 736-4242 or (888) 753-0226; www.angelsinnmotel.com, on Hwy 49*, has modern facilities. **Crusco's $$$** *1240 S. Main St; tel: (209) 729-1440; www.cruscos.com; open Thu–Mon*, in a 150-year-old building has freshly made Italian-influenced fare.

AUBURN

ⓘ California Welcome Center
Auburn *13411 Lincoln Way; tel: (530) 887-2111; www.visitplacer.com. Open Mon–Sat 0930–1630, Sun 1100–1630.*

ⓜ Placer County Court House
Museum *101 Maple St; tel: (530) 889-6500; www.placer.ca.gov. Open daily 1000–1600. Free.*

Like most Gold Country towns, Auburn was an accident. Prospectors headed somewhere else hit pay dirt here first, but unlike hundreds of ragtag tent camps that disappeared as quickly as they sprouted, Auburn endured. Placer gold, panned from stream beds, gave way to hard rock gold, mined underground, which in turn gave way to more enduring riches from the Transcontinental Railroad in the 1860s.

Placer County Museum has excellent regional gold displays and Native American baskets. The real Gold Rush was in **Old Town** (*Lincoln Way*), a warren of narrow streets and 19th-century buildings surrounding the red-and-white-striped **Firehouse No 1** (*Lincoln Way; tel: (530) 505-7725*) and an 1849 **Post Office** (*1583 Lincoln Way; tel: (530) 889-2120*), California's oldest. The **Gold Country Museum** has a demonstration mine shaft as well as period equipment.

Gold Country Museum *Gold Country Fairgrounds, 1273 High St; tel: (530) 889-6500; www.placer.ca.gov/facility/ museums/localmuseums/ goldcountry.aspx. Open Tue–Sun 1100–1600. Free*

Accommodation and food in Auburn

Ikeda's $ *13500 Lincoln Way; tel: (530) 885-4243; www.ikedas.com; open daily 0800 to 1900, 2000 or 2100, depending on season,* is the best stop for burgers and milkshakes.

Bootlegger's Old Town Tavern & Grill $$ *210 Washington St; tel: (530) 889-2229; www.bootleggersauburn.com; open Tue–Sun,* serves an eclectic mix including steaks in Auburn's 1870 City Hall building.

Power's Mansion Inn $$$ *195 Harrison Ave; tel: (530) 885-1166; www.powersmansioninn.com,* is a bright pink mansion built in 1898, serving traditional afternoon tea.

COLOMA

Marshall Gold Discovery State Historic Park $ *310 Back St; Coloma, CA 95613; tel: (530) 622-3470; www.parks.ca.gov. Park open daily 0800–sunset, museum open 1000–1500, to 1630 Apr–Labor Day. In summer or at warm weather weekends Coloma is awash with school groups, family picnickers and river rafters.*

The California Dream started in Coloma, when a sawmill contractor named James Marshall spotted a few shiny flecks in January, 1848. **Marshall Gold Discovery State Historic Park** (*surrounding Hwy 49*) contains about 70 per cent of the once-booming town. Historic buildings are concentrated along Main, Back and Brewery Sts; Marshall's restored cabin is below his hilltop grave and monument.

Start with the visitor centre and an excellent video about the geology of California gold, Gold Rush history and the often ruinous impact of miners digging, blasting and washing everything in sight – 150 years have barely begun to heal the environmental havoc that set California on the path to riches. A working replica of Marshall's sawmill sits on the banks of the American River, which has changed course since 1848. Trails lead to the site of the original mill. Visitors still find traces of gold by panning the riverbank using pans from the visitor centre.

COLUMBIA

Columbia State Historic Park *Columbia, CA 95310; tel: (209) 588-9128; www.parks.ca.gov*

Museum and Visitor Center *Main & Spring Sts; tel: (209) 588-9128. Open daily 1000–1600. Free.*

Columbia California Chamber of Commerce *Tel: (209) 536-1672; www.columbiacalifornia.com*

California's most appealing Gold Rush relic is an almost-ghost town, complete with brick storefronts, iron shutters, wooden sidewalks, spreading trees, stagecoaches and men (plus a few women) in real frontier garb. The park museum and ranger office have free self-guiding tours to the dozens of restored Gold Rush structures and businesses in a real town that never closes.

Accommodation and food in Columbia

City Hotel $$ *Main St; tel: (209) 532-1479* or *(800) 532-1479; www.cityhotel.com,* more resembles the 'Gem of the Southern Mines' that 1856 visitors knew. The **City Hotel Restaurant $$$** is a French-

California culinary delight. The **Fallon Hotel $$** (*see City Hotel contact information*) offers an opulent 1890s look.

COULTERVILLE

Northern Mariposa County History Center *10301 Hwy 49 and 132; tel: (209) 878-3015; http:// home.inreach.com/nmchc/. Open Wed–Sun 1000–1600. Free.*

Coulterville remains a very small mining, ranching and tourist supply town. The **Northern Mariposa County History Center** is a pair of 1865 brick and stone buildings with period guns, Paris gowns and local Chinese furnishings. The 1851 **Sun Sun Wo Company Store** (*Main and Kew Sts*) is the sole survivor of a once-thriving Chinatown. The 1920s goods on the shelves here disguise an opium den behind. The **Whistling Billy** locomotive engine, under the **Hanging Tree** in front of the History Center, once hauled ore from a nearby mine. Gold is still found in town along Maxwell Creek.

Accommodation and food in Coulterville

The **Hotel Jeffrey $$** *1 Main St; tel: (209) 878-3471; www. hoteljefferygold.com*, began as a Yosemite stage stop. Walls are still covered in the original stamped tin.

Right
Brewing up around the campfire, Columbia State Historic Park

JACKSON

ⓘ Amador County Chamber of Commerce & Visitors Bureau *571 S. Hwy 49; Jackson, CA 95642; tel: (209) 223-0350 or (800) 649-4988; www. amadorcountychamber.com. Open Tue–Fri 0900–1630.*

ⓜ Amador County Museum $ *225 Church St; tel: (209) 223-6386; www.co.amador. ca.us/depts/museum. Open Wed–Sun 1000–1600.*

Kennedy Mine Tailing Wheels *N. Main St, in a park 1 mile N. of downtown. Open daily dawn–dusk. Free.*

Kennedy Mine Tours $ *tel: (209) 223-9542; www. kennedygoldmine.com. Tours Sat, Sun and holidays mid-Mar–Oct, bookings required.*

Jackson grew and prospered with the Kennedy and Argonaut Mines, which survived until World War II. The **Amador County Museum** offers a good overview of daily life through the 1920s. The most striking remnant of the past is the **Kennedy Mine Tailing Wheels**, ruins of wooden wheels used to move mine debris (tailings) over several ridges to a holding pond. A well-marked **viewpoint** 1½ miles north of town overlooks what remains of the mine headframe at the top of an abandoned 6000-ft shaft, once the deepest in North America. **Kennedy Mine Tours** explores the surface structures. **White St Sava Serbian Orthodox Church** (*724 N. Main St; tel: (209) 223-2700*) is the oldest Serbian Orthodox church in America.

Accommodation and food in Jackson

Linda Vista Motel $$ *10708 N. Hwy 49, Martell, CA, 1 mile north of Jackson; tel: (209) 223-1096,* is outstanding value accommodation. The **National Hotel $$** *2 Water St; tel: (209) 223-0500,* claims to be the oldest operating hotel in California (since 1862). The **Jackson Rancheria Casino & Hotel $$–$$$** *12222 New York Ranch Rd, Jackson; tel: (800) 822-9466; www.jacksoncasino.com,* Amador County's largest employer, offers (Native American-operated) gaming, lodging and dining.

JAMESTOWN

ⓜ Railtown 1897 State Historic Park $ *Two blocks east of Historic Downtown Jamestown on 5th Ave; tel: (209) 984-3953; www.railtown1897.com. Grounds open daily Apr–Oct 0930–1630, Nov–Mar 1000–1500 for self-guided tours. Call in advance to book weekend steam-train excursions Apr–Oct.*

Gold Prospecting Adventures $$ *18170 Main St; tel: (209) 984-4653 or (800) 596-0009; www.goldprospecting.com. Advance booking required.*

'Jimtown' still uses original false-front buildings and wooden sidewalks, many of which have featured prominently in films such as *Butch Cassidy and the Sundance Kid.* Jamestown's working gold mine, an open-pit operation outside town, is off limits, but **Gold Prospecting Adventures** sells prospecting and panning trips for individuals and families. These can be great fun, but expect to get dirty and wet, and dress accordingly.

Locomotive engines and carriages from **Railtown 1897 State Historic Park** have appeared in more than 200 films. The museum contains the original roundhouse and workshops of the Sierra Railroad, organised in 1897 to serve the Mother Lode.

Accommodation in Jamestown

The **National Hotel $$** *18183 Main St; tel: (209) 984-3446 or (800) 894-3446; www.national-hotel.com,* is an 1859 antique; many of the furnishings are original to the building. The **Jamestown Hotel $$** *18153 Main St; tel: (209) 984-3902 or (800) 205-4901; www. jamestownhotel.com,* is a bed and breakfast of similar vintage.

MARIPOSA

ⓘ Mariposa County Visitors Center
5158 Hwy 140, Mariposa, CA 95338; tel: (209) 966-7081 or (866) 425-3366; www.homeofyosemite.com. Open daily.

This southern gateway to Gold Country is the home of the **California State Mining and Mineral Museum** (*Fairgrounds Rd, tel: (209) 742-7625; www.parks.ca.gov; open May–Sep 1000–1800, Oct–Apr Wed–Mon 1000–1600*), one of the world's finest mineral and gem museums. Government has been holding court in the white **Mariposa County Courthouse** (*Bullion St between 9th and 10th Sts*) since 1854, the state's oldest official building still in use. Most courtroom furnishings are original, including the potbellied stove. **St Joseph's Catholic Church** (*top of Bullion St*) is a striking example of traditional Gold Country church architecture. The **Mariposa County Museum and History Center $** (*5119 Jesse St, tel: (209) 966-2924; www.mariposamuseum.com; call for hours*) has an exhaustive collection, from a working stamp mill to ancient bottles of Guinness®.

PLACERVILLE

ⓘ El Dorado County Visitors Authority Chamber of Commerce
542 Main St, Placerville, CA 95667; tel: (530) 621-5885 or (800) 457-6279; www.visit-eldorado.com. Open Mon–Fri 0900–1700, Sat 1000–1400.

ⓜ El Dorado County Historical Museum $
Next to the Fairgrounds, 104 Placerville Dr.; tel: (530) 621-5865; www.co.el-dorado.ca.us/ museum. Open Wed–Sat 1000–1600, Sun 1200–1600.

Once known as 'Hangtown' for its favoured method of law enforcement, Placerville was more supply centre than mining town, a breeding ground for early entrepreneurs. The town's most famous product is the 'Hangtown Fry', eggs scrambled with bacon and oysters. Look for the historic saloon on Main Street with a 'hangman' suspended outside, visible across the street from the balcony of the beautifully restored 1857 **Cary House Hotel $$** *300 Main St; tel: (530) 622-4271; www.caryhouse.com*. The **El Dorado County Historical Museum** focuses on local manufacturing and other mining support services. **Hangtown's Gold Bug Park & Mine** (*1 mile north via Bedford Avenue and Hwy 50, tel: (530) 642 5207; www.goldbugpark.org; open 1000–1600 daily Apr–Oct, weekends Nov–Mar*) has 352ft of lighted tunnel with wooden floors for self-guided tours, a stamp mill, museum and hiking trails. Nearby **El Dorado wine** valleys are best known for Zinfandel, Syrah and Merlot. The **El Dorado Winery Association** (*tel: (800) 306-3956; www.eldoradowines.org*) has free winery maps and touring suggestions.

PLYMOUTH

Plymouth is a convenient starting point for tours of the **Amador wine country**. **Amador Vintners Association** (*Box 667, Plymouth, CA 95669; tel: (209) 245-6992 or (888) 655-8614; www.amadorwine.com*) has free tasting and touring information in a region renowned for Zinfandels.

SACRAMENTO

Sacramento Convention and Visitors Bureau *1608 1 St, Sacramento CA 95814; tel: (916) 808-7777; www.discovergold.org. Open Mon–Fri 0800–1700.*

Old Sacramento Visitors Center *1002 2nd St; tel: (916) 442-7644; www.oldsacramento.com. Open daily 1000–1700.*

Sutter's Fort State Historic Park $ *27th & L Sts; tel: (916) 445-4422; www.parks.ca.gov. Open daily 1000–1700.*

California State Indian Museum $ *2618 K St at Sutter's Fort; tel: (916) 324-0971; www.parks.ca.gov. Open daily 1000–1700.*

California Museum for History, Women and the Arts $ *1020 O St; tel: (916) 653-7524; http://californiamuseum.org. Open Tue–Sat 1000–1700, Sun 1200–1700.*

California State Capitol *10th St between L & N Sts; tel: (916) 324-0333; www.parks.ca.gov and www.capitolmuseum.ca.gov. Open daily 0900–1700, free guided tours hourly.*

Old Sacramento *28 acres west of 3rd St. to the Sacramento River.*

California State Railroad Museum $$ *2nd & I Sts in Old Sac; tel: (916) 445-6645; www.csrmf.org. Open daily 1000–1700. Train excursions $–$$, Apr–Sep weekends.*

California's capital city began as **Sutter's Fort**, built by Swiss immigrant John Sutter, whose Coloma sawmill sparked the Gold Rush. Sutter's adobe administration building is largely original, but the rest of the fort is reconstructed. The self-guided audio tour is a lively introduction to daily life of the era, aided by interpreters in period dress during summer and holiday periods. The adjoining **California State Indian Museum** has a rich collection of photographs and artefacts. The **California Museum for History, Women and the Arts** draws upon the 120 million items in state archives.

The domed **California State Capitol** is one of the West's most elegant public buildings. It is also an outstanding museum, thanks to extensive 1980s renovations that returned gubernatorial and admin offices to turn-of-the-20th-century splendour. Visitors can watch Senate and Assembly sessions, but the magnificent **Capitol Park** around the building can be more revealing than legislative debates.

Old Sacramento, or 'Old Sac', is Sacramento's original city centre, now almost all a state historic park and national historic landmark. Brick buildings date to the 1850s, skilfully mixed with modern construction, wooden sidewalks and shade trees. The **California State Railroad Museum** is America's largest railway museum, filled with splendidly restored locomotive engines, luxurious private carriages, sleepers and extensive displays on America's first transcontinental railway. A **Waterfront Promenade** links Old Sacramento and the **Crocker Art Museum**, the oldest art gallery west of the Mississippi. The **Aerospace Museum of California**, north of downtown, displays 30 military and civilian aircraft with a flight ride simulator.

Accommodation and food in Sacramento

The **Delta King Hotel $$** *1000 Front St; tel: (916) 444-5464 or (800) 825-5464; www.deltaking.com*, is an original paddlewheel steamboat with hotel, restaurant overlooking the river, and a saloon,

Early Tourism

California has been a popular tourist destination since the 1870s. Thomas Cook included California in its first round-the-world tour in 1872–73, and in 1876 the company ran the first tour of California in its own right. Early tourists visited the Yosemite Valley by stage-coach, before continuing on to San Francisco by train – in fact, only Los Angeles (which began to grow as late as the 1880s) and Disneyland® Resort would have been missing from the list of sights that remain popular to this day.

Crocker Art Museum $ 216 O St; tel: (916) 808-7000; www. crockerartmuseum.org. Open Tue–Sun 1000–1700, Thu to 2100. Free Sun 1000–1300.

Aerospace Museum of California $ 3200 Freedom Park Dr., McClellan Park, McClellan; tel: (916) 643-3192; www. aerospacemuseumofcalifornia. org. Open Mon–Sat 0900–1700, Sun from 1000.

permanently moored at Old Sacramento. **Lucca** $$ 1615 J St; tel: (916) 669-5300; www.luccarestaurant.com; open daily, is a Californian–Italian favourite of Governor Arnold Schwarzenegger. **Amber House** $$$ 1315 22nd St; tel: (916) 444-8085 or (800) 755-6526; www.amberhouse.com, comprising two historic homes, has the latest hotel amenities. **Biba** $$$ 2801 Capitol Ave; tel: (916) 455-2422; biba-restaurant.com; open Mon–Sat, is one of Northern California's better Italian restaurants as well as the star of a television cooking programme. **Il Fornaio** $$$ 400 Capitol Mall; tel: (916) 446-4100 or (888) 482-5426; www.ilfornaio.com; call for hours, serves traditional Italian in a white froth of a dining room, next to the Wells Fargo Museum. **Le Rivage Hotel** $$$ 4350 Riverside Blvd; tel: (800) 323-7500; www.lerivagehotel.com, is luxury with a marina and bocce ball court along the Sacramento River. The sleek **Sterling Hotel** $$$ 1300 H St; tel: (916) 448-1300 or (800) 365-7660; www.sterlinghotel.com, is even better known for its stunning **Chanterelle** restaurant $$$, tel: (916) 442-0451.

SAN ANDREAS

This tiny mining camp was known largely for the capture, trial and conviction of notorious highwayman Black Bart, famous among victims for his courtesy and poetry. The courthouse where the trial was held is now the **Calaveras County Historical Museum** (30 N. Main St; tel: (209) 754-1058; www.calaverascohistorical.com/museum.html; open daily 1000–1600).

SONORA

Tuolumne County Visitors Bureau 542 W. Stockton Rd, Sonora, CA 95370; tel: (209) 533-4420 or (800) 446-1333; www.tcvb.com. Open daily late May–Aug; closed Sun Sep–late May.

Tuolumne County Museum & History Center $ 158 W. Bradford Ave; tel: (209) 532-1317; www.tchistory.org. Open Sun–Fri 1000–1600, Sat to 1530.

Once the wildest town on the Southern Mother Lode, Sonora has remained a busy crossroads with skiers, snowboarders, hikers and loggers mixing with Gold Country tourists.

The **Tuolumne County Museum & History Center**, in the 1857 county jail, has an interesting mix of old photos and curios. **Old Sonora** stretches along **Washington St** from the dark red **St James Episcopal Church** into the town centre. The County Museum has self-guiding walking maps.

Accommodation and food in Sonora

The Gunn House $$ 286 S. Washington St; tel: (209) 532-3421; www.gunnhousehotel.com, built in 1850, is within walking distance of restaurants and two live theatres. Named after the old Stanislaus River, **The Old Stan** $$ 177 S. Washington St; tel: (209) 536-9598; http:// oldstan.com; open Wed–Sun, serves local beer, local live music, and tapas.

SUTTER CREEK

Sutter Creek Visitors' Center *71 Main St, Sutter Creek, CA 95685; tel: (800) 400-0305 or (209) 267-1344; www.suttercreek.org. Open Thu–Mon, call for hours.*

Sutter Creek does not have a very Gold Rush-like appearance. Main St is filled with galleries and antique shops in 19th-century storefronts; side streets are lined with still more original buildings. **Knight Foundry** (*81 Eureka St*) was the last water-powered foundry in America.

Accommodation and food in Sutter Creek

Caffè Via d'Oro $$ *36 Main St; tel: (209) 267-0535; www.caffeviadoro. com; open Wed–Sun*, serves Mediterranean-Californian cuisine and Amador wines.

The Foxes Inn $$ *77 Main St; tel: (209) 267-5882 or (800) 987-3344; www.foxesinn.com*, is one of Gold Country's most popular bed and breakfasts.

Victorian **Grey Gables Inn $$** *161 Hanford St; tel: (209) 267-1039 or (800) 473-9422; www.greygables.com*, is run by a pair of British expatriates.

Sutter Creek Palace $$$ *76 Main St; tel: (209) 267-1399; www.thesuttercreekpalace.com; open Fri–Tue*, is known for steaks and the appearance of occasional ghosts in the Victorian dining room.

YOSEMITE NATIONAL PARK

Yosemite National Park $$ *PO Box 577, Yosemite National Park, CA 95389; tel: 209-372-0200; www.nps.gov/yose.*

Accommodations *Delaware North Companies Parks & Resorts at Yosemite; tel: (559) 253-5635; www.yosemitepark.com*

Yosemite Valley Visitor Center *Yosemite Village; tel: (209) 372-0200. Open daily 0900–1900 in summer.*

Tuolumne Meadows Visitor Center *Tuolumne Meadows; tel: (209) 372-0263. Open early summer–Sep.*

Yosemite has been the target of adoring adjectives since the 1850s – all of them pertaining to waterfalls cascading down sheer, ½-mile-high granite walls, meadows laced with oak, cedar and maple trees, stupendous stands of sequoia redwoods and mountain vistas punctuated by rocky domes and spires.

The only problem is that the most famous sights, **Half Dome, El Capitan, Yosemite Falls, Bridalveil Fall** and more, are in Yosemite Valley. Nearly all of the 3.4 million-plus people who come to Yosemite each year come to Yosemite Valley. The rest of the park is practically deserted, including hiking trails barely beyond shouting distance of the gridlocked valley floor.

If possible, *don't* visit the valley in summer, but if you absolutely must come during high season, park your car, hire a bicycle (about $20 per day) and bypass the traffic jams. Free shuttles make non-stop loops around the valley from 0700–2200 in summer, an even easier alternative to driving. The main visitor centre, as well as most accommodation, restaurants and services, are in **Yosemite Village**.

Instead of crawling through the valley, visit **Glacier Point**. The view is better than anything in the valley, spanning **Vernal Fall, Nevada**

Fall, **Little Yosemite Valley**, **Yosemite Falls** and more. The vista is even better in winter, when the only access is by ski or snowshoe. The 60 miles across Yosemite National Park from **Crane Flat** over **Tioga Pass** and down to **Lee Vining** is one of California's best short drives, threading through lush alpine meadows along the spine of the Sierra Nevada. The road is usually closed by snow in Oct or Nov and seldom reopens before the end of May.

Accommodation and food in Yosemite

All accommodation in Yosemite National Park is run by DNC Parks & Resorts at Yosemite. Advance bookings are essential Apr–Sep and at weekends and holidays all year *tel: (801) 559-4949; www.yosemitepark. com*. Valley choices include **The Ahwahnee $$$**, motel-like **Yosemite Lodge at the Falls $$** and several clusters of tent-cabins, cabins and camping grounds. Choices at the south end of the park include the **Wawona Hotel $$$** and camping. Towns surrounding the park also offer accommodation.

Eating choices within Yosemite are limited to the same concessionaire-operated facilities, ranging from posh at **The Ahwahnee $$$** to fast food and supermarket fare.

Right
Yosemite National Park's
Bridalveil Fall

Suggested tour

**ⓘ Grass Valley
Nevada County
Chamber of
Commerce** *248 Mill St,
Grass Valley, CA 95945;
tel: (530) 273-4667 or
(800) 655-4667; www.
grassvalleychamber.com.
Open Mon–Fri 0900–1700.*

**ⓑ The Northstar
Mine Powerhouse
& Pelton Wheel
Museum** $ *Across Hwy 49;
tel: (530) 273-4255;
www.nevadacountyhistory.org
/htmls/northstar.html. Open
May–mid-Oct 1000–1700.*

**ⓘ Nevada City
Chamber of
Commerce** *132 Main St,
Nevada City, CA 95959;
tel: (530) 265-2692 or
(800) 655-6569; www.
nevadacitychamber.com.
Open Mon–Fri 0900–1700,
Sat 1100–1600, Sun
1100–1500.*

ⓑ Firehouse Museum
$ *215 Main St;
tel: (530) 265-5468;
www.nevadacountyhistory.
org/htmls/firehouse.html; call
for hours.*

**Miners Foundry
Cultural Center** *325
Spring St; tel: (530) 265-
5040; www.minersfoundry.
org. Open Mon–Fri
0900–1600. Free.*

Total distance: 175 miles.

Time: Two days, plus at least one night in Yosemite.

Links: Lake Tahoe to the north; Spine of the Sierra to the east.

Route: From **SACRAMENTO ❶**, take I-80 east across the flat Sacramento Valley **❷** to AUBURN **❸** and the foothills of the **Sierra Nevada ❹**. Follow Hwy 49 south through Gold Country to **COLOMA ❺**, where gold was discovered in 1848, PLACERVILLE **❻**, PLYMOUTH **❼**, JACKSON **❽**, SAN ANDREAS **❾**, ANGELS CAMP **❿**, COLUMBIA **⓫**, SONORA **⓬**, JAMESTOWN **⓭** and MARIPOSA **⓮**. Turn east on Hwy 140 to the canyon of the Merced River and follow the river into **YOSEMITE NATIONAL PARK ⓯**, or take Hwy 120 from south of Jamestown to **Groveland ⓰** and head for **YOSEMITE ⓱**.

Detour 1: Grass Valley and Nevada City prospered on deep mines drilled by immigrants from Cornwall and other European mining centres; Cornish pasties remain a local speciality. Follow Hwy 49 north from Auburn to Nevada City; either return to Auburn on Hwy 49 or take scenic Hwy 20 to I-80 and loop back to Auburn.

Grass Valley grubbed more than $400 million in bullion from tunnels beneath the town. **Empire Mine State Historic Park** $ (*10791 E. Empire St; tel: (530) 273-8522; www.parks.ca.gov; open daily*) has tours of the mine entrance, the 1850 owner's home, formal gardens and other buildings. The **Northstar Mine Powerhouse & Pelton Wheel Museum** is one of the most comprehensive mining museums in the Mother Lode.

Nevada City, 4 miles north, is quieter and more scenic. Don't miss the filagree-balconied **National Hotel** (*211 Broad St; tel: (530) 265-4551; www.thenationalhotel.com*). The white wedding-cake **Firehouse No 1** has pioneer relics, including Donner Party artefacts (*see page 36*). The **Miners Foundry Cultural Center** is an arts centre. **Malakoff Diggins State Historic Park** $ (*54-mile return trip; Hwy 49 11 miles to Tyler Foot Crossing Rd, turn right for 17 miles and follow the signs; tel: (530) 265-2740; www.parks.ca.gov*) is a rust-red badlands created by mining that washed away entire mountains.

Detour 2: Follow Hwy 88 east from Jackson to **Indian Grinding Rock State Historic Park** $ (*14881 Pine Grove-Volcano Rd; tel: (209) 296-7488; www.parks.ca.gov; call for hours*). The park protects an immense limestone slab with nearly 1200 holes worn by generations of Miwok women grinding acorns and other seeds into meal, a reconstructed Miwok village, the **Chaw'Se Regional Indian Museum** (*open daily*), and primitive camping in Miwok-style U'macha'tam'ma' bark houses.

Less than 2 miles away, **Volcano's Daffodil Hill** turns golden with more than 300,000 daffodils in March and April.

Also worth exploring

This backroads route to Columbia passes two of California's finest public caves. **Mercer Caverns $$** (*tel: (209) 728-2101; www.mercercaverns.com; open daily 1000–1630 (in summer, Sun–Thu 0900–1700, Fri–Sat to 1800))* is an intimate hole filled with dripping stalactites, towering stalagmites, congealed waterfalls and delicate strands of limestone pasta. **Moaning Cavern $$** (*5350 Moaning Cave Rd, Vallecito, CA 95251; tel: (866) 762-2837 or (209) 736-2708; www.caverntours.com; call for hours*) has a freestanding 232-step spiral staircase; the more adventurous explorers can abseil 165ft to the bottom. The moaning emanates from bottle-shaped holes at the bottom of the cave. A zip line entertains above ground.

Murphys is centred around the 1865 **Murphys Historic Hotel $$** (*457 Main St; tel: (800) 532-7684 or (209) 728-3444; www.murphyshotel.com*), temporary home to Mark Twain, Brett Harte, J.P. Morgan, Horatio Alger and other Gold Rush luminaries who left bullets in the woodwork. Galleries and wine-tasting rooms are legion.

The 60 miles across Yosemite National Park from **Crane Flat** over **Tioga Pass** and down to **Lee Vining** is one of California's best short drives, threading through lush alpine meadows along the spine of the Sierra Nevada. The road is usually closed by snow in Oct or Nov and seldom reopens before the end of May.

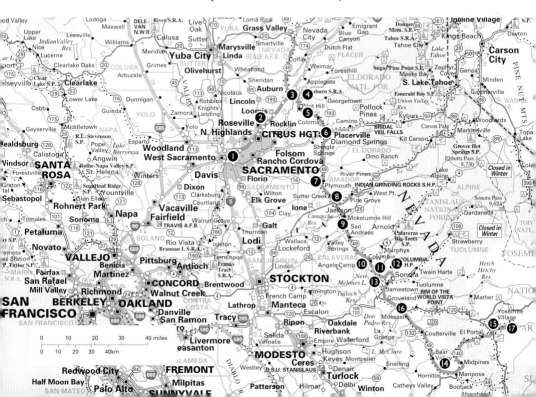

Sequoia and Kings Canyon National Parks

Ratings

Children	●●●●●
Outdoor activities	●●●●●
Scenery	●●●●●
Geology	●●●●○
History	●●●●○
Wildlife	●●●○○
Architecture	●○○○○
Food	●○○○○

These two contiguous parks contain some of California's most spectacular mountain scenery, from the biggest living things on earth to vast tracts of Sierra Nevada wilderness. The human-made attractions of Sequoia and Kings Canyon are warnings: valleys filled with rotting stumps larger than houses, fallen logs big enough to support a car, awe-inspiring views very nearly turned into theme-park ski-runs. Tortuous trails lead eastward over the spine of the Sierra to Mount Whitney and the Owens Valley, but innumerable easier paths wandering a few miles into the wilderness are an indelible introduction to the glories of outdoor California.

BOYDEN CAVERN

Festooned with marble draperies, stalactites and stalagmites, the interior of **Boyden Cavern $$** *(Hwy 180, 22 miles northeast of Grant Grove, Kings Canyon NP in Sequoia National Monument; tel: (866) 762-2837 or (559) 338-0959; www.caverntours.com/BoydenRt.htm; open May–Oct, call for tour times)* is a constant 55°F (13°C), which sends birds, small animals and underdressed tourists into quick hibernation. Walking, rappelling and canyoneering tours are offered. Entrance through Sequoia National Park requires separate admission charges to the park and Boyden Cavern.

CRYSTAL CAVE

Crystal Cave $ is more difficult to reach. Vehicles over 22ft are prohibited on the access road and a steep ½-mile trail leads from the car park to the cave entrance. Marble stalactites, stalagmites and

flowstone adorn the chilly 48°F (9°C) caverns. (*Off General's Hwy, 8 miles south of Giant Forest (Sequoia National Park); tel: (559) 565-3759; www.sequoiahistory.org/cave/cave.htm; open daily mid-May–Oct, closed in winter.*) Day-of-tour advance tickets required from Lodgepole Visitor Center or Foothills Visitor Center (*see page 243*).

FRESNO

ⓘ Fresno City and County Convention & Visitors Bureau, Water Tower Visitor Center 2444 *Fresno St; tel: (559) 237-0988 or (800) 788-0836; www.fresnocvb.org. Open Mon–Fri 1100–1500, Sat to 1400.*

The agricultural heart of California is blazingly hot in summer and blanketed by thick fogs in winter. A third of all US-grown grapes and over half the figs, cotton, nectarines and turkeys come from local farms.

The **Fresno Art Museum $** (*2233 N. First St (Radio Park); tel: (559) 441-4221; www.fresnoartmuseum.org; open Tue–Sun 1100–1700, Thu to 2000*) has collections of French post-impressionist prints as well as American, Asian and Mexican art and sculpture. Asian art and alternating exhibits featuring regional history and European and American still-life paintings are on offer at the **Fresno Metropolitan Museum $** (*1515 Van Ness Ave; tel: (559) 441-1444; www.fresnomet.org; open Tue–Sun 1100–1700*).

Forestiere Underground Gardens (*5021 W. Shaw Ave; tel: (559) 271-0734; www.undergroundgardens.com*) is an underground labyrinth of 50-odd rooms created between 1905 and 1946 to protect fruit orchards

Forestiere Underground Gardens $$ *5021 W. Shaw Ave; tel: (559) 271-0734; www. undergroundgardens.info. Open Apr–Nov, call for hours.*

Meux Home Museum $ *1007 R St; tel: (559) 233-8007; www.meux.mus.ca.us. Open Fri–Sun 1200–1530.*

and other crops from the blistering summer sun. Descendants of builder Baldassare Forestiere conduct the tours.

The **Kearney Mansion Museum $** (*Fresno Historical Society. 7160 W. Kearney Blvd; tel: (559) 441-0862; www.valleyhistory.org; open Fri–Sun for tours 1300, 1400, 1500*) began as an opulent French Renaissance-style mansion for turn-of-the-20th-century raisin mogul M. Theo Kearney. Kearney's extensive canal system introduced industrial-scale vineyards and orchards to Fresno.

Meux Home Museum brought Fresno the latest in urban elegance, 1889-style. The town's first two-storey home and the first embellished with Victorian finery, it remains Fresno's most stylish building.

The self-guided **William Saroyan Walking Tour** (*from the William Saroyan Society; tel: (559) 221-1441; www.williamsaroyansociety.org*) explores many of the sites used by native son and novelist William Saroyan in his tales of Armenian immigrant life in America. Saroyan is best known for *The Human Comedy* and the stage play *The Time of Your Life*.

KINGS CANYON NATIONAL PARK

ⓘ Grant Grove Visitor Center *Grant Grove Village; tel: (559) 565-4307. Open daily; call for hours.*

Cedar Grove Visitor Center *next to Sentinel Campground; tel: (559) 565-3793. Open daily late May–early Sep.*

ⓘ Kings Canyon National Park $ *Sequoia and Kings Canyon National Parks, Three Rivers, CA 93271; tel: (559) 565-3341; www.nps/gov/seki*

The park is named after a gaping canyon ripped into the salt-and-pepper granite of the High Sierra by the raging torrent of the Kings River, then gouged into a broad valley by ponderous glaciers. Just downstream from the confluence of the middle and south forks of the Kings River, the canyon plunges 8200ft from the peak of Spanish Mountain, the deepest gorge in North America.

Right
Kings Canyon Highway

Kings Canyon's most popular attractions are concentrated around Grant Grove. Just one road penetrates the park proper, the Kings Canyon Highway (*Hwy 180*), open only in summer. From the flat river meadow at Roads End, canyon cliffs soar nearly another mile straight up.

Cedar Grove is as close as Kings Canyon comes to civilisation. The seasonal village and visitor centre are named after surrounding groves of incense cedars. The flat valley floor is ideal for leisurely cycling 5 miles to Roads End.

The 'U' shape of Kings Canyon, the unmistakable sign of past glacial activity, is most obvious from **Canyon Viewpoint** (*1 mile east of Cedar Grove*). The 'V' shape of the lower canyon, beyond the reach of glaciers, is typical of canyons carved by rivers.

Knapp's Cabin (*1 mile east of the viewpoint*) stored equipment for opulent fishing expeditions staged by Santa Barbara businessman George Knapp during the 1920s. One mile east of the cabin is the car park for **Roaring River Falls**. An easy 5-minute paved path leads to the falls, roaring (and sometimes trickling) through a narrow granite chute.

The 1½-mile loop trail through **Zumwalt Meadow** is one of the most scenic walks in either park. The trail crosses a suspension bridge to a view over the grassy meadow and **North Dome** (8717ft), then descends through the meadow. Expect to see a variety of birds, as well as a profusion of wildflowers – leopard lilies, shooting stars, violets, Indian paintbrush, lupines and others, depending on the season. Pick up a self-guiding map at the visitor centre.

Just beyond is **Grand Sentinel Viewpoint**, with clear views of one of the most striking rock formations in the area, the Grand Sentinel (8504ft).

Roads End is the literal end of the road and the start of a vast network of trails. Gruelling tracks cross the Sierra over passes above 11,000ft and into the Owens Valley (*see page 116*). The 9-mile return hike to **Mist Falls** is an easier glimpse of the backcountry. The sandy trail is relatively flat, but gains 600ft in the final mile to the largest waterfall in the twin parks. Allow between 4 and 6 hours.

Return to Cedar Grove on the road, or, more interestingly, via the **Motor Nature Trail** on the north side of the river. The rough corrugated road is passable by passenger vehicles but is *not* recommended for RVs.

Grant Grove is administratively part of Kings Canyon National Park, but the dense stand of sequoia, sugar pine, incense cedar, black oak and mountain dogwood looks more like Sequoia National Park. The grove is named after the **General Grant Tree**, officially the world's third-largest giant sequoia and the nation's Christmas Tree at 267ft tall and 107ft in circumference. A ⅓-mile paved path wanders through the grove. Most of the major trees have been fenced off to protect their shallow root systems from trampling by enthusiastic crowds.

The trail also passes the **Fallen Monarch**, which has been a house and a stable, and the **Gamlin Cabin**, a rebuilt 1872 loggers' cabin. A quieter alternative is the seldom-visited **North Grove Loop**, a 1½-mile trail from the Grant Grove car park. The 1½-mile **Dead Giant Loop** (*lower end of Grant Grove car park*) passes a historic lumber mill pond on the way to a giant sequoia that was killed by girdling, or cutting through the living cambium layer (just beneath the bark), which cut the flow of nutrients to the tree. The walk offers an instructive comparison between the ways National Park and National Forest lands are managed.

Big Stump Basin (*Hwy 180, 2½ miles southwest of the visitor centre*) is just what the name suggests, a valley filled with gigantic stumps – how the Grant Grove would appear today had early loggers been allowed to continue. A self-guiding 1-mile **loop trail** highlights regenerating sequoias and other natural features.

The **Mark Twain Stump** is what remains of a giant sequoia felled in 1891 so sections could be displayed in the American Museum of Natural History in New York and the British Museum in London. A similar tree-cutting exercise was conducted for the 1876 Centennial Exhibition in Philadelphia.

The **Kings Canyon Highway** runs from Grant Grove to Cedar Grove. Much of the road follows the canyon of the Kings River, here a sharp 'V' filled with the rushing boom of the river. The sheer granite walls are laced with blue marble, pocked with yellow yucca plants and splattered with green and orange lichen, more easily visible beyond **Junction View**. Numerous lay-bys offer excellent views of the canyon and High Sierra peaks rising in the distance.

Panoramic Point is one of the most accessible vistas across the spine of the high Sierra, with **Lake Hume** to the north below. The 5-mile return **Park Ridge Trail** offers views from the high peaks to the east down the descending western ranges into the Central Valley.

Accommodation and food in Kings Canyon National Park

All accommodation is booked through **Sequoia-Kings Canyon Park Services Company**, *PO Box 907, Kings Canyon National Park, CA 93633; tel: (559) 335-5500* or *(866) 522-6966; www.sequoia-kingscanyon.com*

John Muir Lodge \$\$ is open all year; **Cedar Grove Lodge \$\$** is open May–Oct and **Grant Grove Cabins \$\$**, both rustic and tent, are open in summer. Accommodation is also available outside the park, including **Stony Creek Lodge \$\$\$** and **Kings Canyon Lodge \$\$\$** *Hwy 180; tel: (559) 335-2405*. Advance booking is necessary all year.

In summer, picnic supplies and restaurant meals are available in **Cedar Grove Village \$\$**, **Grant Grove Village \$\$** and **Kings Canyon Lodge \$\$–\$\$\$**. Grant Grove stays open in winter. There are no petrol stations in the park, but Kings Canyon Lodge has a supply at premium prices.

SEQUOIA NATIONAL PARK

Sequoia National Park $ *Sequoia and Kings Canyon National Parks, Three Rivers, CA 93271; tel: (559) 565-3341; www.nps.gov/seki*

Foothills Visitor Center *Generals Highway at Hwy 198; tel: (559) 565-3135. Open daily.*

Free summertime Sequoia National Park shuttles provide easy access to main areas: Green shuttle line: Giant Forest Museum–Wuksachi; Gray shuttle line: Giant Forest Museum–Crescent Meadow–Moro Rock. A 2-hour shuttle $; tel: (877) 287-4453; www.ci.visalia. ca.us/depts/transit/sequoia_ shuttle/general_info.asp, from Visalia saves driving and fuel.

Sequoia has a variety of natural attractions, from caves and Mount Whitney to alpine meadows and crashing rivers – all of which pale next to the dense stands of giant sequoia redwood trees (*Sequoiadendron giganteum*), the largest living things on earth.

Sequoia was created in 1890 to protect these massive trees, then in danger of extinction by logging. **Big Stump Basin**, near the entrance to Kings Canyon National Park and the **Generals Highway**, which leads to Sequoia National Park, is the result of still-current logging techniques.

Three-mile **Crescent Meadow Road** leaves the main road from the former Giant Forest Village. The scenic detour passes several famous sites, but is not recommended for RVs. **Auto Log**, a sequoia felled and flattened for drive-on passenger cars, gives visitors a sense of just how huge sequoias can grow. A set of nearly 400 concrete steps leads 300ft up the side of **Moro Rock** (6725ft) and to a splendid 360-degree view stretching 150 miles from the spine of the Sierra to the Central Valley – save the staircase climb for clear days when valley vistas are visible rather than swathed in haze.

Tunnel Log fell across the road in 1937; crews cut an 8ft-high tunnel through the log the next summer. A bypass accommodates taller vehicles. **Crescent Meadow**, like most naturally grassy areas in the park, is actually a marsh, too wet to support sequoias and other trees. A flat 1½-mile trail circles the meadow to **Tharp's Log**, a sequoia

Right
A few centuries of growth – section through a giant sequoia tree

Lodgepole Visitor Center 2 miles north of General Sherman Tree; tel: (559) 565-4436. Open early spring–late autumn, winter weekends; call for hours.

Mineral King Ranger Station 24 miles up Mineral King Road. Open approximately May–Sep daily.

Giant Forest Village

Giant Forest Village was Sequoia's original centre for visitor services. Recognising that the year-round pounding of traffic and visitors was harming Giant Forest trees, the US Park Services removed accommodation and other services to **Wuksachi**, near the **Lodgepole Visitor Center**, in 1998 and 1999. Car parks and **Giant Forest Museum** (tel: (559) 565-4480) remain, but most of the Village site is being re-seeded and returned to the Giant Forest.

hollowed into a cabin for Hale Tharp, who grazed sheep in the meadow in the 1850s. **Chimney Tree** is a still-living sequoia hollowed out by fire; look inside from the base to see blue sky through the crown. The **John Muir Trail** which follows the crest of the Sierra Nevada crosses 71 rugged miles to Mount Whitney.

Giant Forest (*30 miles from Big Stump Entrance, 16 miles from Ash Mountain Entrance*) was named by John Muir. Four of the largest known sequoias grow in this grove. Most visitors spend their time staring in awe at named trees and dodging other visitors. Fortunately, the many hiking trails through Giant Forest provide a serene, almost deserted introduction to the 8000 or so mature sequoias in the area.

The biggest of them all is the **General Sherman Tree**, 275ft tall and 103ft in circumference. The trunk alone contains more than 52,000 cubic feet of wood, but with so many other slightly less monstrous trees nearby, it's hard to grasp General Sherman's extraordinary dimensions. One of the best easy walks is the 2-mile paved **Congress Trail** (*from the Sherman tree*); pick up a self-guiding trail guide at the Sherman tree or the **Lodgepole Visitor Center**, just north.

Hospital Rock (*5 miles beyond Ash Grove Entrance toward Giant Forest*) marks an ancient Native American village site. Look for **pictographs** on surrounding boulders and 71 mortar holes once used to grind acorns and seeds into flour.

Mineral King (*turn off 5 miles north of Three Rivers, no RVs or trailers*) is a scalloped bowl at 7800ft, the only bit of the park's Sierra high country accessible by vehicle. Walt Disney tried to turn the scenic bowl into a ski resort in 1965. Thirteen litigious years later, it was added to Sequoia National Park instead.

Seven hundred-odd twists and turns in 25 miles of part-paved, part-gravel road discourage most visitors, but the summer-only route along the East Fork of the Kaweah River is worth the time, the driving effort and the occasional terror of meeting another vehicle on a blind corner with neither verge nor guardrail.

Silver City has general supplies, petrol and food, but the only facilities in Mineral King itself are a seasonal ranger station and a basic campground. Hiking into the golden **Sawtooth Mountains** to the east is superb. The ¼-mile **Cold Springs Nature Trail** is a less strenuous alternative.

Accommodation and food in Sequoia National Park

The park hotel, restaurants and other commercial services, including **Wuksachi Lodge $$**, open all year, are operated by **Delaware North Companies Parks & Resorts at Sequoia, Inc.**, *PO Box 89, Sequoia National Park, CA 93262; tel: (866) 807-3598; www.visitsequoia.com.* Seven campgrounds are operated by the National Park Service *tel: (800) 365-2267; http://reservations.nps.gov.* Intrepid hikers go 11½ miles into the Sierra backcountry and stay at **Bear Paw High Sierra Camp** *(www.visitsequoia.com/1776.aspx)* tent cabins.

Montecito-Sequoia Lodge $$ *63410 Hwy 180 (Generals Hwy) between Sequoia and Kings Canyon; tel: (800) 843-8677; reservations: tel: (800) 227-9900; www.mslodge.com,* is open all year, as are motels in the town of **Three Rivers**, *Hwy 180, south of Ash Mountain Entrance.*

Silver City Mountain Resort $$ *tel: (559) 561-3223 (summer)* or *(559) 734-4109 (winter); www.silvercityresort.com* has cabins and chalets on the road to Mineral King in summer.

Meals and picnic supplies are available in Wuksachi Village, Lodgepole and Montecito-Sequoia all year. **Silver City Bakery and Restaurant $$** near Mineral King and an adjoining general store are open in summer.

In 2000, former president Bill Clinton proclaimed a section of national forest south of Sequoia National Park's former Giant Forest Village as **Giant Sequoia National Monument**. The forest service, the timber industry and environmentalists have been at odds over logging in the monument. The monument is accessible from Kernville, near Lake Isabella east of Bakersfield. For information, contact the **Sequoia National Forest** office *(tel: (559) 784-1500; www.fs.fed.us/r5/sequoia/ gsnm.html).* A major draw is the **Trail of a Hundred Giants** within a 355-acre grove *(www.kernvalley.com/news/trail100.htm).* The **Sequoia High Sierra Camp** is open from mid-Jun–early Oct for hiking and fly-fishing.

The Sequoia High Sierra Camp $$$
Giant Sequoia National Monument; tel: (866) 654-2877; www.sequoiahighsierracamp. com, operates mid-Jun–early Oct.

Giant Sequoias

Sequoiadendron gigantea aren't the tallest living things – coastal redwoods top them by 100ft – nor the largest around – a Montezuma cypress in Oaxaca, Mexico, has a larger girth. But in sheer volume, giant sequoia redwoods are the largest living things on earth, and Sequoia National Park has more of them than anywhere else.

Sequoias have high tannin levels that discourage insects and rot; bark nearly 3ft thick is impervious to fire. Even if the heartwood burns away, the tree can survive. The intense heat releases its tiny seeds and burns away brush that would compete with its seedlings.

The sequoia's weakness is its roots, which penetrate only 3–5ft into the soil. High winds or heavy snows can topple the top-heavy giants. Foot or vehicle traffic atop the fragile roots can further weaken the trees.

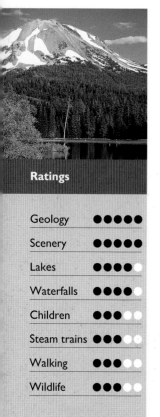

Cascade Volcanoes

Ratings

Geology	●●●●●
Scenery	●●●●●
Lakes	●●●●○
Waterfalls	●●●●○
Children	●●●○○
Steam trains	●●●○○
Walking	●●●○○
Wildlife	●●●○○

California's Cascade peaks, Lassen and Shasta, begin a string of active volcanoes stretching north into British Columbia. This jumble of volcanic peaks, razor-edged river valleys and deep forests is one of California's most alluring – and forbidding – natural areas. Don't be deceived by mild Sacramento Valley weather. A few miles east – and a few thousand feet up – temperatures can drop to freezing in any month. The highway through Lassen Volcanic National Park is closed in winter, though snowploughs keep most other paved roads open.

The Sierra Nevada volcanoes are largely dormant, but the Cascades are very much alive. Mount Shasta last erupted around 1786, but steam vents near the peak are still hot. Lassen Peak erupted between 1915 and 1917, the most recent eruption in the continental US until Mount St Helens (in southern Washington State) blew up in 1980. Bookmakers aren't fixing odds, but geologists are betting on another major California eruption in the next few centuries.

CASTLE CRAGS

Castle Crags State Park *Castella Exit from I-5; tel: (530) 235-2684 or (530) 225-2065; www.parks.ca.gov. Ranger station usually open summer and weekends.*

The granite ramparts of Castle Crags rise dramatically from the west side of I-5, resembling the remnants of some enormous castle wall towering more than 4000ft above. A narrow road twists 2 miles from the park entrance to a wooded **Vista Point** and a cluster of picnic tables with unobstructed views of the Crags and Mount Shasta. The best views are late in the day (Mount Shasta) and early morning (Castle Crags), when the setting sun casts a rich, smouldering glow.

DUNSMUIR

The railway made Dunsmuir a popular mountain resort between the 1920s and 1940s, known as much for its wonderful fly-fishing and mineral water as the pristine mountain scenery and a cinema palace called the California Theater. Celebrities pulled into town by the carriage-load, from baseball home-run king Babe Ruth to Hollywood

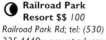

❶ Dunsmuir Chamber of Commerce and Visitors' Center *5915 Dunsmuir Ave, Ste 100, Dunsmuir, CA 96025; tel: (530) 235-2177 or (800) 386-7684; www.dunsmuir.com*

☾ Railroad Park Resort $$ *100 Railroad Park Rd; tel: (530) 235-4440; www.rrpark.com,* features accommodation in boxcars with bay windows or roof-top cupolas.

❶ Café Maddalena $$ *5801 Sacramento Ave; tel: (530) 235-2725; www.cafemaddalena.com; open late-Mar–Dec Thu–Sun for dinner,* serves Mediterranean dishes to rival anything San Francisco can offer.

luminary Clark Gable. As more powerful diesel-electric locomotives replaced steam in the 1950s, Dunsmuir sank into obscurity.

Once I-5 bypassed the town in 1961, most of California forgot it ever existed, until 1991, when the railroad put Dunsmuir back in the spotlight. A Southern Pacific train derailed, spilling tank cars loaded with a powerful herbicide into the Sacramento River. The poison killed everything in the river for 45 miles downstream into Shasta Lake, and nearly killed off the town.

The Sacramento River eventually recovered. So did Dunsmuir, with the help of a hefty financial settlement from the railway. Trophy-sized trout returned to the river while the town refurbished and rebuilt Dunsmuir and Sacramento Aves.

Don't miss **Hedge Creek Falls** (*north edge of town, Frontage Rd*), a 30-ft waterfall cutting through basaltic lava that once flowed down the slopes of Mount Shasta. A gazebo next to the trailhead offers a pleasant view of the Sacramento River Canyon.

Below
Marsh and mountain in Lassen Volcanic National Park

LASSEN VOLCANIC NATIONAL PARK

Lassen Park is the southernmost link in the Cascade volcano chain that runs through **Mount Shasta** and **Lava Beds National Monument** in

ⓘ The **Kohn Yah-mah-
nee Visitor Center**
at the southwest park
entrance opened for year-
round operations in
autumn 2008. There is a
restaurant, restrooms, a
gift shop, exhibits and an
information, permit and
reservation desk.

ⓘ **Lassen Volcanic
National Park $**
*38050 Hwy 36 East,
Mineral, CA 96063;
tel: (530) 595-4444;
www.nps.gov/lavo. Open
Mon–Fri 0800–1630.* Check
the park website for
current road conditions
and summer-only park
opening dates.

Loomis Museum
*Manzanita Lake; tel: (530)
595-4444, ext. 5180. Open
late May–mid-Jun Fri–Sun
0900–1700; mid-Jun–Sep
daily 0900–1700.* Call to
verify that museum is open.

California, north to British Columbia. It is also one of California's least-visited national parks, an eerie, volcanic landscape that is virtually devoid of people, even at the height of summer.

Lassen Peak, the mountain (10,457ft), is a fraction of **Lassen Volcanic National Park**, 100,000 jumbled acres where Cascade volcanoes meet the Sierra Nevada. Prominent features include Lassen Peak and smaller volcanoes, as well as mud pots, fumaroles, hot springs, boiling lakes, emerald-green meadows and stupendous wildflower displays – and that's just what's visible from the highway. Drive slowly (the speed limit is 35mph) and buy the *Road Guide to Lassen Volcanic National Park*, $, at park entrances.

Unfortunately, the road, Hwy 89, is covered by 50ft of snow in winter. From Nov to Jun, it's possible to explore both the north (from Redding) and south (from Red Bluff) edges of the park, but the only permitted forms of transport across this road in winter are snowshoes and cross-country skis.

From the north, the **Loomis Museum** (*tel: (530) 595-4444*) covers regional geology and history. Lassen erupted around 1700, creating the **Chaos Crags**, which were still steaming in 1850, and a vast rockfield called the **Chaos Jumbles**. The mountain went into violent action in 1914, with an earth-shattering eruption in 1915 and small bursts that continued through 1921. The 1915 eruption blasted boulders to Reno, Nevada, shot a plume of dust 25,000ft into the air and cast a pall over Sacramento. Time and advancing vegetation have hidden most visible signs of that last eruption. The best views are from the ½-mile **Devastation Trail** (*Road Marker 44*).

Park rangers lead free naturalist Jun–Aug programmes (guided walks and hikes), and Jan–Apr snowshoe programmes. There are also many self-guiding walks. Remember, though, that nature has a thin skin in Lassen – literally. Most areas of visible thermal activity are vast pools of boiling mud covered by a solid-seeming, but fragile, crust.

One of Lassen's otherworldly sights, **Bumpass Hell** (*3 miles return from Marker 17*), is named after an early Danish explorer who put a foot through the crust and saw his leg cook before he could pull away. *Stay on marked trails and boardwalks!*

One of the best high hikes is the 5-mile return **Lassen Peak Trail** (*5 hours from Marker 22*), a windy, sun-blasted trail that gains 2000ft. Bring sunblock, a hat and plenty of water. An easier 7½-mile return trail climbs **Brokeoff Mountain** near the south entrance. The peak is 1200ft lower than Lassen, but the trail is shaded until the summit.

Best stops for non-hikers are **Manzanita Lake** and **Reflection Lake** (*near the north entrance*) which provide serene reflections of Lassen Peak in late afternoon. Thousands of 19th-century migrants walked **Nobles Emigrant Trail** (*Marker 60*) through the park. The trail can be seen through the chaparral to the northeast. Beyond the **Devastation Area**, look for trees with a curve at their base, the *snow bend*, caused by winter snows bending the trees as saplings.

Deep blue **Lake Helen**, between the Lassen Peak and Bumpass Hell car parks, is frozen white at least eight months of the year. The lake was named after Helen Brodt, the first woman known to have climbed Lassen Peak. Lassen's most accessible thermal field is **The Sulphur Works**, a miniature Bumpass Hell near the south entrance. An easy boardwalk winds past small mudpots and fumaroles.

Accommodation and food near Mount Lassen

Drakesbad Guest Ranch *California Guest Services; tel: (530) 529-1512 ext. 120; www.drakesbad.com*, is a National Historic Landmark.

Sleeping in the park means camping. For a real roof (all must be booked well in advance), try **Hat Creek Resort $$** *Hwy 44 & 89, Old Station; tel: (800) 568-0109; www.hatcreekresortrv.com;* year-round, **Lassen Mineral Lodge $$** *Hwy 36 E., Mineral; tel: (530) 595-4422; www.minerallodge.com;* cabins at **Rim Rock Ranch $$** *13275 Hwy 89, Old Station; tel: (530) 335-7114; www.rimrockcabins.com;* or secluded **Drakesbad Guest Ranch $$$** *Warner Valley Rd, Chester, CA 96020; tel: (530) 529-1512; www.drakesbad.com.* Most visitors drive up from Redding or Red Bluff. The only food in the park is at **Manzanita Lake $$** (*north entrance*), the **Peak Necessities Café and Gift Shop $$** (*south entrance open in summer*) and at the **Kohm Yah-mah-nee Visitor Center** restaurant.

Right
The McArthur-Burney Falls

McArthur-Burney Falls Memorial State Park

McArthur-Burney Falls Memorial State Park $ *24898 Hwy 89, Burney, CA 96013; tel: (530) 335-2777; www.parks.ca.gov. Open year-round for camping and day use.*

The 129-ft double cataract of **McArthur-Burney Falls** cuts through millions of years of moss-covered lava flows in a lush conifer forest. Halfway between Shasta and Lassen, the Falls, like the rest of the region, owe their existence to volcanoes. Shasta, Lassen and other Cascade peaks are noted for their explosive power, generated when thick, sticky lava builds up pressure in underground chambers until it blasts through to the surface.

Shield volcanoes such as these begin life belching a mixture of magma, superheated steam and other gases. Magma shoots into the air, cools quickly and falls back to earth to form steep-sided hills called cinder cones. In later stages, lava floods from vents in vast sheets, building up successive layers called shields. Hwy 89 between Lake Britton and the park entrance cuts through a shield, as do the Falls.

An easy 1-mile **Falls Trail Loop** winds to the bottom of the Falls and back up. The slightly more difficult 1½-mile **Headwaters Loop** passes the point where underground rivers emerge to feed the falls. **Lake Britton**, a reservoir popular for fishing, swimming and boating, is a 1-mile walk or 1½ miles by road (Hwy 89) from the park entrance.

McCloud

McCloud Chamber of Commerce *205 Quincy St, McCloud, CA 96057; tel: (530) 964-3113; www.mccloudchamber.com*

McCloud Ranger District *2019 Forest Rd, Hwy 89 east of McCloud; tel: (530) 964-2184. Open 0800–1630 Mon–Fri, Sat in summer.*

McCloud Railway and Shasta Sunset Dinner Train $$–$$$ *Across from the McCloud post office; tel: (530) 964-2142 or (800) 733-2141; www.shastasunset.com, details Jun–Dec excursions.*

McCloud looks much as it did in 1965, when the McCloud River Lumber Company abandoned the town it had built. Heavy winter snows can cut power and phone lines for days, but urban refugees have revitalised a town that most expected to die.

Among McCloud's most popular attractions are the Upper, Middle and Lower **Falls of the McCloud River** (*near River Loop Rd and Fowlers Campground off Hwy 89, 5 miles east of McCloud*), torrents shooting from crevices in the rock. Lower Falls has carved a deep swimming hole. **Jot Dean Cave** (*9 miles south of Medicine Lake on County Rd 49*), a shallow, collapsed lava tube, is usually cool enough to hold ice in summer but shallow enough to explore without a torch.

The easiest way to enjoy off-road sights is aboard open-air carriages on the **McCloud Railway** Excursion Train, sightseeing trips, or its 3-hour Fri- and Sat-night **Shasta Sunset Dinner Train**.

Accommodation in McCloud

The carefully restored 1916 **McCloud Hotel** $$ *408 Main St; tel: (530) 964-2822 or (800) 964-2823; www.mccloudhotel.com*, a National Historic Landmark building, was originally company-owned housing for mill workers and town teachers. The hotel now offers bed with breakfast in the garden as an option. The **McCloud River Inn Bed and Breakfast** $$–$$$ *325 Lawndale Ct; tel: (800) 261-7831 or (530) 964-2130; www.riverinn.com*, is an historic five-room Victorian inn.

MOUNT SHASTA AND MOUNT SHASTA CITY

ⓘ Mount Shasta Chamber of Commerce and Visitors Bureau *300 Pine St, Mount Shasta, CA 96067; tel: (530) 926-4865 or (800) 926-4865; http://mtshastachamber.com/index.php*

ⓒ Mount Shasta Ranger Station *204 W. Alma St; tel: (530) 926-4511.*

Below
Serene Mount Shasta

Mount Shasta City is a former railway and lumber centre that has turned its attention to tourists and New Age believers. The latter revere 14,164ft **Mount Shasta** as an energy and spiritual centre inhabited by Limurians, ancient escapees from the lost continent of Mu. The rest of us see the tallest and most spectacular peak in Northern California, the source of the Sacramento River and a climbing challenge.

Mt. Shasta Ski Park (*off Hwy 89; tel: (530) 926-8610 or (800) 754-7427; www.skipark.com*) is a pleasant local ski area in winter, popular with mountain bikers in summer and a lift up the mountain in any season. It's also possible to climb the peak in summer, a strenuous, occasionally fatal, trek. Stop at the Ranger Station for advice on climbing, equipment rental or lessons. **Bunny Flat Scenic Trail** (*from Bunny Flat car park*) is a gentle alternative that climbs to Horse Camp, the usual base for peak climbs. A still less strenuous outing is **Mount Shasta City Park** (*north end of town*), where Sacramento River headwaters gush from a lava tube.

Accommodation and food in Mount Shasta

Lily's $$ *1013 S. Mt Shasta Blvd; tel: (530) 926-3372; www.lilysrestaurant.com; open daily*, serves Californian food with Asian touches. Best bets for accommodation are the **Mount Shasta Ranch Bed and Breakfast $$** *1008 W.A. Barr Rd; tel: (530) 926-3870; www.stayinshasta.com*, a 70-year-old ranch, and **Mount Shasta Resort $$** *1000 Siskiyou Lake Blvd; tel: (800) 958-3363; www.mountshastaresort.com*, a golf resort near Lake Siskiyou.

REDDING

ⓘ Redding Convention and Visitors Bureau *777 Auditorium Dr., Redding, CA 96001; tel: (800) 874-7562 or (530) 225-4100; www.visitredding.com. Open Mon–Fri 0900–1700, Sat 1000–1700. Winter, call for hours.*

A railway town that never stopped growing, Redding is the primary gateway to mountain escapes in three directions. The top historic sight is **Shasta State Historic Park** (*Hwy 299, 6 miles west; tel: (530) 243-8194; www.parks.ca.gov; open daily*). Originally Shaster, the area's Gold Rush settlement, was the richest, busiest town in the region until the railway route was built in Redding in 1872. The 1861 **County Courthouse** has been restored as an excellent museum.

Turtle Bay Exploration Park $
840 Auditorium Dr.; tel: (800) 887-8532; www.turtlebay.org. Call for hours.

The best stop in Redding itself is **Turtle Bay Exploration Park**. The civic complex includes the well-designed **McConnell Arboretum & Botanical Gardens**, 200 acres of oak savannah and wetlands laced with walking paths, **Paul Bunyan's Forest Camp**, which celebrates the logging industry, and the **Turtle Bay Museum** with a river aquarium with trout, native perch and sturgeon, and combined collections from the Redding Museum of Art and History and the Carter House Natural Science Museum. Spanish architect Santiago Calatrava designed the **Sundial Bridge**, a translucent glass and tile-covered concrete pedestrian bridge with a sundial-like support pylon, to connect Turtle Bay Exploration Park to the Sacramento River Trail and with the Mediterranean-climate Botanical Gardens addition to McConnell Arboretum.

Accommodation and food in Redding

Redding used to be a stop for petrol between the San Francisco Bay area and Oregon. With the Turtle Bay complex, it has come into its own, but still boasts many moderately priced motels, mostly clustered around I-5 freeway services at Hilltop Drive. **Jack's Grill $$** *1743 California St; tel: (530) 241-9705; www.jacksgrillredding.com; open Mon–Sat 1700–2300*, is a Redding institution for 16oz steaks.

SHASTA LAKE

Shasta Lake Visitor Information Center
14250 Holiday Road, Redding; tel: (530) 275-1589; www.fs.fed.us/r5/shastatrinity/recreation/nra/index.shtml. Open summer Wed–Sun 0800–1630.

Shasta Dam Visitor Center Tel: (530) 275-4463; www.shastalake.com/visitorcenters. Open for tours. Free, call for location and hours.

Lake Shasta Caverns $$ O'Brien, Shasta Dam Blvd exit from I-5; tel: (530) 238-2341 or (800) 795-2283; www.lakeshastacaverns.com. Advance booking required for daily tours.

When full, Shasta Lake has more shoreline than San Francisco Bay. Shasta Lake is used by more than two million people every year, many of whom stay in a houseboat, amongst the world's largest fleet of flat-bottomed homes on water. Activities include trout and salmon fishing, jet-skiing, water-skiing, wake-boarding, and hiking around the shore, resulting in a surfeit of whining jet skis and roaring motorboats near the lake's dozen or so marinas.

Shasta Dam, 3460ft long at its crest, 602ft high and 883ft thick at the base, contains enough concrete to build a 3-ft path around the equator. Behind the dam are five watery arms, stumps of the Sacramento, Pit and McCloud Rivers, dammed for power and irrigation in 1945. The **Visitor Information Center** tells the story of this engineering feat.

It's possible to plumb nature's bowels at **Lake Shasta Caverns**, one of the state's more spectacular caves, complete with 'waterfalls' of solid calcium carbonate, masses of mineral straws that seem to defy gravity and delicate fluted columns. The 2-hour tour begins with a 15-minute catamaran ride across the lake and an 800-ft climb by bus before descending into the chilly cave on foot.

Vulcanism in California

California was born of a 200-million-year collision between North America and the floor of the Pacific Ocean. As the Pacific Plate, one of the great tectonic plates that make up the earth's crust, was forced beneath the North American plate, islands and mountains scraped off against the edge of the continent. At the same time, a fraction of the titanic forces driving the Pacific Plate downward escaped to the surface as volcanic activity. The Sierra Nevada Mountains emerged about 170 million years ago, while the Cascade peaks are still emerging.

In Southern California, vulcanism is most obvious around Mammoth Lakes. Devil's Postpile National Monument is an ancient basalt flow that cooled into striking vertical columns. The hot springs dotting the Sierra are fuelled by geothermal activity, including mineral springs that created the striking tufa towers of Mono Lake. Mountains of black volcanic obsidian, once the source of arrowheads, are now used for fine surgical scalpels.

Suggested tour

Total distance: 225 miles.

Time: One day with no stops, but three days recommended.

Links: The Gold Country (*see page 226*) and Lake Tahoe (*see page 122*) both lie to the south (follow I-5 to Sacramento, or Hwy 89 to Truckee). The Coast Redwoods (*see page 196*) are to be found by driving due west from Redding.

Route: Take I-5 north from Redding, climbing from soporific Sacramento Valley scenery towards **LAKE SHASTA ❶**, **CASTLE CRAGS ❷** and the riverside town of **DUNSMUIR ❸** to **MOUNT SHASTA CITY ❹**, at the base of **MOUNT SHASTA ❺**. Follow scenic Hwy 89 east into the Cascades to the former logging town of **MCCLOUD ❻**, then gradually turn south along the federally designated Volcanic Legacy Scenic Byway through lava flows and pine forests to **MCARTHUR-BURNEY FALLS MEMORIAL STATE PARK ❼**, **Hat Creek ❽** and **Old Station ❾** to **LASSEN VOLCANIC NATIONAL PARK ❿**. In winter, take Hwy 44 west to Redding. In summer, continue south through the park to Hwy 36, then turn west to **Red Bluff ⓫**.

Also worth visiting

Mount Shasta Loop

A network of gravel roads loops around the north and east sides of Mount Shasta, making it possible to circumnavigate the mountain in a single day – but only in good summer weather and never in an RV. Check road conditions and maps before setting out. Local vehicles travel the back roads regularly, but most have high clearance and four-wheel drive. If rangers or the Visitors Bureau advise against the drive, heed their caution – blizzards can occur in summer.

Fortunately, paved roads offer a taste of Mount Shasta's more spectacular north face. Take I-5 north from Mount Shasta City past **Black Butte ⓬** (6325ft), a volcanic plug cloaked with broken rock called talus. A 2½-mile trail leads to the peak, with sweeping views of Mount Shasta just east, the Sacramento Valley south, the Klamath Mountains west and **Weed ⓭** just north. Continue 5½ miles north to the Central Weed exit, Hwy 97.

A lumber baron named Weed picked the windiest spot in the upper Sacramento Valley for a mill so the newly sawn lumber would dry quickly. Hwy 97 bypasses the late 19th-century town centre, which remains largely intact. The best Shasta views lie along the first 15 miles of Hwy 97 between I-5 and Military Pass Rd, just beyond the Hwy 99–Hwy 97 Cutoff.

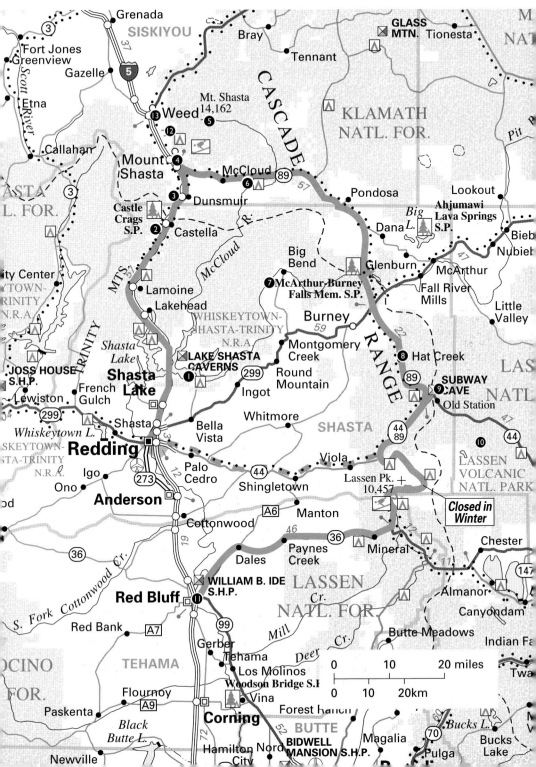

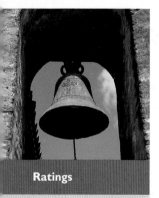

California Missions

Ratings

Architecture	●●●●●
Historical sights	●●●●●
Scenery	●●●●●
Art	●●●●○
Churches	●●●●○
Gardens	●●●○○
Children	●●○○○

'Always go forward and never look back' was the personal credo espoused by Fra Junípero Serra, the 18th-century Franciscan priest, university professor and missionary who created California.

Serra's missions are California's most visible link to the past, a chain of 21 whitewashed churches that define the state's most important highway as well as its very existence. For despite its secular excesses, modern California was born as a religious enterprise whose branches still flower in popular mythology and architecture.

In 1769, the Spanish crown sent Serra and military commander Gaspar de Portolá to head Spain's first attempt to settle Alta, or upper, California. It was called The Sacred Expedition, a gruelling desert march from Baja (lower) California to San Diego in midsummer.

Serra's mission was simple and direct: Christianise the local tribes, teach them the Spanish language and European mores, put them to work and then start over again until California had been civilised under Spanish rule.

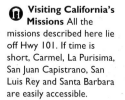

Visiting California's Missions All the missions described here lie off Hwy 101. If time is short, Carmel, La Purisima, San Juan Capistrano, San Luis Rey and Santa Barbara are easily accessible.

User-friendly websites provide historical and cultural information – some even have samples of Native Americans' purported plainsong! Here are several sites to enhance the mission experience: *missions.bgmm.com; www.californiamissions.com; www.ca-missions.org*

History

Serra founded a chain of 21 missions, stretching 600 miles north to Sonoma, just below Russia's southernmost settlement of Fort Ross (*see page 189*). Each outpost was a day's travel from the next, linked by *El Camino Real*, The King's Highway, a rough trail that became Hwy 101. Individual missions flourished and grew wealthy, but the system failed.

Supplies and equipment from Mexico often arrived late or disappeared. Earthquakes levelled adobe buildings. Imported diseases killed Native American converts, called *neophytes*, by the thousands.

The final blow came in 1834, when a then-independent Mexico secularised Church property. Mission holdings were sold or given as land grants. Most of the mission buildings dissolved back into the adobe mud from which they had sprung, surviving only as the names of the towns which had grown up around the long-vanished churches.

Nostalgic 19th-century artists pushed for the missions' restoration, aided by commercial interests, recognising profit in 'Old California'.

San Francisco Solano

San Rafael Arcángel

San Francisco de Asis

Santa Clara

San José

Santa Cruz

San Juan Bautista

San Carlos Borromeo del Rio Carmelo (Carmel)

Nuestra Señora de la Soledad

San Antonio de Padua

San Miguel Arcángel

San Luis Obispo de Tolosa

La Purisima Concepción de María Santisima

Santa Inés

Santa Barbara

San Buenaventura

San Fernando Rey de España

San Gabriel Arcángel

San Juan Capistrano

San Luis Rey de Francia

San Diego de Alcalá

0   10   20   30   40 miles
0 10 20 30 40km

PACIFIC OCEAN

PACIFIC OCEAN

Mission Carmel (San Carlos Borromeo del Rio Carmelo) $ *3080 Rio Rd, Carmel; tel: (831) 624-1271; www.carmelmission.org. Open Mon–Sat 0930–1700, Sun 1030–1700.*

Nuestra Señora Dolorosísima de la Soledad *36641 Ft Romie Rd, Soledad; tel: (831) 678-2586. Call for hours. Admission by donation.*

San Juan Capistrano was converted back from a hay barn, San Luis Obispo from a gaol, while Carmel was rebuilt from a rubble heap.

The Mission Style, whitewashed walls, red-tile roofs, rounded arches and massive sprays of bougainvillaea, became the architectural rage from California to Florida. Generations of cinema-goers grew up with the imposing façade of Mission Santa Barbara as their image of Early California – modern pink paint apparently photographed better than the original whitewash.

Many missions have common names, shown below in parenthesis.

Missions

Mission San Carlos Borromeo del Rio Carmelo (Mission Carmel)

Carmel (1770) is a nearly perfect image of what a mission ought to be – golden sandstone, Moorish towers and contemplative gardens, all set off by splashes of brilliant bougainvillaea. Fra Serra is buried beneath the floor in front of the main altar; the rebuilt padre's quarters include Serra's spartan cell and a library with volumes dating to 1534. Carmel is also one of the most visited of the missions. Try to go early in the day before the crowds arrive. The church is closed during services, though the large courtyard remains open and popular.

Nuestra Señora Dolorosísima de la Soledad (Mission Soledad)

Soledad (1791) is better known for its state prison than its mission, which is little more than a restored chapel, museum and adobe ruins in a pleasant, pastoral setting.

Right
Father Serra's parlour in the San Carlos Borromeo del Rio Carmelo Mission

Why Missions?

Spain had little interest in California when Serra and Portolá were sent north to establish a chain of missions. Generations of Spanish monarchs had happily ignored Alta California since Sebastián Vizcaíno visited Monterey in 1602. But in the 1760s, Spain saw a new threat in the Pacific: Russia.

Russian fur-seal hunters were slowly making their way south from Alaska, posing a potential threat to undefended Alta California. A chain of missions and *presidios*, military forts, could block Russian advances.

The Russians got as far south as Fort Ross (see page 189) in 1812. What impact the missions had is unclear. After Mission Solano (Sonoma) was established a decade later, Fort Ross became a major buyer of California flour, beef and wine to provision Alaskan fur bases.

When the fur trade declined from overhunting along the entire Pacific Coast, the Russians unloaded Fort Ross on John Sutter, best known as the owner of Sutters Fort where the Gold Rush began in 1848. Sutter returned the favour by neglecting to pay most of the agreed selling price. The missions themselves went out of business in 1834, when Mexico secularised Church property.

La Purisima Concepción de María Santisima $
La Purisima Mission State Historic Park, 2295 Purisima Rd (4 miles north of Lompoc); tel: (805) 733-3713; www.lapurisimamission.org. Open daily 0900–1700.

San Antonio de Padua
$ 23 miles southwest of King City, Mission Rd, Jolon; tel: (831) 385-4478; www.missionsanantonio.net. Open daily 0900–1700.

San Buenaventura $
211 E. Main St, Ventura; tel: (805) 643-4318; www. sanbuenaventuramission.org. Open Mon–Fri 1000–1700, Sat 0900–1700, Sun 1000–1600. Admission by donation.

La Purisima Concepción de María Santisima (La Purisima)

La Purisima (1787) was rebuilt as a public works project in the 1930s, but it is the most authentic restoration amongst the missions. Workers used period tools and methods to bring an archaeological site back to life. The darkly ornate (but unconsecrated) church is furnished and painted as it would have been at its height in the 1820s. The kitchen garden is planted with typical food and medicinal plants, from garlic and chillies to elderberries and myrtle. Even the farm animals are period, down to the four-horned churro sheep that have come closer to extinction than the missions themselves.

San Antonio de Padua

Sitting in a small valley surrounded by Fort Hunter Liggett, a quiet military reservation, San Antonio (1771) is more serene now than when it was a famed horse-breeding centre. The founding Franciscans are long gone, though the rough, rebuilt adobe arches and promenades match 19th-century photographs of the original building. Modern renovators have removed the candles, flowers and other devotional objects that once crowded the simple chapel, and stencilled designs along the walls and altar are based on original colours.

San Buenaventura

The stone church and surrounding gardens have been restored to a good approximation of their original appearance (1782). The tiered bell tower, topped by a striped dome, echoes Moorish motifs that distinguish California Mission styles from similar Mexican buildings. The museum has many of the mission's original furnishings, including the only wooden bells used in any of the 21 missions.

San Diego de Alcalá $ 10818 San Diego Mission Rd, San Diego; tel: (619) 281-8449; www.missionsandiego.com. Open daily 0900–1645.

San Fernando Rey de España 15151 San Fernando Mission Blvd, Mission Hills; tel: (818) 361-0186. Open daily 0900–1700.

San Francisco de Asis $ 3321 16th St, San Francisco; tel: (415) 621-8203; www.missiondolores.org. Open daily 0900–1600.

San Francisco Solano $ 114 E. Spain St, Sonoma State Historic Park, Sonoma; tel: (707) 938-9560; www.parks.sonoma.net/sonoma.html. Open daily 1000–1700.

San Gabriel Arcángel $ 428 S. Mission Dr., San Gabriel; tel: (626) 457-3035; www.sangabrielmission.org. Open daily 0900–1630.

San José de Guadalupe $ 43300 Mission Blvd, Fremont; tel: (510) 657-1797; www.missionsanjose.org. Open daily 1000–1700.

San Diego de Alcalá (Mission San Diego)

This was California's first mission (1769), and the first to be moved out of the reach of presidio soldiers. Not a wise move in San Diego's case, for the mission was sacked by *neophytes* (*see page 256*) and unconverted tribes in 1775. Rebuilt with high adobe walls, the mission prospered until secularised in 1834, when it fell into ruin. The blindingly white walls were raised again in the early 20th century. San Diego buildings were particularly narrow because of the acute shortage of tall timber needed to span wider structures.

San Fernando Rey de España (San Fernando Rey)

The graceful buildings and lush gardens of San Fernando (1797) seem to have survived the test of time, but the church is actually the youngest in the mission system. It is a copy of an 1806 church demolished by an earthquake in 1971. The mission once grazed more than 21,000 head of cattle in the San Fernando Valley, supplying candles, soap and leather goods to other missions. San Fernando's *convento*, or guest and missionary quarters, is the largest surviving mission building in the state. Bob Hope is buried at the San Fernando Mission Cemetery.

San Francisco de Asis (Mission Dolores)

Usually called 'Mission Dolores' after a nearby lake that disappeared decades ago, the mission (1776) is San Francisco's oldest building. It is also among the most ornate, with a chapel restored to the 1791 period. The small mission museum holds artefacts from the colonial period, as does the cemetery, including California's first native-born Mexican governor (Luís Antonio Arguello), the city's first Mexican mayor (Francisco de Haro) and last Mexican mayor (José Noé).

San Francisco Solano (often called Sonoma Mission)

This last of the missions to be established (1823) was also destroyed by a Native American uprising and rebuilt in more durable adobe. All that remains of the rebuilt complex are the chapel and part of the priests' quarters, restored about 1913.

San Gabriel Arcángel (Mission San Gabriel)

San Gabriel (1771) has the oldest cemetery in Los Angeles County (1778) and has survived more earthquake damage than any major structure still in use locally. The original vaulted roof was damaged by a quake in 1804, as were the replacement in 1812 and its replacement in 1987. The choir loft, baptistery, sanctuary, sacristy and pulpit are all original. Landscaped grounds contain numerous ruins, including the original bell tower, which collapsed in an early earthquake.

San José de Guadalupe (Mission San Jose)

This copy was built on the site of the original mission church (1797). The interior shows the 1830–40s period, complete with ornate sculptures and gold-leaf replica furnishings.

San Juan Bautista
406 2nd St, San Juan Bautista Historic Park, centre of town; tel: (831) 623-4528; www.oldmissionsjb.org. Open daily 0930–1630.

San Juan Capistrano
$$ 26801 Ortega Hwy, San Juan Capistrano; tel: (949) 234-1300; www.missionsjc. com. Open daily 0830–1700.

San Luis Obispo de Tolosa *782 Monterey St, San Luis Obispo; tel: (805) 781-8220; www. missionsanluisobispo.org. Open daily 0900–1700.*

San Juan Bautista

If this largest of the California missions looks familiar, with its ponderous bells in the tower and an extended arcade fronting the monastery wing, it probably is. San Juan Bautista (1797) was used for the climactic stairway chase in Alfred Hitchcock's classic *Vertigo*. The bear and coyote tracks in the tiles along the church's central aisle were made while the tiles were drying in the sun nearly three centuries ago. The mission and surrounding square are one of the best surviving examples of an early 19th-century California town.

San Juan Capistrano

Forget the syrupy song and made-up legend about the swallows returning to Capistrano on 19 March. The mission (1775) is better remembered for its fountains, lush gardens, peaceful courtyards, the 1777 Serra Chapel, the oldest building still in regular use in California, and the ruins of the Great Stone Church which collapsed during morning Mass in an 1812 earthquake. San Juan Capistrano is also one of the most popular missions. Get there at opening and flee when the tour buses start arriving.

San Luis Obispo de Tolosa (Mission San Luis Obispo)

You'd never know by looking that Mission San Luis Obispo (1772) served time as the town gaol. Once among the richest of the missions (renowned for its wines), an 1830 earthquake sent San Luis' fortunes tumbling. It was eventually returned to the Roman Catholic Church, renovated into a vaguely New England-ish chapel, and finally returned to its adobe form from the 1930s. The imitation marble *reredos*, the decorated area behind the altar, is especially dramatic. So are the outstanding Chumash Native American exhibits that are displayed in the mission museum.

Mission Organisation

Spain had more than a century of mission experience in New Mexico, Texas, Baja California and elsewhere before moving into California. The basic scheme combined religious, military and civilian authority.

Missionaries were to Christianise and Hispanicise the natives and turn them into a docile workforce. Civilian settlers were responsible for creating a *pueblo*, or town, to instil civil authority, while soldiers built a *presidio*, or fort, to protect mission and town.

The scheme fared poorly in California. Early settlers and soldiers were largely conscripts who deserted at the earliest possible moment. The padres soon learned to establish missions as far from *pueblo* and *presidio* as possible to avoid abuse of their converts. Civilian and military authorities were just as distrustful of the missions, which seemed to concentrate on amassing wealth rather than building a new order.

None seemed to give more than a passing thought to the Native Americans they subdued, converted and unknowingly killed by way of imported diseases, poor sanitation and worse diet. Whether by design or by accident, the missions effectively destroyed every Native American group they encountered.

San Luis Rey de Francia $ 4050
Mission Ave, San Luis Rey
(Oceanside); tel: (760) 757-
3651; www.sanluisrey.org.
Open 1000–1600.

San Miguel Arcángel
801 Mission St, San Miguel;
tel: (805) 467-3256;
www.missionsanmiguel.org.
Open daily 0930–1630.

Right
Mission Santa Barbara

San Luis Rey de Francia (Mission San Luis Rey)

The King of The Missions (1798) was the largest building in all of California for more than half of the 19th century. It is still the largest mission, its scalloped white façade almost a glaring mirage beneath the Southern California sun. The quadrangle once sprawled across 6 acres and mission fields stretched 15 miles. A unique wooden dome sits atop the cruciform church, an eight-sided lantern with 12 dozen panes of glass. The mission museum claims America's largest collection of old Spanish vestments and the sole surviving mission-era walking staff and padre's hat.

San Miguel Arcángel

San Miguel (1797) is a beloved mission, but was a structurally poor church building with the 21 missions' best-preserved original interior artwork – murals with mineral pigment bound with cactus juice – before it took a heavy hit in a 6.5 Richter-scale earthquake on

San Rafael Arcángel *1104 Fifth Ave, San Rafael; tel: (415) 454-8141; www.saintraphael. com. Open daily 1100– 1600. Free.*

Santa Barbara $ *2201 Laguna St, Santa Barbara; tel: (805) 682-4149; www.sbmission.org. Open daily 0900–1700.*

Santa Clara de Asís *Santa Clara University, 500 El Camino Real, Santa Clara; tel: (408) 554-4023; www.scu.edu/mission. Open daily.*

Santa Cruz Mission State Historic Park *Santa Cruz; tel: (831) 425-5849; www.santacruzstateparks.org/ parks/mission. Open Thu–Sun 1000–1600.*

Santa Inés $ *1760 Mission Dr., Solvang; tel: (805) 688-4815; www.missionsantaines.org. Open daily 0900–1700.*

22 December 2003. The church still stands. Moisture swelled the cracked adobe and damaged the murals. Restoration is under way with parts completed and visitors welcome.

San Rafael Arcángel (Mission San Rafael)
Built as an *asistencia*, or branch, to Mission Dolores, San Rafael (1817) was primarily a sanatorium for its San Francisco parent house. The original mission was razed in 1870; the replica – on approximately the same site – was built in 1949.

Santa Barbara
Unique among the missions, Santa Barbara (1786) has remained a parish church from the day it was consecrated. Called 'Queen of The Missions' for its classic Roman façade (borrowed from a 27 BC architectural encyclopaedia), the mission starred in dozens of early films – it was convenient to Hollywood's favourite holiday destination, Montecito. The pink-hued, sandstone church is complemented by the lush courtyard gardens within and a spectacular city rose garden in front.

Santa Clara de Asís (Mission Santa Clara)
The current church, built after fire destroyed the earlier building (1777) in 1926, mirrors an impressive mission building. The roof is covered in red tiles salvaged from the ruins of earlier mission structures. The wooden cross (inside a redwood frame) standing in front of the church dates to the founding of the original mission. Olive trees, roses and wisteria around the quadrangle beside the church have been growing since the mission days.

Santa Cruz
Santa Cruz (1791) was the smallest of the missions, but not this small – what you now see is a half-size replica built in 1931 to house a mission museum. The mission itself collapsed in 1857 from earthquake damage. The best reason to visit is **Santa Cruz Mission State Historic Park** (*144 School St; tel: (831) 429-5849*). A seven-room barracks is California's only remaining housing for mission *neophytes* (*see page 256*). The building was later used by *Californio* and Irish residents.

Santa Inés
Santa Inés (1804) was admired for its cattle herds, fine leatherwork and delicate jewellery until 1824, when a guard chastised a convert with too much obvious enthusiasm. The *neophyte* community set fire to the church and mission affairs never recovered. Restoration began around the turn of the 20th-century, including a *trompe-l'oeil* painting behind the sanctuary. The marble panels separated by Ionic columns are actually flat plaster.

Ratings

Gambling	●●●●●
Nightlife	●●●●●
Scenery	●●●●●
Architecture	●●●●○
Children	●●●●○
Shopping	●●●○○
Food and drink	●●○○○
History	●○○○○

Greater Las Vegas

The ads claim that Las Vegas never sleeps. It's true. The lure of 'easy' money, clattering slot machines and flashing neon may slow in the hours just before dawn, but 'Vegas' has barely paused for breath since Nevada legalised gambling in the early 1930s.

'Show the suckers a good time and send 'em home broke' is how an early casino-owner might have put it. The public responded by turning what was once a dusty, sun-blasted oasis in the middle of nowhere into one of the most-visited, most talked-about cities on earth.

Vegas mirrors America's changing visions of itself, especially the 3-mile stretch of Las Vegas Blvd South lined with 40-plus casinos known simply as The Strip.

In the 1990s, circus acts and fairytale castles pushed half-naked showgirls and other more traditional attractions into the background. The social pendulum is swinging back with shows and nightclubs that expand the limits of public sensuality. Extravagance, opulence and entertainment are today's watchwords, concepts that Las Vegas is more than happy to indulge with yet another round of bigger, grander and glitzier hotel-casinos.

Getting there and getting around

ⓘ Las Vegas Convention & Visitors Authority (LVCVA) *3150 Paradise Rd, Las Vegas, NV 89109; tel: (702) 892-7575 or (877) 847-4858; www. visitlasvegas.com. Open daily 0800–1700.*
The airport, car rental offices, hotels, restaurants, casinos, museums and shops are also overflowing with brochures.

ⓢ Las Vegas Monorail *$ east of The Strip from MGM Grand to the Sahara; tel: (702) 699-8200; www.lvmonorail.com. Trains run daily Mon–Thu 0700–0200, Fri–Sun to 0300.*

McCarran International Airport (LAS) *tel: (702) 261-5211; www. mccarran.com,* is south of the Strip, 5 miles from the city centre. Taxi to Strip hotels averages $8–20. **Gray Line** *(tel: (800) 634-6579 or (702) 384-1234; http://airport.graylinelasvegas.com)* airport bus is slightly less for a return journey. **I-15** is the main access highway from California and the Grand Canyon.

Public transport
The Regional Transportation Commission of Southern Nevada *(tel: (800) 228-3911 or (702) 228-7433; www.rtcsnv.com/transit)* offers Citizens Area Transit (CAT) bus service to most of Las Vegas; a **Deuce** double-decker bus down the Las Vegas Strip; and in 2009, debuts **ACE** rapid transit bullet-shaped buses with dedicated lanes and stops adjusted for passenger flow between downtown, the convention center, Las Vegas Strip, Henderson and North Las Vegas. The **Las Vegas Monorail** *(www.lvmonorail.com; $5 per ride)* connects seven hotel-casinos along the

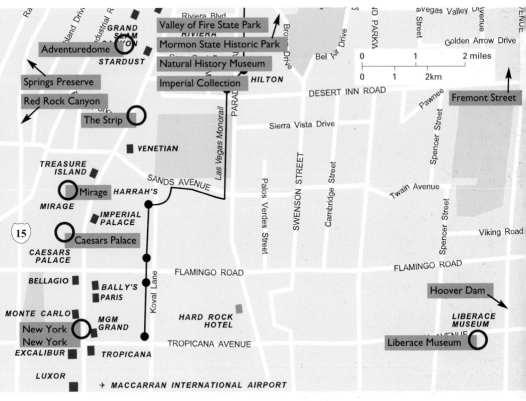

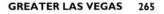

east side of Las Vegas Blvd South, better known as The Strip. The elevated line runs *behind* resorts from the MGM Grand (at Tropicana Ave) to the Sahara (at Sahara Ave), with stops for Bally's and Paris; Flamingo and Caesars Palace; Imperial Palace and Harrahs; the Las Vegas Convention Center, Hilton and the Sahara. Riding the air-conditioned carriages beats inching through Strip traffic, especially in summer, but stations are at the rear of each hotel stop. Allow for a 15–20-minute hike to get from the monorail to The Strip. **Strip Trolleys $** (*www.striptrolley.com*) serve Strip casinos half-hourly until 0200. Traffic along The Strip grinds to a crawl mid-afternoon to late evening.

Parking

Parking is plentiful, convenient and cheap. Casino car parks are well lit, patrolled 24 hours daily and almost always free. Free valet parking is available at the main entrance to all casinos; tip the attendant $2–$5 when the vehicle is returned. Car parks which do charge, such as the **Fremont Street Experience** (*see page 266*) lot, normally waive the fee with validation (a stamp or paste-on sticker) from a nearby casino or merchant.

Fremont Street Experience
Downtown, 425 Fremont St; tel: (702) 678-5777; www. vegasexperience.com. Light and sound shows nightly.

Hoover Dam & Lake Mead 30 miles east of Las Vegas on Hwy 93; tel: (702) 494-2517 or (866) 730-9097; www.usbr.gov/lc/hooverdam. Dam visitor centre open daily 0900–1800. Tours $$. Lake Mead National Recreation Area is open 24 hours.

Imperial Palace Auto Collection $$ Imperial Palace, 3535 Las Vegas Blvd S.; tel: (702) 794-3174; www.autocollections.com. Open 0930–2130.

Las Vegas Natural History Museum $ 900 N. Las Vegas Blvd; tel: (702) 384-3466; www.lvnhm.org. Open daily 0900–1600.

Above
Las Vegas pastiche – the skyline of the New York New York Hotel

Sights

Fremont Street Experience
Four blocks of Fremont St have been transformed into the **Fremont Street Experience**, a walking street topped by a 90-ft canopy set with 12.5 million synchronised LED modules that explode into light and sound shows after dark. Downtown casinos are generally less flashy than their Strip counterparts, less expensive and less noisy.

Hoover Dam
About 726ft from base to dam-top highway, Hoover Dam is one of the highest concrete dams ever built. Finished in 1936, it backs the Colorado River into **Lake Mead**, a 140-mile strip of blue in the beige, grey and red landscape of the Mojave, Great Basin and Sonoran deserts that meet along its shores. The lake is a popular boating and outdoor recreation area from spring to autumn.

The **Dam Visitor Center** has a self-guided **Discovery Tour** with exhibits, a film on dam construction, the power plant generators and overlooks from both sides and the middle of the dam. Several river-rafting companies in Las Vegas offer easy whole- or half-day raft and canoe trips down the Colorado River from just below the dam.

Imperial Palace Collections
One of the West's finer car collections (each vehicle is for sale!) includes an 1897 Haynes-Apperson. Rotating exhibits have featured a 1928 Delage limousine owned by the late King of Siam, US President Dwight Eisenhower's parade limo and one of the world's largest collections of Model J Duesenbergs.

🎹 **Liberace Museum**
$$ *1775 E. Tropicana
Ave; tel: (702) 798-5595;
www.liberace.com. Open
Tue–Sat 1000–1700, Sun
1200–1600.*

**Old Las Vegas Mormon
State Historic Park** $
*Washington Ave and Las
Vegas Blvd; tel: (702) 486-
3511; http://parks.nv.gov/
olvmf.htm. Open
0800–1630.*

**Red Rock Canyon
National Conservation
Area** $ *20 miles west,
off Charleston Blvd;
tel: (702) 515-5350;
www.nv.blm.gov/redrock
canyon. Scenic Drive loop
open Nov–Feb 0600–1700;
Mar and Oct to 1900;
Apr–Sep to 2000. Visitor
Center open daily
0800–1630.*

**Springs Preserve
Free–$$** *333 S. Valley
View Blvd at Alta Dr;
tel: (702) 822-7700;
www.springspreserve.org.
Gardens (3701 W. Alta Dr.)
open daily 0800–1800.
Call to check hours.*

⭘ **The Strip** *Las Vegas
Blvd S., Stratosphere to
Mandalay Bay. Never closed.*

Las Vegas Natural History Museum
The museum is a good introduction to the plants and animals indigenous to Nevada as well as marine life from around the world.

Liberace Museum
Liberace was a classically trained pianist, technically astute and addicted to grand gestures of dazzling spectacle – audiences loved him. The museum displays many of his flashiest costumes, jewelled accessories, automobiles, pianos and other accoutrements.

Old Las Vegas Mormon State Historic Park
This is where the entertainment began. In 1855, Mormon traders opened a fort in an isolated desert meadow ('Las Vegas' is 'meadows' in Spanish) to cater to pioneer wagon trains headed for California. The fort was eventually selected as a railway stop (steam locomotive engines needed regular infusions of water), which prompted an initial round of land speculation that resulted in today's Las Vegas. The Museum includes a late 19th-century Mormon living room.

Red Rock Canyon National Conservation Area
Best known for a 13-mile driving loop that winds through some of the most spectacular desert scenery within easy reach of Las Vegas, the conservation area is named after the 3000-ft high Red Rock Escarpment, as popular with rock climbers as with sightseers. Self-guided hiking trails lead to a spring, a waterfall, several small canyons and what remains of an old homestead. Wild *burros* frequent the loop road in search of handouts.

Springs Preserve
The Strip has an antidote: a 180-acre stop west of Downtown with botanical gardens; trails; a desert living centre; Mojave Desert ecology, Native American history, and water use in an ORI-GEN centre; concert space; and the Nevada State Museum (Las Vegas), constructed on an historic water-source landmark area that still provides most of Downtown Las Vegas's water supply.

The Strip
The Strip *is* Las Vegas for most visitors, 3 miles of boulevard glitz lined with more than 40 hotel-casinos and acres of neon. Traffic tends to move slowly, but the only way to see the full scope of creative casino architecture is to park and walk, or take the monorail.

Above right
Man versus mountain in Red Rock Canyon

Valley of Fire State Park $

55 miles northeast of Las Vegas, off I-15, near Overton; tel: (702) 397-2088; http://parks.nv.gov/vf.htm. Park open dawn–dusk, visitor centre open 0830–1630.

Valley of Fire State Park

This rugged valley is filled with eroded red sandstone formations that seem to catch fire in the sunlight – the effect is most spectacular at dawn and sunset. Some rocks and cliffs are covered with prehistoric petroglyphs. The most easily accessible set of petroglyphs lies along the ¼-mile trail to **Mouse's Tank**, a natural basin named for a Paiute Indian who successfully eluded capture in the natural maze.

Shopping in Las Vegas

Most stores and shops in Las Vegas open at 1000; along The Strip, most remain open to 2300 or 2400. As shopping evolved to become one of America's favourite forms of entertainment, casinos began to create their own themed shopping opportunities. Amongst the glitziest of the shoppertainment palaces are **The Grand Canal Shoppes** (*The Venetian, 3377 Las Vegas Blvd S.; tel: (702) 414-4500; www.thegrandcanalshoppes.com*) and **The Forum Shops at Caesars** (*Caesars Palace, 3570 Las Vegas Blvd S.; tel: (702) 893-4800; www.harrahs.com/casinos/caesars-palace/casino-misc/the-forum/shops-detail.html*). The Grand Canal is modelled on Venice, complete with gondoliers in red-and-white striped shirts poling gondolas along meandering canals, St Mark's Square, living statues, and Renaissance-inspired singers and actors. The Forum Shops offers Italianate streetscapes beneath hand-painted barrel vaulting that cycles through the day from sunrise to sunset. Faux-marble statues come to life on the hour with Vegas' own twist on Roman mythology. **The Shoppes at the Palazzo** (*The Palazzo, 3327 Las Vegas Blvd S.; tel: (702) 414-4525; www.theshoppesatthepalazzo.com*) touts 60 upscale shops including Barneys New York. **Miracle Mile Shops** (*Planet Hollywood, 3667 Las Vegas Blvd S.; tel: (888) 800-8284; www.miraclemileshopslv.com*) boasts a regularly scheduled rainstorm at Merchant's Harbor.

Fashion Show Las Vegas (*3200 Las Vegas Blvd S.; tel: (702) 784-7000; www.thefashionshow.com*) is the largest mall on The Strip, with more than 250 speciality and department stores. A few blocks west of Downtown Las Vegas, the **Las Vegas Premium Outlets** (*875 S. Grand Central Parkway; tel: (702) 474-7500; www.premiumoutlets.com*) provides a chance to 'collect' from more than 150 designer stores.

Accommodation and food in Las Vegas

Las Vegas is the hotel capital of the planet, with 133,000 rooms and still counting. Accommodation is concentrated along The Strip (*Las Vegas Blvd S.*) and **Downtown** (*Fremont St and nearby*). New Strip hotels are the most luxurious, the most touted and the most expensive;

The Word
The best single source of practical and up-to-the-minute Vegas information is the *Las Vegas Advisor* 3665 S. Procoyon Ave, Las Vegas, NV 89103; tel: (702) 252-0655 or (800) 244-2224; *www.lasvegasadvisor.com.* The monthly newsletter is filled with accommodation and show deals, gambling strategies, non-gaming activities and tips on local bargains – no adverts allowed.

downtown hotels are less expensive. Prices drop even further at motels west of I-15.

Visit midweek for the best value, but always book ahead to avoid major conventions or sporting events, which drive accommodation prices sky-high. The Sunday *Los Angeles Times* travel section is the single best source of current accommodation deals.

Casino food and drink prices have crept upward in recent years, but casino buffets are still good value for any meal. The **Fiesta**, **Rio** and **Station** (**Boulder**, **Palace**, **Sunset**, **Texas** and **Santa Fe**, plus the **Green Valley Ranch**) casinos get high marks for good food as well as good buffet prices.

Drinks are free to gamblers, though service is generally slow. Expect to pay standard prices at casino bars, where service is generally very good. The drinking and gambling age is 21 and alcohol may be served 24 hours a day.

Gambling

Gambling, or 'gaming' as the politically correct prefer, fuels the flash, the glitter and the hype that keeps Las Vegas moving. Take the rows of slot machines standing like sentries at the airport (locals warn the odds are terrible), petrol stations, supermarkets and wedding chapels as a hint: Vegas is a money machine oiled by the mathematical certainty that, in the long run, the player *always* loses. The only question is how long it takes.

Below
Antique slot machine in Las Vegas

In general, the easier the game, the higher the house edge, or advantage. The house keeps around 45 per cent of the money bet on keno, less than 0.5 per cent of the cash bet on blackjack, Vegas's most popular card game. Most casinos offer free lessons for **blackjack** (also called '21' for the perfect hand) and **craps** (a high-speed dice game). Try to graduate to low-stakes tables at slack periods, breakfast to mid-afternoon, before jumping into the heady night-time whirl.

Most gamblers opt for the ubiquitous **slot machines**, which require neither skill nor a rulebook. Pump in quarters, dollars or banknotes (occasional nickel slots are around) and pull the handle or push a button to set the reels spinning. If a winning combination appears, bells ring, lights flash and coins clatter reassuringly into a metal hopper. **Video poker** machines operate similarly, but require some knowledge of the rules of poker.

Other popular games include **baccarat**, a European card game similar to blackjack where the goal is nine rather than 21; **keno**, a lotto-like game; **roulette** and a number of different **poker** games. It is also possible to bet on sporting events at any casino sport book.

Casino themes

Most Vegas casinos have become gigantic theme parks in order to set themselves apart in a highly competitive market. The basic amenities are the same – accommodation, casino, restaurants, bars, cabarets and shows – but the packaging varies dramatically to lure different kinds of punters. And there are always new hotel-casinos opening or changing themes.

Bellagio *3600 Las Vegas Blvd S.; tel: (702) 693-7111 or (888) 987-6667; www.bellagiolasvegas.com.* An opulent village transplanted from Italy's Lake Como to Nevada. No one under 18 is admitted except registered guests, unless eating at a resort restaurant or attending a show or other event.

Caesars Palace *3570 Las Vegas Blvd S.; tel: (866) 227-5938; www.harrahs.com/casinos/caesars-palace/hotel-casino/property-home.shtml.* Togas and other glories of Imperial Rome plus fabulous shopping.

Circus Circus *2880 Las Vegas Blvd S.; tel: (877) 434-9175; www.circuscircus.com.* Vegas's original family casino with circus acts, games and the **Adventuredome $$$** Theme Park to keep the kids occupied.

Excalibur *3850 Las Vegas Blvd S.; tel: (702) 597-7777 or (877) 750-5464; www.excalibur.com.* Camelot on The Strip, complete with strolling dragons.

Luxor *3900 Las Vegas Blvd S.; tel: (877) 386-4658; www.luxor.com.* Ancient Egypt within a black glass pyramid, complete with a Sphinx crouching over the entrance.

Mandalay Bay *3950 Las Vegas Blvd S.; tel: (877) 632-7800; www. mandalaybay.com.* The world's top tropical resorts distilled in the desert, with a separate no-gaming **Four Seasons Hotel $$$** *3960 Las Vegas Blvd; tel: (702) 632-5000 or (877) 632-5000; www.fourseasons.com/ lasvegas,* to raise the tone.

MGM Grand *3799 Las Vegas Blvd S.; tel: (702) 891-7777 or (877) 880-0880; www.mgmgrand.com.* Cinema magic made real inside.

The Mirage *3400 Las Vegas Blvd S.; tel: (702) 791-7111 or (800) 374-9000; www.mirage.com.* Look for the erupting volcano outside at night, the tropical rainforest inside and dolphins and white tigers in the Secret Garden.

New York New York *3790 Las Vegas Blvd S.; tel: (702) 740-6969 or (866) 815-4365; www.nynyhotelcasino.com.* The New York City skyline compressed around a casino. The roller coaster looping round the Statue of Liberty is real.

Palms Casino Resort *4321 W. Flamingo Rd; tel: (702) 942-7777 or (866) 942-7777; www.palms.com.* A season starring in MTV's *Real World* put The Palms on the map as Las Vegas's hippest, sexiest, must-be-seen party hotel, complete with a bookable recording studio.

Paris *3655 Las Vegas Blvd S.; tel: (702) 946-4405 or (877) 796-2096; www.harrahs.com/casinos/paris-las-vegas/hotel-casino.* All the romance of early 20th-century Paris, from steak frites to cobblestone streets, plus every mod con a casino can dream up. The Eiffel Tower is one of the hottest restaurants in town.

Rio All-Suite Hotel & Casino *3700 W. Flamingo Rd; tel: (866) 746-7671; www.harrahs.com/casinos/rio/hotel-casino.* Mardi Gras takes off seven days a week just west of The Strip.

Treasure Island *3300 Las Vegas Blvd S.; tel: (702) 894-7111 or (800) 288-7206; www.treasureisland.com.* Caribbean fantasies for adults, including an epic sea battle in front. In *Sirens of TI®,* sexy shipboard sirens vanquish renegade pirates four times nightly.

The Venetian *3355 Las Vegas Blvd S.; tel: (702) 414-1000 or (877) 883-6423; www.venetian.com.* Renaissance Venice, complete with St Mark's Square, gondolas, the Doge's Palace and the Grand Canal.

That's entertainment!

Entertainment is the name of Las Vegas's game. The idea began with mobster Bugsy Segal, who imported musicians and comedians to give customers another reason to gamble in *his* casino. The ploy worked, then started feeding on itself. Casinos competed to create the flashiest shows and the most outlandish décor. Elegant drives were eclipsed by acres of neon, which gave way to erupting volcanoes, battling frigates and crooning gondoliers. Fantasy became a prelude to reality.

Big-name stars, 'headliners' in Vegas-speak, come and go regularly. Traditional shows, **Folies Bergere $$** (*Tropicana; tel: (800) 829-9034; www.tropicanalv.com*) and **Jubilee $$** (*Bally's; tel: (800) 237-7469; www.harrahs.com/casinos/ballys-las-vegas/casino-entertainment*) rely on lavish sets, singing, dancing and bare breasts. Most offer early-evening covered versions with topless shows later. Sextravaganzas such as **Zumanity $$$** (*New York New York; tel: (866) 606-7111; www.nynyhotelcasino.com*) or **Fantasy $$** (*Luxor; tel: (800) 557-7428 or (702) 262-4400; www.luxor.com*) are adult-only and uncovered.

A few casinos have held on to child-orientated spectacles. The most lavish is the **Tournament of Kings $$** (*Excalibur; tel: (702) 597-7600; www.excalibur.com*), a dinner show with jousting knights. Vegas's finest magic show is **Lance Burton $$** (*Monte Carlo; tel: (877) 386-8224 or (702) 730-7160; www.montecarlo.com*), one of the world's top illusionists.

Lavish productions, like those by **Cirque du Soleil** (*www.cirquedusoleil.com*), are expensive supershows with elaborate technical effects and superb athletic performances. Cirque's Las Vegas productions, all $$$ and amongst the most popular entertainment in town, include: **The Beatles LOVE** (*The Mirage; tel: (800) 963-9634 or (702) 792-7777; www.mirage.com*); **Kà** (*MGM Grand; tel: (877) 264-1844 or (702) 796-9999; www.mgmgrand.com*); **Mystère** (*Treasure Island; tel: (800) 963-9634 or (702) 796-9999; www.treasureisland.com*); **O** (*Bellagio; tel: (888) 488-7111 or (702) 693-7722; www.bellagio.com*); **CRISS ANGEL Believe** (*Luxor; tel: (800) 963-9634 or (702) 792-7777; www.luxor.com*); and **Zumanity** (*New York New York (see above)*).

The glitz capital also has high culture: **Bellagio Gallery of Fine Art $$** (*Bellagio; tel: (877) 957-9777 or (702) 693-7871; www.bellagio.com/amenities/gallery-of-fine-art.aspx*) has several museum-quality exhibitions each year.

Vegas for kids

Vegas is the archetypal playground for adults, but children don't get left out entirely. Easy hikes at **Springs Preserve**, **Red Rock Canyon $**, **Valley of Fire $**, and **Lake Mead/Hoover Dam** are a good way to run off excess energy. Nearby Henderson (on the way to Hoover Dam) has a free attraction for kids of all ages; **Ethel M® Chocolate Factory & Botanical Cactus Garden** (*1 Sunset Way; tel: (888) 627-0990 or (702) 458-8864; www.ethelm.com*) has free tours (and samples) of fine chocolate production, with a well-labelled cactus garden outside.

Thrill rides are Vegas's latest attraction for grown-up kids. **Adventuredome** **$$** (*Circus Circus; tel: (702) 794-3939; www.adventuredome.com*) has its share of screamers, but the top ride is the **Stratosphere Tower** **$$** (*Stratosphere; tel: (702) 380-7711; www.stratospherehotel.com*), with a roller coaster and two free-fall rides atop the 1149-ft tower. Best indoor-outdoor roller coaster is **New York New York** **$** (*www.nynyhotelcasino.com/entertainment/entertainment_ therollercoaster.aspx*), which runs through the lobby and around the New York skyline.

For artificial reality, kid-style, **Excalibur** **$** (*www.excalibur.com/ attractions/spongebob4d.aspx*) has SpongeBob Squarepants 4D™ ride and Luxor has popular IMAX® Ride films. The 'Klingon Encounter' and 'Borg Invasion 4D' in **Star Trek: The Experience** **$** (*Las Vegas Hilton; tel: (888) 462-6535; www.startrekexp.com*) could have come straight from the latest *Star Trek* space battles.

For free attractions, check out the dancing **Fountains of Bellagio** (*Bellagio*) that perform a water ballet day and night, and the **Volcano** *at The Mirage* that erupts every 15–30 minutes after dark. **St Mark's Square**, at the end of **The Grand Canal**, *at the Venetian*, offers a variety of strolling minstrels, jugglers and mimes to keep the crowds amused; or look for buskers in quiet corners throughout the Grand Canal Shoppes. Downtown, the **Fremont Street Experience** (*Fremont St; tel: (702) 678-5777; www.vegasexperience.com*) explodes into an overhead parade of moving images at dusk.

The Mirage offers animal attractions (*tel: (702) 791-7188; www.miragehabitat.com*). The **White Tiger Habitat** has views of tigers at play, asleep and being themselves. **The Secret Garden** **$** is a small zoo with white tigers and other endangered large cat species. **Dolphin Habitat** **$** is a large pool with trained bottlenose dolphins.

Below
Excalibur Hotel, Las Vegas

Showcase Mall (*3785 Las Vegas Blvd S.*) has three child-friendly attractions. **GameWorks** **$–$$** (*tel: (702) 432-4263*) is Vegas's largest video arcade, designed primarily for teenagers and young adults. **Everything Coca-Cola** **$** (*tel: (702) 270-5952*) is just what the name implies, everything you ever wanted to buy (or to know) about Coca-Cola. **M&M's World** (*tel: (702) 736-7611*) is the ultimate M&M's candy shop, with colours available nowhere else.

Grand Canyon, Bryce and Zion

Ratings

Geology	●●●●●
Scenery	●●●●●
Sunsets	●●●●●
Children	●●●●○
History	●●●●○
Walking	●●●●○
Food and drink	●●○○○
Architecture	●○○○○

The Painted Desert vision of the American Southwest springs to life in these three National Parks. All were regarded as aberrations of nature and roadblocks to orderly development until recent decades. Today's visitors are more likely to stare with awe and vertigo into the mile-deep Grand Canyon, wonder at the fairy-like hoodoos of Bryce Canyon and gaze in silence at the mountain patriarchs of Zion – at least until the next tour bus or RV caravan pulls into the car park.

The region ... is altogether valueless. It can be approached only from the south, and after entering it, there is nothing to do but leave. Ours has been the first, and will doubtless be the last, party ... to visit this profitless locality.

Thus wrote a member of the 1858 US government survey team, summing up the perceived economic value of the Grand Canyon. Today the Canyon receives more than four million visitors annually, all come to wonder at the red, white, buff, grey, yellow, orange, brown, pink and black rock.

BRYCE CANYON NATIONAL PARK

🄱 **Bryce Canyon National Park $$**
Box 640201, Bryce Canyon, UT 84717;
tel: (435) 834-5322;
www.nps.gov/brca

ⓘ **Visitor Center**
1½ miles south of Park Entrance. Open Nov–Mar 0800–1630; Apr and Oct 0800–1800; May–Sep 0800–2000, verify hours in the Hoodoo park newspaper, also online at the park website.

Bryce is an 18-mile canyon lined with hoodoos – ancient cliffs that have been eroded into parallel rows of sharp-edged pinnacles tinged with red, gold and chalk. Endless ranks of hoodoos form fanciful forests of stone that seem at times to resemble natural amphitheatres rimmed by fairy-tale cities of sheer-sided minarets, turrets, steeples and towers.

The drive south from the Park Entrance rises 1100ft to **Rainbow Point**. The road (Hwy 63) offers numerous lay-bys where you can pull in and enjoy the view, but longer-term parking is extremely limited. Arrive before 1000 if you are planning to park and explore from **Sunrise, Sunset, Inspiration, Bryce** or **Paria Viewpoints** during the spring to autumn. Trailers are not permitted beyond Sunset Campground, midway along the canyon drive. RVs longer than 25ft are prohibited from Paria View, at the end of the road, because of lack of turning space.

UTAH

Minersville

15   89

12

Boulder

Paragonah   Panguitch

130   Parowan

Modena   143   63

Newcastle   Summit   Brian   12   Bryce   Bryce Canyon National Park
           Head   Hatch   12   Escalante

56   Cedar   14   89   Henrieville
Enterprise   City
                        Bryce   **Sunrise Point**
Kanarraville   Canyon   **Sunset Point**
                        89   Rainbow Point   National   **Inspiration Point**
Kolob Canyons   Canyons   Junction   Park   **Bryce Point**
                Alton   **Paria View**
Veyo   15   Zion   Orderville   Glendale
           National
18   Zion National Park   9   Mt Carmel   89   89
                Mt Carmel
Hurricane   9   Springdale   Junction
St George   Washington   59   Kanab

15   Fredonia   Page
Littlefield
                        Marble Canyon   98
Mesquite   389
nkerville   89
                Jacob Lake   89
                                Colorado River
                    North Rim
                Road closed
                in winter   89
        Tuweep

Pierce   Grand   Phantom Ranch
Ferry   Grand Canyon National Park South Rim   Canyon   Tuba Cit
                National   North
                Park   160
            Grand   Grand Canyon Village   Desert View
            Canyon   Village   64
    18   Tusayan   Cameron
                                Gray Mountain
        Fraziers Well   Grand
                Canyon   180
                Railroad

ARIZONA

Peach Springs   180   89
        Grand Canyon Caverns
66   64
Valentine
        Seligman   **Williams**   Parks   40
40   Ash Fork
                                40
Kingman   93   89   Sedona   Munds Park   **Flagstaff**
                        17

Arriving at dawn

Sunrise is one of the most striking times of day to see the hoodoos and the easiest time of day to park. Park at **Sunrise Point** (*less than a mile beyond the Visitor Center*) to watch the low rays of light begin to pick out the spires, then follow the **Rim Trail** down between the hoodoos to **Sunset Point, Inspiration Point** or **Bryce Point**. Return via the main road.

During the day

Drive directly to **Rainbow Point**, where visibility can exceed 100 miles and early visitors occasionally spot mountain lions. The 1-mile **Bristlecone Loop Trail** threads through stands of rare bristlecone pines.

The return drive offers many lay-bys, most with hiking trails. **Agua Canyon** has several named hoodoos, including **Hunter** and **Rabbit**. One of the park's biggest draws is **Natural Bridge**, an 85-ft arch 6 miles north of Rainbow Point.

Bryce Point was named for Mormon settler Ebenezer Bryce, who farmed the Paria Valley for a short time in the 1870s and told the world of the mystical wonders that lay just to the south. **Inspiration Point** is best known for **Silent City**, a formation of 200-ft hoodoos packed in dense rows like some high-rise city emptied of people.

Arriving at sunset

Sunset Point is the obvious point from which to enjoy the sunset, though parking is a problem in summer. Vistas curve east towards **Queen's Garden, Wall Street** and an illusory balanced rock called **Thor's Hammer**. Allow 2 hours to

Bryce Canyon Shuttle provides free transport daily *0900–1800 late May–Sep* between the Ruby's Inn business area (Hwy 63), the park Visitor Center and the most famous viewpoints and trailheads in the Main Amphitheater. Park roads remain open to private vehicles, but summer traffic moves slowly.

Garfield County Tourism Office *55 S. Main, Panguitch, UT 84759; tel: (435) 676-1160 or (800) 444-6689; www.brycecanyoncountry. com*

Opposite
Walking the Navajo Trail in Bryce Canyon National Park

walk the 1.3-mile **Navajo Loop Trail** that wanders past Thor's Hammer, through the narrow clefts separating the hoodoos and through forests of pygmy Douglas fir trees. The easiest canyon trail is a 1.8-mile stroll through Queen's Garden from Sunset Point.

If schedules are tight, the best 1-hour park visit is **Fairyland Point**, just beyond the Visitor Center (also good for Nordic skiers). The stunning view is a preview of the magical scenery that lies beyond. Astronomy programmes and full-moon walks are popular, and Bryce Canyon horse riding is a unique way to see the hoodoos.

Accommodation and food in Bryce

The only non-camping accommodation in the park is **Bryce Canyon Lodge $$** *Xanterra Parks & Resorts, 6312 S. Fiddlers Green Circle, Ste 600N, Greenwood Village, CO 80111; tel: (303) 297-2757 or (888) 297-2757; www.brycecanyonlodge.com; open Apr–Oct*. Nearby choices include **Best Western Ruby's Inn $$** *1 mile north of the Park Entrance on Hwy 63; tel: (435) 834-5341 or (866) 866-6616; www.rubysinn.com*, and **Bryce Canyon Pines** *12 miles west on Hwy 12; tel: (800) 892-7923; www.brycecanyonmotel.com*. Other accommodation is available in **Tropic**, east of the park on Hwy 12.

Best local restaurant, and well worth the 6-mile drive, is **Cowboy's Smokehouse Bar-B-Q $$** *95 N. Main St, Panguitch, Utah; tel: (435) 676-8030; open Mon–Sat 1130–2200*, for authentic wood-smoked meats and enormous slabs of home-made pie. **Bryce Canyon Lodge Restaurant $$** is the only restaurant in the park open all year. **The General Store $$, Sunrise Point**, sells snacks and drinks mid-Apr–Oct.

GRAND CANYON NATIONAL PARK

Grand Canyon National Park $$ *Box 129, Grand Canyon, AZ 86023; tel: (928) 638-7888; www.nps.gov/grca and www.nps.gov/archive/grca/ grandcanyon*

The Grand Canyon is larger than it appears. The popular South Rim and the less-frequented North Rim are just 10 miles straight across the Canyon and 215 miles by highway. It is possible to see the Grand Canyon in a day, less if on a flightseeing package from Las Vegas, but the ever-changing colours and the utter vastness of the canyon beg to be absorbed at leisure, far from the vast crowds who stop at the South Rim and Grand Canyon Village. At the very least, skirt the crowds by walking or cycling the **South Rim Trail** from **Hopi Point** east to Grand Canyon Village and **Mather Point**. A free shuttle (*www.nps.gov/grca/planyourvisit/shuttle-buses.htm*) on five South Rim routes eases the return.

Bright Angel Trail began as a Native American trail from the rim down to the springs at Indian Gardens. Private developers widened the trail in 1891 and began the mule rides that remain one of Grand Canyon's most popular organised activities.

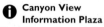

Canyon View Information Plaza
South Rim 6 miles north from the South Entrance, open daily 0800–1700, 1800 in summer. Access is by shuttle bus, walking or by bicycle.

Desert View Information Center, Kolb Studio, Yavapai Observation Station *and* **Tusayan Museum** *keep similar hours, i.e. 0800 or 0900–1700. Verify hours online.*

Road and Fire Conditions *Tel: (928) (928) 638-7888 or* **Arizona Road Conditions:** *tel: (888) 411-7623; www.dot.state.az.us. Ask for The Guide, free at visitor centres.*

North Rim Visitor Center *Near Grand Canyon Lodge. Open 0800–1800 mid-May–mid-Oct.*

Grand Canyon Railway $$
233 N. Grand Canyon Blvd, Williams, AZ 86046; tel: (928) 773-1976 or (800) 843-8724; www.thetrain.com. Operates daily.

The Park runs a **free shuttle bus** system *year-round through the Village and the West Rim. Shuttle routes, seasons of operation, and times can change. Check www.nps.gov/grca/planyourvisit/shuttle-buses.htm*

The **Grand Canyon Railway** (*tel: (800) 843-8724*) runs to the South Rim from Williams, 65 miles south of the Park. The 1901 line, originally run by the Santa Fe Railway, provided the easy access that turned the Grand Canyon from geographic curiosity into an American icon. A vintage steam locomotive engine pulls the restored 1920s Harriman carriages in summer; a 1950s diesel does the duty in winter.

Grand Canyon Village Historic District is the central section of Grand Canyon Village from **Bright Angel Trailhead** east to **Verkamp's Curios** and the **First National Park Service Administration Building**. Many Village structures are historic landmarks, including the **Kolb Studio** and **Lookout Studio**, perched on the canyon rim, **Red Horse Station, Bright Angel Lodge**, the **El Tovar Hotel**, the **Santa Fe Railway Station, Verkamp's Curios** and the **First National Park Service Administration Building**. Hopi House's Native American rugs, jewellery, pottery and tourist souvenirs are museum-class, as is the southwest-style adobe building.

Mule Trips (*Xanterra Parks and Resorts®; tel: (303) 297-2757* or (*888) 297-2757; year-round one-day rides and 1–2 nights overnight to Phantom Ranch*) have been popular for generations. Riders must be at least 4ft 7ins tall and weigh less than 200lbs. Advance booking is essential year-round, but there *may* be last-minute cancellations the morning of the ride (*tel: (928) 638-2631; www.grandcanyonlodges.com/mule-trips-716.html*).

One-day trips lead from the stone corral at the head of Bright Angel Trail to Tonto Platform and Plateau Point, 3200ft below. The blue-green Colorado River twinkles another 1300ft down. The ride takes about 7 hours.

Phantom Ranch rides stay overnight or two nights at Phantom Ranch cabins on Bright Angel Creek at the bottom of the Canyon. Two-night trips take a different return route.

The **North Rim**, 1000ft higher than the South Rim, is a different world. While the South Rim bakes in desert heat, the North Rim enjoys a cooler, mountain summer with spruce, fir and quaking aspen. And when the South Rim is dusted with snow, the North Rim is frozen beneath 25ft of white. The Grand Canyon Lodge and other North Rim facilities are open mid-May–mid-Oct; the park itself remains open longer, snow permitting.

A shorter season and more roundabout access mean that North Rim crowds are a tenth of South Rim mobs. The quickest way to enjoy the relative serenity is on foot. Easiest walks are the ½-mile **Bright Angel Trailhead** and the 1½-mile **Transcept Trail**. **Mule Rides** are another option; **Canyon Trail Rides** (*Grand Canyon Lodge Trail Rides Desk; tel: (435) 679-8665*) offer hour and half-day rides along the Canyon Rim or half- and full-day rides into the Canyon.

Rafting the Colorado River (*tel: (928) 638-7888*) remains the most adventurous way to see the Grand Canyon. Allow a full day for a

Above
The North Rim of the Grand Canyon

The **Grand Canyon Field Institute** offers classes, some with in-park lodging, most months of the year. Check schedules, itineraries and costs on *(866) 471-4435* or *(928) 638-2485; www. grandcanyon.org/fieldinstitute*

Canyon Trail Rides $$$
Tel: (435) 679-8665; www.canyonrides.com, uses mules for various-length rides in Bryce, Grand Canyon North Rim and Zion National Parks.

smooth-water float, including a picnic lunch. Water trips last from between one and eighteen days. Most outfitters depart from Lees Ferry, upstream from the park. A few outfitters ride the river all year. Contact the Park *(tel: (928) 638-7888; www.nps.gov/grca/grandcanyon/trip_planner.htm)* for a free *Trip Planner* that includes contact information for approved concessionaires, details on length and put-in and take-out points and permits. Or check with local chambers of commerce. Summer trips book out early in the season. The waiting time for private 'non-commercial' river-running permits can be several years.

Outside park boundaries, the **Hualapai in Grand Canyon West** *(tel: (877) 716-9378* or *(702) 878-9378; www.destinationgrandcanyon. com)* offers tours of the **Skywalk**, suspended 4000ft above the canyon floor, an Indian village, rafting and lodging. Beautiful, sacred **Havasu Falls** is on the **Havasupai Indian Reservation** *(Havasupai Tourism Office; tel: (928) 448-2121; www.havasupaitribe.com)*. Access the tribal centre by hiking, riding a horse or taking a helicopter from Hualapai Hilltop to Supai Village, where tourists camp or stay in a lodge and take a tour to several waterfalls.

Accommodation and food in Grand Canyon

Book as early as possible (6–12 months) to ensure a place to sleep at America's most popular National Park. South Rim is open year-round; North Rim is open mid-May–mid-Oct. All park accommodation and restaurants are operated by **Xanterra Parks & Resorts®**, *tel: (303) 297-2757* or *(888) 297-2757; www.grandcanyonlodges.com*

Grand Canyon National Park Lodges, *tel: (928) 638-2631*, handles information and same-day bookings for the South Rim Queen of the lot is the historic **El Tovar Hotel $$$** near the railway station. **Bright Angel Lodge and Cabins $$$** is near the Rim; **Thunderbird Lodge**

$$$ and **Kachina Lodge $$$** offer a choice of canyon-side or park-side rooms. **Maswik Lodge $$** and **Yavapai Lodge $$** are removed from the Village. Accommodation is also available in **Tusayan** (just outside the Park's south entrance), **Valle, Williams, Flagstaff** and **Sedona**.

All of the park hotels have restaurants, from the formal **El Tovar Dining Room $$$** to the ever-popular **Bright Angel Fountain $** with long midday queues for ice cream. Best stop for picnic and other supplies is **Canyon Village Marketplace**, in the Market Plaza.

The North Rim hotel is **Grand Canyon Lodge $$$** *tel: (877) 386-4383 or (480) 337-1320; www.grandcanyonlodgenorth.com; open mid-May–mid-Oct.* Outside-the-park possibilities are **Kaibab Lodge $$** *HC 64, Box 30, Fredonia, AZ 86022; tel: (928) 638-2389; www.kaibablodge.com,* and **Jacob Lake Inn $$** *40 miles north of the Park's North Rim at the junction of Hwy 67 and Hwy 89; tel: (928) 643-7232; www.jacoblake.com.* The only North Rim restaurant is the **Grand Canyon Lodge Dining Room $$$** but the lodge also has a deli and a snack shop. The **General Store**, *North Rim Campground,* carries picnic supplies.

ZION NATIONAL PARK

ℹ Zion Canyon Visitor Center
½-mile north of the South Entrance; tel: (435) 772-3256. Open daily, 0800–1700, to 1800 or 2000, depending on season.

Kolob Canyons Visitor Center *Park Entrance near I-15. Open daily 0800–1630 or 1700.*

🅿 Zion National Park $$$ *Springdale, UT 84767; tel: (435) 772-3256; www.nps.gov/zion*

🚍 Zion Park Shuttle is the only access to the 6-mile Zion Canyon Scenic Drive Apr–Oct, with stops at scenic viewpoints and trailheads. Shuttle routes begin at car parks in Springdale and the park Visitor Center. Zion Canyon Scenic Drive is open to private vehicles Nov–Apr. The remainder of the park is open to private vehicles all year.

Like Grand Canyon, Zion has two units: **Zion Canyon** (south) and **Kolob Canyons** (north). It is possible to combine the two in a single exhausting day, but more rewarding to allow at least a day for each.

Kolob Canyons is best known to backcountry hikers, but the easy 5-mile drive up Hurricane Fault to the picnic area at **Kolob Canyons Viewpoint** is not to be missed. Look for stunning views of mesa formations dropping sheer to the Lower Kolob Plateau. The *Kolob Canyons Road Guide $* at the visitor centre offers excellent explanations of Kolob geography and geology.

Zion Canyon is filled with names like Abraham, Isaac, Jacob and Moroni (the Mormon angel). The biblical names for the imposing formations were actually chosen by a Methodist minister, Frederick Vining Fisher, who explored the North Fork of the Virgin River.

The **Zion Canyon Scenic Drive** follows Fisher's route up the canyon, starting from **The Watchman** (6546ft), a mountain wedge standing sentinel near the South Entrance. A short path leads from the car park to the **Court of the Patriarchs**, the aforementioned Mounts **Abraham, Isaac, Jacob** and **Moroni** to the west.

Almost directly across from the Zion Lodge Complex lie the **Emerald Pools**, the lower pool at the base of a waterfall an easy ½-mile from the road. A more strenuous 1-mile trail leads to a larger pool at the base of the cliffs.

The natural hanging gardens of **Weeping Rock** are a ¼-mile from the car park. The gardens are watered by mists and rivulets seeping from the sandstone. Take a moment to duck beneath a well-watered overhang to see Zion's serrated peaks shimmer through the mist.

ⓘ Cedar City Area Chamber of Commerce Visitor Center *581 N. Main St, Cedar City, UT 84720; tel: (435) 586-4484; www.chambercedarcity.org*

Cedar City-Brian Head Tourism and Convention Bureau *581 N. Main St, Cedar City, UT 84720; tel: (435) 586-5124 or (800) 354-4849; www.scenicsouthernutah.com*

Zion Canyon Visitors Bureau *Box 331, Springdale, UT 84767; tel: (888) 518-7070; www.zionpark.com*

St George Area Chamber of Commerce *97 E. St George Blvd, St George, UT 84770; tel: (435) 628-1658; www.stgeorgechamber.com*

Grand Circle Association *Box 750392, Torrey, UT 84775; tel: (888) 254-7263; www.grandcircle.org*

Climbers cling like ants to the cliffs beyond Weeping Rock that lead to the **Temple of Sinawava**, end of the road and start of a 1-mile **Riverside Walk** along the Virgin River to another hanging garden.

Accommodation and food in Zion

Zion Lodge $$$ *4 miles north of the South Entrance; tel: (888) 297-2757 or (435) 772-7700; www.zionlodge.com,* is the only indoor accommodation in the park. Reservations are essential.

Other accommodation is available in Springdale, just beyond the South Entrance, and the nearby towns of Hurricane and St George. Most convenient accommodation for Kolob Canyon's visitors is in Cedar City.

The **Castle Dome Café $** and the **Red Rock Grill $$$** *(tel: (435) 772-7760)* are the only park restaurants. Picnic supplies can be purchased in nearby towns.

Right
Pitting human strength and agility against sheer rock in Zion National Park

Language

How To Talk Californian

Alternate: Means 'alternative', not 'every other' – sometimes a source of confusion when reading timetables.

Bed & Breakfast (or 'B&B'): Overnight lodging in a private home, usually with private facilities and almost always more expensive than nearby hotels and motels.

Brewpub: A tavern that brews its own beer.

Buffalo wings: Chicken wings, usually fried and served with a spicy sauce as an appetiser or as bar food.

California cuisine: Anything the chef wants it to mean, as long as it's expensive, but usually based on fresh, organically grown foods.

Chili dog or chili burger: Hot dog or hamburger disguised with chili, onions and cheese.

Chimichanga: A pseudo-Mexican concoction of a fried tortilla filled with meat, beans, cheese, tomatoes and lettuce.

Chips: Crisps, usually made from potatoes, but also from corn, taro, casava, rice or other starches.

Corn dog: Hot dog dipped in corn meal and fried. Usually served hot on a stick.

Dead head: Fans of the band the Grateful Dead; also a term for hippies.

Designer water: Pejorative term for bottled water.

Downtown: City or town centre.

Holiday: A public holiday, such as Labor Day, not a private holiday, which is a vacation.

Lodging: The usual term for accommodation.

Natural ingredients: Food that has been grown, processed and prepared without pesticides or other chemical additives.

Outlet shopping: Shopping at large stores specialising in factory overruns at reduced prices. Sometimes, factory outlets are simply low-priced retail stores selling direct from the factory.

Resort: A fancy hotel which specialises in leisure activities such as golf, tennis and swimming.

Road kill: Literally, animals killed by passing cars, but usually used to describe bad restaurant food.

Californian driving terms

Big rig: A large lorry, usually a tractor pulling one or more trailers.

Boulevard stop: Slowing at a stop sign, but not stopping.

CHP California: Highway Patrol, the state road police force.

CNG: Liquefied petroleum gas used as fuel.

Crosswalk: Pedestrian crossing.

Connector: A minor road connecting two freeways.

Curve: Bend.

Divided highway: Dual carriageway.

DUI: Driving Under the Influence of alcohol or drugs, aka Drunk Driving. The blood alcohol limit in California and Nevada is 0.08% and is very strictly enforced.

Fender: Bumper.

Freeway: Motorway.

Garage or parking: Garage car park.

Gas(oline): Petrol.

Grade: Gradient, hill.

Highway: Trunk road.

Hood: Bonnet.

Metering lights: Traffic signals controlling access to bridges, freeways, etc.

Motor home: Motor caravan.

Pavement: Road surface. A UK 'pavement' is a US sidewalk.

Ramp: Slip road.

Rent: Hire.

Rubbernecking: Slowing down to peer while driving past the scene of an accident or some unusual event.

RV (recreational vehicle): Motor caravan.

Shift (stick): Gear lever.

Shoulder: Verge.

Sidewalk: Pavement.

Sig-alert: An official warning of unusually heavy traffic, usually broadcast over local radio stations.

Switchback: Serpentine road.

Traffic cop: Traffic warden.

Trunk: Boot.

Yield: Give way.

Index

Acknowledgements

Project management: Cambridge Publishing Management Limited
Project editor: Karen Beaulah
Series design: Fox Design
Cover design: Liz Lyons Design
Layout and map work: Concept 5D/Cambridge Publishing Management Limited
Repro and image setting: PDQ Digital Media Solutions Ltd/Cambridge Publishing Management Limited
Printed and bound in India by: Replika Press Pvt Ltd

We would like to thank the following photographers and organisations for the photographs used in this book, to whom the copyright in the photograph belongs:

Maxine Cass (pages 6, 8, 12, 13, 16, 17, 18, 22, 23, 24, 30, 32, 33, 34, 35, 36, 39, 42, 45, 47, 48, 51, 52, 59, 60, 62, 64, 66, 70, 73, 76, 78, 81, 85, 86, 89, 90, 94, 97, 98, 101, 102, 104, 109, 110, 121, 122, 127, 128, 134, 136, 139, 140, 142, 146, 148, 152, 154, 157, 159, 164, 166, 168, 171, 172, 176, 178, 181, 183, 186, 188, 191, 193, 196, 199, 200, 203, 206, 214, 216, 218, 219, 221, 226, 229, 235, 238, 240, 243, 246, 251, 252, 258, 262, 267, 270, 274, 276 and 281);
Ethel Davies (page 279);
Fred Gebhart (pages 54, 58, 74, 114, 118, 124, 131, 248, 256, 264, 266, 269 and 273).

Feedback form

We're committed to providing the very best up-to-date information in our travel guides and constantly strive to make them as useful as they can be. You can help us to improve future editions by letting us have your feedback. Just take a few minutes to complete and return this form to us.

When did you buy this book? ....
....

Where did you buy it? (Please give town/city and, if possible, name of retailer)
....
....

When did you/do you intend to travel in Scotland? ....
....

For how long (approx)? ....

How many people in your party? ....

Which cities, national parks and other locations did you/do you intend mainly to visit?
....
....
....
....

Did you/will you:
❏ Make all your travel arrangements independently?
❏ Travel on a fly-drive package?
Please give brief details: ....
....

Did you/do you intend to use this book:
❏ For planning your trip?   ❏ Both?
❏ During the trip itself?

Did you/do you intend also to purchase any of the following travel publications for your trip?
A road map/atlas (please specify) ....
Other guidebooks (please specify) ....

Have you used any other Thomas Cook guidebooks in the past? If so, which?

....

....

Please rate the following features of *Drive Around California* for their value to you (circle VU for 'very useful', U for 'useful', NU for 'little or no use'):

The *Travel Facts* section on pages 14–23	VU	U	NU
The *Driver's Guide* section on pages 24–29	VU	U	NU
The *Highlights* on pages 40–41	VU	U	NU
The recommended driving routes throughout the book	VU	U	NU
Information on towns and cities, National Parks, etc	VU	U	NU
The maps of towns and cities, parks, etc	VU	U	NU

Please use this space to tell us about any features that in your opinion could be changed, improved, or added in future editions of the book, or any other comments you would like to make concerning the book:

....

....

....

....

....

....

....

....

Your age category: ❏ 21–30   ❏ 31–40   ❏ 41–50   ❏ over 50

Your name: Mr/Mrs/Miss/Ms ....

(First name or initials) ....

(Last name) ....

Your full address (please include postal or zip code):

....

....

....

....

....

Your daytime telephone number: ....

Please detach this page and send it to: Drive Around Series Editor, Thomas Cook Publishing, PO Box 227, The Thomas Cook Business Park, 9 Coningsby Road, Peterborough PE3 8SB.

Alternatively, you can e-mail us at: *books@thomascook.com*